P9-DNK-954

SIGNS AND WONDERS

Jesus therefore said to them:
Unless you see signs and wonders,
you do not believe.

JOHN IV, 48

Signs AND Wonders

A STUDY OF THE MIRACULOUS ELEMENT IN RELIGION

LOUIS MONDEN, S.J.

Foreword by Avery Dulles, S.J.

DESCLEE COMPANY

New York · Paris · Tournai · Rome

This work originally appeared in Flemish under the title *Het Wonder* (Antwerp: De Standaard; Utrecht: Het Spectrum) from which a French version, *Le Miracle, Signe de Salut* (Bruges: Desclée de Brouwer, © 1960), was made by the author, with additions to text and bibliography, for the series "Publications du Museum Lessianum," Theological Section, no. 54.
It is from the author's French version that the present translation into English has been made. Moreover, the bibliography has been adapted for the English-speaking reader.

Imprimi potest
February 18, 1966
J. Hoing, Praep. Prov.

Nihil obstat: Daniel V. Flynn, J.C.D.

Imprimatur: Terence J. Cooke, D.D., V.G.
Auxiliary Bishop of New York
February 10, 1966

The nihil obstat and imprimatur are official declarations that a book or pamphlet is free of doctrinal or moral error. No implication is contained therein that those who have granted the nihil obstat and imprimatur agree with the contents, opinions or statements expressed.

Library of Congress Catalog Card Number: 66–17860

Manufactured in the U.S.A.

FOREWORD

by Avery Dulles, S.J.

Ever since biblical times miracles have held a central place in Christian theology and apologetics, and it is safe to say that as long as the Gospels are honored they will continue to command attention. Every Christian believer, if he dares to face the implications of his own faith, must come to terms with the evidence for the miraculous in the Bible and in Christian history.

For the ancient and medieval mind miracles were not a problem; their occurrence was taken for granted. But for modern man the authenticity of any miracle story is automatically suspect. Science is understandably reluctant to admit those anomalies which men of faith have commonly dubbed miracles. And the fact that miracle stories are part of the stock-in-trade of practically every religion casts additional doubt on the case for the Christian miracle. On what grounds can a man credit the miracle stories in his own religious tradition and not those of other faiths? Do the miracle stories form an essential part of the Christian message, or can we construct a modern, "demythologized" Christianity purged of these questionable ingredients?

The problem of miracles—and it is a real problem today for believers as well as unbelievers, for Catholics as well as other Christians—will not be solved by any single book. But if there is any one book which comes close to doing the job, I am convinced that this is it.

Since its appearance in Flemish in 1958 Father Monden's *Het Wonder* has been translated into French, German, and Spanish. It has been hailed by theologians of many nations as the outstanding work on the subject. The French Dominican, N. Dunas, calls it "the best theological synthesis of the problems presented by miracles."[1] The Hungarian Jesuit, L. Boros recommends it as "probably the most important monograph on the question of miracles."[2] The Anglican Ian T. Ramsey, professor of the philosophy of the Christian religion at Oxford, declares: "It is a most valuable contribution to the philosophy of miracle and will undoubtedly rank as a definitive work."[3] *The Heythrop Journal*, in a review of the French translation, states: "The author deserves every congratulation on his success in providing us with the most thorough and comprehensive treatment of miracles in modern times."[4] And *The Clergy Monthly* is no less enthusiastic: "Father Monden's work is, to date, simply *the* book on miracle, and we can only express the hope that the English edition may be available soon."[5]

Among the qualities for which this book has been widely praised one may point out, first of all, its extraordinary comprehensiveness. Monden treats the problem of miracle in all its main dimensions. He investigates miracles in the Bible, miracles in the Church, and the evidence for the miraculous outside the Church, whether in non-Catholic Christianity, in other religions, or in purely secular situations. In his doctrinal treatment, Monden surveys the views of the ancient Fathers, the medieval doctors, the modern theologians, and the official documents of the Church. Not content with this, he touches on the theme of the miraculous in modern fiction, even in the cinema. His chapter on the Lourdes healings is a model of clarity and compression. On practically every phase of the problem, Monden's compact footnotes provide invaluable leads for those

[1] N. Dunas, O.P., *Connaissance de la Foi* (Paris: Cerf, 1963), p. 100.

[2] L. Boros, S.J., *Der Anwesende Gott* (Olten: Walter Verlag, 1964), p. 228, note 36.

[3] Ian T. Ramsey, book review in *Theology*, 64 (1961), 74.

[4] W. Donnelly, book review in *The Heythrop Journal*, 1 (1960), 336.

[5] J. Bayart, S.J., book review in *The Clergy Monthly*, 25 (1961), 395.

who wish to go into the matter more fully. In the preparation of this translation the footnotes have been carefully adapted, supplemented, and brought up to date, under the author's personal guidance, to make them more serviceable to English-speaking readers.

A second remarkable feature of this book is that, instead of stopping short with an apologetical approach to miracles, it examines the meaning and value of miracles to those who are already convinced believers. As Canon Thils puts it, "One of the great merits of the author is that he has at long last, and without hesitation, set forth a dogmatic theology of miracles alongside of the apologetic, and has given primacy to the dogmatic." [6] Monden makes it clear that, over and above their value as confirmatory signs, miracles are to be esteemed as channels through which God communicates with us. They are, in effect, a dramatized form of speech which powerfully brings home to us the message of the Gospel. If nature is God's prose, miracles may perhaps be called his poetry. Just as words dance and sing for the poet of genius, so nature glows with a new radiance when God makes use of it to show his personal presence and thus to effect a salvific encounter with man.

This book has also been justly praised for its exceptional balance in steering a middle course between a credulous avidity for miracles and an attitude of hypercritical aloofness. Monden is firm and positive in his positions, but never aggressive. He wins the reader's confidence by his scrupulous care neither to exaggerate nor to minimize the actual strength of the case. Conscious that faith is always a free assent, in no way coerced by the evidences, he is content to appeal to the reader's prudence and good judgment. This is an honest type of apologetics—one that commends itself to an age for which the integrity of personal choice is a prime value.

A final merit of this work, which it shares in common with all superior theological writing, is the reverence with which the author treats his subject matter. If God is present in his wonderful deeds, we must, like Moses, take off our shoes. The place on which we are standing is holy ground (cf. Ex. III, 5). Unless we are receptive to things new and unexpected we shall never succeed in discerning the meaning of miracles. Our eyes will be held.

[6] G. Thils, book review in *Ephemerides Theologiae Lovanienses*, 36 (1960), 509.

To some it may appear that the whole theme of miracles has had its day. Have we not all been surfeited with the old controversies about the possibility and historicity of miracles? What has been the result of these centuries of polemics and counter-polemics except that believers and unbelievers have agreed to disagree? Why then disturb the truce and reopen these unpleasant disputes?

If Monden were simply repeating the old-line apologetic, these objections would strike home. If he began with the usual a priori approach to the effect that God is God and can therefore suspend the laws of nature at will; or if he tried to argue that the Christian miracles surpass the powers of any created agent and must therefore be attributed to God's omnipotence—all this has been said often before, and has failed to win the assent of candid men. But Monden's line of reasoning is far more subtle and will strike most English and American readers as new. His whole approach is through the philosophy and theology of sign. It is not necessary for me to defend this approach; Monden is his own best advocate.

Above all, let it not be said that the question of miracles is irrelevant. In an age when we hear on every side the complaint that God is silent and that men must resign themselves to his absence from the world, we ought to study with particular care any indications that perhaps after all it may be his "delight to be with the children of men" (cf. Prov. VIII, 31).

A certain type of Protestant theology, during the past generation, has concentrated almost exclusively on the God who speaks. For all that these theologians have done to make us aware of the salvific power of God's word, we can feel only gratitude. For them, at least, God is not silent. But if one stops here, he has stated only half the truth. The God of Israel and of Christianity is, above all else, a God of deeds. He is the God who acts. With the first Christians we are called upon to celebrate not only the words but the "mighty deeds of God" (Acts II, 11). Among all his deeds, those which most specially manifest his power, his fidelity, and his redemptive love are those which theology calls miracles.

Let us put away for a while the hackneyed definition of miracle as a "violation of the laws of nature." Let us instead go back with Father Monden to a richer, more biblical, and more theological definition. Let us call miracle, as the French title of this book did, "sign of salvation."

Physical miracles, to be sure, are not the sum and substance of Christianity. In themselves they are not the total salvation to which they point. But they inescapably call attention to the fact that salvation is not just a theory or an idea; it is a concrete reality which affects the whole man, body and soul alike. To drop out the miraculous element from Christianity is, inevitably, to mutilate the Gospel.

I earnestly hope that this book will be studied and discussed by a wide audience. I hope that it will be criticized and commented upon from every point of view—by biblical scholars and theologians of every confession, by philosophers, ethnologists, historians, psychologists and physicians. Only by a many-sided dialogue involving experts in all these fields can the problem of miracle be illumined as it must be. Such a conversation, I am sure, will strongly confirm many of Monden's conclusions; perhaps it will enable us to refine or correct what he says on certain points.

But if this is a book to be studied and debated it is also a book to be read and enjoyed. While ministers and students of religion will surely appreciate this book, *Signs and Wonders* is far too informative and inspiring to be monopolized by professionals. It is a book for lay readers as well as for scholars and theologians. It speaks to the heart as well as to the mind.

AVERY DULLES, S.J.

LETTER-PREFACE TO THE FRENCH EDITION

by Léon-Joseph Cardinal Suenens

REVEREND AND DEAR FATHER:

After reading the original Flemish edition of your book, *Signs and Wonders,* I felt that I should encourage you to publish it in French and several other languages. For men do not light a lamp and put it under the measure. You answered my letter immediately, stating that the French edition was almost ready to go to press, and also taking advantage of my remarks to ask me to write a preface for it. I couldn't possibly refuse, I welcome, in fact, the opportunity to repeat how remarkable and very timely this book is which presents an old subject in contemporary garb. More truly than ever, the miraculous remains the sign of God's presence among men in our world today. To understand the meaning and importance of this sign, one must place it in the proper perspective, and ask the Church how she interprets the miraculous and at what level she places it. Failure to clarify the theological notion of the miraculous has often produced a cheap and equivocal type of apologetics. The question that had to be resolved first was this: Does the miraculous belong in the natural or the supernatural order? In assigning it fortunately to the supernatural order, your answer at once makes irrelevant all the objections of rationalism which, especially in the

19th century, attacked the miraculous as an appendage to creation, an act of retouching unworthy of the Creator or an attempt to remodel his own handiwork. At once also, the miraculous appears as a divine sign in all its fulness and with the wealth of its religious meaning. Man in his curiosity dwells unduly long on the apparent, spectacular, and purely physical aspects of the miraculous. It was important to place the miraculous within its proper context as a religious sign.

The horizon of your readers will widen with every page, for the realm of the miraculous is immense. In speaking of miracles, we tend to restrict them to the limited area of the apologetic miracle where miracles are expected to be clear-cut and demonstrable by precise criteria. But this is merely a part of the whole truth, as you have pointed out so correctly. Your answer to these basic questions makes it all the easier for the reader to accept your answer to a further question, the one modern man will ask before all else: Are miracles subject to scientific verification?

Your answer is both yes and no, depending on the meaning of the word "science." If we call science only the medical, biological and experimental sciences, that is those branches of science which by definition and method study only the laws of nature and the succession of phenomena, leaving aside all that is not subject to experimentation and thus does not reveal any causal relationships, then we must say that scientific verification of the miraculous is a contradiction in the very words.

We can draw the same negative conclusion from an analysis of the miraculous itself. If miracles are divine signs for men, every man with a live religious sense and an open heart must be able to understand them; scientists could not have a monopoly on seeing and understanding, for instance, a sudden cure. Since truth calls for a total commitment of the human soul, man must take along his entire self for meeting God in the miraculous.

For these two reasons it does not pertain to science to discern the miraculous as such.

This, however, does not mean that we may altogether take the miraculous out of the scope of scientific inquiry. We are merely assigning to science its proper task which doesn't consist in determining whether a miracle has taken place or not, but to check the facts as rigorously as possible. When the respective areas of competency are thus clearly defined, the Church asks that scientists perform their own proper task with the greatest consciousness and in all rigor; she could have no use for anything but the most absolute scientific loyalty.

While a miracle is not a purely scientific event in which a scientific aspect could be isolated in its pure state, it is a sign-event which does have an observable scientific aspect. We want this scientific inquiry to be as thorough as possible, absolutely open and clear, with no reservations and no illusions. Let us beware of hasty conclusions and irrational enthusiasm.

Science is expected to check the reality of the event itself, for instance, a sudden cure, and establish its exceptional nature, i.e., its inexplicability. Miracles are by definition signs that God gives to men by achieving an exceptional feat. This feat can be scientifically established as exceptional, but not as it is a sign.

Science is called upon to establish a link between the exceptional event and a prayerful religious context characterized by high moral standards and attitudes, for the study of this constant factor also belongs in the domain of science.

Finally, it pertains to science to demonstrate that the relationship between the exceptional fact and the religious context is an exclusive one, i.e., that this relationship is the only constant and stable link science can uncover between the facts.

Your book explains all of this in a masterly manner and in a language accessible to the learned public, with all the theological shadings and precisions necessary for the understanding of this complex subject. Reverend and dear Father, yours is a theological achievement of the first order; you have put the miraculous back in its chosen place in contemporary apologetics. May God bless you for it.

Sincerely yours in Our Lord,

✠ L. J. SUENENS

CONTENTS

· INTRODUCTION

The miraculous element in Christianity is a subject of current interest about which both believers and unbelievers have notably revised their views during the last half-century.

This change of opinion is most striking among unbelieving scientists. At the beginning of the present century it was thought good form in scientific circles to oppose to any recounting of miracles a firm attitude of disavowal, or to appeal in the name of science to the notion of suggestion, or to that of magnetism or of some other psychological panacea, in order to discredit the miraculous. Nowadays, men no longer refuse to admit facts; for although science may continue its attempt to find an explanation of the miraculous within the framework and according to the principles of natural psychology, it nevertheless acknowledges that Catholic miracles bring before such a court a challenging problem, a problem as yet unsolved. The Catholic interpretation is rejected as vehemently as ever it was; but there is general agreement that the miraculous must be taken seriously, that it must be handled as a problem which science is to consider. Let us recall how Alexis Carrel has told us that about the year 1900 "it was difficult for a young doctor, and dangerous for his future career" for him to take any serious interest in the fact of Lourdes,[1] while, on the other hand, in 1930 a medical dissertation on the miracles of Lourdes was accepted by the University of Paris. Moreover, in 1937, Dr. Smiley Blanton was actually sent to Lourdes by a section of the Academy of Medicine of New York which devotes itself to the subject *Medicine and Religion,* in order that he might gather together complete documentary evidence on the spot. This contrast in viewpoints serves as a gauge by which the distance which divides them may be measured.[2]

Not less striking is the re-evaluation of the miraculous among Protestants. At the end of the last century, it was fashionable to be skeptical not only in respect to contemporary miracles but even in the face of those which are recorded in the Gospel. As late as 1908 Seeberg observed in a Protestant encyclopedia: "The wonder was once the cornerstone of apologetics, then it became a kind of wooden leg, and today it must be regarded as the cross of apologetics." [3] On the other hand, in 1933 we find G. Marquardt ending his study of the miraculous according to contemporary Protestant theology with the statement: "Were one to take the Catholic notion of the wonder as a kind of outside limit, the depiction by a graphic curve of the course of Protestant theological thought would indicate that, despite occasional differences, there is a slow but ever ascending tendency to converge with it." [4] Since these words were written, the same tendency has become more marked. No doubt, a far from negligible group of Protestant theologians has come under the influence of the *Entmythologisierungstheorie,* that effort at demythologization which, on a basis of rationalistic preju-

[1] A Carrel: *Man the Unknown* (New York, 1935), p. 148.

[2] H. Monnier: *Étude médicale de quelques guérisons survenues à Lourdes* (Paris, 1930). In 1939 A. Guarner offered to the University of Algiers his dissertation, *De l'instantanéité des guérisons de Lourdes* (Algiers, 1939). See A. Vallet: *La vérité sur Lourdes et ses guérisons miraculeuses* (Paris, 1944), pp. 56-60, on the subject of these two theses. F. Leuret and H. Bon give a rather full list of academic theses on Lourdes in their *Modern Miraculous Cures* (New York, 1957), ch. II, n. 6, pp. 203-204, as does also A. Deroo: *Lourdes, cité de miracles ou marché d'illusions* (Paris, 1956), pp. 15-22. On Dr. Blanton's visit, see A. Vallet: *op. cit.*, pp. 66-67.

[3] *Realencyclopädie für protestantische Theologie und Kirche* (Leipzig, 1908), vol. XXI, p. 562.

[4] G. Marquardt: *Das Wunderproblem in der deutschen protestantischen Theologie der Gegenwart* (Munich, 1933), p. 322.

dices, forthrightly declares that *miracles are impossible.*[5] According to these theologians, the miraculous is no more than a mythological adornment of the Christian Gospel, the product of a superseded framework of thought and imagination. They think that modern Christian thought is always well advised to pry away the existential kernel of the evangelical message by digging it out of this mythical pulp. Nevertheless, Protestant thought, as it concerns itself with the miraculous, continues on the whole to approach Catholic doctrine. Among post-war theologians a renewed interest in the miraculous is closely allied to their re-evaluation of the sacramental idea, something which is quite apparent in Protestant writing in our day.[6]

Anglicanism, which is generally closer to traditional teaching than is Continental Protestantism, seems at one with Catholic theology in respect to the miraculous. Some of the most representative Anglican writers have developed a doctrine which can only be described as being fully Catholic.[7]

Insofar as Catholic theology is concerned, the fluctuation of opinion has also been great. During the nineteenth century, when confronted by the open disavowals of non-believing scientism, Catholic apologetics emphasized especially the physical side of the miraculous. It was believed that in this way natural science would be brought to admit the scientific demonstration of the abrogation of Nature's laws and, consequently, the transcendent intervention of the Creator of those laws. The omnipotence of God working through nature was something which such apologists thought

[5] Such are the words of R. Bultmann, the author of the theory of demythologization; cf. W. Bartsch (ed.): *Kerygma und Mythos*, II (Hamburg, 1952), p. 182. Along lines similar to Bultmann see R. H. Fuller: *Interpreting the Miracles* (London, 1963). Among the criticisms of Bultmann's view of the miraculous, see especially: L. Malevez: *The Christian Message and Myth: the Theology of Rudolf Bultmann* (London, 1958), esp. pp. 125-140; J. de Fraine: "Evangelische boodschap en modern denken" *Strievcn*, 7/2 (1953), 203-216; and James Mark: "Myth and Miracle, or the Ambiguity of Bultmann," *Theology*, 66 (1963), 133-140.

[6] See below, ch. VI, note 1, where reference is made to articles by O. Cullmann, P. H. Menoud, and G. Fitzer.

[7] I am thinking particularly of the fine book of C. S. Lewis: *Miracles: A Preliminary Study* (New York, 1947). See also the inaugural lecture delivered at the University of Oxford in 1951 by I. T. Ramsey: *Miracles: An Exercise in Logical Mapwork* (Oxford, 1952).

themselves able to capture on the wing. Hence they strove to base their demonstrations on the type of evidence which the science of the age attributed to scientific proofs. Miracles were therefore presented as undeniable facts—as arguments which an adversary could evade only by recourse to deception or bad faith.

Since that time it has been learned that it is not wise to accept scientific developments as definitive. Our own age makes a sharper distinction between the realms of science and metaphysics. The synthetic mentality has become prevalent, and apologetics proceeds on the basis of a theological view in which miracles are assigned their due place in God's redemptive plan. Further, it has been recognized that the chief element in the miracle, namely its religious meaning, was overlooked in discussions which treated them merely as perceptible factual occurrences subject to scientific control. More and more, Catholic theologians are agreed in looking on the sign-function of the miracle as primary. Its apologetic value is perceived not by the methods of experimental science, but inasmuch as a man seeking religious truth discerns its reality as a sign. By the same token, such an apologetic method is more modest: instead of conducting its inquiries under the harsh light of the scientific laboratory, it now honors that zone of light and shade in which personal confrontation is achieved through the veil of signs.

The evolution of opinion among Christians and non-believers alike, which has just been sketched, has had particular effect on specialists and men of science, while so far as the mass of the public is concerned, the situation is quite otherwise.

"Popular science" writings, especially in the post-war period, have served to instill deeply into the mind of the man in the street a blind trust in scientific theories, a kind of trust which true scientists have long since cast aside. Such trust ascribes to scientific theories the power to explain all things, and inclines many contemporaries—among them even some fervent Catholics—to treat of the miraculous with aggressive misgiving and open skepticism: they are ready to look at the wonder as if it were no more than a mere marginal gloss to be rejected as a parasitical excrescence on religious truth.

Austere consciences are seemingly justified in this skepticism in view of the popular tendency among our contemporaries to look for marvels, for occult manifestations, for prophecies, for apparitions, and for signs of the coming of doom. Racine might indeed speak to our time with new implications in his words: "Was ever an age so fecund in the miraculous?" It appears as if superstitious hopes, eradicated by science and unbelief, seek their revenge in this stickly confusion. Even within the Catholic Church, excesses in popular devotional life have shown themselves in such guise as to require that warnings be issued from very high quarters in order that this fevered search for the marvelous be discountenanced.[8]

Outside the communion of the Catholic Church there has been manifested a most virulent exhibition of this taste for wonders in what has justly been dubbed "the invasion of the sects."[9]

Even among the neo-paganized populations of our refined cities there exists an open market for astrologers, soothsayers, spiritistic mediums and radiaesthetists. Indeed, we learn from a trustworthy source that in France alone faith-healers outnumber by five or six thousand those medical practitioners who are recognized as such by law.[10]

In the present juncture it therefore appears that the time is ripe to essay a basic study of the Christian miracle, a study which will bring us face to face with current problems and which will weld into one whole the traditional principles of theology and its more recent findings.

The very plan of this book is dictated by new insights: my idea is not to begin by plunging at once into apologetic demonstration, but rather by establishing, first of all, a full dogmatic basis for the Christian miracle; it is on the foundation of this dogmatic basis that proofs will be built up. Too frequently discussion with non-believers is vitiated by a misunderstanding; the apologist and his

[8] The most influential such warning was that given by Msgr. [now Cardinal] Alfredo Ottaviani, secretary of the Holy Office, which appeared in *Osservatore Romano* of February 4, 1951. A French translation was published in *La Documentation Catholique* of March 25, 1951, cc. 353-356 [and there are several available English versions; cf. *The Tablet* (London) 197 (February 24, 1951), 144-145; *American Ecclesiastical Review*, 124 (May 1951), 321-326; *Irish Ecclesiastical Record*, 5th ser., 75 (April 1951), 334-339.]

[9] Cf. H. C. Chéry: *L'offensive des sectes* (Paris, 1954); R. Rouquette: "Le problème des 'sectes' ", *Etudes*, 285 (1955), 381-395.

[10] M. Oraison: *Médecine et guérisseurs* (Paris, 1955), pp. 32-34.

adversary have fundamentally different concepts of the miraculous. Now, it is the Catholic Church which appeals to the miracles produced within its fold as being signs testifying to the authenticity of the religious teaching which it delivers. The Church, therefore, is alone capable of stating what it considers a miracle to be, what is its function in the whole complexus of her religious doctrine. Only the Church can stipulate what is to be required for a miracle to be regarded as authentic, how it is to be recognized, and precisely what value it has as testimony to the truth. The Catholic apologist shares with the nonbelieving inquirer the need to find out whether such things as miracles do actually occur—not things which are more or less analogous, not happenings upon which man arbitrarily imposes his own conditions, but those very occurrences which the Church itself recognizes as miracles—and to discover if there is a possibility of discerning in these things, with certitude, the meaning which the Church wishes to give to them. I shall accordingly begin by stating the question in terms of Catholic doctrine, seeking to discover from it what is the nature and meaning of the miraculous. One advantage of this method is that it takes us at once to the center of almost every great religious problem.

In the second part I shall set forth the apologetic aspect of the miraculous, seeking to establish the historic truth of the facts alleged and to demonstrate how they can be recognized as divine signs.

The manner in which this work is presented to the reader is, likewise, somewhat unusual. I wish to make the matter easily understood by the educated reader who is not a specialist; and at the same time I seek to satisfy the demands of scientific scholarship. It is rather in the manner of the essayist than in the fashion of the writer of a treatise that I shall proceed; and I shall try to avoid, as much as possible, language which is overly technical or purely academic. Nevertheless, it is my hope not to overlook any important problem in the field. The logical succession of thought will be emphasized by adherence to a systematic plan plainly indicated by headings and sub-headings; otherwise it might be obscured by the involved character of certain discussions. Those, be they specialists or not, who may wish to peer more thoroughly into one or another question will find ample bibliographical notes. In order not to stretch the text to inordinate length, some technical matters have likewise been relegated to the notes.[11]

I am moved to state my particular indebtedness to Père E. Dhanis whose unpublished treatises on Faith and on Miracles, so frequently referred to in this work, are outstanding among the writings which I have consulted.

In reverent homage to one whom Scripture salutes as "the great Sign," I offer these pages to Her whose name is inextricably interwoven with the miracles which have taken place within the past one hundred years.

[11] The bibliography has been brought up to date [and English bibliographical indications have been given in some places by the translators.]

PART 1

The Theology of the Miraculous

1 · BASIC CONSIDERATIONS: MIRACLES AND THE DATA OF FAITH

The fundamental point of departure of a theological investigation of the data of faith is necessarily the living consciousness of the Church, as expressed through the agency of its contemporary teaching authority. From this point there are two paths which may be followed in penetrating more deeply into the mystery.

The first method seeks to return to the very sources of revelation, in which the earliest expressions are found, as yet vague and confused, and then to trace the process of development which links the primitive manifestation to the fuller expression of received belief, be it either complete or in process of completion. The steps of such growth are marked by more or less overt declarations of the teaching authority as well as by ritual and by liturgy, and by the witness of the Church Fathers and theologians, by the whole prayer life of the Christian community down through the centuries. The advantage of such a method is more than negative: as well as exposing every misunderstanding of the significance and scope of dogmatic definitions, it also serves notably to enrich our understanding of the matter under consideration. Even in the natural order one must begin with the germ and the growth of anything about which thorough knowledge is desired. This is even more true of mysteries which surpass our merely human reasoning to such an extent as to elude, in great degree, the grasp of our conceptual and dialectical powers. How better can we uncover the mysterious suggestiveness of God's Word than by surprising it, as one might say, on his very lips and by tracing, step by step, the work of the Spirit of Truth in making that word manifest? Christ has himself promised to teach his Church by that Spirit "who will bring to your mind whatever I have said" and thus lead his Church toward the apprehension of that whole truth which it "cannot yet bear." [1] We, therefore, put ourselves in touch with the Church as the recipient of the primitive revelation; and, in our faith, we confront the faith of the early Christians. By following the line of continual development which characterizes this or that truth of faith we become aware of, and grasp, the fuller expression of truth.

In respect to the miraculous element in religion this method returns to the wondrous facts narrated in the Old and New Testaments, especially to Christ's own miracles, and it seeks to abstract from them the doctrinal truth to which they testify. This does not mean reducing these miracles to their least common denominator and in this way forming a definition. Any such projection of modern theological conceptions into writings expressing a different universe of thought would be at the antipodes of sound theological method. Rather are we to look upon each and every miraculous occurrence as a facet of a whole which is extremely rich and varied; and it is the total view of the whole matter which will stand out sharply against the background of the Christian Gospel.

The living complexity of the Gospel miracles has remained a feature of the Church's life, and Christian thinkers have gradually evolved a self-consistent doctrinal expression of it. Only at the First Vatican Council was this doctrine declared in its authentic and infallible form. Before the nineteenth century the teaching authority had not pronounced upon the question.[2] It is therefore neces-

[1] Cf. John XIV, 26 and XVI, 12-13.

[2] Even controversy with the Protestants has left scarcely any traces in ecclesiastical documents. The attacks launched in the age of the Enlightenment and by the Encyclopedists did not evoke any doctrinal decision, and they were met only by the canonical norms and the very strict and wisely critical principles of procedure which Benedict XIV decreed for canonical enquiries into

sary, if we are to trace the stages of development, to look, first of all, to what the Fathers have to say of the Gospel miracles, to the norms which the Church has established for the acknowledgment of the miraculous, and to the spontaneous expression of the Christian community when confronted with the enduring existence of miracles within the Curch.

A theological investigation of the data of faith may also be attempted along another path.

Taking the Church's authoritative declaration as a point of departure one may integrate it organically in the Church's living doctrine and in a considered synthesis of the faith. In other words, and to quote the Fathers of the First Vatican Council: "When reason, enlightened by faith, carefully, devoutly, and modestly inquires, it does by God's gift acquire some understanding of revealed mysteries, and that a most profitable one. It achieves this by the analogy of things known by natural means, by the interrelationship of the mysteries among themselves and by their connection with man's last end." [3]

According to this method, concepts like those of sign and transcendent divine intervention throw light on the nature of the miraculous as it is defined by the Church and accepted by believers. Moreover, miracles are contemplated in the redemptive plan in such a way as to clarify their structure, their distinctive characteristics, and bearing on men's lives.

Actually, the two methods are not to be separated one from the other; for rather than being two independent procedures, they are the complementary approaches, constantly overlapping, of a unified theological investigation.

Tradition is not the mere act of passing on a series of proposi-

the authenticity of miraculous occurrences, something to which reference must be made later in this work.

[3] So has the First Vatican Council outlined for us the theological task: "*Ac ratio quidem, fide illustrata, cum sedulo, pie, et sobrie quaerit, aliquam Deo dante mysteriorum intelligentiam eamque fructuosissimam assequitur, tum ex eorum, quae naturaliter cognoscit, analogia, tum e mysteriorum ipsorum nexu inter se et cum fine hominis ultimo*" (Denzinger-Schönmetzer: *Enchiridion symbolorum* [Freiburg i. B., 1963] 3016. This work is hereinafter cited as *DSch*).

tions; dogma is not a game determined by the arbitrary machinations of dialecticians.

Receptivity to the word of God, as preserved by Tradition, must be completed by reverent meditation. The obedience of faith and the understanding of faith assist and complement each other; theological speculation, docile in its audacity, "preserves the maiden purity of the Word of God." It is only to the patience inherent in prolonged thought that Tradition will yield its unfathomed richness. By ceaseless confrontation of this thought with the true Word our theological speculation will show itself exempt from the self-sufficiency and the posturings of a kind of knowledge which is self-intoxicated. The result will rather be a wisdom born of God and ever directed toward him.

It is the aim of the present study to put this true theological method into practice. The chapters which follow will therefore present, first, a dogmatic study of the miraculous and only after that, a consideration of the Gospel miracles. Such a method of procedure is not chosen by the author simply in terms of his own predilection: the subject can be presented in no other way.

At the First Vatican Council, the Church, through the agency of her infallible teaching authority, summed up in a short formula the data of faith in regard to the miraculous.

After first defining the act of faith and emphasizing its supernatural character, the Council goes on: "Nevertheless, so that the obeisance of our faith might be consonant with reason, God has been pleased to supply, besides the interior aids of the Holy Spirit, external evidences of his revelation, namely divine acts, especially miracles and prophecies. In splendidly displaying God's omnipotence and infinite knowledge, these constitute most certain signs of divine revelation, attuned to the understanding of all men." [4]

Later the Council points by implication to the miraculous in referring to "all those things, so numerous and so marvelous, which

[4] "*Ut nihilominus fidei nostrae obsequium rationi consentaneum esset, voluit Deus cum internis Spiritus Sancti auxiliis externa iungi revelationis suae argumenta, facta scilicet divina, atque imprimis miracula et prophetias, quae cum Dei omnipotentiam et infinitam scientiam luculenter commonstrent, divinae revelationis signa sunt certissima et omnium intelligentiae accommodata*" (*DSch* 3009).

God has provided to render the Christian faith evidently credible." [5]

The same doctrine reappears in the condemnation as heretical of propositions which are in contravention of this article of faith: "Should anyone say that the divine revelation cannot be rendered credible by external signs, and that therefore men should be led to faith only by their own inner experience or by private inspiration: let him be anathema." "If anyone should say that all miracles are impossible and that consequently all accounts of them, even though found in the Holy Scriptures, are to be taken as fabulous and mythical, or that miracles can never be known with certainty, and that they do not provide valid proofs of the divine origin of the Christian religion: let him be anathema." [6]

The Council did not actually attempt a definition of the miraculous: it rather indicated three essential elements which must be incorporated into any theological definition.

The first of these elements, that one about which the Council is most insistent, is its function as a *sign*—a sign, moreover, intended to assist reason in adhering to faith by proving, through external evidence, the credibility of revelation. In giving primary emphasis to this function, the Council evidently did not mean to exclude other functions or meanings of the miraculous.

The decree of the Council states that miracles are signs "attuned to the understanding of all." The significance of the Council's words is not apparent at first glance, and commentators have interpreted it in various ways. The obvious reading would be that the proof can be grasped both by men of education and by the unlettered. Yet nothing in the *Acta* of the Council serves to support this interpretation.[7] The anti-Modernist oath imposed by Pius X

[5] "*Omnia quae ad evidentem fidei christianae credibilitatem tam multa et tam mira divinitus sunt disposita*" (*DSch* 3013).

[6] "*Si quis dixerit, revelationem divinam externis signis credibilem fieri non posse, ideoque sola interna cuiusque experientia aut inspiratione privata homines ad fidem moveri debere: anathema sit*" (*DSch* 3033).

"*Si quis dixerit, miracula nulla fieri posse, proindeque omnes de iis narrationes, etiam in Sacra Scriptura contentas, inter fabulas vel mythos ablegandas esse; aut miracula certo cognosci numquam posse nec iis divinam religionis christianae originem rite probari: anathema sit*" (*DSch* 3034).

[7] This is the interpretation defended by E. A. de Poulpiquet: *Le miracle*

repeats the words of the Council and explains them in this fashion: "signs most perfectly attuned to understanding all ages and men, even of this time." [8] It is evident that this further explanation draws its inspiration from Modernist notions which were not yet current when the Council was held; and, as the explanation has no real basis in the conciliar texts, it must be regarded as an extension whose authority is derived from that of the document (i.e., the anti-Modernist oath) in which it is found.

A recent commentator on the constitution "Dei Filius"—from which document this text is taken—thinks that the expression "attuned to the understanding of all men" has the same meaning as the words in the first draft of this constitution, "things perceptible by man as signs of God's word, even before the act of faith is elicited." [9] This explanation is plausible, since Msgr. Simor, the chairman of the Commission, who carefully studied the text, declared that this paragraph has reference to those who deny the persuasive value of external signs, "or who will only admit them to be of accessory value, after the act of faith has actually been elicited." [10] The commentator himself admits that this interpretation is an hypothetical one; there exists no decisive indication why the text was changed.[11] Therefore the words of the Council do not lend certain authority to any choice among these varying interpretations.

---

et ses suppléances (Paris, 1913), pp. 204-205; by A. Vacant: *Études théologiques sur les Constitutions du Concile du Vatican* (Paris, 1895), II, pp. 49-50; and with greater subtlety by S. Harent in his article, "Foi", *DTC*, c. 229.

[8] "*Externa revelationis argumenta, hoc est facta divina, in primisque miracula et prophetias admitto et agnosco tanquam signa certissima divinitus ortae christianae religionis, eademque teneo aetatum omnium atque hominum, etiam huius temporis, intelligentiae esse maxime accommodata*" (*DSch* 3539).

[9] R. Aubert: *Le problème de l'acte de foi* (Louvain, 1945), pp. 168-169.

[10] Mansi: LI, c. 47, B.

[11] What is the exact signification of the expression in question if we do adopt this interpretation? Does it mean that natural reason, unaided by any grace accompanying faith, is able to discern the probative or evidential value of miraculous signs? The expression used in the pro-synodal draft, "etiam ante fidem susceptam" was clearly directed against the *fideism* of Abbé Bautain. He had contended that it is only after man has received the grace of faith that he has a sense of the divine and becomes capable of knowing the meaning and the probative value of the miracle as of other signs authenticating revelation. In the case of a man without faith, the Abbé Bautain thought that these signs would be worthless. The Church deemed it necessary to reject such opinions. Bautain was required, on several occasions, to sign certain propositions laid be-

There does exist, however, a doctrinal statement upon the role of faith in the discernment of the miraculous, although the statement is not itself an expression of the infallible teaching authority. It is to be found in a later document, the encyclical "Humani Generis." In its turn, this statement looks back to the words of the Council; but it adds a proposition which declares plainly that the probative value of a miracle does not depend upon the grace of faith. Actually the encyclical speaks of "the many and marvelous external

---

fore him, first by his bishop, then by the Congregation of Religious. These statements affirm clearly that "the use of reason is antecedent to faith and leads man to it by revelation and by grace" (*DSch* 2755); and again, "reason is able to establish with certitude the authenticity of revelation" (*DSch* 2756). In order best to accomplish this task, should reason be aided by the help of grace, and does the necessity of grace derive from the physical or merely moral powerlessness of natural reason when confronted by divine signs? The text does not settle this point, no more than does the encyclical "Qui pluribus" of Pius IX. There is no doubt that some rationalists of the school of Hermes have interpreted a passage from this encyclical (*DSch* 2778) as a statement by the Church of the demonstrability of revelation by the unaided reason of man, apart from the help of grace. But the allocution, "Singulari quadam," pronounced shortly thereafter by the Pope (cf. Denzinger-Rahner: *Enchiridion Symbolorum*, 1642) which emphasized the moral weakness of reason consequent upon original sin, is unanimously taken to express a direct contravention of this opinion of the Hermesians. The fourth chapter of the constitution "Dei Filius," of the First Vatican Council does no more than repeat the text of "Qui pluribus" by stating that right reason (*recta ratio*, which that text opposes to reason illumined by faith, *ratio fide illustrata*) or natural reason "can establish the foundations of faith." But does reason do so with or without the help of grace? Again it must be confessed that the text itself does not tell us (*DSch* 3019), and therefore the statement has to be understood—just as is the case of what is said in "Qui pluribus"—in the light of the complementary explanations offered in "Singulari quadam." The probability remains, therefore, that the whole bent of these texts tends clearly in the direction of recognizing the physical capability of natural reason to attain to knowledge of certitude by means of signs but seems, at the same time, to affirm that this effort of human reason is, in actuality, always aided by grace and would remain morally powerless without that aid. Thus these texts apply to miracles and to other probative signs of revelation the principles established by the Council on the subject of a purely natural knowledge of God's existence (*DSch* 3004-3005). A phrase in "Humani Generis": *vel solo naturalis rationis lumine*, i.e., *by light of natural reason alone*, might seem to resolve the debate in this sense. Yet some have justifiably questioned whether a remark inserted, in passing, into an encyclical could resolve a question disputed for centuries by differing schools of Catholic theology, especially inasmuch as many earlier documents had always avoided taking a stand on this point. [See on this head F. Malmberg: "Zelfs met het natuurliik redelicht alleen. Notities bij een passage van de encycliek 'Humani Generis,'" *Bijdragen* (1950), 202-211.]

signs given by God, from which the divine origin of the Christian religion can be proved, even by the merely natural light of reason." [12]

The miraculous sign, as the Council declares, is a sign which is beyond denying, for it can be recognized as such with certitude: it validly establishes the credibility of revelation. We may note that, according to the Council, the fact of revelation is not established by the sign, but the credibility of that fact is. This distinction is significant: we shall return to it.[13]

To sum up: the teaching authority regards the miraculous as an undeniable sign of God's supernatural revelation, the probative force of which does not presuppose the presence of faith, but is rather to be apprehended by any man of good judgment.

The second element in the miraculous which the Council proposes for our consideration is its *transcendent* character.[14] It is a *divine act*, a *showing forth of God's power*. To regard this transcendent intervention of God as impossible, to reject wholly the miraculous element in Christianity, especially that of which the Scriptures speak, is to incur condemnation.[15]

[12] *DSch* 3876.

[13] Here one should note the difterence between the formula to which Abbé Bautain was required by his bishop to assent and that imposed upon him, three years later, by the Roman Congregation of Religious. According to the first, he was made to declare that "reason can establish with certitude the authenticity of revelation." The second formula adopted, for the first time, the expression which Vatican I was to make its own: "the means which render divine revelation evidently credible" (see the texts in *DSch* 2756 and 2768). True enough, the earlier formulary is also repeated in the encyclical "Qui pluribus," and it thence passed into the Vatican text already cited (cf. above n. 11). But the *Acta* of the Council (Mansi: LI; c. 369, emendatio 22) clearly establish that the word "demonstratio" should be taken in the broad, traditional sense of a moral or prudential certitude, and that this earlier formulary only states less precisely what the second more exactly expresses. The discussion about the use of the word "evidentem" in the text of the constitution "Dei Filius (Mansi: LI; cc. 219-265, *passim*), leaves no uncertainty on this head. See the summary of the discussion in R. Aubert: *loc. cit.*; pp. 198-200.

[14] This point was affirmed obliquely (*in obliquo*) rather than directly (*in recto*), which is to say that it is found not in a principal statement but in one subordinate and explanatory; and it therefore does not, properly speaking, form part of the definition. Nevertheless, it is still a part of the doctrine definitely stated by the Council.

[15] The expression "consequently" which joins the second phrase of the

In the view of the Council, the intervention of divine power is considered to be a necessary condition of the fact that the miraculous occurrence is a divine sign. There is, in the text, no other indication of a relationship between the characteristic of a miracle as *transcendent* and its function as a *sign*. Does this manifestation of power presuppose the direct intervention of God, or may it be mediated by a creature? This is a point in respect to which the Council takes no position. Does this act of divine intervention presuppose that the natural laws have been broken? There is not a word in the conciliar text which refers to this matter.

A third element in the miraculous is rather suggested than explicitly named by the Council. The word "miraculum" is introduced without any further explanation. We must therefore understand it according to common usage as meaning a fact beyond the ordinary, a *prodigy* or *wonder*; but here the term is tied into its religious context, for the Council associates it with "acts of God."

To the man in the street this third element is important, for is it not precisely by the unusual, by the spectacular, note in a miraculous occurrence that he is struck? The more sensational a wonder is, the more it shows a departure from the normal course of events, the more it seems to transcend the limits of what is possible, so much the more spontaneously does he acclaim it as a "miracle."

The Church itself looks upon this marvelous note as being a necessary characteristic of the miraculous; but it does not belabor the point and rather concentrates attention upon the sign and the fact of God's transcendent intervention in human affairs which the miraculous act itself makes evident. The prodigy is only the outer shell of a reality which has deeper implications.

The doctrine of the Church in this matter is, furthermore, strictly in agreement with the language of the Gospel. The evangelists made use of a vocabulary more precise than our own, a language, moreover, which leans upon that of the Old Testament.

---

canon to the first one indicates that this second part falls under condemnation only insofar as it is to be deduced as a conclusion following upon the first phrase. In the technical sense the second phrase is said to be condemned "in sensu composito" and not "in sensu diviso," or, in other words, only if held conjointly with the first, and not if held separately.

So it is that, while in English one may speak almost indifferently of a *miracle* or of a *prodigy*, the New Testament makes use of three very distinct terms: it speaks of prodigies (*prodigia, portenta*), of acts of power (*virtutes, opera*—it is true, of course, that the latter word includes, in a larger sense, the whole of Christ's mission, in which his miracles are only one element), and of signs (*signa*; the Greek word σημεῖον has the more exact meaning of a distinctive mark or stamp of approval).[16]

It is worthy of remark that the word "prodigium," as indicating only the marvelous aspect of the miraculous, is never used by itself; it is always coupled with one of the other two terms; at times it is even linked to both of them. In the triad: act of power, prodigy, sign, emphasis is clearly laid on the first and third terms.

In its Christian meaning the miracle is not only or even primarily a baffling occurrence; it is basically, as faith teaches, an act of divine power at work among mankind, and a sign of the divine message of salvation.

Prior to constructing from these elements a valid theological definition, a preliminary question must be faced: Is the miracle, as we have attempted thus provisionally to describe it, a plausible or an improbable element in the whole complexus of Christian revelation? Does it fit into place in the Christian system?

[16] On the language applied to the miraculous in the Old Testament, see C. Tresmontant: *Études de métaphysique biblique* (Paris, 1955): Excursus I: La notion du miracle, pp. 223-228. For the New Testament, see, *inter alia*, L. Fonck: *Die Wunder des Herrn* (Innsbruck, 1903), pp. 50-51; P. Dausch: "Die Wunder Jesu," *Biblische Zeitfragen*, 11-12 (Münster, 1912), 5-6; P. Menoud: "Miracle et sacrement dans le N. T.," *Verbum Caro*, 6 (1952), 142. On the meaning of σημεῖον, cf. H. Thielicke: *Das Wunder* (Leipzig, 1939), pp. 22-24; F. Zorell: *Lexicon Graecum Novi Testamenti* (Paris, 1937), c. 1198; S. V. McCasland: "Signs and Wonders," *Journal of Biblical Literature*, 76 (1957), 149-152.

2 · THE MEANING OF THE MIRACULOUS

On the assumption that God were to create a purely natural world order, sound theology can give no good reason why miracles should ever occur.[1] For such an order is verified precisely in the constancy and regularity of the course of events. Would not any change wrought in it by God, whether intended as a remedy for some malfunctioning in the order—if such may be admitted in view of God's omnipotence!—or as a capricious display of power, be an occasion of disorder in the universe and a contradiction of God's

[1] A. Van Hove: *La doctrine du miracle chez S. Thomas* (Paris, 1927), pp. 132f.; ID: *Het Mirakel* (Brussels, 1932), pp. 49-53, offer evidence from the texts that such was the opinion of St. Thomas. Even before him, J. Huby: "Miracles et lumière de grace," *Recherches de science religieuse*, 8 (1918), 63 f., had made similar studies. Later he undertook a deeper examination of two texts which Van Hove had considered as unfavorable to his own interpretation and he reached the conclusion that they fitted perfectly into the scheme of Thomistic thought as he and Van Hove had interpreted it; cf. J. Huby: "De la finalité du miracle. A propos de deux textes de S. Thomas," *Recherches de science religieuse*, 19 (1929), 298-305.

The theologians and apologists who followed St. Thomas were mainly of the contrary opinion, right up to the beginning of the present century. In the third chapter of the present work I shall examine their faulty outlook in its historical context: we will see then that their mistake was an inevitable consequence of a false apologetic concept of the miraculous.

wisdom? A king who lightly disregards his own laws is an unworthy tyrant; an inventor whose machine requires dubious shifts to make it work is a miserable botcher.

Truly if God's last word were the creative act by which he had launched the world in being, we should have to agree with those who, "looking up . . . at the night sky . . . feel it almost impious to suppose that God should sometimes unsay what he has once said with such magnificence." [2]

I · THE MIRACULOUS AND THE SUPERNATURAL

Yet the very core of the Christian Gospel is the certitude that God has given voice to a new word: he has called man, whom he had made king over the universe, to a relationship with himself undreamed of, unmerited, a relationship beyond any hope of man: this is what we call grace.

The initial chapter in human history is a holy one: God walks in the Garden of his creation; he initiates man into the mysteries of his triune life, which the wisdom of the ages would have been powerless to unlock.

Because of this the world in which man exists is built up into an area infinitely greater than it had been; it becomes the theater of a divine confrontation, of a colloquy through which are wrought the interchanges linking God and his creatures.

Therefore what had seemed a complete and unchangeable order of things becomes involved in a wholly new adventure. It is made part of a plan grander than before: as a matter of fact, God gives to

[2] Cf. C. S. Lewis: *Miracles,* p. 115. This was an objection constantly raised during the eighteenth and nineteenth centuries. Thus we find Voltaire saying: "God does nothing unreasonable, and how, therefore, could he find a cause for temporarily disfiguring his own work? . . . Why should God work a miracle? In order to accomplish a particular end in respect to some living thing. He is thus made to say: 'By making the world, by my divine purposes, and by my immutable laws I have failed in the accomplishment of a particular end; I will change my eternal ideas, my unchangeable laws, in order that I may try to accomplish what I have been unable to do by means of them? This would be rather an avowal of weakness than of strength; and it is evident that it admits in God an inconceivable contradiction." (Voltaire's article on "Miracles" in the *Dictionnaire philosophique*). J. S. Lawton: *Miracles and Revelation* (London, 1959) has very clearly shown how these objections of the Enlightenment arose from a notion of revelation distorted by Rationalism.

it a mission to embody a mystery infinitely more splendid than that to which the magnificent but limited ambit of natural laws testifies.

Will this new call mutilate the previous order or on the contrary perfect and expand it, adapting it to the pattern of a reality which is divine?

The transcendent nature of the miraculous then expresses, in the world which we perceive, that infinite love by which God manifests his election of man in admitting him to supernatural life: it demonstrates that in God's eyes the immutable glory of his creation is a paltry thing when weighed against his least sign of love for the child born of his grace.[3]

II · THE MIRACULOUS AND THE INCARNATION

Once recognized as plausible within the framework of man's supernatural calling, miracles become immeasurably more probable in view of the concrete act which makes this calling a reality—the redemptive act of the divine Incarnation. For "God, who at sundry times and in diverse ways has spoken in the past to our forefathers by the Prophets, has spoken in these latter days to us by his Son, whom he has chosen as the heir of all things, the heir of all the ages."[4] Thus God entered visibly into history's stream; he speaks to us, in human tongue, by his everlasting Word: "The Word was made flesh; and dwelt amongst us."

In all men the body and the material world which is its extension are at one and the same time instruments which the spirit employs and mirrors in which the spiritual is reflected. Now, this double function being granted, the body becomes the *sign* which binds men together, the mediator which makes communication among men possible. By himself taking on human flesh, the Word of God

[3] "(The miracle) is the harbinger of that divine 'philanthropia' of which St. Paul speaks, whereby God, condescending to make use of a language intelligible to man, lets his abnormal goodness shine through abnormal signs." M. Blondel: art. "Miracle" in A. Lalande: *Vocabulaire technique et critique de la philosophie*[5] (Paris, 1947), p. 615. B. De Sailly: "La notion et le rôle du miracle," *Annales de phil. chrétienne,* 154 (1907), 352 f., develops similar ideas.

[4] Hebr. I, 1-2.

has made of that body an instrument of eternal purpose, a mirror wherein the divine is reflected in human form. The body born of the holy Virgin—and in its wake all earthly things—becomes the great and efficacious Sign, the all-sufficing Sacrament whereby God is leagued with us. God has willed, by the sharing of his whole self, to make a sign to us: in all the closeness of human contact he has come to us as human beings.

Are not the words which the Christmas Preface of the Roman liturgy employs to express the basic purport of the mystery of the Incarnation—"that as we behold God in visible form, we are snatched up into the love of that which is unseen[5]—are not these words suited to express, as well, the religious significance of the miraculous? At even first glance, it is clear that a miracle is to be envisioned as a direct prolongation of the Incarnation, as a perceptible showing forth of God's redemptive love.[6]

God knows well of what clay he has made us. He knows how our eyes and our hearts are fixed on the countless wonders which tempt our senses, on the tasks of survival, on the mere routine of daily life; he knows that we are fixed to the extent of being blinded. He knows how a searching glance, the charm of a countenance, the appeal of a being who can be seen, heard, and touched, will captivate the human mind which by its nature is so subject to sensory

5 ". . . *ut dum visibiliter Deum cognoscimus, per hunc in invisibilium amorem rapiamur.*" This is a thought which recurs in Augustine: "*quia illa quae non videbantur non credebantur per ista temporalia quae videbantur, aedificabat fidem ad illa quae non videbantur*" (*Sermo* 88, n. 1; ML XXXVIII, c. 539). And in another place: "*Quapropter Deus qui fecit visibilia coelum et terram, non dedignatur facere visibilia miracula in coelo vel in terra, quibus ad se invisibilem colendum excitet animam adhuc visibilibus deditam*" (*De Civitate Dei*, X, 12; ML XLI, c. 291).

6 "Every particular Christian miracle manifests at a particular place and moment the character and significance of the Incarnation" (C. S. Lewis, *Miracles*, p. 131). Inversely, Tertullian saw in the miracles of the Old Testament a kind of preparation for, or allurement to the Word in his human relationship with us: "*Ipse enim (Verbum scil.) et ad humana semper colloquia descendit, ab Adam usque ad patriarchas et prophetas, in visione, in somnio, in speculo, in aenigmate, ordinem suum praestruens ab initio, semper quem erat persecuturus in fine. Ita semper ediscebat et deus in terris cum hominibus conversari, non alius quam sermo, qui caro erat futurus; ediscebat autem, ut nobis finem sterneret, ut facilius crederemus filium Dei descendisse in saeculum, cum et retro tale quid gestum cognosceremus. Propter nos enim sicut scripta sunt ita et gesta sunt, in quos aevorum fines decurrerunt*" (*Adversus Praxeam*, XVI; ML II, c. 174).

perception. He knows how impoverished are our eyes when we open them to the dazzling light sent forth by the Most High, the Invisible, the All Holy. That he might share with us his own life, he bent to our weakness and manifested a condescension motivated only by love. He did not, by some violent act, detach our hearts from earthly things; he did not force our eyes to gaze upon the pure and awesome brilliance of his glory; instead he himself descended to the measure of his creation; and, despoiling himself of his divine majesty, he took human flesh upon himself. From that time eyes which desire to see him here have not needed to sever themselves from the love of material things, from the joys and beauties of this earth; for God, in being made man, becomes a fellow wayfarer with us. We, as well as John, can testify to "what we have heard, what we have seen with our eyes, what we have thought upon, and what we have handled: the Word of Life." [7] To have heard that word we are not required to be deaf to the music of this earth, for in human language God speaks to us "as no man ever spoke." We need never fear, in our converse with him, that he will not understand our words: all our human speech is known to him. There are eyes which meet mine; there is a voice in my ear; there is a hand upon my shoulder: the glance, the words, the hands are a man's . . . but I know that they are God's.[8] In this process by which God's schools us—by a pedagogy which baffles description because it so lends itself to our human weakness—the miracle is yet a further step: it extends to its uttermost limit the divine condescension of the Incarnation.

In having made himself approachable and near to us in the Word made flesh, God remained, nonetheless, disguised and an enigma. He hid himself under what Paul has termed "the form of a

[7] I John I, 1-3; John I, 18.

[8] J. Mouroux, *The Meaning of Man* (New York, 1948), pp. 81-84. St. Athanasius (*Or. III contra Arianos*, n. 32; MG XXVI, c. 392) turns these figures to the consideration of Our Lord's miracles: "The hand indeed by which he cured Peter's mother-in-law of her fever was a hand impelled by a human act; but it was divine power that subdued illness. So also, when he cured the man born blind, he made use of spittle drawn from his human mouth, but it was God's intervention which, by means of this slime, gave sight to the sightless eyes. And, when he summoned Lazarus from the tomb, he spoke as a man in human language; but it was as God that he recalled him to life."

servant." The body taken up by the Word is not a glorious body radiant with divinity: it is the body of sinful and disinherited man. The Incarnate Word became, in all things except sin, a man like other men.[9] Faith alone pierces the veil, recognizing God present in the carpenter's son and catching in his words the message of the divine heart.

Yet, if God be so deeply united to humanity, will not his care for us lead him, in the very moment of requiring the commitment to him which is made by our act of faith, to accommodate himself yet further to our frailty and to strengthen our faith in a way we are able to perceive? Is it only by the purity and the depth of his teaching or only by the moral grandeur of his personality that he will show himself? Must one not rather expect that he will manifest himself in a brief flash of the glorious brilliance of his body or in the transfiguration of things which that body touches? Is it not thus that he will make himself accessible to our near-sighted eyes?

If it be true, as St. Bernard says,[10] that "the chief reason which led God to take human flesh upon himself is that he might attract to the love of his saving humanity those to whom human love alone appeals, that they might, little by little, be drawn to spiritual love," does not such a motivation lend support to the probability of miracles?

Christ understands how our poor sight is fascinated by visible things, how it is captivated to what lies on the surface: it is even likely that, when the God of love shows himself to us in the flesh of man, we may fail to know him unless he sometimes lets us glimpse his mighty power by compelling our capricious and easily distracted gaze to rest on him. Our hands cling to material things, which we wish to enjoy and to own: was it not obvious that we would hardly consent to relinquish earthly in favor of divine glory unless we briefly glimpsed it in the person of the Lord? Why else did God establish in man a heart perceptive of every bodily pres-

[9] Hebr. IV, 15.

[10] St. Bernard, *Sermo XX in Cantica*, n. 6; ML CLXXXIII, c. 870: "*Ergo hanc arbitror praecipuam invisibili Deo fuisse causam, quod voluit in carne videri et cum hominibus homo conversari, ut carnalium videlicet, qui nisi carnaliter amare non poterant, cunctus primo ad suae carnis salutarem amorem affectiones retraheret, atque ita gradatim ad amorem perduceret spiritualem.*"

ence and every intimate relationship, if it were not that he might thus summon human feeling to confront his own divine heart?

Like the Church and the sacraments, miracles are thus set in that line which is the normal prolongation of the Incarnation. The "loving kindness and the humaneness of God our Saviour" know how to make use of human frailty and to adapt themselves perfectly to the weakness of our mortal flesh; that "divine philanthropy" speaks to us directly "so that, casting off the heedlessness and the lusts of this world, we set our hearts on the blessed hope of the coming of glory in our great God and Saviour, Christ Jesus." [11]

The word of God prolongs his historical presence in another presence—seen but veiled—that of the Church and the sacraments. Does this not even increase our need of the support of a presence we can perceive? Sacramental rites, which put us in touch with the redemptive act, surely betoken a presence we can perceive; but the mystery of the Redemption is open only to those whose faith is vital. The very character of the divine plan, as is made clear by the Incarnation, seems to make it likely that the veil will sometimes be lifted so that our eyes may briefly glimpse something of the Reality which lies beneath the sacramental sign and that our faith may thus be confirmed.[12]

III · THE MIRACULOUS AND THE REDEMPTION

The meaning of the miraculous becomes even more apparent if it be viewed against the background of the concrete form in which the Incarnate Word is sent to us. Mankind, whose life the Word comes to share, is sinful and fallen from grace; in order to make men share in his divine life he has first to cure, purify, and ransom them. Thus the miraculous, as a perceptible sign of this divine message, must carry a redemptive significance. It forms a part of the redemptive work whenever things visible are in the forefront: at the very beginning of life when the body serves as the instru-

[11] Titus II, 12-13; III, 4.

[12] In recent years it is Protestant theologians especially who have so forcefully drawn our attention to the relationship between the miraculous and the sacramental. See the works cited in ch. VI, note 1, below. Some suggestions are made, from the Catholic viewpoint, in G. Söhngen: *Symbol und Wirklichkeit im Kultmysterium* (Bonn, 1940), pp. 82-94.

ment of redemption, and at its close when glory takes complete possession of the whole body and when it knows its final flowering.

It is the flesh that is the theater of the redemptive work. Sin and bodily distress are closely linked: "the wages of sin is death." The consequences of sin are most sharply sensed in the realm of man's bodily feeling. Sickness, misery, and death especially, are the marks of sin. Because of sin the world which the senses perceive becomes a screen which cuts us off from God, rather than a mirror in which we may glimpse his glory. Concupiscence holds our bodies in its thralldom and pinions the wings of our free flight to God: the natural universe becomes *a vale of tears* wherein humanity, exiled from heavenly grace, vainly tries to establish itself in joyfulness and peace. The Redemption fulfills the "divine philanthropy" of the Incarnation by entering into the center of our alienation from God, into our human anguish. God, in his turn, walks the path trodden by fallen man: *homo igitur cecidit, sed Deus descendit*; for what was in the case of man a fall becomes for God a descent. God comes to us in the very body of sin in order that he may regain his own possession, man; he draws unto himself all flesh in order that he may direct the man's return to the Father of a world gone astray. From the enslaved body he fashions an instrument of ransom, an earnest of reawakened life. He turns all the burdens of weariness, sorrows, and sufferings into wounds which heal. In himself drinking the very dregs of the chalice of death itself, he transforms death into the roots of divine life. He "binds the salvation of mankind to the Tree of the Cross; from a tree came death: from the Tree comes life, so that the demon who conquered man by the tree of Paradise is himself brought low by the Tree of the Cross." [13]

Such is the part taken by the flesh in the work of redemption. The body becomes the axis on which the fate of mankind so turns that man may return to his true source. To use the expression employed by Tertullian, the body is the hinge of salvation—*caro salutis cardo*[14]—the hinge on which the gates of life re-open to the vista of a regained paradise.

[13] "*qui salutem humani generis in ligno crucis constituisti, ut unde mors oriebatur inde vita resurgeret, et qui in ligno vincebat, in ligno quoque vinceretur, per Christum Dominum nostrum*" (The Preface of the Holy Cross in the Roman Liturgy).

[14] *De Carnis Resurr.*, VIII; ML II, c. 806.

This function of the body—that it serve as a focal point and an instrument of redemption—is a fundamental principle of the divine plan of salvation. Likewise, in the Mystical Body of Christ, the Church, the visible structure, serves as the instrument by means of which grace is shared. The sacraments are like the body's external organs, exterior rites being instrumentalities by means of which the grace they signify is conferred. Hilary of Poitiers expressed this notion most strikingly when he declared that "just as Christ, who is God, subsisted in bodily form, so do we, in our turn, become divine through our human bodies." [15]

In this respect too, the miraculous fits perfectly into God's plan, inasmuch as by it the body becomes symbol and instrument of a spiritual rebirth. Our bodies are seen to be suddenly freed of their ills, our material woe is relieved; the anguish which encompasses us in the midst of life's trials is unexpectedly lifted; by the hand of God the blemishes of sin, sorrow, wretchedness, and death are effaced. But such benefits do not exhaust their own meaning: they are indications of healing on a deeper level. What comes to us through our bodies is the certitude that God's will is to heal the whole man: God desires to awaken us to a recognition of his goodness, to excite faith in his saving purposes, to arouse confidence and lead us to commit ourselves to him.

A miracle is something that happens in the physical world; but its true significance springs from its spiritual meaning. Bodily healing is always a sign and a work of God; by it he makes known his redeeming intention, adapting himself to our weakness and making use of "this body of death." Thus it is that, when we are in despair because of the extremity to which we are reduced by sin and death, the first stirrings of renewed life come to awaken us to the promise of its flowering.

And, in yet another sense, the body is a sign of salvation: it is no mere transitory implement to be put aside when its first work is done; for once salvation has been attained, grace and glory are not confined within the realm of the spirit: they flow out beyond it,

[15] "*Non ille eguit homo effici, per quem homo factus est: sed nos eguimus ut Deus caro fieret, et habitaret in nobis, id est, assumptione carnis unius interna universae carnis incoleret. Humilitas eius nostra nobilitas est, contumelia eius honor noster est: quod ille Deus in carne consistens, hoc nos vicissim in Deum ex carne renovati.*" (*De Trinitate*, II, n. 25; ML X, c. 67).

subduing the entire cosmos by their brightness and their power.

Christ's body was transformed by his resurrection into a glorious body. Because of her assumption, the body of the holy Virgin shares in the glory of her unspotted soul. And we know, as well, that "the Lord will conform our wretched bodies to the pattern of his glorious body by that power which he has over all things that are." [16] When all is finished, our bodies will at last be transfigured in glory; "death is the last enemy which shall be destroyed." [17] On that day, there will be "a new heaven and a new earth" bright with the glory of the presence of Christ the Lord. Today, "all creation groans in travail to bring forth the revelation of the sons of God" and we, also, we "groan within ourselves, in the expectation of the redemption of our bodies." [18] The Church walks forth along the dim-lit path of faith: she suffers anguish and pain of body and of soul; she bears, with Christ, his redeeming Cross, down the long chain of years even to the end of time.

But God would not be the God of the Incarnation and of the Redemption if, even in the midst of this long *Via Crucis*, there were not an occasional glimpse of the glory that is to be, if the dawn of the resurrection did not sometime pierce through the clouds which obscure this valley of tears, if our misery were not consoled, if our weakness were not aided.

During his life on earth, Christ on Mount Tabor, although still "clothed in the form of a servant," revealed for a moment to his chosen apostles a reflection of the glory which had been his at the right hand of the Father, from before the beginning of the world. His object was not to spare them the Cross; he rather sought to teach them to bear it with strength, trust, and faith.[19] In their dark-

[16] Phil. III, 21.

[17] II Peter III, 12-13 (echoing Is. LXV, 17; LXVI, 22); I Cor., XV, 26: "*novissima autem inimica destruetur mors.*"

[18] Rom. VIII, 20-23.

[19] This thought is often taken up by the Fathers in sermons on the Transfiguration; cf., for example, the words of Leo the Great (*Sermo LI*; ML LIV, c. 310): "*In qua transfiguratione illud quidem principaliter agebatur, ut de cordibus discipulorum crucis scandalum tolleretur; nec conturbaret eroum fidem voluntariae humilitas passionis, quibus revelata esset absconditae excellentia dignitatis. Sed non minore providentia spes sanctae ecclesiae fundabatur, ut totum Corpus Christi agnosceret qualis esset communicatione donandum, et eius sibi honoris consortia membra promitterent, qui in capite praefulsisset.*" See also St. John Chrysostom (*Hom. LVI in Matth.*, n. 1

est hours, the remembrance of Tabor would shine as "a light gleaming in the darkness of the night and awaiting the dawn, until the hour when the day-star would show itself to all hearts." [20]

Every Christian miracle embodies this spark which points the way to eternal glory. It shares not indeed in the full glory of the resurrection but in the lesser light of Tabor. No more than the apostles, are we able to bear the bright light of this glory but we are assured of its existence, real if hidden: we know that we ourselves are its weak containing vessels. The miracle remains a thing exceptional, for the Cross is not to be laid down during our earthly pilgrimage. Nevertheless the unexpected occurrence of the miraculous enlightens our faith, sustains our hope, and renews our love.

Augustine, speaking with reference to the cure at the pool of Bethsaida[21] expatiates upon the meaning of the miraculous. This

---

and n. 4; MG LVIII, c. 549 and cc. 554 f). Here again, miracle and sacrament are regarded as being closely united in the same eschatological perspective. What is said, in the *Oratio secreta* appointed in the Roman Missal for the Mass of Tuesday in Passion Week, in respect to the Eucharist can be said also of the miracle: "*Hostias tibi, Domine, offerimus immolandas: quae temporalem consolationem significant; ut promissa non desperemus aeterna.*"

[20] II Peter I, 16-19; see also II Cor. III, 18.

[21] "*Magis gaudere ac admirari debemus, quia Dominus noster et Salvator Jesus Christus homo factus est, quam quod divina inter homines Deus fecit. Plus est enim ad salutem nostram quod factus est propter homines, quam quod fecit inter homines: et plus est quod vitia sanavit animarum, quam quod sanavit languores corporum moriturorum. Sed quia ipsa anima non eum noverat a quo sananda erat, et oculos habebat in carne unde facta corporalia videret, nondum habebat sanos in corde, unde Deum latentem cognosceret; fecit quod videre poterat, ut sanaretur unde videre non poterat. Ingressus est locum ubi jacebat magna multitudo languentium, caecorum, claudorum, aridorum, et cum esset medicus animarum et corporum, et qui venisset sanare omnes animas crediturorum, de illis languentibus unum elegit quem sanaret, ut unitatem significaret. Si mediocri corde, et quasi humano captu et ingenio consideremus facientem, et quod ad potestatem pertinet non magnum aliquid perfecit, et quod ad benignitatem, parum fecit. Tot jacebant, et unus curatus est, cum posset uno verbo. Quid ergo intelligendum est, nisi quia potestas illa et bonitas illa magis agebat quid animae in factis ejus pro salute sempiterna intelligerent, quam quid pro temporali salute corpora mererentur? Corporum enim salus quae vera exspectatur a Domino, erit in fine in resurrectione mortuorum: tunc quod vivet, non morietur; tunc quod sanabitur, non aegrotabit; tunc quod satiabitur, non esuriet aut sitiet; tunc quod renovabitur, non veterascet. Nunc vero in illis factis Domini et Salvatoris nostri Jesu Christi, et caecorum aperti oculi, morte clausi sunt; et paralyticorum membra constricta, morte dissoluta sunt, et quidquid sanatum est temporaliter in membris mortalibus, in fine defecit; anima*

text splendidly sums up the role which the miraculous plays in the divine economy of our redemption:

"That Christ Our Lord became man ought arouse in us more joy and more wonder than to behold divine prodigies wrought among men. What, for the sake of men, he became is of greater significance to our salvation than are the works which he did among men: it is a greater thing that he should have healed the wounds of our souls than the bodily ailments of men who are destined for death. But, for the very reason that the soul itself is unaware of him to whom it owes its health because it perceives by means of carnal eyes, attuned to bodily things, rather than through spiritual eyes capable of recognizing the hidden God, he has brought before the fleshly eyes wonders which are able to cure the eyes of the spirit from the blindness which keeps them from seeing. And, therefore, upon reaching the place in which there lay a great multitude of the blind, the halt, and the lame, he who was the destined physician of soul and body alike, having come to save the souls of all who believe, then selected one among the afflicted in order that, in him, there might be symbolized the unity in which all mankind is linked.

"Is it with selfish hearts and from the narrow viewpoint of merely human wisdom that we are to gaze upon Jesus working his miracles? We would then have to conclude that he had made but slight use of his power and had given only little rein to his goodness. Of the multitude lying there in anguish, he gave health to but one, even though he might have called upon all to rise. But we ought rather to conclude that his power and goodness were more mindful of what souls required to be saved than of what bodies needed for their temporal health.

"That health of body which we expect to receive from Our Lord will be granted to us on the last day, in the resurrection of our bodies. The life then to be given can never more know death; the cure, then to be wrought, cannot again succumb to sickness; the fulfillment, then to be given, can never yield to thirst or hunger; the youthfulness then regained can never grow old.

---

vero quae credidit, ad vitam aeternam transitum fecit." (*In Jo. tract.* XVII, n. 1; ML XXXV, c. 1527; and the similar passage of *Sermo* 88, n. 1; ML XXXVIII, c. 539).

"Those who were cured of blindness by Our Lord and Saviour Jesus Christ, during his life on earth, have long since closed their eyes in death; those whose withered limbs were restored in time have again yielded them to the dissolution brought by death; every cure of mortal members, granted in time, has in time fallen away; but the soul which has believed has passed over into the life that is eternal."

3 · THE STRUCTURE OF THE MIRACULOUS

On the basis of the scriptural terminology and of what has been defined by the teaching authority of the Church, the first chapter of the present work has set forth a description of the miraculous. We directed our attention to the value of the miracle as a sign; its character as a manifestation of divine power; and its quality as a prodigy or wonder. Now that, in my second chapter, the miracle has been set into the framework of the Economy of Salvation, it is fitting that the organic interdependence of these three elements be more precisely explored, in order that the *structure* or *shape* of the miracle may be theologically explained.

I · THE STRUCTURE OF THE MIRACLE, CONSIDERED AS A DIVINE SIGN

On the basis of the considerations developed in chapter II an initial conclusion may be drawn: the principal element of the structure of the miracle consists in its value as a sign.

A sign is commonly defined as an object leading to the knowledge of something else. However, this is but a derived and a weakened sense of the word. Actually, the relationship between the sign and the thing signified does not arise of its own accord. Nor is this relationship established by the knower; rather, he recognizes a pre-established relationship and, in a certain sense, rediscovers it. A sensibly perceptible "thing" (*res*) becomes, in the philosophically *formal* sense, a "sign" only insofar as it is inserted into a spiritually dynamic relationship between subjects, which is accurately termed the *sign-act*. It thus becomes, for persons who are in touch with one another, an element in their communication.

The miracle is a sign in the full sense of the word. Often it is discussed as though we first perceived it as an intervention of divine power and only later, by a process of reasoning, made use of it as a proof or indication, so that it becomes a *sign-object* of the revelation to which it points. But the function of the miracle in the redemptive economy, as described above, implies that it is a sign in a deeper and a more meaningful sense. Whenever the power of God shows itself in a perceptible manner, its prime purpose is to indicate to us, in a fashion wholly personal, his tidings of salvation. The purpose of miracles, then, is less to show his sovereign power than to signify his redemptive love. Therefore, the act which makes of the miracle a divine sign is not the activity of human reasoning following upon the intervention of God in the world; it is rather the *sign-act* wrought by God himself involving himself in nature in order to signify our salvation.

Let us examine more closely God's action in "making signs" to men.

Spiritual matters are apprehended by man only through the mediation of perceptible things. If we are to know and love spiritual reality, which is not of itself sensibly perceptible, we must approach it along the lines of imagery, an imagery which without being arbitrary is nevertheless not ineluctably linked to the reality which it betokens, but leaves a certain liberty to our choice in making signs. This imagery, chosen by the will, becomes the means of mediation through which we attain spiritual reality; and to it we give the name *symbol*.[1]

[1] On the symbol in religion see the study by L. Vander Kerken: *Religieus gevoel en aesthetisch ervaren* (Brussels, 1945), ch. 3: "De religieuze aktiviteit"; P. Tillich: "Theology and Symbolism" in F. E. Johnson (ed.), *Religious Symbolism* (New York, 1955); A. Vergote: "Le Symbole," *Revue phil. de Louvain* 57 (1959), 197-224; J. V. Langmead Casserley: "Event-Symbols and Myth-Symbols," *Anglican Theological Review*, 38 (1956), 127-136; K. Rahner:

Such imagery never measures up to the idea which it expresses; of its very nature it is unable to do so. Fundamentally, it is opposed to this idea; and it expresses it only in and through this contrast. Doubtless, the imagery must, in a sense, be adapted to the notion it symbolizes: there must be a point of contact between the image and the spiritual reality which it pictures. Yet, it is only under this particular form of *sign-act,* which we call *symbol-act,* that the sign and the thing signified become, in and beyond their antithetical appearances, the object of a single, undivided act of understanding. The sign and the thing signified are experienced in unison; or to express it even more clearly, in the undivided unity of a single act we apprehend through and in the sign a reality which is and remains greater than the sign itself.

For example, a handclasp is not the complete and necessary expression of the spiritual reality which we call friendship. No doubt, in order that reciprocal offering and mutual union of minds be expressed, there are affinities between the gesture of grasping the hand and the spiritual attachment which it bespeaks. I am able, therefore, to take the handclasp as being the freely chosen image, the symbol, of friendship. When I have so taken it, it becomes a symbol-act through which in a unique and single action, in and through a bodily gesture, I offer my spiritual friendship to someone else. If he apprehends the meaning of the gesture I make, then this handclasp is sufficient, without any further action, to put my friendship before him. He may accept or reject it; but, in and by my gesture, it is offered to him as a reality directly confronting him.

"Zur Theologie des Symbols," *Schriften zur Theologie,* IV (3rd. ed., Zurich, 1962), 275-311; A. Van Leeuwen: "Enige aantekeningen over het symbool," *Bijdragen,* 20 (1959), 1-14; S. Wisse: *Das Religiöse Symbol* (Essen, 1963); On the subject of "symbolic" causality in the sacramental system, see L. Monden: *Het misoffer als mysterie* (Roermond, 1948), esp. pp. 109-131; ID.: "Symbooloorzakelijkheid als eigen causaliteit van het sacrament," *Bijdragen,* 13 (1952), 277-285; P. Schoonenberg: "The Sign," *Lumen Vitae* (Eng.), 14 (1959), 9-18. Some useful insights, even though at times they appear somewhat imprecise, are to be found in the book of E. Masure: *Le Signe* (Paris, 1953), esp. pp. 17-38. On the structure of the miraculous sign consult: J. Kijm: "Apologetische notities bij het wonder," *Bijdragen,* 14 (1953), 148-155; T. F. Beaudry: "Miracle and Sign," *Studia Montis Regii,* 3 (1960), 65-94.

Actually, no relationship between God and man is effected except by means of symbols. It is symbolism alone which can bridge the chasm dividing a pure spirit from one who can never entirely cast aside the limitations of the senses. Man wishes to know God; he desires to become one with him in prayer or in giving of self; he yearns to make God known to other men: this he must always do by means of symbols. God himself so expresses himself; and he is known, on the human level, only through his creation which speaks to the senses.

If God wishes to disclose to us, in a more intimate revelation, the secrets of his triune life, the symbolic form is no less necessary. But for this further step, ordinary symbols cease to be adequate. Signs of our natural knowledge, they are suited for and limited to the expression of merely natural meaning. Should God wish, nevertheless, to make them the vehicles of supernatural reality, it seems that this can be done in only two ways. He might make use of the unchanged symbols while enlarging our capacity to receive them and raising us to a new understanding of them. Or alternatively he can leave our knowing powers untouched, but so modify the sensible reality which serves as a sign that it will express more than it could naturally do.

In his entire revealed message God speaks to us in the first way. In order that he may make known to us mysterious realities above the reach of reason, he employs ordinary human signs. But he also elevates our understanding and enlarges our intelligence by giving us new insight so that we become fitted to discern a new meaning in the old symbol. This higher path of understanding is called Faith.

Our ordinary daily language must suffice to transmit divine revelation or the inspired message of the prophets or of Holy Writ, as well as to express the personality of the God-Man and the infallible dogmatic definitions of the Church.

This language makes known to us, for example, that God is "Father." According to natural human thought, this word expresses a well-defined and certain reality. But when God teaches us, by the words of Christ, that he is a "father," paternity in the natural order becomes the symbol of a reality whose full meaning cannot be conveyed by realities of the natural order. Nevertheless, by making full use of the concept of fatherhood, God strengthens our understanding so much that the unchanged word conveys to us an apprehension of God's fatherhood according to his own nature, even though we are unable to describe it. Then are we able to say: "Our Father, who are in heaven"; for it is no longer we ourselves, in our merely natural state, but the Spirit of God within us who prays: "Abba, Father." [2]

The same considerations apply to sacramental symbols. Bathing in clear water naturally signifies a desire for moral and spiritual purification. But when the immersion in, or pouring on of, water symbolizes burial with the slain Christ and resurrection with him to divine life, we have a meaning which God alone can attach to this symbol, a meaning which is perceptible only to a living faith.

The case is otherwise when God, still speaking to man's natural reason, wishes to open to us the realm of the supernatural and thus to prepare the path to faith. The supernatural must then divest itself of itself, without however losing a jot of its transcendent character. Such a paradox is possible only if God allows the supernatural to pierce through the natural: God so modifies a natural thing as to suggest, by some unusual manifestation, something which transcends the normal meaning of the symbol; this remarkable occurrence, and the religious framework into which it is set, make it possible for there to be, in the very midst of nature, a reference to the supernatural.

The miracle, then, does not depend on divine revelation or the higher vision of faith to disclose its meaning. It confronts the nonbeliever directly; and, if it appeals to the believer also, it is in order

[2] In this sense, any dogma might be called a symbol. But I avoid the use, nevertheless, of the word *symbol* in describing dogmatic formularies in order that I may not be misunderstood. The Modernists actually termed dogmas "symbols," but in a sense wholly subjective and void of substance. According to their view, these symbols are no more than a provisional, fluctuating, and necessarily incomplete expression of a personal religious experience—one lacking any objective representational value as regards the content of faith. In the orthodox view, dogmas are, contrariwise, expressions employed by God himself or, at the least, resting upon his warranty, as permanently and objectively valid, which serve in a real sense—if only by a remote analogy—to make known to us his ineffable mysteries. On the radical difference between these two ways of looking at the matter, consult A. Gardeil: *Le donné révélé et la théologie* (Juvisy, 1932), pp. 41-114.

to offer an external support to his faith: God makes use of it chiefly as a toothing stone, as a connecting link between faith and what is perceptible to the senses. It is a divine symbol-act wherein the supernatural shows itself to natural knowledge: the supernatural is expressed in what is open to natural perception.

This symbolism implies that the natural course of events is changed without being subverted, in the sense that the natural is transcended. In the light of its own character and of the ambit in which it occurs, this change immediately appears as being symbolic of a divine intention other than that shown in the normal course of events. Clearly, any such divine intention can be effective only as a special activity of God, as an act of his divine power.

In concluding, we might sum up, in technical fashion, the structure of the miraculous as we see it now. The miracle is no mere intervention of divine power transfigured after the event, into a symbol by a sign-act on the part of man. Its significance comes from a sign-act placed by God, one which necessarily takes the form of a transcendent intervention, for it serves as a symbol of the supernatural in the perceptible world of nature.

II · HISTORICAL NOTE ON THE THEOLOGY OF THE MIRACULOUS

This theological enquiry suggests some landmarks for a summary history of the theology of miracles. We shall see that at different times one emphasis on one element in the structure of the miracle gives way to another, and that perfect balance has not always been maintained.[3]

The Gospels put primary emphasis on the function of the miracle as a sign. The Gospel of John, to which we shall later return, is thoroughly characteristic in this regard. The note of transcendence is seen as an indispensable aspect of the symbolism which marks a miracle; more than this, the wondrous aspect embodies the specific manner which draws our attention to the meaning of the miraculous.

[3] Cf. A. Michel: "Miracle," *Dict. de théologie cath.*, X, cc. 1801-1812; J. A. Hardon: "The Concept of Miracle from St. Augustine to Modern Apologetics," *Theological Studies*, 15 (1954), 229-257.

The Church Fathers of the earlier centuries[4] were prone to insist strongly upon the miracle as a sign of salvation rather than as a manifestation of divine omnipotence. This is not to say that they incorporated the miraculous into an apologetic system, but when they made passing reference to it they considered it as being primarily the seal of true revelation or else they saw it as a fulfillment of prophecy, insisting primarily on its significance as a sign. In respect to any superiority of the Christian miracle over the wonders known to the pagan world, they gave the former priority in connection with its function in the religious context of the Gospel, which brings out its significance, rather than as a manifestation of power.[5]

Generally speaking, they approached the consideration of the miraculous from the point of view of faith. The miraculous plays a lesser role in their theologically speculative work than it does in their sermons and meditations. Rather than giving themselves to an analysis of the miracle as an occurrence, they prefer seeking to discern its purpose and its significance for the Christian who walks the path of faith. Moreover, the whole tone of their thought is Platonic: less insistence is laid upon what links cause to effect than upon the relationship of present existence to its archetypical form, hence to its symbolic nature.

The first to set up a systematic doctrine was St. Augustine, whose influence on all who treated of this subject extended even until the twelfth century. His doctrine was thoroughly traditional.[6]

[4] Many texts, interpreted however from a Protestant standpoint, may be found in H. Schlingensiepen: *Die Wunder des Neuen Testamentes. Wege und Abwege ihrer Deutung in der Alten Kirche bis zur Mitte des fünften Jahrhunderts* (Gütersloh, 1933); A. Fridrichsen: *Le problème du miracle dans le christianisme primitif* (Strasbourg, 1925).

[5] On the miracles as fulfilling the prophecies, cf. Justin: *Apol.*, I; 30, MG VI; c. 376; Tertullian: *Adv. Judaeos,* IX, ML II, c. 616; *Adv. Marcionem,* III; 3; IV, 39; ML II, cc. 324, 455. On their superiority to pagan wonders, see Origen: *Contra Celsum,* I; 68; II, 4; III, 27. Augustine often reverts to this idea, e.g., *De Civitate Dei,* X, 12; X, 17; X, 18; XXII, 10; ML XLI, cc. 291, 296, 297, 772.

[6] A good treatment of the question and more ample bibliographical information is supplied by P. de Vooght in his "La notion philosophique du miracle selon S. Augustin," *Rech. de théologie ancienne et médiévale,* 10 (1938), 317-343; ID: "Les miracles dans la vie de S. Augustin," *ibid.,* 11 (1939), 5-16; ID: "La théologie du miracle selon S. Augustin," *ibid.,* 11 (1939), 197-222.

He stresses the significance of the miracle as a sign so forcefully that some commentators feel he has wholly cast into the shade its transcendent nature. As a matter of fact, St. Augustine did face the question of divine intervention; but he did not look upon it as an act of God's creative power: he saw in it God's activity stirring up the seeds and capacities which his own hand had, once and for all, actually sown into the nature of things.[7]

Miracles, therefore, are set apart from natural happenings not by the fact that they demonstrate a manifestation of power, but rather because their unusual nature makes them better fitted to be signs. According to St. Augustine, we might consider even natural occurrences as miracles in a wide sense, for each of them speaks of the power and goodness of God; but he himself says: "those things alone are properly called miracles which, although they are as material as are other aspects of nature, are offered to our perception in order to convey to us a divine message." [8] Their center of gravity rests precisely on their value as signs; by reason of the unusual quality which marks them, God attracts our attention and invites us to a salutary union with himself, making use of invisible things to bring us to things which are not seen: "Let us take advantage of

[7] Commentators on St. Augustine have expressed divergent opinions on this point. Here I adopt the interpretation which P. de Vooght defends in the first of the articles cited in the preceding note; it appears to me the most probable. According to this view, St. Augustine makes a distinction between the ordinary and immediate capabilities of natural things (*semina*, e.g., the grains of wheat in respect to the ear into which it flowers) and those deeper, and more productive, capabilities (*semina seminum*, e.g., the water mentioned in Genesis in respect to the fish to which it gave birth). The "semina" are at the root of the ordinary course of things; the "semina seminum" ordinarily initiate the action of natural things but are also able—by reason of divine intervention whether direct or indirect—themselves to become directly active. Because of the "semina seminum" the miraculous therefore finds in nature its positive fulcrum. Some passages in "De genesi ad litteram" (e.g., IX, c. 18; ML XXXIV, cc. 406-407) which certain writers (A. Van Hove: *La doctrine du miracle chez S. Thomas*, pp. 31-32; A. Darmet: *Les notions de raison séminale et de puissance obédientielle chez S. Augustin et S. Thomas d'Aquin* [Selley, 1934], pp. 35-43) rely upon to support the idea that the "seminum semina" are no more than merely obediential powers, having a purely negative potentiality to become the object of a miraculous intervention, appear to me to fit better into De Vooght's explanation.

[8] "*Illa quae quamvis ex eadem materia corporali, ad aliquid tamen divinitus annuntiandum nostris sensibus admoventur, quae proprie miracula et signa dicuntur*" (*De Trinitate*, III, 10, 19; ML XLII, c. 879).

the steps which Divine Providence has been pleased to prepare for us. For, while we were absorbed in our playthings and imaginings, losing ourselves in fond thoughts and reducing our lives to the level of vain fancies, God, in his unspeakable mercy, was pleased to make use of reasonable creatures subject to his laws, by speech and writings, by fire, by smoke, by cloud, and by pillar—all, so to speak, being visible words—that he might meet us, his children, on our own level and play with us the game of parable, so that with this kind of slime he could cure the ills of our inner eye." [9]

A well-known passage in his commentary on the Johannine Gospel attempts a synthesis of all these matters in what is said there of the multiplication of the loaves: "Our Lord's miracles are divine acts which raise man's soul on high, teaching him to discern God's presence through visible signs. God is no material being who can be seen by fleshly eyes, and the wonders by which he governs the whole world in the ruling of his domain are now so familiar to us as to appear unworthy of attention; so that scarcely anyone notices how wondrous is God's power in the development of a grain of wheat. For this reason, mindful of his mercy, he decided in his good time, to work wonders surpassing the ordinary course of natural events, so that man, grown too accustomed to the wonders that daily surround him, might be struck by happenings not more grand but more unusual. Actually, the government of the universe is a greater deed and a more extraordinary one than is the act of feeding five thousand men with five loaves. Nevertheless, the former passes unnoticed, while everyone is struck by the latter. And this is not because the second of these accomplishments is greater, but rather because it is rarer. For in presently nourishing the whole world, does he not empower a few grains to produce a harvest? Therefore, it is as God that he has acted; for the same power,

[9] "*Utamur gradibus quos nobis divina providentia fabricare dignatus est. Cum enim figmentis ludicris nimium delectati evanesceremus in cogitationibus nostris, et totam vitam in quaedam vana somnia verteremus; rationali creatura serviente legibus suis, per sonos ac litteras, ignem, fumum, nubem, columnam, quasi quaedam verba visibilia, cum infantia nostra parabolis ac similitudinibus quodammodo ludere et interiores oculos nostros luto huiuscemodi curare non aspernata est ineffabilis misericordia Dei*" (*De vera religione* 50, 98; ML XXXIV, c. 165).

which everyday brings forth rich harvests from simple seedlings, multiplies on this occasion the five loaves under his hands. This divine power was in Christ, and he treated the loaves like seeds, except that, instead of sowing them in the earth, he, as Creator of the world, multiplied them as they were held in his hands. By this act, Our Lord compels our attention and attracts our thoughts to him; he has shown his power in order to make us think. It is his desire that his visible gestures will draw us to marvel at the Creator who is unseen, so that, aroused to faith and purified by faith, we may wish to see with the eyes of our souls the invisible one whom we recognized when he wrought these wonders before our bodily eyes."[10]

More precisely, and in line with their more systematic spirit, the mediaeval scholastics, in their heyday, took up this point, and offered an answer to the question, *What is a miracle?* However, they approached it from a different angle. They were as yet scarcely concerned with apologetics, and did not systematically use miracles for this purpose. But the whole theological climate had changed. The Platonic outlook of the Fathers had yielded to the influence of Aristotelian philosophy—newly recovered by the Western world—and, little by little, Platonism fell into the background. Under Aris-

[10] "*Miracula quae fecit Dominus noster Jesus Christus sunt quidem divina opera et ad intelligendum Deum de visibilibus admonent humanam mentem. Quia enim illi non est talis substantia quae videri oculis possit, et miracula ejus quibus totum mundum regit universamque creaturam administrat, assiduitate viluerunt, ita ut pene nemo dignetur attendere opera Dei mira et stupenda in quolibet seminis grando; secundum ipsam suam misericordiam servavit sibi quaedam, quae faceret opportuno tempore praeter usitatum cursum ordinemque naturae, ut non maiora, sed insolita videnda stuperunt, quibus cotidiana viluerant. Maius enim miraculum est gubernatio totius mundi, quam saturatio quinque millium hominum de quinque panibus: et tamen haec nemo miratur: illud mirantur homines, non quai maius est, sed quia rarum est. Quis enim et nunc pascit universum mundum, nisi ille qui de paucis granis segetes creat? Fecit ergo quomodo Deus. Unde enim multiplicat de paucis granis segetes, inde in manibus suis multiplicavit quinque panes. Potestas enim erat in manibus Christi: panes autem illi quinque, quasi semina erant, non quidem terrae mandata, sed ab eo qui terram fecit multiplicata. Hoc ergo admotum est sensibus, quo erigeretur mens, et exhibitum oculis ubi exercetur intellectus, ut invisibilem Deum per visibilia opera miraremur, et erecti ad fidem et purgati per fidem, etiam ipsum invisibiliter videre cuperemus, quem de rebus visibilibus invisibilem nosceremus*" (*In Joannis Evangelium*, tract. XXIV, 1; ML XXXV, cc. 1592-3).

totelian leading, theology began to think, more and more, in terms of cause and effect. It ceased to be primarily a wisdom of the faith subsisting on devotion, and it set itself to reflecting upon its own nature, its function, and its method. Thus, step by step, it achieved the status of a science—an ordered body of knowledge.[11] Henceforward, theology was to rely on reason enamored of the metaphysical rather than on docility of the heart.

The main question was no longer: *What is God's purpose in the miracle?* or, *How can man best reply to this purpose within the ambit of his devotional life?* It rather became: *What exactly is the nature of the divine intervention which the miracle involves?*

In order that such a question might be handled properly, the aspect of the miracle as a sign had, perforce, to yield so that due prominence might be given to the transcendent act of God's power which the miracle represents. The first indication of this new viewpoint is found in the twelfth century in St. Anselm, and it was brought to fulfillment by St. Thomas Aquinas.[12]

It is true that St. Thomas recognizes the three constituent elements of the miracle and thus points them out: "We can distinguish two aspects in the miraculous: first of all, what it is that has taken place, i.e., so to speak, something beyond the powers of nature—for which reason miracles are called acts of divine power—and secondly the end which the miracle is designed to serve, that is to say, the manifestation of something supernatural—for which reason it is called a sign. The extraordinary character of the miracle, moreover, causes it to be termed a wonder or a marvel." [13] Elsewhere, we find St. Thomas presenting the miracle as a kind of di-

[11] Cf. M. D. Chenu: *La théologie comme science au XIIIe siècle* (Paris, 1943).

[12] The principal passages in which St. Thomas treats of the miraculous are: *De Potentia,* q. VI; *Summa Contra Gentiles,* III, cap. 98-100; *Summa Theol.* I, q. 105, a. 6-8 and III, qq. 43-44. On the Thomistic doctrine of miracles see: A. Van Hove: *La doctrine du miracle chez S. Thomas et son accord avec les principes de la recherche scientifique* (Paris, 1927).

[13] "*In miraculis duo possunt attendi: unum quidem est id quod fit, quod quidem est aliquid excedens facultatem naturae, et secundum hoc miracula dicuntur virtutes; aliud est id propter quod miracula fiunt, scilicet ad manifestandum aliquid supernaturale, et secundum hoc communiter dicuntur signa; propter excellentiam autem dicuntur portenta vel prodigia, quasi procul aliquid ostendentia*" (*Summa Theol.* IIa IIae. q. 178, q.1 ad 1).

vine witness.[14] Yet, there is no allusion to the sign-function in his definition of a miracle: "An occurrence is miraculous when it surpasses the power of every created thing." [15] This definition is concerned only with the note of power; the matter of being a sign is relegated to an accessory place. The primary note is that God is the author of the miraculous; we, by reasoning, constitute it as a sign. The biblical conception—an intervention which God himself intends to be significant—is practically abandoned.

This debased conception remained dominant in theology and in apologetics until the end of last century. In periods marked by rationalism the breach between the note of power and the sign-function was further enlarged.

St. Thomas was early led to a conclusion as surprising as it is revealing: mysteries of faith, like the Incarnation and Transubstantiation, which exceed the grasp of the senses and are not consonant with the concept of the miracle as a sign, are nevertheless regarded as miracles, solely because they rest upon God's power, which surpasses all created power.[16]

The transcendent character of the miraculous is conceived of by St. Thomas in a much stricter fashion than tradition might have suggested to him. In his eyes there is no miracle unless its result exceeds not only the powers of material nature but all created power, all of which means that the event must be attributed to God's direct intervention. Later on, theological speculation returned to a less narrow and more traditional view, and recognized as miraculous whatever exceeded the competence of material na-

[14] *De Potentia*, q. VI, a. 5, in c.

[15] "*Aliquid dicitur esse miraculum quod fit praeter ordinem totius creaturae*" (*Summa Theol.*, I, q. 110, a. 4, in c). A more explicit definition is thus given: "*Miraculum dicitur quasi admiratione plenum, quod scilicet habet causam simpliciter et omnibus occultam; haec autem est Deus. Unde illa quae a Deo fiunt praeter causas nobis notas miracula dicuntur*" (*Summa Theol.*, I, q. 105, a. 7, in c).

[16] See, for example, concerning the Eucharist: *Summa Theol.*, III, q. 29, a. 1 ad 2; *De Potentia*, q. VI, a. 2 ad 2, etc.; concerning the Incarnation: *Summa Theol.*, q. 31, a. 1 ad 2; *De Potentia*, q. VI, a. 2 ad 3 and ad 9; a. 9 obj. 9. Compare these texts with traditional doctrine such as, for example, is expressed by Paschasius Radbertus who, in *De corpore et sanguine Domini*, XIII, ML CXX, c. 1316, cleaves to it faithfully: "*Quod si carnis species in his visibilis appareret, iam non esset fides aut mysterium, sed fieret miraculum.*"

ture.[17] It must be added that, from time to time, St. Thomas expresses this view.[18]

The problem of discerning how God's intervention is to be recognized seems scarcely to have occurred to St. Thomas.[19] This should not astonish us. The question never presented itself to him because in his day the transcendent intervention of God in certain events was unanimously admitted. Had the problem arisen, it would doubtless have led him to the traditional concept of the miracle as a sign. This is established by the way in which he treats the related question of the difference between a divine prodigy and a demonic prodigy. He resolves this question, explicitly faced, in full conformity to traditional views, by appealing to the context and the essential significance of miraculous occurrences.

Before long the transcendence of the miraculous became a matter of controversy. On the threshold of the eighteenth century, and within the framework of Cartesian rationalism, what were at first sporadic attacks gradually united into a common offensive against the probative value of the miracle. Whether the attacker be called Spinoza, Pierre Bayle, Voltaire, or Hume,[20] the basic argument is

[17] Thus Benedict XIV, for example, who distinguishes between major and minor prodigies: "*Nos discimus miracula maiora excedere vires totius naturae creatae, et miracula minora excedere vires naturae tantum corporeae et visibilis*" (*De Servorum Dei beatificatione et beatorum canonisatione,* lib. IV, pars I, c. I, n. 15; see also: c. II, n. 7).

[18] For example, *De Potentia,* q. VI, a. 5, in c.

[19] A. Van Hove: *loc. cit.;* pp. 310, and 312: "A principal conclusion which follows an examination of the writings of St. Thomas is that we must not hope to find in them a definitive solution of the problem of how a miracle can be recognized . . . In his day the problem never arose, and it did not arise because the entire body of the doctrine of the miraculous rested upon an age-old tradition which hardly required that the problem be considered."

[20] The cultural and historical background in which this negation of the miraculous is set has been very well described by P. Hazard: *The European Mind, 1680-1715* (London, 1953), pt. 2; ch. II, pp. 155-179, and J. S. Lawton: *Miracles and Revelation* (London, 1959). The chief works alluded to above are: Spinoza: *Tractatus theologico-politicus* (published anonymously at Hamburg, 1670), "Praefatio" and ch. VI: "De miraculis"; P. Bayle: *Pensées diverses à l'occasion de la comète qui parut au mois de décembre 1680;* D. Hume: *An Enquiry concerning Human Understanding* (1758), ch. X: "Essay on Miracles"; F. Voltaire: *Dictionnaire Philosophique ou la raison par Alphabet* (*ca.* 1770), s. v. "Miracles." A. Michel in his article "Miracle" in the *Dict. de Theol. Cath.* also cites J. J. Rousseau as being among those opposed to the possibility of miraculous happenings, and he offers a text from his

the same: miracles are impossible because they imply a violation within the fabric of Nature's unalterable law. In the face of the dominating power of the determinism which governs the world, human interests are paltry and negligible. So strongly is this put that any suggestion that the Almighty would alter the nature of things for the benefit of man is made to seem sacrilegious. "Man cannot hope," declares Spinoza,[21] "that Nature will become the partner and sharer in his folly." Voltaire goes him one better by saying: "To suppose that God will work miracles is to insult him with impunity."[22]

And Hume, laying stress upon the thirst for marvels always displayed by the unlettered masses, their credulity in receiving extravagant accounts, the deceitful and ridiculous occurrences which have taken place, and the frequent scandals which have ensued, seeks to bring the whole matter under general disapproval by the pronouncement that "There is not to be found, in all history, any miracle attested by a sufficient number of men, of such unquestioned good-sense, education, and learning, as to secure us against all delusion in themselves; of such undoubted integrity, as to place them beyond all suspicion of any design to deceive others."[23] "The very same principle of experience," he concludes, "which gives us a certain degree of assurance in the testimony of witnesses, gives us also, in this case, another degree of assurance against this fact, which they endeavor to establish; from which contradiction there necessarily arises a counterpoise, and mutual destruction of belief and authority."[24]

In replying to these attacks, an apologetic in defense of the miraculous gradually took form, but dealt with the essential element —the miracle in its function as sign—in an adequate fashion.

Lettres écrites de la montagne (1765), Lettre III: "Can God work miracles? That is to say, can he abrogate laws which he has established? To treat this question seriously would be impious, if it were not absurd" (*loc. cit.*, c. 1807). But, as a matter of fact Rousseau continues: "To punish anyone who resolves this question negatively would be to make too much of him; it should be enough to lock him up"; and actually the meaning is exactly contrary to what Michel wishes to read into it.

[21] B. Spinoza: *loc. cit.*, Praefatio: "*quasi tota nature cum ipsis insaniret.*"

[22] F. Voltaire: *loc. cit.*

[23] D. Hume: *loc. cit.*, at the beginning of the second part of the chapter.

[24] *Ibid.*, at the conclusion of the first part.

Hence, it became impossible to take account of the deepest meaning of the miracle, as the tidings proclaiming "a new heaven and a new earth." A good many apologists of that age went so far as to hold that miracles would be possible even if the universe were not ordered to a supernatural end.

Furthermore, it became impossible to lay due stress upon the importance of existential choice and connaturality with the reality signified as a condition for recognizing the sign.

Finally, it became impossible to insist upon the moral quality of any certitude which is based upon signs or upon the indispensable function of this certitude in our lives.

In the midst of the triumphant chorus of rationalism, only the voice of Pascal is raised to recall briefly the echoes of biblical and Augustinian tradition.

Pushing to its logical extremity this mutilated concept, Catholic apologists met their adversaries on the ground which they had chosen. That favorite gibe of the Age of Enlightenment, "an infraction of Nature's laws" appeared to them to verify, in an empirical way, the fact of God's transcendent intervention. They thought they could not only establish the metaphysical possibility of this infraction, but that they could even furnish scientific demonstration that it took place in certain miracles.

The miracle they defined simply as being a fact plainly contrary to natural law and hence necessarily stemming from the Creator. Its religious meaning is passed over in worldly discussion about natural law, and the apologist—in reality more a metaphysician than a scientist—bound himself in chains to the rationalistic world he fancied he was escaping.

At the close of the last century, when philosophical criticism began to show deeper interest in the essence and in the limits of scientific knowledge, it was recognized that Catholic apologetics had been led into a blind alley. It must be agreed that scientific finding and metaphysical reflection take place on different planes, and that the passage from one to another cannot be justified. Not unreasonably were apologists of the miraculous reproached for having transformed the lack of a scientific explanation into a metaphysical inexplicability. And the philosophy of science raised the objection that to prove by scientific means a transcendent causal intervention is nothing but a contradiction in terms. In order to declare that an unexplained fact is inexplicable, one must abandon scientific investigation and carry the case into another court by appealing to the sign-aspect of the miracle.[25]

At the beginning of the present century, the best thinkers felt it incumbent upon them to take up again the tradition rooted in Scripture and in the Church Fathers, and to reinstate, as an essential element in the definition of the miracle, its function as a sign.

The perfect blending of the two elements was not at once rediscovered: sometimes the function of the miracle as a sign was so accentuated as to cast into the shade its transcendent aspect. This is especially true of the outright Modernists, for whom the miracle seemed an extraordinary but wholly natural occurrence which the religious man construed as a symbol of his subjective longing after God;[26] but the same may be said of even some Catholic writers, as for instance Le Roy and Laberthonnière.[27]

[25] This concept of the miracle is still held by most of the manualists; for example, R. Garrigou-Lagrange: *De Revelatione*[3] (Rome, 1929), II, pp. 35-136; H. Dieckmann: *De Revelatione christiana* (Freibourg, 1930), pp. 291-328; S. Tromp: *De revelatione christiana*[4] (Rome, 1937), pp. 112-122; L. Lercher—F. Schlagenhaufen: *Institutiones theologiae dogmaticae*[3] (Innsbruck, 1939), I, pp. 56-72; A. Dorsch: *Institutiones theologiae fundamentalis* (Innsbruck, 1930), I, pp. 378-428; A. Lang: *Fundamentaltheologie* (Munich, 1954), I: "Die Sendung Christi," pp. 100-119.

Up until the Second World War, most monographs on the miraculous presented matters in similar style; for example: Cardinal Lépicier: *Le miracle, sa nature, ses lois, ses rapports avec l'ordre surnaturel* (Paris, 1936); G. Joyce, *The Question of Miracles* (London, 1934); F. Pauwels: *Het wonder* (De Katholieke Kerk) (Utrecht, 1940); G. Kafka: *Naturgesetz, Freiheit und Wunder* (Paderborn, 1940); H. Pinard de la Boullaye: *Conférences de Notre-Dame de Paris de l'année 1931* (Paris, 1932); F. Desiderio: *Il valore apologetico del miracolo; Studio critico* (Rome, 1955); Z. Aradi: *The Book of Miracles* (New York, 1956); V. Marcozzi: "Il miracolo," *Problemi e orientamenti di teologia dommatica* (Milan, 1957), 1, pp. 105-142. There are other writers who, while they hold firmly to the classic definition, have nevertheless tended to adhere to a movement which would return to the idea of the miracle as a sign. So, for example: J. H. Newman: *Two Essays on Miracles*[11] (London, 1897); J. de Tonquédec: *Introduction à l'étude du merveilleux et du miracle*[2] (Paris, 1916); A. Van Hove: *Het mirakel* (Brussels, 1932).

[26] Cf. K. Pfeifer: *Das Wunder als Erkenntnismittel der Glaubwürdigkeit der göttlichen Offenbarung in der modernen katholischen und protestantischen Apologetik* (Aschaffenburg, 1936), pp. 52-62.

[27] E. Le Roy: "Essai sur la notion du miracle," *Annales de la philosophie chrétienne,* 153 (1906-1907), 5-33; 166-191; 225-259. The ideas set forth in these articles were made the subject of a discussion at the *Société française de*

The strongest stimulus to return to the traditional concept was provided by M. Blondel, who rediscovered it thanks to the philosophical principles of his apologetic of immanence.[28] Spurred by the controversy aroused by the ideas he had advanced, he was forced to bring into better perspective the transcendent element which he had understated at first, and to express with greater precision its necessary connection with the sign-function.[29]

On the other hand, and at about the same time, there began among the proponents of classic Scholasticism a vigorous renewal in which the sign-function of the miracle was restored to its rightful place in the understanding of what it is that constitutes a miracle. This is especially true of the thought of A. Bros, of L. de Grandmaison, and of those who shared the views of P. Rousselot.[30]

---

philosophie, at a meeting on 28 December, 1911. See the report of the discussion. "Le problème du Miracle," *Bulletin de la société française de philosophie* (1912), 85-168. The report of the meeting includes an exposition of the position of L. Laberthonnière.

[28] M. Blondel first expounded his opinions in *Action* (Paris, 1893), 392-398, and then again in his "Lettre sur les exigences de pensée contemporaine en matière d'apologétique," *Annales de philosophie chrétienne* (1895-1896), vol. 33, pp. 337-347, 466-482, 599-616; vol. 34, pp. 131-147, 255-267, 338-350. (These articles are reprinted in book form in English translation: *The Letter on Apologetics* [New York, 1965].) In reply to the articles by Le Roy, cited in the preceding note, there appeared a synthesis clearly inspired by Blondel, although signed B. de Sailly: "La notion et le rôle du miracle," *Annales de philosophie chrétienne,* 154 (1907), 337-361. Blondel was not present at the meeting of the *Soc. franç. de philos.*, but a letter from him was read there, and it is to be found in the Report (pp. 152-162). In it he takes a stand against Le Roy, once again expressing his own views; and his fully matured opinions were finally restated in contrast with those of other participants in the discussion in a note on the word "miracle" in A. Lalande: *Vocabulaire technique et critique de la philosophie*[4] (1932), I, pp. 469-471. To these documents there must be added a brief but important text, a letter sent to the *Revue du Clergé français,* 38 (April 15, 1904), 405. The principal texts have been put together, with an interpolated commentary by Y. de Montcheuil: *Maurice Blondel, Pages religieuses* (Paris, 1942), pp. 114-122; F. Rodé: *Le Miracle dans la controverse moderniste* (Paris, 1965).

[29] On this point see P. De Locht: "Maurice Blondel et sa controverse au sujet du miracle," *Eph. Theol. Lov.,* 30 (1954), 344-390; B. Welte: "Maurice Blondel," *Theologische Revue,* 51 (1955), 5-12; F. Rodé: Le Miracle dans la controverse moderniste (Paris, 1965).

[30] A. Bros: "Comment constater le miracle?" *Annales de philosophie chrétienne,* 152 (1906), 250-267; L. de Grandmaison: *Jesus Christ* (New York, 1937), III, pp. 3-32. Among authors who emphasize the value of the miracle as a sign, I should point out particularly: J. Clémence: "Le miracle dans l'économie chrétienne," *Etudes,* 227 (1936), 577-589; J. Wéhrlé: "Le

During recent years, the return of theological study to biblical sources has helped much to re-set the true and traditional concept of the miracle within an authentically scriptural and patristic framework. The theology of the miracle is thereby faced with increased opportunities of expressing a new synthesis which will unite the traditional heritage with the results of the theological task to form an harmonious whole, impressive in its religious value.

---

miracle, Sa nature, Sa finalité, Sa fréquence," *Etudes religieuses*, 112 (1924); G. Söhngen: "Wunderzeichen und Glaube," *Catholica*, 3 (1935), 145-164, reprinted in *Die Einheit in der Theologie* (Munich, 1952), pp. 265-285; J. Kijm: "Apologetische notities bij het wonder," *Bijdragen*, 14 (1953), 148-155; F. Taymans: "Le miracle, signe du surnatural," *Nouvelle Revue théologique*, 77 (1955), 225-245; A. Dondeyne: "The Existence of God and Contemporary Materialism," in J. Bivort de la Saudée: *God, Man and the Universe* (New York, 1953), pp. 22-31; H. Dolch: *Das Wunder: Eine Hilfe für den Unterricht* (Paderborn, 1953); A. Liégé: "Réflexions théologiques sur le miracle," *Pensée scientifique et foi chrétienne* (Paris, 1953), pp. 206-218; ID.: "Réflexions pour une apologétique du miracle," *Revue des sciences philos. et théol.*, 35 (1951), 249-254; H. Fortmann: "Wonder en geneeskunde: I. Theologisch aspect," *Annalen van het Thijmgenootschap* (1955), 217-226; J. Delmotte: "Het mirakel," *Collat. Brug. et Gand.*, 1 (1955), 289-310, 492-509; P. Schoonenberg: *Het geloof van ons Doopsel*, II ('s Hertogenbosch, 1956), pp. 137-166; *Réflexions sur le miracle*: special number of *Lumière et Vie*, 33 (July, 1957); H. Thibeaud: *A Dieu et à Jésus-Christ par la philosophie* (Paris, 1956), pp. 297-324; J. H. Walgrave: "Geloof en wonder," *Jong-Kultuurleven* (1958), 305-310; ID.: "Wonder en wetenschap," *ibid.*, pp. 346-351; C. Dumont: "Unité et diversité des signes de la Révélation," *Nouv. Rev. Theol.*, 80 (1958), 133-158; R. Guardini, *Wunder und Zeichen* (Würzburg, 1959); J. F. Beaudry: "Miracle and Sign," *Studia Montis Regii*, 3 (1960), 65-94; R. W. Gleason, "Miracles and Contemporary Theology," *Thought*, 37 (1962), 12-34. A whole flock of writers sharing views expressed by P. Rousselot concerning the psychology of the act of faith in his "Les yeux de la foi," *Rech. de science rel.*, 1 (1910), 241-259, 444-475, have strongly stressed the value of the miracle as a sign, but have ascribed to faith alone the power of fully discerning this meaning and its probative value. Among such may be instanced: J. Huby: "Miracle et lumière de grâce," *Recherches de science religieuse*, 8 (1918), 36-77; E. Masure: *La grand'route apologétique* (Paris, 1938); P. Tiberghien: *La science mène-t-elle à Dieu* (Paris, 1933), pp. 158-168, 183-212; H. Bouillard: "The Christian Idea of the Miraculous" in P. Flood, O. S. B. (ed.), *New Problems in Medical Ethics* (Westminster, Md., 1953), I, 247-259; J. Coventry: *Faith Seeks Understanding* (London, 1951); E. Masure: "Le miracle comme signe," *Revue des sc. philo. et théol.*, 43 (1959), 273-282.

III • GOD'S TRANSCENDENT INTERVENTION THROUGH MIRACLES

Following upon this attempt to establish a synthesis on the shape or structure of the miraculous, it will be fitting, once again, to look into the several elements of this structure. As a matter of fact, the nature of each element is determined and modified in accordance with the organic function it fulfills in the whole. The next chapter (IV) will set forth in detail the conditions to be fulfilled by a prodigy as externally manifested in order that it may be a true structural element. The sign-function, as it is related to Christian faith and life, will also be considered in a separate chapter. Presently, we limit our consideration to the third element: God's transcendent intervention. What is the nature of this incursion? What must it be in order to constitute a miraculous sign?

In order to answer this question, can we observe the perceptible fact and argue immediately to the reality and nature of the divine intervention? I do not think so. Actually, the facts which we establish are of the physical order; our grasp of them is achieved on the plane of the spontaneous or scientific knowledge of nature, not at all on that of a metaphysical view of being or of things. It is therefore beyond us to deduce from these facts the nature of the cause which underlies them. For example—I am speaking now, not from the scientific, but from the metaphysical viewpoint—what is it that occurs in a sudden cure, in the multiplication of the loaves, in the resurrection of someone from the dead? Is it a new creation? Is it an actuation of pre-existing natural potencies or a total departure from the natural causal sequence? Vainly would we seek to make logical deductions concerning these matters or to erect, on a basis of the scientific data, a structure of metaphysical ideas.

The expression "an infraction of natural laws" is, moreover, easily misunderstood. By "natural laws" do we understand the principles which determine the metaphysical and ontological structure of matter? These, after all, are beyond our perception; they leave our ordered and systematized knowledge far behind. Contemporary science more and more admits this: "The new mathematical formulae no longer describe nature itself but *our knowledge* of nature"; "when we speak of the picture of nature in the exact science of our age, we do not mean a picture of nature so much as *a picture of our relationships with nature.*" [31] If we regard natural laws as constants of observation, resulting from our scientific researches, it is not easy to admit that the affirmation of a fact not amenable to these laws—supposing such affirmation be possible—can be of any value in determining the nature of the metaphysical causality which is at the root of the occurrence.[32]

Only one means remains by which we can determine the nature of the divine intervention: we must begin with the structure of the sign which marks the miracle. This structure is established by theological means and is the source of theological deductions. We may, therefore, state without fear of error that a natural occurrence can express and signify more than its nature can account for. This surplus of meaning must be rooted in the divine intention which is the cause of the event. A solid springboard in nature is needed to guarantee this surplus, but it is only the participation of nature in a divine act and in a divine intention by means of an extension of its natural meaning, that confers upon the natural phenomenon its quality as a supernatural sign.[33] In order to express this kind of

[31] W. Heisenberg: *The Physicist's Conception of Nature* (New York, 1958). The passages cited here are found on pp. 25 and 29.

[32] Modern scientific notions about the purely statistical character of the laws of nature do not in any wise weaken this thesis. Received physical theories oblige us to conclude that phenomenal determinism in the macrophysical scale is only the consequence of an infinite number of reactions in the microphysical order, and that these reactions are each, in themselves, not merely indeterminate but irrevocably indeterminable. The calculus of probability nevertheless attributes to the global resultant of these reactions such statistical probability as is practically equivalent to an absolute determinism. Such a modification in the conception of natural determinism has the great advantage of inclining the majority of men of science to be less indisposed to admit the notion or concept of a divinely transcendent intervention in natural affairs. Yet it can teach us nothing about the true nature of this intervention. It is actually a question of purely scientific indeterminism and not of metaphysical liberty of any sort whatsoever; the statement of this indeterminism belongs entirely within a framework of scientific knowledge, and is not to be situated on the plane of the metaphysical; it cannot now nor can it ever justify any conclusion whatsoever respecting the structure of the being responsible for this indeterminism nor respecting the possibility of referring this indeterminism to a transcendent cause in any precise sense. In the fourth chapter of the second part of this book I shall return to this question.

[33] On the matter of instrumentality considered as "intentional participa-

participation in a higher causality, there is only one word which is sufficiently general and yet not too vague: this is the word "instrument." God, then, makes use of material natures as instruments in executing his plan of salvation. This he may do directly or by the intermediary activity of creatures he selects. The saint or the divine messenger who works miracles does so as an instrument or minister, carrying out God's salvific designs.

Are we able to carry our analysis yet further and define even more precisely the relationship between the normal activity of nature and that which it suddenly exhibits as a divine instrument? We have seen that the transformation which the natural undergoes in the miraculous foreshadows, momentarily and in a particular instance, the final eschatological renewal by which nature will share in heavenly glory. Thus one may apply to miracles the axiom: *gratia supponit naturam*—grace does not destroy nature; it rather frees it, ennobles it, makes it divine. In this world of ours, a world not purely natural because it is wounded and unbalanced by sin, the coming of divine glory necessarily takes place as a violent invasion, as an upsetting of the established order, more precisely of the "established disorder." But, in its full meaning, this invasion means liberty; this upsetting involves an elevation to the divine. Nature then comes to reflect not merely the world of the spirit, but the very life of God himself in us; by going beyond itself, the natural becomes perfected. As St. Ambrose puts it, God is a good archi-

---

tion" see L. Monden: *Het misoffer als Mysterie* (Roermond, 1948), pp. 123-127. In his *La causalité instrumentale dans l'ordre surnaturel*[3] (Paris, 1924), pp. 173-204, E. Hugon applies to the miraculous the concept of instrumental causality, taken, however, in a sense which is much too strict. Père E. Dhanis in a recent article ("Qu'est-ce qu'un miracle," *Gregorianum*, 40 [1959], 201-241) asks (p. 217, note) if I have not actually abandoned the physical transcendence of the miracle in favor of a merely semiological transcendence. In reality, in the miracle, as I understand it, nature, *as nature*, becomes a symbol of the supernatural; semilogical transcendence can only come to be by physical transcendence. But it seems to me impossible to express this transcendence in terms of positive science, and hence I am reluctant to express it by saying that a miraculous event is "withdrawn from the governance of natural laws." The closely reasoned argumentation by which Père Dhanis sets himself to establish this particular kind of transcendence in the case of miraculous happenings apparently rests upon an appeal, at the decisive moment (p. 215), to the use of a middle term which pertains to the metaphysical or semiological rather than to the scientific order.

tect who does not destroy the house in order to add another story; but rather re-enforces the foundations.[34] The Saviour does not contradict the Creator; in the order of grace (into which the miracle is inserted), nature sees itself "wondrously" (*mirabiliter*) restored to its wholeness; by the miracle, as by grace, Christ is come among men "not to destroy the Law but rather to fulfill it."

[34] "*ut ipsum se ostenderet Creatorem qui opera operibus intexeret, et prosequeretur opus, quod ipse iam coeperat; ut, si domum faber renovare disponat, non a fundamentis, sed a culminibus incipit solvere vetustatem. Itaque ibi prius manum admovet, ubi ante desierat . . .*"—Ambrosius: *Lib.* V *in Lc.*, n. 58; ML XV; c. 1630). The rest of this text is concerned with the Mass prayer: "*Deus qui humanae substantiae dignitatem mirabiliter condidisti et mirabilius reformasti,*" and with the assurance given by Our Lord that he "came not to destroy the Law but rather to fulfill it" (Matt. V, 17).

4 · CHARACTERISTICS OF THE CHRISTIAN MIRACLE

As we have seen in the foregoing chapters, not every prodigy is to be regarded as a sign of salvation, as bearing a message from God.

Both the event itself and its religious context must satisfy certain specific conditions.

I shall begin in this chapter to examine these conditions. It is my purpose to establish, from the standpoint of faith, strict criteria suitable for distinguishing a true miracle from a false one. In the course of this process, I shall point out a number of misunderstandings and prejudices which are deeply seated in Catholic thought.

The first section of the present chapter approaches the subject in negative fashion: it will point out those characteristics which, according to the Christian view of the matter, mark many wondrous things as false miracles. The second section will set forth, in a positive fashion, some characteristics of the authentic Christian miracle.

I · NEGATIVE CHARACTERISTICS

To begin with, we must exclude whatever, by any kind of *unsuitability,* contradicts the salvific meaning of the miraculous, and whatever tends to shift the center of attention toward the worldly and profane.

Hence, it is evidently impossible that the notes characteristic of the Christian miracle be encountered in any phenomenon which is occurring in a context that is unhealthy, disturbed, indecent, or immoral. Equally to be shunned is whatever smacks of sickly enthusiasm, of mere drollery, or of childishness. So also in regard to anything redolent of charlatanism, trickery, magic, or illusion. And, finally, we must reject out of hand wonders which subserve the material profit of the pretended wonder-worker or which foster either his pride or his sensuality.[1]

It must, moreover, be recognized that anything which presents a mere appearance of being part of a religious context, although it actually has no inherent relationship to it and may even contradict it in some sense, has no place among Christian miracles.

There is no doubt that the religious signs which are accepted by mankind often are marked by a certain incoherence. If I learn that, in a certain land, highway robbers and harlots are accustomed to pay devotion to a figure of the Madonna in order that they may be favored with good hunting, I must take into account, before I pass judgment, that waywardness of the human heart which oft-times is at the root of strange contradictions in life. But if our concern is with a divine sign, then perfect integrity is required; whatever contradicts integrity is not to be tolerated any more than would be elements absolutely alien to a religious meaning. In other words, the unusual aspect of the outward form of the prodigy must not show the kind of extravagance and eccentricity which is in evident contradiction with the salvific nature of the divine message which the prodigy is intended to express.

Dorothy Sayers has devoted a chapter to the internal integrity of a miraculous event; and she compares this quality to what the novelist or dramatist strives for in order that he may achieve psychological truth in the presentation of his characters. She points to the "irrelevancy" of some wonders; and, as a type of the extraordinary act which lacks relation to the meaning which it should have, she instances what the mocking Jews would have required of the Crucified Saviour: "We may ask ourselves how much power would be

[1] Cf. L. de Grandmaison: *Jesus Christ* (New York, 1937), III, p. 21.

left in the story of the crucifixion, as a story, if Christ had come down from the cross. That would have been an irrelevant miracle, whereas the story of the resurrection is relevant, leaving the consequences of action and character still in logical connection with their causes." [2]

The apocryphal gospels, especially those concerned with the childhood of Jesus, are full of miracles which are out of character and which lack relevancy. What messianic meaning can be discovered in the tale that God would permit that his Incarnate Word, while yet a child, should model birds of clay and give them life by the whim of his creative breath? [3] The same lack of meaning is to be found in a good many legends, be they ancient or modern. If science had not established that the transportation of the holy house of Nazareth to Loretto is no more than a legend, we might very easily guess it to be such from the nature of the wonder itself. The mission of the angels in the redemptive plan is surely not that they might serve as benevolent house-movers.[4]

Another essential characteristic of the Christian miracle is that it must not be marked by excessive sensationalism, but should rather display a real discretion. It is generally thought—and even devout Christians fall victims to this error—that the divine intervention is most clear and most convincing when it departs in sensational fashion from the normal order.

This easily leads to the attitude of mind which looks at the most abnormal as being the most *convincing* miracle and evokes recollection of the witty sally of Anatole France: "Being at Lourdes during August, I visited the grotto where countless crutches are hung up as emblems of cures which have been effected. My companion pointed out these trophies to me, and whispered: 'Just one wooden leg would say more than all these.' " [5]

[2] D. Sayers: *The Mind of the Maker* (Living Age Books, 1956), p. 86.

[3] Cf. C. Tischendorf: *Evangelia Apocrypha* (Leipzig, 1876); C. Michel and P. Peters: *Evangiles apocryphes* (Paris, 1924); M. R. James, *The Apocryphal New Testament* (Oxford, 1953).

[4] H. Thurston in his article, "Loretto" in Hastings: *Encyclopaedia of Religion and Ethics* (Edinburgh, 1915), VIII, cc. 139-142, emphasizes "the intrinsic improbabilities of the legend itself." On the subject of Loretto, consult the two volumes of G. Hueffer: *Loretto: Eine Geschichtkritische Untersuchung der Frage des Heiligen Hauses* (Münster, 1913-21).

[5] A. France: *Le jardin d'Épicure* (Paris, 1897), pp. 203-204.

But, as a matter of fact, an excessively sensational miracle would no longer be Christian; for its external aspect would command all our attention, and so serve to obscure its religious significance.

A comparison will make this clear. Symbolic rites and symbols themselves represent a religious reality: the sign which is experienced displays, beyond itself, the mystery (*Mysterium*) which it veils. Yet how simple and plain are the symbols which Christ chose and which the Church adapts to her liturgy.

Christ seems to have hesitated to gratify our senses by an overly luxurious symbolism; for, rather than drawing us beyond it to a realization of the truth which it signifies, it might make us prisoners to sensory symbols. Rather than being revealing signs these symbols would then have become merely elaborate screens, hiding what is really significant. The plain appearance of bread is something which, for example, attracts our attention just sufficiently to draw it, by means of the bread, to the Christ who is present because of it. Are there not some baroque monstrances which display so tasteless a refinement of elaboration in symbolizing the inner richness of the Eucharistic mystery that they all but succeed in distracting our attention from its essence? The same may be said of miracles. They do attract attention, in some sense, by the fact that they are unusual, by the sense of surprise which is evoked by the unaccustomed; but excessive sensationalism would make them miss the mark. No doubt, a great effect will be produced to the extent that they satisfy man's thirst for the marvelous; but such an effect would inevitably be enmeshed in the passion of worldly curiosity, and, far from drawing attention to the real meaning of the miraculous occurrence, would force it into the background.[6] Even when

[6] Analogous ideas have been expressed, particularly in Germany, in respect to the recent controversy about the advisability of televised Masses, especially when there is question of showing the act of consecration. See: "Apparatur und Glaube," *Ueberlegungen zur Fernübertragung der heiligen Messe, Christliche Besinnung,* 8 (Würzburg, 1955). R. Guardini and K. Rahner are notable for their insistence, in the articles they have contributed to the discussion, on the fact that certain gestures and actions, charged with the weight of personal and intimate communication, are stripped of this weight and profaned when the wholly personal communication which they bespeak is opened to undiscriminating public view (cf. esp. pp. 36-42). In another essay, *Die Sinne und die religiose Erkenntnis* (Würzburg, 1950; published in French under the title *Les sens et la connaissance de Dieu* [Paris, 1954]), R. Guardini, without making explicit reference to the miraculous, has developed a similar point.

he works miracles, God dwells more in the depths of silence than in the raging storm; his work does not lay itself open to that criticism of the Greek philosopher which is often so apt in regard to our frivolous and restless day: "the sound of your words prevents me from hearing what you are saying."

Men's thirst for the most amazing and indubitable wonders actually stems from a desire for a faith without shadows, for a crown without a cross. This is what the Jews of old desired when they clamored for "a sign from Heaven."

A miracle is Christian only if it helps us to believe rather than relieve us of the necessity of faith. God does not overwhelm his creature and coerce him. He calls to man in the core of his own freedom, and he bids him listen. Athanasius spoke to the unwise and told them that "they must learn that Christ is not come to make a parade of his power, but rather that he might cure and teach weak and ignorant men. It would have required display on his part, had he sought only to thrill his hearers. As Physician and Teacher, he bound himself not only to come among them, but also to involve himself in their need and show them how to bear their limitations. As a matter of fact, if the manner of his coming had not been within the bounds of mankind's own weakness, even the Incarnation would have been of no avail to them." [7]

If it is to be a Christian miracle, moreover, it should not give the impression that this passing world is now already glorified, that Paradise has already been regained. The miracle must rather give a glimpse of what is to come; it is a kind of smile by which God lightens the path of his Church as it follows the *Via Crucis* which is mortal life.[8] The sudden growth of a new leg, strikingly sensa-

[7] "*Discant illi Dominum non venisse ut se ostentaret, sed ut infirmos simul et ignaros curaret et doceret. Ostentantis enim fuisset, solummodo apparere et spectantes stupore percellere: at sanantis et docentis erat, non tantum advenire, sed indigentium commodo prospicere, atque ut illi ferre possint apparere; ne si modus ipse laborantium excederet, illos potius perturbaret, atque ita Numinis adventus ipsis fieret inutilis*" (Athanasius, *Oratio de Incarnatione Verbi*, n. 42; MG, XXV, c. 171). See on this point, J. Guitton: *Jésus* (Paris, 1957), pp. 208-210.

[8] See J. Levie: *Sous les yeux de l'incroyant* (Brussels, 1944), pp. 39-43, on the links which bind the discretion characteristic of the Christian miracle and the plan of salvation. In Msgr. Kerkhofs's book, *Notre-Dame de Banneux* (Tournai, 1950), p. 55, Père Scheuer comments on Our Lady's words by writing: "She will not abolish suffering; this would not be expedient; *non*

tional as this might be, would express but ill God's grace; it would be less suitable to our fallen status, it would be less a sign of salvation, than are the ordinary examples of healing at Lourdes. Ofttimes these leave even traces of scars, and thus recall to us the marks upon his blessed body which our risen Saviour wished to preserve in order that they might recall to his disciples the strength of the bond that unites the state of glory to the redemptive work of the Holy Cross.

Furthermore, it would be foolish to think that the more sensational the miracle, the stronger the force it exerts to compel belief. Such miracles encounter the self-same resistance that meets others: they are repulsed by the same blindness and pre-judgment, by the same lack of spiritual discernment. Whatever is sensational encourages all the manoeuvres of bad faith, and increases the flight from the truth that plagues the troubled spirit. The concluding words of the parable of Dives and Lazarus reveals deep knowledge of human psychology: "Even though someone should arise from the dead and come unto them, they would not believe." [9]

Pascal showed a splendid sense of this divine discretion when he wrote: "God wills to be found by those who seek him in singleness of heart, and to be unseen of those who fly from him. Therefore has he so arranged it that the indications of his presence are visible to those who seek him, and invisible to those who do not. To those who wish only to see, he gives all needed light." [10]

Another similar prejudice must be avoided. God, in the miracle, bends to our weakness and he strengthens our faith. The miraculous is, consequently, not a necessary path to faith. Man has no real claim to it. Anyone who would make of a miracle a prerequisite of

---

expedit. On the contrary, for ever since Calvary it is the Cross which cures and saves. What she will do is to give comfort in suffering; she will lighten the burden." St. Augustine has expressed in telling fashion the law of the "forma servi" which the miracle must respect, when he said: "*Signum eius est humilitas eius. Per stellam eum Magi cognoverunt; et erat hoc signum de Domino datum, celeste atque praeclarum; noluit stellam esse in fronte fidelium signum suum, sed crucem suam. Unde humiliatus, inde glorificatus; inde erexit humiles, quo humiliatus ipse descendit*" (*In evang. Joannis*, Tract. III, 2, ML, XXXV, c. 1396).

[9] Luke XVI, 31.

[10] B. Pascal: *Pensées*, ed. by Brunschvicg, no. 430. This notion is, indeed, a sort of leading theme throughout all Pascal's work.

his own going to God would thereby abandon Christianity; for he would set at naught the gratuitous or essentially free nature of the miracle: it is something that God grants when and as he wills.

Even more evidently, miracles are not experiments by which we can manipulate God at our discretion and check up on his testimony. Only a devout attitude of humble openness is fitting to man and invokes God's condescendence. An age of over-confidence in its own knowledge voiced, through the words of Renan, the conditions on which it would accept the miraculous:

"Let a thaumaturgist present himself tomorrow with testimony sufficiently important to merit our attention; let him announce that he is able, I will suppose, to raise the dead; what would be done? A commission composed of physiologists, physicians, chemists, persons experienced in historical criticism, would be appointed. This commission would choose the corpse, make certain that death was real, designate the hall in which the experiment should be made, and regulate the whole system of precautions necessary to leave no room for doubt. If, under such conditions, the resurrection should be performed, a probability almost equal to certainty would be attained. However, as an experiment ought always to be capable of being repeated, as one ought to be capable of doing again what one has done once, and as in the matter of miracles there can be no question of easy or difficult, the thaumaturgist would be invited to reproduce his marvelous act under other circumstances, upon other bodies, in another medium. If the miracle succeeds each time, two things would be proven: first, that supernatural acts do come to pass in the world; second, that the power to perform them belongs or is delegated to certain persons." [11]

But we need have no fear: not only did a miracle of this kind never come to pass; it never will. Such an occurrence would not be a Christian miracle, nor, for that matter, a religious event at all; it would be quite meaningless. Any wonder brought to pass under such conditions would be nothing more or less than a mere capitulation of God, yielding to the impertinent importunity and the self-willed pride of a creature. The Psalmist had long ago expressed God's reply to such a challenge: *Deus irridebit eos*; "God

[11] E. Renan: *Life of Jesus* (New York, 1864), pp. 44-45. See, as well, the anecdote recounted by J. Guitton: *Jésus*, pp. 190-191.

shall laugh them to scorn." Scornfully indeed will God refuse his gifts to our grotesque self-sufficiency. On the other hand, upon those who are humble he showers blessings with the freedom and the generosity of one who is truly a great Lord.

God rules out all demands, even the cautious and circumspect demands of the man of good will. From the very beginning, the apparitions at Lourdes were a source of disturbance to Abbé Peyramale. In speaking to Bernadette, he showed himself skeptical and harsh; but inwardly he felt crushed by the burden of his priestly responsibility: faith and doubt were at war within his heart. He brusquely told the little girl who asked, in the name of Our Lady, that a chapel be built: "Tell the Lady that she ought to make the wild-rose bushes in the grotto flower." On the morrow, Bernadette made his demand known, and at noon she reported to the Rector what the Lady's reply was: "She smiled when I told her that you wanted a miracle. She smiled again when I asked that she make the wild-roses bloom. In any case, what *she* wants is a chapel." [12] This smile veiled an undisguised refusal: to the demands of a creature Heaven replies by its silence; but it is a silence which is full of understanding for the man of good faith, such as this pastor was. The Virgin could smile; for she could read the future, and she could foresee the torrent of miracles which the sovereign freedom of God will later shower down upon millions of pilgrims. The wild-roses did not bloom; yet the sign was given. Lourdes was soon to become a name synonymous with the word miracle; and the whole world was to turn its eyes toward the ever-smiling Virgin, always Immaculate.

It is such a consideration which best guides us in the practical discernment of the miraculous. The authenticity of any miraculous event which would be constantly at the disposal of Christians or which is produced at regular intervals will appear, at the least, unlikely. It seems to me, for example, that the hypothesis of those who believe the liquefaction of the blood of St. Januarius at Naples to be due rather to miraculous intervention than to some natural chemical process is tainted by the flaw of inherent unlikelihood. God makes use of the miracle according to the norms of his sovereign freedom: it is difficult to defend the notion that he would

[12] M. Auclair: *Bernadette* (New York, 1958), pp. 132-133.

make of it a plaything to satisfy the idle curiosity of the children of men.[13]

In his novel, *Father Malachy's Miracle*,[14] Bruce Marshall, an author whose refined psychological insight is joined to a charmingly theological humor, has presented to us an account of a typical pseudo-miracle which sums up all the defects and all the improbabilities which I wish here to underline. Wholly sensational, and quite wanting in any connection with the message of the Gospel, this miracle is foisted upon heaven with naive impetuosity. Yet it is the prototype of the *ideal miracle* dreamed of by many Catholics and by many opportunistic apologists.

A good Benedictine monk, Dom Malachy Murdoch, who is as naive as he is pious, is sent by his Abbot to do parish-work in Edinburgh. During a discussion with an Anglican priest he binds himself to prove that miracles are as possible today as ever they were aforetime, and he promises to uproot, at eleven-thirty on the following evening, a nightclub called *the Garden of Eden*, where young people dance and dissipate in scandalous proximity to his presbytery. He promises to transport, in the twinkling of an eye, to any place chosen by the heretical clergyman, all the pleasure seekers, the whole orchestra, and the young women who so freely share their charms with the guests of the place. He tells his plan to his Rector and to his fellow-priests, and in justification he adds: "One little spectacular miracle and we shall prove to the world, in a manner so sure as to be irrefutable, that we have the Light and the Truth and are the divinely appointed guardians of the Way. One little spectacular miracle . . . and we shall be able to go and teach, not only Scotland, but all nations with the certainty that they will listen to us."

On the following evening Dom Malachy prays with confidence, and he accomplishes his miracle by means of a silent litany. A breathtaking miracle, the miracle of the century, a miracle clear to everyone, is the result of his prayer; for the Garden of Eden shakes

[13] On this point see the fine articles of H. Thurston: "The Blood Miracles of Naples," *The Month*, 149 (1927), 44-55, 123-135, 236-247; ID.: "The 'Miracle' of Saint Januarius," *The Month*, 155 (1930), 119-129.

[14] B. Marshall: *Father Malachy's Miracle* (Garden City, 1931).

upon its foundations, it slowly rises up, and it glides over the clouds to land on the top of the Bass Rock—a rocky little island in the Firth of Forth—just as the Anglican clergyman had stipulated. The surprised young people within the club stop dancing and nearly fall headlong into the water; lifeboats are put out to sea to bring back the assemblage to the mainland, while a little later, during the darkest hour of night, four priests entone a triumphant *Te Deum* in an empty parish church. This last is an act prophetic of the effect produced by this miracle.

There is actually no hope whatever of the accomplishment of the expected general conversion of all mankind. The miracle causes talk, as does any miracle; but the publicity given to it makes the talk more than usually intemperate and widespread. It is rather the opinions and the actions of those involved in it than any religious aspect which evokes attention. Everyone is interested in the miracle from his own self-centered point of view; and each man forms his estimate of it in accordance with his own self-interest. The descent into the profane is unhesitating and complete, for the sensational aspect denies the religious aim of the occurrence. One young unbeliever, a brother of a bishop, who had actually witnessed the miracle of Dom Malachy, gave the prelate an account of it, and ended by saying unexpectedly: "Ah didn't believe a word of all yon humbuggery and nonsense." The owner of the Garden of Eden and the manager of the nightclub, who had been ruined by the miracle, put in claims for damages; a rascally entrepreneur worked out the amount which he supposed he could gain by the reproduction of such doings and he unblushingly sought from Dom Malachy the secret of the trick, being, as he said, ready to purchase exclusive rights to it, in order that he might incorporate it into a romantic film which he purposed to make. Journalists had much to say of the wonder; for this unexpected manna had fallen to them in the midst of the dog days when there was little about which they might write. Anglican Church dignitaries suggested that the miracle was due to auto-suggestion or to collective hypnosis, and others asserted that it was mere trickery. The public as a whole expressed a great diversity of opinions on this topic: businessmen announced it as something opposed to the common sense of the British people; ladies became indignant at what they considered papistical fables; and, for a while, among the strollers on Prince's Street the story became a byword with the comment that life would be very amusing if all these religious tales were "truly true."

Fr. Malachy had to learn by experience that "man will not be convinced of a miracle in one day." He had firmly stated, in the presence of his bishop, that "all unprejudiced people will be convinced that the Garden of Eden could not possibly have been brought to rest on the Bass Rock by natural means," only to hear his Rector drily interrupt him by remarking: "My dear Fr. Malachy, I fear that among mortal men there are very few who are unprejudiced." In the midst of universal unbelief, it was but a wretched consolation to attribute this or that conversion to the miracle. The rosaries muttered by the old church hens who flocked to the hole left by the displaced nightclub were more of a scandal than a satisfaction.

Poor Dom Malachy's embarrassment was complete when the owner of the miraculous nightclub, who was not to be at a loss for ideas wherever his own profit was concerned, decided to make the place a center of rather dubious attractions. He organized a series of special events during which one female of his troupe, after having sung a ballad about the miraculous transportation, announced that she would raffle off, on the stroke of midnight, the silk stockings which she had worn when the Garden of Eden first took flight. Fr. Malachy, in a prayer which was a kind of act of contrition, besought the Lord that he would not further allow these people "to turn his miracle into an occasion of sin," and the Garden suddenly arose again into the air and came back to the place where it had originally been. This led the Anglican Dean of London to declare that the reappearance of the Garden of Eden on the spot from which it had been missing proved beyond peradventure that it had never been elsewhere.

If I have lingered over this amusing tale it is only because it proves, by the well-known device of the *reductio ad absurdum*, the total uselessness in the realm of religion of a sensational event devoid of spiritual significance. Dom Malachy himself took to heart the lesson given him by the whole matter when he declared: "Indeed I blame nobody but myself who was presumptuous enough to imagine that I could cure by one burst of celestial fireworks what twenty centuries of saintly Catholic lives have failed to remedy."

There is only one thing in this novel which passes belief, and that is that such a miracle could ever have taken place. Fr. Malachy thought that it had been wrought by the power of the Holy Spirit; but few would have been like-minded, for the nightclub impresario vainly asked just who is this Holy Spirit about whom the good priest had so much to say, and why was it that he would never agree to display the Spirit's photograph to him. The "miracle" of Dom Malachy could never have come about: it would not have been a Christian miracle, and there are no others. One may, however, profit from the story in the same way as did the poor priest himself: "Perhaps He allowed me to do it in order to show me that his ordinary means were best after all . . . Almighty God intended to teach me a lesson and I must say that he's done it pretty thoroughly."

II · POSITIVE CHARACTERISTICS

How can the salvific character of the miraculous sign show itself, in a positive way, through the visible event? I think that there are three ways in which this can be: one, in the person by whom the miracle is wrought; a second, in the circumstances surrounding it; and a third, in the very nature of the wondrous event itself.

Should the miracle be wrought through instrumentality of a human being, it follows, of necessity, that this *wonder-worker* must be a person transformed by Christian revelation: he must himself be a sign of God's salvific purposes; and the miracle will issue from his ordinary conduct and will appear as a sort of overflow of the divine life within him. Actually, there are two cases which fulfill such a requirement: one is that of personal sanctity; the other of apostolic mission. The miracle which is linked to human instrumentality shows itself usually by the work of a saint or an apostle, for it is in such alone that there exist an aptitude and a fitting ground in which the salvific character of the wonder can best and most fully be discerned.

Holiness and the miraculous are plainly linked together; this is certainly so if we are to take the word "holiness" in the strict sense. Every Christian, ransomed by Christ and so a co-redeemer with him, may loosely be termed to be "holy." Nevertheless, we ordinarily take the word "holy" in a stricter sense, reserving it and the title of "saint" for those who, by a life of renunciation and heroic charity, show that they are untainted by human frailty and can display a perfection of spiritual beauty wholly superior to the virtues of mere humanism, a perfection expressive of divine grace to so perceptible a degree that they evidently show forth the very Christ within themselves and so become a kind of sacramental sign of the indwelling Trinity. Such holiness corresponds in the moral order to that which miracles effect in the material order. Holiness and the miraculous are therefore adapted to each other, like body and soul. As seen by faith, the sensible sign, which is the miracle, and the spiritual sign, which is holiness, are regarded as each extending into the other. Is it not, therefore, to be expected that from one who is intimately linked to Christ and his Cross there would shine forth the first fruits of the Redemption? Is it not normal that those whose faith verges on vision should show forth in their bodily action some tokens of the glory that is to be? Does not heaven lean closest to earth at precisely those points in which the earth rises nearest to heaven?

In the life of a saint, moreover, miracles are better protected from misinterpretation and sensational exploitation: the whole context of holiness casts out such connotations. There is here no danger that the wonder-worker will give himself over to complacency and to pride in the work of his own hands, to a feeling that what he does, he does of his own power. In miracles wrought by the means of holy men, one is drawn beyond the personality of the doer, and is unmistakably led by both the activity and the very person of the wonder-worker to the greatest of all signs and wonders, that of divine love.

The personal qualities of the wonder-worker seem less closely knit to the miraculous event when that event occurs to testify to a *divine mission*, to a message or to a doctrinal pronouncement. In such a case, the miracle may be likened to the credentials shown by an ambassador. It is the mission and the message which are certified to and not the personal worth or the talents of the ambassador himself. Such miraculous events testify rather to the divine desire to transmit the message than to the qualities of the chosen instrument. Thus they do not, of necessity, rule out those dangers of too great self-complacency or inordinate self-esteem which can ensnare the wonder-worker. The apostles, newly commissioned by Our Lord to carry out the work he had confided to them, were exceedingly joyful that in his name they were able to cast out devils. Yet Christ tempered their joy when he said: ". . . 'I beheld Satan fall like a lightning-flash from heaven. Behold I have given you power to tread upon the serpents and scorpions, and over all the might of the enemy, and nothing shall harm you. Nevertheless, rejoice not at this, that the spirits are subject to you; but rejoice that your names are written in the heavens.' "[15]

A man, who far from being a saint may even be a sinner, could therefore perform miracles if the office with which he is charged despite his personal failings, so requires. But such cases are exceptional.[16] Will God, who reads the innermost heart, mark with the seal of his grace—except in very unusual circumstances—a mission which is in the hands of an unworthy instrument? The question is all the more pertinent inasmuch as the Christian Gospel is no abstract doctrine but rather a witnessing which is strongly linked to the person of the witness. I think we may even say that a miracle cannot confirm the mission of a man whose unworthiness is so patent that it compromises or deforms the testimony he offers. There is always the danger that such a miracle might be interpreted as being a mark of approval of his unworthiness, or at least as tantamount to declaring that belief and life can be divorced. Our Lord appar-

[15] Luke X, 17-20; see also Matt. VII, 21-28.

[16] It seems to me that these cases are even more exceptional than the older authors thought. See, for example, *Summa Theol.* I, I, q. 43, a. 3 and 4; Benedict XIV: *De servorum Dei beatificatione et beatorum canonisatione*, lib. IV, pars 1, c. 3, par. 20. They were concerned less with dogmatic preoccupations than with the instancing of marvelous events, either actual or fictive; and either a want of the critical spirit or too great respect for popular credulity impaired their judgment of some alleged miracles. When reference is made to context, it will be seen that the scriptural texts which they cite in support of their thesis are concerned with emphasizing the dangers of vanity or self-complacency to the wonder-worker and the spiritual ruin to which this might lead, rather than with the assertion that the doing of miracles may go hand in hand with the state of sin.

ently confirms this by declaring: ". . . there is no one that shall work a miracle in my name and shall be able to speak ill of me." [17] The man born blind plainly stated: "We know that God heareth not sinners." [18]

Therefore, any miracle which is not linked to moral integrity in the doer of it is to be regarded with extreme suspicion. St. Paul, in speaking of signs, of wonders, and of mighty works, as guaranteeing the preaching of a divine message, always links them together, and he never attributes worth to them unless they are confirmed by a major criterion: the religious personality of the witness and in the way in which he carries out his mission. He must be loyal and faithful; he must be spiritually bold and patient; he must show self-sacrificing devotion to the service into which he has been called.[19]

Whenever it is no longer a question of preaching within an ordered and hierarchical framework, whenever it is a matter of a mission guaranteed rather by personal charismatic gifts than by apostolic office, or of a private revelation confirmed by miracles, then the rule cited above is to be applied rigorously. In such a case it is not merely the marvelous signs which authenticate the preacher's mission but also, even more importantly, the personal qualities and other credentials of the alleged messenger which authenticate the signs themselves. By this I do not mean to say that the criterion is always found in considerations of natural talent or intellectual ability. On the contrary, we may find a convincing force, a divine warranty, in testimony whose deeper meaning, inner consistency, and organic interdependence upon its constituent elements wholly surpasses either the intellectual ability or the acumen

[17] Mark IX, 39.

[18] John IX, 31.

[19] E.g., II Cor. XII, 12; I Cor. I, 5-6; IV, 15; XIV, 22-25; II Thess. I, 10; etc. In his "Remarques sur la foi dans S. Paul," *Revue apologétique*, 65 (1937), 123-136, J. Mouroux very justly remarks: "The miracles must be united to the message; they are parts of a whole: wonders are not to be regarded as something in themselves, they are rather enmeshed as gifts which show themselves in every part of the total human experience" (p. 133). The first and chief sign—and he amasses a number of texts to establish this—is the witness himself; his bearing, his whole life, above all, his loyalty, his bravery, and his patience are to be considered. It is only after the weighing of all these that Mouroux speaks of miraculous signs, and he introduces the point with this phrase: "As part of such a life, other signs may be noted: divine prodigies" (p. 135).

of the witness. The externally observed wonder, in such cases, prolongs a divine initiative already apparent in the message itself, revealing with greater clarity its salvific significance. Thus we ofttimes find in divine secrets entrusted to an unlettered and ungifted child a purity and a convincing credibility, precisely because through the soul of that child the purely gratuitous or *free* nature of the divine gift, so characteristic of the miraculous, has taken upon itself form and life: *pauperes evangelizantur*; the poor have the Gospel preached unto them.[20]

Just as it affects the personality of the wonder-worker, so too the salutary significance of the miracle must pervade the *context* in which it occurs.

Surely, the most normal and fitting context is that of *prayer*. By prayer man expresses his hope of salvation in single-mindedness and in strength: the miracle thus comes into being as God's clear response to the cry of our need. However, it seems that, if the saving meaning of God's reply to our petition is to be preserved, prayer must not confine itself to material need, to the desire for health or bodily well-being, but must express our need for a larger health, a health which will serve the aspiration of the soul for that grace which cures and elevates. No doubt, this way of looking at things is correct. The meaning of the miraculous is most clear

[20] It is not possible to doubt that this is true in Bernadette's case. M. Auclair in *Bernadette* (p. 249) is quite faithful to historical verisimilitude when she puts upon the lips of Bernadette this prayer: "For the spelling I never learned, the knowledge I never had, for my ignorance and my stupidity, thank you! Because had there been in this world a girl more ignorant and more stupid than I, you would have chosen her." As far as the apparitions at Banneux are concerned, Msgr. Kerkhofs (*op. cit.*, p. 176) significantly declares: "Obviously, both the facts and the message conveyed at Banneux are beyond the powers of the untaught and uncouth child who did not even understand the meaning of some telling words. Nevertheless, during the series of eight apparitions, which comprised actions and words of great importance, Mariette Beco, a young girl of little talent, was never at a loss. That the message should be so sublime is in itself a marvel. But that it should be without the slightest flaw or weakness is still more astonishing. In the best of human endeavors do we not find some imperfect details? But here we have not the work of man, but a work of the Blessed Virgin." See the detailed proof of this assertion as it has been set forth by R. Leijs: "Le sens des paroles de Banneux Notre-Dame" in *Notre-Dame de Banneux;* II: *Les faits de Banneux N.-D.* (Liège, 1959), pp. 77-121.

when prayer is fashioned after the mind of Christ, in accordance with the order of petition expressed by the *Pater noster* which asks that, first of all, God's will be done, and only then expresses our earthly hopes. It is not unusual for a sick person to feel impelled to renounce his own cure in order to obtain that of another and to gain, by means of the prayer of complete self-abandonment, the healing of someone even entirely unknown to him. Both the nobility of such an act, and the mystery of the redemptive Cross thus clearly emphasized, are strikingly impressive in our eyes. It would, however, be erroneous, were we to set this high self-abnegation as the norm of all prayer under such circumstances.[21] Actually the mi-

[21] O. Karrer in *Gebet, Vorsehung, Wunder* (Lucerne, 1941) goes yet further when he stigmatizes as non-Christian any prayer offered with a view to obtaining a miracle. In his opinion, there is but one kind of prayer wholly Christian, and that is the prayer of complete self-abandonment, for the sake of God's kingdom, to his will and his providential leading (pp. 123-124). Prayer which seeks first the kingdom of God is convinced that all the rest will be added as increment. On the subject of the less perfect kind of prayer of which I have spoken, he expressly declares: "Prayer which arises from merely instinctive need, unconnected with the desire for eternal salvation, fails to fulfill the fundamental conditions which make its being answered possible" (p. 119). These exaggerated opinions are founded, it seems to me, on a twofold error in perspective: a misunderstanding of the meaning of the miraculous, and a misunderstanding of the true worth of the prayer of petition.

The axis upon which Karrer bases his argument is quite correct: there can be no miracle in the absence of a supernatural desire for salvation. But, if one requires in the beneficiary so clear a consciousness and so entire an abandonment to this saving intention, is not something forgotten? Is it not the aim of the miraculous event precisely to awaken to the supernatural the man who is enmeshed in the material and taken up by worldly concerns? Such a requirement would suppose that what God hopes to achieve by the miracle is already realized; and it would make the miracle a vain and senseless thing. It is also wrong to believe that every prayer which issues from the anguish of one whose situation is felt to be desperate is not true prayer. Such a view betrays a misconception of the psychical complexity of human reaction to suffering as well as to the mysterious confrontation between the grace of God and human freedom. Moreover, it is untrue to pretend that the prayer of wholehearted abandonment to the divine will is incompatible with insistent and confident petition for a miracle. The whole of the Gospel, to which Karrer so often appeals, makes this clear. One has only to read, for example, the deeply human account of the resurrection of Lazarus to realize this. As I hope to show in the following chapter, the role of the miraculous in the life of Christians is not limited, as Karrer seems to suggest, to the arousing of faith; it rather plays a part in the fullness of the Christian life.

All Karrer's conclusions on the subject of the miraculous flow from his erroneous notion of the meaning and value of the prayer of petition, a notion

raculous is a sign from a God who desires to speak to us in the depths of our sinfulness, who wishes to solace our bodily misery, to know our need. Is it not precisely for those who are least aware of the need of redemption, for those astray in the painful by-paths of sin, who, like a wounded beast, cry out in pain for Someone who can draw the dart from out of their flesh; is it not mainly for such that the miracle offers the only possible evidence of salvation? Do not such estranged souls unknowingly express their need for salvation as they groan and weep in what is actually prayer? The shock of the miraculous turns their eyes from the paltry things of earth, and it awakens them to the goodness of God, lovingly bending down to heal their wounds.

Let us not deceive ourselves. Neither lack of vision nor selfishness, neither the animalistic self-centeredness nor the earthiness of the prayer offered by the mass of men stand in the way of a miracle being wrought. On the other hand, pride, presumption, the pharisaical consciousness of being better than others—each of these has, in every generation, been the chief obstacle to true prayer and to its miraculous fulfillment.

A concrete example may show us how prayer exceeds, in itself, the expectation of man, aware of a definite answer to his spiritual need. The Breviary tells us, on the feast of St. Callixtus, how "while he was in prison he miraculously cured the soldier, Privatus, who suffered from ulceration in all his flesh, and thus won him to Christ. Shortly after being baptized, Privatus was flogged to death." [22] What could have initially impelled Privatus to pray other than his human desire for a cure of the bodily ills under which he languished? Yet God's grace touched his soul as well as his body; all the generous instincts of his soul responded to the unexpected call of the Lord, and he joyfully offered up the health he had so ardently desired, and even his very life, that he might gain the

---

which merited for his book the disapprobation of the Congregation of the Holy Office.

22 ". . . *missus est in carcerem, ubi Privatum militem, ulceribus plenum, admirabiliter sanitati restitutum, Christo adiunxit; pro quo idem, recens adhuc a fide suscepta, plumbatis usque ad mortem caesus occubuit*" (second nocturn lesson of the festival of St. Callixtus, October 14). Karrer (*op. cit.*, p. 144) also cites this text, but gives only its latter portion, without noting how the beginning contradicts the theory which he espouses.

precious pearl of everlasting life, revealed to him in his miraculous cure. This is a magnificent example of the deeper meaning of God's wish for our salvation: that wish, the bountiful mercy of the Lord, "outruns" (as the Collect puts it) "both the merits and the desires of those who cry unto Him." [23]

As well as that of prayer, there is another context in which the miraculous often occurs: it is that of a doctrine, a *message*, of a testimony to be confirmed or authenticated. I have already pointed to the qualities which such miracles require in the person of the messenger. I should like now to indicate two other guarantees which the message itself must furnish.

The first of these is bound up with the value and the truth of the doctrine itself. We may take it as evident that God could not seal with miraculous approval a teaching that is false. With the certainty of faith, we may affirm that a miracle invoked to confirm error in the profession of doctrine, the announcement of a message, or the communication of a private revelation which contradicts the divine revelation which the infallible teaching of the Church presents to us, is merely an illusion and an imposture. On this question Pascal justly remarked: "Miracles are the test of doctrine, and doctrine the test of miracles." [24] Nevertheless, a question remains to be faced. To what extent may a Christian truth—such as, for example, God's fatherly care of us, or the impetratory power of prayer—be confirmed by a miracle when that occurs apart from the context of Chistianity, in connection, even, with either heretical doctrine or pagan belief? This question brings up the whole matter of the possibility of miracles occurring outside the Church, and hence requires a carefully balanced answer. I prefer, therefore, to treat of it in a special chapter.

The second of the two guarantees to which I have referred above is concerned with the tie that binds doctrine and miracle so that each is able to confirm the other. This has to be an essential and intrinsic relationship: a merely external coincidence between miracle and message would not suffice. Let us take as an example some particular revelation such as an apparition of Our Lady. The occur-

[23] "*. . . qui abundantia pietatis tuae et merita supplicum excedis et vota*" (collect for the eleventh Sunday after Pentecost in the *Missale Romanum*).

[24] B. Pascal: *Pensées*, ed. Brunschvicg, n. 803.

rence of cures at the site of apparitions does not, of itself, establish the authenticity of the apparition. The context of prayer and of confidence in Mary might suffice to obtain the miracle even though the apparition were the result of some involuntary error, some illusion, or even of a pathological hallucination undergone in good faith.[25] The case is entirely different when the miracle is directly bound up with the apparition. Such is the case, for example, with the Lourdes cures, which are customarily granted through the use of Lourdes water. Even more evident is this link between apparition and miracle when the miracle is prayed for expressly as a sign confirming the apparitions. Some of the events at Banneux should, it would seem, be considered as falling into this category.[26] So is it also when the miracle is predicted and announced—as was the miracle of the sun at Fatima—as a confirmation of the apparition.

Just as the Christian miracle enforces its requirements in respect to the person of the wonder-worker and the attendant circumstances, so too the *wondrous fact* must be in harmony with the salutary meaning which it expresses. If it is to be a vehicle of the Word of God, it is not enough that it be merely an out-of-the-ordinary occurrence; it must be such in a religious sense. Although the circumstances of the wondrous happening and the agent by whom it is wrought can strongly set their seal upon the act itself by orienting it in a definite direction of meaning, it is nevertheless true that, in the final analysis, it is the wondrous fact itself which carries the religious message. Therefore its natural symbolism must be closely enough allied with its salvific symbolism so that, when it is raised above itself in its instrumental activity, it will be able to convey that message. In other words the wondrous happening must itself display an analogy with the supernatural reality which is salvation. Let us recall, for a moment, the function of the body in the redemptive plan, and thus make clear in what this analogy consists. Man's need to be redeemed has left marks in his flesh: he is in want, he is subject to illness, to pain, and to death. On the other

[25] On this point, see K. Rahner: *Visions and Prophecies* (New York, 1963), p. 31 ff.

[26] Msgr. Kerkhofs: *op. cit.*, p. 176; the facts to which I have made allusion are to be found on pp. 123, 133, 140, etc.

hand, it is the body which has been selected for redemption as the instrument and the cornerstone of salvation. Once the body is redeemed, glory shall shine through it and dwell within it. The miraculous phenomenon will be fit to express redeeming reality, if it symbolically shows forth in the bodily order the liberating effect of grace or if it prefigures that "new heaven and new earth" which is promised.

This principle must be applied very prudently and cautiously, for we run the risk of confining divine signs within the narrow limits of our human comprehension, or of resisting those signs because of the blindness of an age that has lost all sense of the symbolic.

In miraculous cures, provided they avoid sensationalism, the symbolism of redemption is clear. The same can be said of the alleviation of material woe, and the providing of money or food for the poor, at least when it is a matter of relieving a real need and not a display of ostentatious and wasteful opulence. In nature-prodigies, it is often less easy to establish a connection with the supernatural. The symbolism of calming a tempest is immediately evident. The gushing fountain of a stream of water, as at Lourdes and Banneux, reveals, in lucid symbolism, Christ and his sacramental signs.[27] But it is much less simple to behold in the solar miracle of Fatima,[28] to cite one instance, any clear function as a sign of the supernatural. Yet, when we consider the cosmic wonders which Scripture presents almost as rubrics of God's coming, we must realize that, in its own way, this miracle is in the line of the biblical tradition.

In any case, the astonishment and wonder which the Christian miracle arouses cannot be wholly worldly: its primary effect must

[27] Christ as the fountain source is a classic image in Scripture. See K. Rahner: "Flumina de ventre Christi. Die patristische Auslegung von Joh. VII, 37-38," *Biblica*, 22 (1941), 269-302 and 367-403; ID.: "On the Biblical Basis of the Devotion," in J. Stierli (ed.): *Heart of the Saviour* (New York, 1957), pp. 15-35; M. F. Boismard: "De son ventre couleront des fleuves d'eau (Jo. VII. 38)," *Revue biblique*, 65 (1958), 523-546; P. Grelot: "De son ventre couleront des fleuves d'eau. La citation scripturaire de Jean VII, 38," *Revue biblique*, 66 (1959), 369-373. The image of Mary as an "aquaduct" is one which often occurs in the Fathers. See the treatment of the stream of water in the Banneux apparitions which is expressed by Père Scheuer in Msgr. Kerkhofs's book, *Banneux*, pp. 38-40, and 43.

[28] Cf. E. Dhanis: *Bij de verschijningen en het geheim van Fatima* (Bruges, 1945), p. 27.

have a spiritual result; it must confront man with his divine Saviour; it must spur him to surrender of self and to spiritual renewal. Every Christian miracle, solely as an occurrence, must arouse that holy awe which causes man to fall upon his knees and to cry out: "Depart from me, O Lord, for I am a sinner." It is only on this condition that the miracle will make clear Our Lord's response: "Fear not; it is I."

5 · MIRACLES AND THE CHRISTIAN LIFE

A miracle is wholly subordinate to the supernatural reality which it signifies. Like the other signs of revelation, which also call us to a life of union with God, the miraculous has a definite function. In seeking to discover exactly what a miracle means, I have sketched out the broad lines of this function. Now we must consider it in greater detail.

It would be a mistake to be misled by a shortsighted view of apologetics into using miracles only as a weapon in controversy with unbelievers and other adversaries. Useful though it is in controversy, the miracle is still more important in the life of believers and in the whole context of Christian living.

I shall, therefore, first of all examine the problem of the relations between faith and signs, and then pass on to a consideration of the special role of the miraculous sign, especially as it affects the awakening of faith, its gradual growth, and the whole complexus of the religious life which issues from it.

I · FAITH AND SIGNS

In an official declaration of the First Vatican Council, faith is thus defined: "The Catholic Church professes that faith, which is the beginning of human salvation, is a supernatural virtue by which, with the inspiration and help of God's grace we believe that what he has revealed is true—not because its intrinsic truth is seen by the natural light of reason, but because of the authority of God himself who reveals it, since he can neither deceive nor be deceived." [1]

Faith is "the beginning of human salvation." As a response on our part, to God who has called us, faith introduces us to the dialogue of the Father with the Word, in the unity of the Holy Spirit. Thus we share with him the innermost secrets of his own life. Merely natural knowledge can attain only to a God who remains yet afar off: by faith, we come into his presence, the source of all our joy: we confront the God who saves. In this new dialogue, faith is the first step on the path to salvation. It is both our discovery of and our initial commitment to, the saving love which is offered to us. As this conversation continues, faith remains ever on the alert, perduringly attentive to this privileged presence and nourished by the certitude of listening to Him to whom man has, by the act of faith, linked his own destiny.

As is obvious, the certainty of this assent cannot be based upon human reasoning, nor upon merely natural probative arguments. Our nature is lacking in any capacity which is, of itself, able to grasp and understand a supernatural expression.

It needs must be, then, that the word of God arouse in us a new method of knowing, that his grace set aflame in our being a brighter light, a kind of understanding which is above the natural and which will be able to unveil his presence and to decipher the new tongue in which he speaks to us. This supernatural capacity to say "Amen" to God's call is what we call the grace of faith. Its certitude has its whole basis in "the authority of God himself as revealer." The light of grace, the witness of himself which God gives, takes the form of a mysterious attraction, not rooted in human reasoning but springing into being under the heavenly touch of the finger of God, our Saviour.[2] A supernatural virtue, faith is

[1] "*Hanc vero fidem, quae humanae salutis initium est, Ecclesia catholica profitetur, virtutem esse supernaturalem, qua, Dei aspirante et adiuvante gratia, ab eo revelata vera esse credimus, non propter intrinsecam rerum veritatem naturali rationis lumine perspectam, sed propter auctoritatem ipsius Dei revelantis, qui nec falli nec fallere potest*" (*DSch* 3008).

[2] On this subject see: J. H. Walgrave: "Geloofwaardigheid en apole-

also a theological virtue: it seeks God as its direct and immediate end, not as an end to be attained through the medium of created things. Hence, the certitude of faith goes beyond the certitude which is merely natural, and it shares in God's own certitude. The divine call serves, mysteriously, as its own guarantee, by its actuality to us, as the interior light of grace reveals it to us.

Yet, if the uncreated attraction of God, our Salvation, be the motive of our yielding to him, and if it offer to us the greatest possible certitude we can know in this life, being, in effect, a sharing in his own sovereign truth, what further need have we of signs and arguments to be supports for our faith? This question is answered by the First Vatican Council immediately after its definition of faith: "Nevertheless, in order that the obeisance of our faith be consonant with reason, God has been pleased to supply, besides the interior aids of the Holy Spirit, external evidences of his revelation, namely divine acts, especially miracles and prophecies." [3]

By the light of faith we see not clearly, but *as in a glass, darkly*; it affords not full knowledge but an obscure and veiled apprehension of its object. Doubtless, the divine attraction could, through a very

---

getica," *Theologica, Voordrachten en discussies van het Vlaams Werkgenootschap voor Theologie* (Ghent, 1953); Humanus (J. H. Walgrave): "Het mysterie van het geloof," *Kultuurleven* (1952), 261-268; P. de Letter: "Faith and Apologetics," *Irish Ecclesiastical Record*, 82 (1954), II, 310-321; L. Malevez: "Théologie dialectique, théologie catholique et théologie naturelle," *Recherches de science religieuse*, 28 (1938), 527-540; M. de la Taille: "L'Oraison contemplative," *Recherches de science religieuse*, 9 (1919), 273-292; E. Dhanis: "Le problème de l'acte de foi," *Nouvelle revue théologique*, 68 (1946), 26-43. An increasingly large number of contemporary writers are in agreement in seeing in this interpretation the authentic expression of the notions held by St. Thomas Aquinas on this head; see, *inter alia*: M. D. Chenu: "Pro fidei supernaturalitate illustranda," *Xenia Thomistica*, III (Rome, 1925), pp. 297-307; ID.: "La psychologie de la foi dans la théologie du XIIIe siècle," *Études d'histoire littéraire et doctrinale du XIIIe siècle* (Ottawa, 1932). The same may be said, with some reservation in regard to important points, of the following: A. Stolz: "Glaubensgnade und Glaubenslicht nach Thomas von Aquin," *Studia Anselmiana*, I (Rome, 1933); H. Lang: *Die Lehre des Hl. Thomas von Aquin von der Gewissheit des übernatürlichen Glaubens* (Augsburg, 1929).

[3] *"Ut nihilominus fidei nostrae obsequium rationi consentaneum esset, voluit Deus cum internis Spiritus Sancti auxiliis externa iungi revelationis suae argumenta, facta scilicet divina, atque imprimis miracula et prophetias"* (*DSch* 3009).

singular grace, flood man's consciousness with a clear light; but we would then be dealing with an exceptional case. In the normal course of things, this light is not enough to make clear the necessity, as a moral duty plainly perceived, of passing from the state of spontaneous inclination to that of willed faith. The conscious awakening of faith is normally[4] effected by the operations of reason endeavoring to come to grip with external signs: the interior call then asserts itself more clearly within the mind and arouses a definite sense of obligation. The assent to the invitation once given, faith would meet many difficulties if it relied exclusively on an interior attraction and avoided all rational inquiry. It would even run the risk of foundering, if objections increased and doubts arose, as may easily happen because of pagan surroundings, or ceaselessly progressing secular culture, or considerations of temporal advantage. To strengthen its grasp, the motivation of faith must be implanted in a solid rational structure. Thus, by stern effort faith will erect an outer fortress for its certitude, confirming itself by external evidences, so that the believer is able to justify on reasonable grounds the impulse to believe which grace has granted him. Nevertheless, these rationally probative evidences which serve to bolster faith are not actually a part of the strictly supernatural motive which evokes our faith: God's uncreated call is of itself the real warranty of its own witness. Rational motivation is of another order: it is built upon human certitude and human prudence, and cannot take equal rank with divine testimony. Yet it stands near the original motivation, and is closely linked to it: man, through the use of his rational faculties, transposes into the realm of human capacity that immediate certitude, received by him as a consequence of God's uncreated call. This intellectual effort helps one's faith to come to *personal* fruition.[5]

[4] I say "normally" so as to allow for the possibility of the light of grace all at once seizing upon the consciousness, thus making unnecessary any effort to reason things out. This possibility was plainly affirmed at the First Vatican Council, and the Conciliar Fathers engaged in spirited criticism of the text of the prosynodal draft which appeared to be setting such a possibility aside. See Mansi, vol. L, and the summation of these discussions in R. Aubert: *Le problème de l'acte de foi*, pp. 146-149.

[5] J. H. Walgrave: "Geloofwaardigheid en Apologetica," p. 20, regards the needfulness of a judgment of rational credibility as "a particular application of the Christian humanism of St. Thomas, according to whom grace does not

The light, then, in which the probative value of external signs shows itself is not the light of faith which grace affords, but rather the light of natural human reason.[6] Likewise, the signified reality

---

destroy nature, but respects and perfects it." In regard to the necessity of harmony between the adhesion which is proper to faith and the rational justification of it, he expresses himself thus: "The cross of faith is that it cannot healthily grow within the human mind unless the ascending movement of its adhesion ("assensio") be ceaselessly traversed by discursive reason ("cogitatio")." (J. H. Walgrave: "Het kruis van het geloof," *Kultuurleven* [1954], 173.)

[6] A good number of authors (see the writings of Huby, Masure, Tiberghien, Bouillard, Coventry, cited in note 30 of chapter III) hold that the full value of the sign and, in consequence, the probative force of the miraculous, cannot be perceived except by an intelligence already enlightened by faith. Almost without exception, they rely upon the psychology of faith developed by Père Rousselot (see the articles cited in the same footnote). The analysis of faith put forward by the Scholasticism of the nineteenth century was clearly infected by Rationalism: it placed the essential motive of faith in the rational evidences of the fact of revelation, a "fides naturalis" which was subsequently raised and transformed, in one way or another, by grace, into a free, supernatural and meritorious act. (On the genesis of these theological theories see F. Schlagenhaufen: "Die Glaubensgewissheit und ihre Begründung in der Neuscholastik," *Zeitschr. für kath. Theol.*, 56 [1932], 313-374 and 530-595; P. Rousselot: "Remarques sur l'histoire de la notion de foi naturelle," *Rech. de sc. rel.*, 4 [1913], 1-36). It is the great merit of Rousselot that he restored to honor, in the face of these Rationalist theories, the traditional Thomistic doctrine that an act is specified by its formal object. At the same time, he revived, to a very great extent, the authentic Thomistic theology of the act of faith. In agreement with St. Thomas, he holds that the supernatural object of faith cannot be known except by a knowing faculty which has been intrinsically supernaturalized; the formal motivation of this supernatural faith cannot, therefore, be seated in a judgment of rational credibility, nor may it even be something dependent upon it: it must have been communicated in and by the very light of faith itself. Likewise, his interpretation of the part played by the "lumen fidei" in the construction of the supernatural motivation of faith is rooted, as well, in the purest Thomism. He maintains that it is the uncreated call of God our Saviour which produces an inclination of the will in which the intellect joins. By its assent, which is also an act of consent, the intellect, while affirming its objects, co-affirms—at least, implicitly and *exercite*—as the determining motivation of its assent, that divine attraction to which it yields. In other words, there is in faith a certain form of cognition by connaturality. But Rousselot goes even further in his interpretation; and here it is that, as it seems to me, he departs from the great Thomistic tradition, and is imprisoned, in his turn, within the very Rationalism which he wishes to combat. (H. Lang: *op. cit.*, p. 146, while accepting Rousselot's theory, admits that it cannot be established from St. Thomas's texts themselves.) Although traditional Thomism restricts the motivation of faith solely to uncreated testimony, Rousselot is unable to conceive of a faith which would not be intrinsically rational and wherein

glimpsed in signs is not the supernatural element as such, but rather the supernatural as a naturally knowable fact. Man, while still unbelieving, is brought face to face with the message and the tidings of divine supernatural salvation. He yet lacks the capacity

---

the motivation of rational credibility would not play a determining role. Hence, his principal thesis: the divine calling guarantees faith, in the last analysis, "not as an interior fact which is seen, but as eyes for the seeing of the external fact" (*art. cit.*, p. 244, note). If it be admitted that the external motives of credibility form an integral part of the motivation of faith, and that the divine call cannot make itself felt as the motivation of adhesion except insofar as it is immanent in external signs, then Rousselot's conclusion cannot be gainsaid. But I hold that the uncreated call of God is co-affirmed—if implicitly, yet nevertheless directly and without the meditation of any created motivation whatsoever—in the act of affirming the object of faith. I hold, further, that it is affirmed as being a presupposition of the voluntary inclination which causes our affirmation and is thus co-affirmed as something "a priori" with respect to that very inclination of the will. Thus it is the divine summons to belief, itself, which—mysteriously, no doubt, and in implicit fashion—directly and without any mediation on the part of signs or external motivation, itself witnesses to itself as being the root motivation of faith. What is the reason for adhering to this thesis? It is because the light of faith must essentially be of the same nature as is the light of glory, however much it must be distinguished from it, and because it must be avowed that there ought to be, between these two lights, a real participation functioning analogically. Just as does the light of glory, the light of faith must then require—even though it do so in its own fashion—a moment or point of direct confrontation with God, without there being any created intermediary. A cognition by signs can precede the act of faith as a sort of preparation or propaedeutic; it may also follow the act of faith, being the view faith takes of the reality signified. But the judgment of supernatural credibility (to keep the usual, albeit inadequate, terminology) cannot be built up, as Rousselot imagines it can, in the same manner as is cognition by signs. (Cf. the many texts wherein St. Thomas calls faith an anticipatory participation in the beatific vision, an "inchoatio vitae aeternae." On this point see A. Stolz: *op. cit.*, pp. 36-83. We may cite, in particular, a significant text: *In Joannem IV*, lect. 5, n. 2: "*Inducunt nos autem ad fidem Christi tria: primo quidem ratio naturalis . . . secundo, testimonia legis et prophetarum . . . tertio, praedicatio apostolorum et aliorum . . . Sed quando per hoc manuductus credit, tunc potest dicere quod propter nullum istorum credit, nec propter rationem naturalem, nec propter testimonia legis, nec propter praedicationem aliorum, sed propter ipsam veritatem tantum*").

Some recent writers, such as de Broglie and Malmberg, are in agreement with Rousselot in considering grace as a necessary element in the discernment of signs, not merely morally necessary, but physically, as well. However, they part company with him in that they attribute such functioning not to the grace of faith itself, but rather to a prevenient grace—"*gratia praeveniens fidei.*" See, for example, F. Malmberg: "'Apologetica' als theologische wetenschap," *Bijdragen*, 1 (1938), 104-145; ID.: "Apologetische zekenheid en geloofsgenade," *Bijdragen*, 7 (1946), 256-267.

to grasp the full sense of these tidings; but what he does perceive represents to him a plausible natural significance; this expression conveys something which exceeds the existential ambit which he has, hitherto, considered as the boundary of his destiny. The miracle or other external sign is manifestly and closely linked to the mysterious reality which is being preached; through them this reality beckons to him in one way or another. The reality itself still escapes him, despite all this, however; for his ability to know is not equal to it. On the level of natural cognition he comes to the conclusion: these are tidings in which I ought to believe. But the word "believe" has as yet no more than a natural sense. However, on the level of rationality, he is now prepared for the reception of the actual invitation to belief which will come through the direct and uncreated attraction which God will exercise upon him.

G. Söhngen has very happily pictured this relationship between the natural comprehension of signs and supernatural faith by the figure of the Court of the Gentiles at the Temple of Jerusalem. The signs themselves introduce us into a kind of parvis of Revelation: "This parvis is neither the 'Holy One' himself, nor the 'Holy of Holies' where God speaks, nor the 'Holy Place' in which he is heard by faith. Nevertheless, the Gentile who has come into the outer court does see the 'Holy Place' from without; in the parvis he becomes aware that he is near the 'Holy Place' which calls to him; yet the holiness and the very presence of God will not grip him until he has actually come within the sacred precincts." [7]

It goes without saying that the certitude which this natural view of the sign presents to us cannot be an evidential certitude. What is initially in question is a knowledge through signs. There is an essential line of separation between the sign and what it signifies; the image is, of necessity, alien and inadequate in respect of a reality which surpasses all representation. This fact endows the sign with a certain polyvalency, a many-sidedness, an ambiguity which

[7] G. Söhngen: *Wunderzeichen und Glaube*, p. 270. G. Bertram, in the *Theol. Wört. z. N. T.*, vol. III, p. 39, *s. v.* Θαῦμα speaks of the religious wonderment aroused by the miracles of Jesus, and expresses himself in the same sense: *"Der Staunende bleibt im Vorhof; die menschliche Haltung des Staunens gegenüber dem numinosen Erlebnis ist noch nicht Glaube, ist höchstens die Vorstufe dazu, ist, psychologisch gesehen, der Anstoss, der den Glauben wecken, aber auch Zweifel hervorrufen kann."*

only the free decision of the viewer can overcome. Such a form of knowing is incompatible with evidence pure and simple. This is all the more true because the signified reality does not unveil itself in its own supernatural being, but only as that is transposed to the level of nature. The distance between the sign and what it signifies is enhanced; and it excludes, even more decisively, any possibility of evidential knowledge. What the signs make evident is not the fact of revelation itself, but only the credibility of that fact. The First Vatican Council indicated as much when it referred to "all those things, so many and marvelous, which God has provided to render the Christian faith evidently credible." [8] The "evidence of credibility," taken in the traditional sense of the term[9]—a sense which was moreover explicitly recalled in the course of the discussions of Vatican I, but which, unhappily, the nineteenth century readily forgot—has reference only to prudential certitude, a certitude which does not exclude all doubt, but does exclude any prudent uncertainty; since it is necessary in the choice of action in concrete moral matters, it is commonly called "moral certitude."

It would be foolish, moreover, to underestimate the worth of this kind of certitude. Far from being a second-class certitude, it is eminently human; it is the most important, in fact, once we have turned aside from abstract considerations, and enter the zone of existential commitment. The intersubjectivity of persons in their meetings, in conversation, and in love expresses itself by imperfect signs, never entirely "univocal" and, hence, more or less ambigu-

[8] "*omnia, quae ad evidentem fidei christianae credibilitatem tam multa et tam mira divinitus sunt disposita*" (DSch 3013).

[9] Concerning this concept and traditional usage see J. H. Walgrave: *Geloofwaardigheid en apologetica*, pp. 17-18. Pius XII, in his address to the Roman Rota on October 2, 1942, gave a very precise definition of this "moral certitude" (*A.A.S.*, 34 [1942], 340). On this point, also, Rousselot has been led into error by the terminology of St. Thomas, who often called this moral certitude "*opinio fortificata rationibus*." Modern exegetes of Aquinas have no doubt that such expressions concern *certitude*, properly so-called. See, for example, A. Stolz: *op. cit.*, p. 47: "*Mit opinio kann Thomas den gleichen Gewissheitsgrund bezeichnen, den die moderne Theologie certitudo moralis nennt.*" See also H. Lang: *op. cit.*, pp. 132-135. I am in agreement with the definition of J. Maréchal, who in "Crédibilité et philosophie," *Mélanges Maréchal* (Paris, 1950), I, pp. 357-363, remarks that it is "that true human certitude with which we content ourselves, in other departments of life, for arriving at decisions of real importance."

ous. Mutual openness and an underlying likeness one to another allow of a clear interpretation of signs and expressions and justify a choice about their concrete meaning being made with full assurance; and this kind of certitude is much less a prey to doubt and to error than is the most infallible kind of abstract dialectic. To a stranger, it might be said, the signs made by the new-born child, who casts himself into his mother's arms, are enigmatical and dark; but watchful mother love discerns in them a definite language because her sensitivity and insight put her in communion with him. There is no kind of scientific analysis of these infantile babblings which could equal the certitude of a loving mother.

However, prior to the attainment of this certitude, the discernment of signs requires, above and beyond any other form of cognition, an *interior attitude*, compounded of honesty, spiritual health, and unprejudiced openness. In the domain of miraculous signs these dispositions are all the more necessary inasmuch as the ambiguity latent in the sign can be the basis of a real temptation to its misunderstanding. Although the supernatural allures us by the magnificent perspectives it opens up, at the same time it powerfully unsettles us in our need for security and spiritual consolation. We always have some premonition of the sacrifices, renunciations, the whole mystery of death and resurrection, to which the divine call impels us. How easy is it to conceal our fear of the risks involved and our resistance to grace behind the mask of so-called rational objections or behind a fortress which demands geometric proof before assent be given! On the level of human love, we have all known people who are unable to find satisfactory certitude or any warranty which justifies full commitment. What they actually reject is the risk of self-abandonment, the joining with another for better or worse, which marks real love. So is it, likewise, with an involvement in the supernatural: a good many speculatively grounded doubts are no more than an adroit camouflage, a half-conscious flight from the risk that is the price of abandonment to God's love.[10]

In order to express with precision the relationship between the natural cognition of signs and the supernatural light afforded by

[10] On this point see J. Guitton: *Le problème de Jésus et les fondements du témoignage chrétien* (Aix-en-Provence, 1948), pp. 224-226.

faith, I have, hitherto, been concerned with matters from an abstract point of view. In actual reality, whether on the side of God or on that of man, signs are steeped in grace which permeates them through and through. Insofar as God is concerned, signs are salvific acts beyond the grasp of human reason unless it be simultaneously aided by the interior testimony which grace affords. The economy of redemption clothes all nature in an atmosphere of grace: thus miracles, as a natural propaedeutic, are likewise steeped in grace. It is not that grace raises our cognition of signs of the supernatural level, for only the direct illumination proper to faith can do this; but it does cleanse our natural cognition and endows it with open-mindedness and singleness of eye which enable us to face up to things which gravely threaten our worldly security.[11] The unity of God's redemptive plan is shown, therefore, in the collaboration of reason and grace: what we have to deal with is not two isolated and successive acts pursuing their own ends; for reason and grace are rather two moments in one process, attuned one to another, and mutually complementary.

II · MIRACLES AND THE BIRTH OF FAITH

In the setting up of the prudential motives of faith, the miracle plays a primary role. The First Vatican Council recognized its privileged place among those "divine acts" which establish the credibility of revelation and underscored this by affirming that miracles "are attuned to the understanding of all men." [12]

First of all, the miraculous element does not require either such intellectual preparation or such scientific knowledge as is necessary

[11] To the external motivation for credibility there might be applied, *a fortiori*, what the First Vatican Council says in regard to the natural cognition of God: "*divinae revelationi tribuendum est, ut ea, quae in rebus divinis humanae rationi per se impervia non sunt, in praesenti quoque generis humanae condicione ab omnibus expedite, firma certitudine et nullo admixto errore cognosci possint*" (*DSch* 3005). In technical terminology, I might say that reason has the *physical* capacity necessary for the discernment of the signs, but that grace is *morally* necessary for man, in his concrete situation (consequent upon the Fall), to attain to the full exercise of this capacity.

[12] "*. . . omnium intelligentiae accommodata*" (*DSch* 3009). I may refer the reader back to my first chapter for a discussion of the exact meaning of this expression of the Council.

for the comprehension of historical or philosophical argumentation which is appropriate to a cultivated minority of men. The tongue in which the miracle speaks is understood by the least cultivated, and it maintains its persuasive force for the more learned.

It is likewise less dependent on the evolution of thought or the progress of scientific knowledge. For example, that kind of apologetic which is based upon historical considerations must constantly take account of new problems, turn over new documentation, address itself to new objections, but, on the contrary, the disappearance of a cancerous tumor or the sudden healing of a malign wound has today the very same force as an evident sign that it had twenty centuries ago. The miracle makes use of a language which is equally clear to the men of every age.

Other kinds of argumentation presuppose, above all, a personal initiative on the part of man: they imply an active and conscious search, a deliberate setting forth upon a path leading to God. The miracle, on the other hand, itself comes to confront man in the midst of his own indifference and weariness. It confronts him as a face which cannot be denied. He who makes no effort to seek contact with the divine and who, in fact, avoids it on countless pretexts, is brought face to face with it, willingly or not. While the worldly, the merely sensual man, disregards God, shuts himself up in material concerns and is wholly occupied with the trivial round of his work-a-day world, the miracle rudely intrudes on the very field of his preoccupation and compels his attention. While the man of science encloses himself within the fastness of his own field of specialization, the miracle opens a crack in the very center of the fortress which he had thought impregnable and thus upsets his intellectual self-sufficiency.

Finally, the miracle vindicates itself as the most communicable of arguments, as being that most accessible to the mass of mankind: it is of all signs the widest in its appeal.

So universal is the hearing that the miracle receives, so strong is its persuasive force to man in his inborn weakness and sinfulness, that it undoubtedly deserves that prime place which the First Vatican Council accorded it among all the signs of Revelation. Although it is an argument for which there can be no substitute, it is, nevertheless, neither the deepest nor the most pure; for the most lively and the most perduring faith does not rely upon it. On the contrary,—and on this I must insist—in its relation to revelation, the miracle is *the most external of signs*. Signs which are more directly linked to faith, as, for example, the content of the revelation or the person who makes the revelation, are so much the closer to what is signified that they hardly involve any danger of abuse, but the miracle, due to its external character, may all the more readily prove to be a distraction from the religious signification which is intended.

Anguish in the face of, and resistance to, what the supernatural requires may oft-times fetter man; but the elation which he finds in tangible contact with the divine so appeals to him that he may be tempted to repose in the supra-sensible feeling which it has aroused, all the while he fences himself off from the risks which contact with the supernatural bespeaks. He no longer regards the sign as being the witness to a deeper religious reality: he chooses to stop at it and with it, as though it embodied the very essence of his communion with God. Thus is the sign made a substitute for the mysterious reality which it signifies.

But what is worse even than man's closure of his understanding of the true meaning of the miraculous is his sad avidity to make the wonderworking power of God the plaything of his own fancy. He constructs for himself a magical world from which the truly sacral element has fled and in which the most worldly inclinations to pathological impulses and deviations are given full play. Even among Christians, there is a real danger of the perversion of what is sacred by contamination with all the aberrations of superstition, illuminism, and magic, with their appeal to eroticism and aggressiveness.[13] It is not surprising that the Church does not grant to

[13] In the article cited in the introduction to the present work (footnote 8), Card. Ottaviani declared: "For some years past we have been witnesses to an increase of popular hankering for the wonderful, even when it concerns religion. The faithful repair in vast crowds to places where visions and wonders are supposed to have taken place and, at the same time, abandon the Church, the sacraments, and instruction. People who are ignorant of the first words of the Creed set themselves up as ardent apostles of religiosity. Some of them do not hesitate to speak of the Pope, the Bishops, and the clergy in terms of severe reprobation and then grow indignant when the latter do not take part, together with the mob, in all the enthusiasms and outbursts of certain popular movements. Although this is a displeasing situation, it is not one that causes

private judgment the decision on the validity of the miraculous. Instead it seeks, by a strict and conscientious control, to guide the faithful and to warn against illusion and error. In this way false prodigies and fanaticism are prevented from bringing genuine miracles into discredit or casting doubt upon their value.

Does not Our Lord, in more than one place in the Gospel,[14] suggest to us that we ought not think too highly of the miraculous? The Church Fathers and the theologians, on their part, have stressed the merely incipient, provisional, and extrinsic character of the miraculous as a starting point of man's turning toward God. "Not all the saints," says Augustine, "have been thaumaturges, lest the weaker among you be betrayed into baneful error; for such would it be were you to think that this gift is of greater import than is the righteous life by which everlasting bliss is won." [15] St. Thomas praises those whom the Pharisees sent to arrest Jesus and who returned empty-handed because the personal gifts of Jesus had so captivated them that they declared: "Never has man spoken like him"; and he remarks: "There are three reasons for commending them: in the first place, we have to consider what it was that moved them to admiration. This was not the miracle, but rather

---

surprise. Man's feelings are natural, even those towards religion. Just as man is a rational animal, so he is a political and religious animal. By bringing disorder and confusion into the nature of man and all his feelings, original sin has attacked, so to speak, religious feelings also. This is the explanation of the deviations and the errors of so many natural religions, no more and no less than the explanation of so many other distortions in the history of man. But it is a fact that errors of this kind are much more troublesome where religion is concerned . . ." [as translated in *The Tablet* (London) 197 (24 Feb. 1951), 144]. See also A. Léonard: "La métamorphose du sacré dans la superstition," *Supplément* to *Vie Spirituelle*, 7 (1954), 5-29. There are innumerable cases illustrative of that kind of mental outlook to which Card. Ottaviani refers; see for example: H. Thurston: *Beauraing and Other Apparitions* (London, 1934), pp. 41ff., on Onkerzele and so forth; H. Woltereck: *Das Tor zur Seele* (Seebruck, 1951), pp. 237-240, on Heroldsbach; O. Karrer: "Wundererscheinungen in aller Welt," *Orientierung*, 20 (1956), 13-15; A. Van Cutsem: "Les merveilles du Padre Pio," *Nouv. Rev. Théol.*, 78 (1956), 955-962; "Heiligenverehrung und Aberglaube," *Orientierung*, 20 (1956), 111-112.

[14] Cf. chapter VI.

[15] "*Non omnibus sanctis ista tribuuntur, ne perniciosissimo errore decipiantur infirmi, existimantes in talibus factis maiora dona esse quam in operibus iustitiae, quibus aeterna vita comparatur*" (*Lib. de div. quaest. oct. trib.*, 79, 3; ML XL, c. 92).

the doctrine of Christ. Thus they drew closer to Truth and further from those Jews who were seeking for signs." [16]

On the other hand, why ought we underestimate the value and the compelling force of the miraculous, when we consider the actual psychology of human kind? We are spirits enclosed within bodies. Why then—as was so often the case in the last century—view with suspicion the demands of our senses as if they displayed a weakness humiliating to an essence aspiring to a purely spiritual state? [17] The fact that God has employed miracles is a precise indication of his regard for the human spirit as being conjoined to human flesh: it constitutes a divine recognition of our total humanity. If Christ made the matter of the Jews' hunger after miracles a matter of reproach to them, it was because he saw in it a symptom of their unbelief. He, himself, wrought a continuous succession of miracles, and he appealed to them as guarantees of his divine mission. Both internal and external signs have each their own worth, and it is a complementary one: as Pascal has put it, "Miracles and truth are alike necessary, for the whole man must be brought to belief, his body as well as his soul." [18]

To put it briefly, the argument from miracles is not one which cannot be otherwise supplied. Neither the individual Christian nor the whole Church can lay claim to it by strict right. Yet, it seems in harmony with the redemptive economy; and it is likely that, within the Church, miracles as effectual invitations to belief will never desist. As something humanly unpredictable, it ever bears the mark of God's own sovereign freedom. But, from generation to genera-

[16] "*Ubi redduntur commendabiles ex tribus. Primo ex admirationis causa: quia non propter miracula, sed propter doctrinam Christi mirabantur: ex quo propinquiores efficiuntur veritati, et recedunt a consuetudine Judaeorum, qui signa quaerunt . . .*" (*In Joannem*, lectio V, n. 6. See, as well, lectio III, n. 9).

[17] Is not somewhat this attitude revealed in the words of A. D. Sertillanges in his *L'Idée de création et ses retentissements en philosophie*, p. 204: "It is a case of God condescending to our weakness. He is pleased to come to the help of our blindness, our hardness of heart or thoughtlessness, to give tokens to our sensory nature, which needs unusual jolts. This is the whole meaning of miracles, and it is not very sublime. The value of miracles is founded in our weakness. If they bear witness to God, their testimony is directed chiefly to men who are unable to receive God's great testimony—that of creation in its unity, in the splendor of the eternal order which it reflects, and in the goodness to which it bears witness in spite of the mysteries it contains."

[18] Blaise Pascal: *Pensées*, ed. Brunschvicg, n. 806.

tion, in varying types of community, miracles continue to occur, most frequently in times and situations when they will have the fullest effect. Miracles thus become one of those characteristic manifestations which make it possible for the Church to be "a sign lifted up among the nations." [19]

The concrete persuasive force of the miraculous is, to a large measure, bound up with this regular irregularity. Skepticism in the face of an isolated miraculous occurrence remains a matter of honest doubt: it is impossible to guard absolutely against error or imposture. The beneficiary of an alleged miracle may be, in reality, deceived by his imagination or by a rare coincidence of circumstances. But such a possibility is dissipated when the examined facts are seen to be links in a series, so that, without losing anything of their exceptional nature, they nevertheless occur according to some sort of canon. The moral certitude engendered by some new prodigy is sustained and confirmed by the whole series of signs which have gone before, and every new sign reinforces, in its turn, the evidence to which the anterior members of the series have attested.

Thus is to be explained the attitude of the Church: it requires that we believe in the possibility of the miraculous and in its probative value; but it leaves each mind free to judge the worth of any particular miracle, as such. When, therefore, after a meticulous examination of the facts, the Church declares a miraculous occurrence to be authentic, it is far from wishing to force the consent of the believer or, a fortiori, to bind him to an act of faith. She intends only to lend strong confirmation to his personal religious conviction. She defends the faithful against the risks of unreliable information and hasty conclusions; she protects them against that intemperate zest for wonders which seems to be seated in man.[20]

[19] "*Quo fit ut ipsa (ecclesia) veluti signum levatum in nationes, et ad se invitet, qui nondum crediderunt, et filios suos certiores faciat, firmissimo niti fundamento fidem, quam profitentur*" (First Vatican Council, *DSch* 3014).

[20] Cfr. C. M. Henze: "Neue Wunder. Wer hat das Recht ein neues ausserordentliches Geschehen als Wunder zu bezeichnen?" *Freiburger Zeitschrift für Phil. und Theol.*, 1 (1954), 411-419; A. Michel: art. "Miracles," *Dict. de Théol. cath.*, cc. 1856-57; K. Rahner: *Visions and Prophecies*, pp. 11-13, note.

III • MIRACLES AND THE GROWTH OF THE LIFE OF FAITH

It might seem that the miracle, as an external sign, would be influential only on the threshold of conversion in order that it might arouse the indifferent conscience or masked incredulity. As faith increases, does not the attention of the believer shift from the sign itself to the reality it symbolizes and its lifegiving worth? This way of looking at things is not entirely accurate; for the miracles retain their value for men whose lives are animated by faith.

The rational motivations of faith are marked by some degree of independence from its supernatural motivation. For this reason we must engage in a continual effort to bring the motives of our faith into contact with our worldly notions, with life as we experience it, and with the exactions which our surroundings and the times impose upon us.[21] The rational basis of faith is not to be thought of as a treasure to be locked up in a strongbox, nor as an answer to a problem once and forever given. It is a living conviction, wholly personal and complex, which differs in proportion to individuals, to their milieu, to their era. In the objective sense, the motives of faith remain the same; but they have to be made personal, they must become part of the dynamism of life. A sincere believer can encounter many a crisis during his lifetime; the equilibrium between his beliefs and his surroundings may be upset by a too unilateral development of either; and, in unfavorable circumstances of such sort, all his interior certitudes may appear to fail him at the same moment: it is then that the believer in search of a rational basis for his faith may make use of the argument from miracles to overcome his discomfiture.[22]

"Cradle-believers" receive, with their baptism, the grace of faith, and they usually develop it quite smoothly in favorable surroundings. Their transition to adulthood presents a risk as it excites in them a difficult crisis: the awakening of strong emotional forces coincides with that of an untutored critical sense, and when prac-

[21] Cfr. J. H. Walgrave: "Het kruis van het geloof," *Kultuurleven* (1954), 163-173.

[22] I have elsewhere expatiated on this theme; cfr. L. Monden: "Weifelend geloof," *Streven*, 6 (1952), II, 147-158.

ticed belief is brought sharply face to face with indifferent or hostile surroundings, the result may be a complex situation. At such a time miracles may return to prominence among the motives of credibility; during this period of crisis they can provide a temporary support for faith.

Just as crises of this nature present themselves in the lives of individuals, so do they also in the religious life of a community. From this point of view, the apologetic worth of the miraculous is thrown into sharp relief for such an age as our own.

During its history, Christianity has known times when men's lives and thoughts, their conception of the world of mankind, formed a harmonious whole: the relationships between secular society and the world of faith were clearly marked in the minds of individuals as well as in that of the Church, and in both preaching and apologetics. At such times, the argument based on the miraculous might readily slip into the background, yielding to criteria more interior in their nature. However, at other periods of history, the world has been in a rapid and disconcerting state of change with the result that the commensal relation between faith and reason seemed to be constantly changing. There can be no doubt that it is in just such an age that we, ourselves, are living. The whole spirit of our time—its changed social attitudes, the advances made in positive science and in psychology, ideological and political changes, the general breakdown of traditional patterns of thought and life, the overwhelming ascendancy of technology, an increased awareness of problems on a world scale, the tendency of men's minds to become immersed in irrational and existential matters—has split the barrier built around the formalized and routine religion of many Christians. Contemporary man is ceaselessly confronted with questions which are too ill-formulated to be satisfactorily answered, but which are, nevertheless, sufficiently vexing to bring insecurity and doubt in their train.

The miracle is a sign which speaks to all conditions of men. Its palpable reality protects it from the danger of being "rationalized away" and its power to effect personal contact endows it with existential value. Moreover, it presents a real basis which makes it possible for men, despite their unsettled state, to recover interior balance and slowly to sift problems of the moment. The interest which surrounds the miraculous in our own time is, in large part, accounted for by these facts. No longer is the miracle left to be treated by specialists in theology: we find novelists and dramatists, ever aware of what the mass of men find moving, selecting miracles as the focus of dramatic treatment and of their religious enquiry.[23] Less than a century ago, when Rationalistic Positivism was at its height and fancied it would soon be able to offer a scientific explanation of man and the world, such interest in the miraculous would have been unthinkable. Although that passion for wonders which is always latent in the mass of men is likely to degrade this renewed realization of the miraculous, so that, in fact, the Church has been obliged to issue warnings, is not this aspect of the larger issue a merely marginal—if inevitable—one, the price of a happy development in Occidental religious thought? And, in any event, it is not forbidden to think that God comes to help our sorely tried faith by showering upon us a host of perceptible signs.

Perhaps this very thought explains the fact that so many contemporary miracles are linked to apparitions or messages of Our

[23] By the way of illustration, and without any pretension to completeness, I cite here some works which clearly show an involvement in the problem of the marvel. As far as novels are concerned, I might point, in addition to the books of B. Marshall and E. Langgässer already named, to the following: G. Bernanos: *La joie;* A. J. Cronin: *The Keys of the Kingdom;* H. Ghéon: *Les jeux de l'enfer et du ciel;* G. Walschap: *Zuster Virgilia;* A. Majocchi: *Vie de chirurgien;* G. Cesbron: *Vous verrez le ciel ouvert;* J. L. Martin Descalzo: *La frontière de Dieu;* M. West: *The Devil's Advocate;* W. Barrett: *The Empty Shrine.* In scoffing mood, like the now almost-forgotten novel of E. Zola: *Lourdes,* whose appearance once caused so great a stir, are A. Gide: *Les caves du Vatican;* R. Peyrefitte: *Les clés de S. Pierre;* R. Brulez: *De verschijning te Kallista;* Louis Bromfield: *The Strange Case of Miss Annie Spragg.* In the theater, as well, many writers, and those not among the least important, have shown increased interest in the problem raised by the miraculous: for example: B. Björnson: *Ueber die Kraft;* E. Lavery: *The First Legion;* A. Manzari: *Il miracolo;* G. Sion: *Le voyageur de Forceloup;* L. Fodor: *The Vigil;* B. Shaw: *Saint Joan;* J. P. Sartre: *Le diable et le bon Dieu;* Kaj Munk: *Ordet* (The Word); G. Greene: *The Potting Shed,* etc. On the moving picture screen the theme of the miraculous seems to have attracted the very best directors. Quite at random, one might mention Vittorio de Sica: *La porta del Cielo;* Marcel Blistène: *Le sorcier du ciel;* Roberto Rossellini: *Il miracolo* (scenario by Fellini); Henry King: *The Song of Bernadette;* Ladislao Vajda: *Marcellino, pan y vino;* Carl Dreyer: *Ordet* (based on *The Word* by Kaj Munk); and, quite recently: Berlanga: *Los jueves milagros (A Miracle Every Thursday);* B. Wicki: *Das Wunder des Malachias* (based on the novel of B. Marshall).

Lady. Marian devotion always affords an ideal terrain for the blossoming forth of the miraculous. Her perfect purity provides the very best religious context in which to set the miracle. Of all the saints, Mary is closest to God; and by her, heaven comes closest to earth. That she is Mother means that she is ready to hear every cry for help, for she knows all our spiritual and bodily ills. The weak and the neglected turn to her of their own accord as a source of the maternal protection and love of which they are in need. All that is good in us, weak and threatened as it may be, expands by her help. It is she who responds to our craving to be understood; it is her motherly heart that hears us in sorrow or remorse. The interior quality of Marian devotion guarantees the whole background of prayer, humility, and silence which fit the soul for the divine ascendancy.

Yet there is a deeper significance to the frequency of the Marian miracle: it depends on the place which belongs to Mary in the redemptive economy. Truly did the Fathers call her "*aurora Christi.*" Her Immaculate Conception is a form of the visible presence of the Saviour even before His own arrival. Our Lady is herself that Advent: it is she in whom Christ comes to meet man; it is she, on behalf of all mankind, who by her *fiat* welcomes Him. It is in Mary's affirmative response and by it that humanity is wedded to Christ in His Church. Is it not, therefore, to be expected that, in the growth and development of the Church of which she is the archetype, Mary's hand should be felt in the work by which Christ is awaited and foreshadowed? On the threshold of turning to him, at the dawning of faith, after falling into sin, after apostasy—Mary is there. By the very nature of her calling she was, and still is, the gate of heaven and the refuge of sinners.[24]

Now, the rule of the miracle is the same: it kindles the initial sparks of faith and delivers us from the grip of unbelief, our doubt, and the perplexities of this life. Thus can we see that link by which God has wished to join Mary and the miraculous. It is a link so striking that Benedict XV did not hesitate to say "the intervention of Mary in any miraculous occurrence must never be ruled out,

[24] On this point, see Père Scheuer in Msgr. Kerkhofs's book, *Notre-Dame de Banneux*, pp. 35-37.

even when it seems that the particular miracle was obtained through the intervention of some other saint."[25]

Hence, it is easy to understand how the disturbed West, puzzled by atheism, clouded by nausea and despair, has greater need than ever before of Mary's intervention. Once again, by means of messages, apparitions, and miracles, she prepares the way on which Christ comes to save his people, gone astray. And is not this Marian presence and function the first glimmering of dawn, which dispels the darkness of night and prophetically announces His new coming to old Europe and the whole world?

IV · MIRACLES AND THE DEVOTIONAL LIFE OF THE BELIEVER

The miracle is not confined in its frame of reference to unbelievers or to believers who are shaken by doubt and by indifference: it is more likely to occur in a context of solidly grounded faith and trust in God.

More than any external buttress of faith, the miracle is a divine sign of salvation; as such, it has a sacramental character which makes of it the embodiment of an actual intimacy of relationship between God and his creatures.

The miraculous thus has for the believer a deeper meaning, based upon the fact that in the light of faith he *sees* it quite differently. He is not blind to its natural significance, but he can also fathom its inner and supernatural significance. As we have seen, the miracle announces the beginnings of redemption; it is the first step in the realization of bodily glory. To the worldly mind the notion that man's body will actively share in the Redemption and its fruits, seems no more than a dream; but, to the believer, the miracle discloses the mystery of the Incarnation in which it is rooted: *the loving kindness of God our Saviour for mankind, and his mercy to men* are thus manifested in a way which is at once veiled and yet accessible to the senses.

So too, from the naturalistic point of view, the transforming

[25] On the occasion of granting approval of a miracle obtained at Lourdes before the canonization of Joan of Arc. See Msgr. Cruysberghs: *Magnificat* (Louvain, 1954), pp. 136-137.

power of grace and its ennobling effect upon the body of material things seem to satisfy no more than some instinctive and unsubstantial yearning. Faith, however, sees in the miraculous an earnest of the glory which will fill *the new heaven and the new earth:* faith discerns therein the love of God *who shall be all in all;* it finds in the miraculous the certification of *that hope which dwells within us.*[26] Like dogmas and sacraments, so too a miracle becomes a symbol of faith and a supernatural expression of God's Word. In distinction to the dogmatic statement, it is a *symbolic act,* a "word-event"—*parole-évènement*—as Jean Guitton felicitously says. While the sacrament gives external forms to divine action, the *word-event* expresses the divine speech. It imparts not an infusion but a message of grace. In a legitimate sense, therefore, we may speak of a miracle, apprehended by faith, as a "dogmatic symbol," [27] or as a "sacrament." Being at once sign and reality, it anticipates what is promised and announces that our definitive salvation is at hand.

Christian tradition very plainly distinguishes the knowledge faith has of the miracle from its apologetic signification. St. John clearly indicates the difference between "seeing" the miracle before the assent of faith has been made, and "seeing" the same miracle in the light of faith.[28] This is something upon which we find the patristic writers insisting with frequency. As St. Gregory puts it: "What the miracles show forth as acts of divine power is one thing; what they bespeak to us as mysteries of faith is quite another." [29] St. Augustine, in commenting upon the second verse of Psalm IX: "*narrabo omnia mirabilia tua*" expresses the distinction even more precisely by saying: "The visible aspect of the miracle

[26] Cfr. I Cor. XV, 28, and I Peter, III, 15.

[27] J. Guitton: *Le problème de Jésus,* II: Divinité et résurrection (Paris, 1953), p. 245. G. Söhngen in his *Symbol und Wirklichkeit im Kultmysterium*[2] (Bonn, 1940, pp. 82-94) makes use of the expression "dogmatische Symbole" and from this point of view compares miracle and sacrament.

[28] In the following chapter I shall treat the Johannine texts in detail.

[29] "*Sed miracula Domini Salvatoris nostri sic accipienda sunt, fratres carissimi, ut et in veritate credantur facta, et tamen per significationem nobis aliquid innuant. Opera quippe eius et per potentiam aliud ostendunt, et per mysterium aliud loquuntur*" (Greg. the Great: *Quadr. Homiliarum in Evangelia,* lib. I, Hom. II, ML, LXXVI, c. 1082). The fact that in applying this principle the Fathers very often become allegorical in a purely subjective sense does not at all weaken the worth of the principle.

serves as an invitation to the light of grace, while the invisible aspect enlightens him who has responded to that invitation: it is only he who, having trusted in what he sees, has penetrated into the knowledge of what he does not see, who can recount all God's wondrous doings."[30] He points up the distinction by the striking image he gives us in a celebrated passage: "Should we happen to gaze upon a portion of a beautiful manuscript, we do not rest satisfied at mere admiration of the scribe's talent, at the regular and attractive formation of the letters he has made: we read them, so that we may also know what they mean. So is it also with some wonderful divine doing: whoever is confronted with it finds pleasure in its beauty and admires its author; but he who understands it, grasps its meaning. There is thus a differentiation between a picture and a piece of writing. When faced with a picture, one who has seen it and admired it has plumbed it; but this is not so in regard to a piece of writing: it must be read. As a matter of fact, if one sees something written and cannot read, he will ask how it is to be understood. He asks what is the meaning of what he has seen, and another who is able to read will unveil to him the meaning of what he has seen. Is this because the eyes of one differ from those of another? Do not both see the letters? They do indeed; but each is not able to grasp the sense signified in the same fashion. One beholds and wonders, the other sees, wonders, and then by reading understands. Hence, since we can all see and admire, let us also read and understand."[31]

[30] "*Sed quoniam visibile miraculum ad illuminationem animam vocat, invisibile autem eam quae vocata venit illuminat; omnia narrat mirabilia Dei, qui credens visibilibus ad intelligenda invisibilia transitum facit*" (St. Augustine: *Enarrat. in Ps.* IX, v. 2.; ML. XXXVI, c. 118).

[31] "*Sed quemadmodum si litteras pulchras alicubi inspiceremus, non nobis sufficeret laudare scriptoris articulum, quoniam eas pariles, aequales, decorasque fecit, nisi etiam legeremus, quid nobis per illas indicaverit: ita factum hoc qui tantum inspicit, delectatur pulchritudine facti ut admiretur artificem; qui autem intelligit, quasi legit. Aliter enim videtur pictura, aliter videntur litterae. Picturam cum videris, hoc est totum vidisse, laudasse: litteras cum videris, non hoc est totum; quoniam commoneris et legere. Etenim dicis, cum videris litteras, si forte non eas nosti legere: Quid putamus esse quod hic scriptum est? Interrogas quid sit, cum jam videas aliquid. Aliud tibi demonstraturus est, a quo quaeris agnoscere quod vidisti. Alios ille oculos habet, alios tu. Nonne similiter apices videtis? Sed non similiter signa cognoscitis. Tu ergo vides et laudas; ille videt, laudat, legit, et intelligit. Quia ergo vidimus, quia*

In the face of the miraculous sign, whose hidden meaning he has plumbed, the believer takes a new *attitude*, compounded at once of familiarity and disinterestedness.

To the true believer the miracle is no longer the brutal shock which startles and puzzles: it is the sudden revelation of an expected presence, a delicate aspect of the divine overshadowing; it has the nature of a gift that it joyfully received, for it is an earnest of true love. One's whole being is permeated with the sense and assurance that no other nation knows a God so close. As a mark of the link which binds man to his Lord, it becomes an expression of interior union and consolation.

However strange it may seem, this sense of ease and *at homeness* with wonders is at the antipodes of that thirst for marvels with which nonbelievers are wont to tax Catholics. In proportion as this kind of relationship with God regards the miracle as a normal manifestation of his power, so is it assured that it is, nevertheless, something of its nature exceptional and rare. Instinctively, it distrusts the multiplication of the miraculous. It refuses to be aroused by the sensational, or to rest in subjection to the overcharged imagination. The reaction of a Catholic confronted by the miraculous has nothing in common with that tense and excited climate in which Björnson, for once, paints the expectation of the miracle in his *Ueber die Kraft.*[32] Alexis Carrel, while still an unbeliever, insisted in his *The Voyage to Lourdes* on the robust common sense of the Catholic hospital attendants at Lourdes. As a witness to the curing of Marie Ferrand, he tells us that he was all thunder-struck, but the attendant, Mademoiselle d'O., "was watching it as calmly as a doctor watching the setting of a broken bone. She had seen such things before." [33]

This kind of piety is ever disposed to submit to being left un-

---

laudavimus, legamus et intelligamus" (St. Augustine: *In Joann.* Tract. XXIV, n. 2; ML, XXXV, c. 1593; see also the same passage in *Sermo* 98, c. 3; ML, XXXVIII, c. 592).

[32] The dramatic evocation, in this play, of the psychological and theological problem which the miracle poses is very striking, but the author's solution is in the tradition of pure Protestantism. Yet the atmosphere which he creates and the harsh explosion of the miracle itself has not the slightest correspondence with the ordinary context of the true Christian miracle.

[33] A. Carrel: *The Voyage to Lourdes* (New York, 1950), pp. 32-33.

cured, to foregoing the reception of any temporal favor; for what it seeks in the miracle is not to evade the Cross but rather that it may be encouraged to bear it in more generous faith. It trusts in God as knowing better than we what proofs of his love he can give us and what he ought deny us lest he spoil the children of his own heart.

In her poignant tale of a young blind beggar E. Langgässer has perfectly expressed this kind of detachment. Men call this man *the blind believer* because his heart is overflowing with child-like joy and unclouded trust in God. At his Pastor's behest, he goes to Lourdes to ask to be cured. He is actually cured; but shortly afterwards, he prays to Our Lady that he may be made again blind; and his prayer is heard. The unbeliever, Casculade, recounts the event to his friend, Marinier: "While I was sitting next to the blind man in the carriage where he was awaiting the sacristan who had gone to drown his disappointment at the tavern, this young man opened his heart to me. In simple language he revealed his secret; he had no wish to have his fleshly eyes restored, for he hoped rather to accomplish the destiny bespoken by the name he had been given. It was only obedience which bound him to carry out his priest's wish, and he knew beforehand that in exchange for the earthly sight which had been restored to him, all that he had seen with his inner eye had been taken away. He was a mystic, and his blindness served him, just as it had the Desert Father or the early eremite, as an unfathomed solitude, as the darkness of the cell in which the solitary is immured. He found the experience a torture, a kind of spiritual death; for he had bartered the darkness of his retirement, lived in the presence of God, for something of no value at all, and all this in deference to human weakness, to man's dryness, to his faint-heartedness, to his unbelief. His eyes had grown unaccustomed to the sight of earthly things, and were stupefied by all that seems indispensable to us; they rejected the gift of earthly vision. He had obeyed, but she who has opened the blind eyes of so many in this place, closed his again. The real miracle was his prayer: that he might remain *the blind believer*. Dear friend, it is this blind faith that is at the basis of every miracle." [34]

Is not this symbol reproduced in the life of St. Bernadette? As a

[34] E. Langgässer: *Das unauslösliche Siegel* (Hamburg, 1946), pp. 145-146.

Sister at Nevers she suffered from a tumor in her knee; but, with strange obstinacy, she refused to seek a cure in the place to which she had led the world: "That spring is not for me." All Christians do not attain, in their association with the miraculous, to the total self-abandonment which we find in the life of many a saint, even apart from those of whom legends tell us. Yet there are many simple souls who have achieved that fervent faith which makes it needless for them to seek support in miracles; they look only for God's deeper purposes; and they submit, thankfully, to the love and expectation of the Word made flesh by making of their weakness an act of consecration of body, soul, and feeling, of all their being.

Viewed from this new angle, the miracle fulfills yet another *function*. Far from being a merely outward support, it enlightens and fosters the soul's desire to know God; it immerses the soul in faith, hope, and charity. This new function has two aspects: one is *incarnational*, the other, *eschatological*.

J. Clémence brings out the *incarnational* aspect very clearly. Following St. Augustine and St. Thomas, he points out the value of the miracle as a starting ground for beginners; but, for those of more robust faith, as he then says, "miracles are a prerequisite for the highest form of Christian living. We are all in need of them. As do ritual and liturgy, although in a fashion wholly its own, the miracle allows us to maintain that harmonious tension of our being in the search for God; it wars against the tendency to anarchy which marks the very core of our sensitive faculties; it infringes upon that monotonous and rigid regularity into which they so readily slip by disposing them to the exercise of their deeper capacities in submitting to the more supple and ever-new rhythm of the Spirit and grace." [35]

For the believer the miracle is, likewise, an invitation to *eschatological* consideration: it speaks of that abiding place we seek; and, like the scouts of the Old Testament narrative, appearing on the horizon, their hands full of clusters of the fruit of the Promised Land, it recalls to us that, here on earth, we are as pilgrims and

[35] J. Clémence: "Le miracle dans l'économie chrétienne," *Etudes*, 227 (1936), 585.

wayfarers. Every miracle is, as it were, watermarked with the words: "Behold, the Bridegroom cometh!" This cry pierces the night of faith and warns us to keep our lamps alight, and ceaselessly to resist sleep, for He whom we await is indeed nigh.[36]

In this connection we may note still another reason for the frequent occurrence of miracles in modern times. The Church is surrounded by men who imagine that they have found an abiding place, by those who delude themselves with the thought that they can reconstitute Paradise on earth. To reveal this mirage for what it is, the Church has proclaimed the dogma of Mary's Assumption, as a new sign in the heavens to arouse the expectation and the hope of mankind. The plenteousness of miracles once more sets a seal upon what Mary has done. God calls to his Church, urging that it be watchful and keep vigil through the long term of its life, remaining erect in prayer, filled with hope and expectation of that final day when there shall be revealed the mystery hidden in the world's heart: *Marana tha—Come, Lord Jesus!*

[36] It would be very interesting to study, from the viewpoint of spiritual theology, the solution which might be advanced to the acridly debated problem about the balance which should exist in the Christian life between the incarnational and eschatological aspects, a solution based on the Christian miracle as well as on the sacramental system. But this would carry us far beyond the scope of the present work.

6 · JESUS THE WONDER-WORKER

The theology of the miraculous must constantly return to its genuine springs: it is the Gospels which tell us of the mighty works of the God-Man, of the signs of his love at work in the world. His miracles are the archetype and the norm for all true miracles. Only by careful study of them were we able to identify the principles and characteristics of the Christian miracle and analyze it theologically. Theology follows, line by line, the miracles of Our Lord. The present chapter might very well have been made the first of all; but I am inserting it in this place in order to follow a logical plan.[1]

[1] Together with some older works, largely superseded but still useful in some respects, like L. Fonck: *Die Wunder des Herrn* (Innsbruck, 1903), and L. Fillion: *Les miracles de J. C.* (Paris, 1910), the following should be consulted: L. de Grandmaison: *Jesus Christ* (New York, 1937), III, pp. 97-154; J. Bonsirven: *Les enseignements de J. C.* (Paris, 1946), pp. 457-461; G. Bichlmair: *Der Mann Jesus*[4] (Vienna, 1948), ch. X: "Mächtig im Wort und Tat," pp. 79-92; J. Schmid: *Das Evangelium nach Markus* (Regensburg, 1938), pp. 33-35; L. F. Hartman, articles "Jesus Christ" and "Miracles" in *Encyclopedic Dictionary of the Bible* (New York, 1963); J. de Fraine: "Het ethos der evangelische wonderverhalen," *Streven* (1946), 1-10; R. Stock: *Zoeklichten over het Evangelie* (Antwerp, 1952), pp. 249-285; F. Tillmann: *Das Joannes-evangelium* (Bonn, 1931), pp. 34-37; M. Meinertz: *Theologie des Neuen Testamentes* (Bonn, 1950), I, p. 83 and pp. 186-191; L. Cerfaux: "Les miracles, signes messianiques de Jesus et oeuvres de Dieu, selon l'Évangile de S.

I • THE MIRACLE, SIGN OF SALVATION

The miracles of Jesus are directly concerned with his *mission* and the claims which he made for himself: it is in the light of these miracles that his power as a worker of wonders is to be understood.

This is established, first, by the brevity of the *period* which was marked by miraculous works. In contrast to the apocryphal gospels, wherein miracles are multiplied from the time of Our Lord's infancy, none of the four authentic Gospels has a word to say of any miracle before the public life or during the Passion. Moreover, Jesus himself connects the miracles with his "time" and with his "hour." From the standpoint of worldly need and activity, the time is "ever-present"; but, on the other hand, his miracles are based on the notion that "his hour" has come, that the point fixed by the Father for the Son's accomplishment of the mission which is his

---

Jean," *L'Attente du Messie* (Bruges, 1954), pp. 131-138; J. P. Charlier: "La notion de signe dans le quatrième évangile," *Revue des sc. phil. et théol.* 43 (1959), 434-448; R. E. Brown, "The Gospel Miracles," in J. L. McKenzie (ed.), *The Bible in Current Catholic Thought* (New York, 1962), pp. 184-201. There is an abundance of Protestant literature on this subject, inasmuch as the question of New Testament miracles is the only aspect of the problem of the miraculous which interests—and indeed preoccupies—the Protestant theologians in general. In my present chapter, I am deliberately avoiding the apologetic aspect of the question; and I shall mention only those works which, from the point of view of the theologian and the exegete can be welded into a Catholic synthesis. It will often be that such elements are those upon which Catholic writers have been less disposed to place stress. I may refer, first of all, to: A. Fridrichsen: *Le problème du miracle dans le christianisme primitif* (Strasbourg, 1925); H. Schlingensiepen: *Die Wunder des Neuen Testamentes.* Wege und Abwege ihrer Deutung in der alten Kirche bis zum Mitte des fünften Jahrhunderts (Gütersloh, 1933); F. Torrance: *Expository Studies in St. John's Miracles* (1938); A. Richardson: *The Miracle Stories of the Gospels* (London, 1941); Ph. H. Menoud: "La signification du miracle selon le N. T.," *Revue d'hist. et de phil. rel. de Strasbourg,* 28-29 (1948-49), 173-192; ID.: "Miracle et sacrement dans le N. T.," *Verbum Caro,* 6 (1952), 139-154; O. Cullmann, "La délivrance anticipée du corps humain dans le N. T.," *Hommage et reconnaissance à K. Barth,* pp. 31-40; G. Fitzer: "Sakrament und Wunder im N. T.," *In Memoriam Ernst Lohmeyer* (Stuttgart, 1951), pp. 169-188; G. Delling: "Zum Verständnis des Wunders im N. T.," *Zeitschr. f. Syst. Theol.,* 24 (1955), 265-280; E. Stauffer: *Jesus and His Story* (London, 1960), pp. 18-21 and 84-86; W. Staehlin: *Symbolon.* Vom gleichnishaften Denken (Stuttgart, 1958), the chapter, "Ueber das Wunder," pp. 152-166; and finally the comprehensive monograph, H. van der Loos, *The Miracles of Jesus* [Suppl. to *Novum Testamentum,* VIII] (Leiden, 1965).

has arrived.[2] "While it is day, I must do the work of him who sent me" [3] declares Jesus in curing the man born blind. His miracles therefore belong to the "time" of preparation, or of his personal manifestation, during which his light shone in the world, offering to each man the opportunity to accept or to refuse him. The time would come when choice would be a thing of the past, "the night in which no man may work": this is the hour which would require of him no more miracles but only that he would "drink the chalice the Father would send him." At first blush, this would seem to be the hour of his enemies rather than his own; and, indeed, at the time he was taken, he said: "This is the hour of the power of darkness." At that time, the miracles which he had already worked would clearly prove that his will to suffer was not a mark of weakness; it signalized rather the hour often predicted when the Father would be glorified in his Son.[4]

Jesus frequently pointed out, by *foreshadowing* or *allusions*, how his miracles were linked to his mission. On his part, the evangelist notes that Jesus looked mercifully upon the crowd of people and upon the unfortunates who thronged about him; he went about doing good.[5] Was this a sympathy expressive only of a sensibility which was disturbed by the sight of suffering or of mere compassion aroused by natural emotion? No doubt the Master was sensitive to suffering; but his miracles manifested rather "the loving kindness of God our Saviour and his love for men." [6] The redeeming love of the Saviour "looked in pity on the crowds because they were as sheep without a shepherd";[7] and he wanted to lead them

[2] Cf. John VII, 6-8; see also John II, 4; V, 17; VII, 30-34; XII, 27 ff. In the Synoptic Gospels the parallel notion is that "it must be," e.g., Matt. XVI, 21. This does not express any natural or human determinism; it signifies the absolute necessity of the divine exaction which is the Father's will. The patristic writers often lay great stress upon this "kairos" marking the miracles of Jesus (cf., e.g., Theodore of Mopsuestia, in MG, LXVI, c. 756A). On Jesus's "hour" see H. Van den Bussche: "De betekenis van het uur in het vierde Evangelie," *Collat. Gandav*, 2 (1952), 97-108; ID.: *Jesus' woorden aan het afscheidsmaal* (Tielt, 1955), pp. 38-39.

[3] John IX, 4-5.

[4] John I, 9-10; IX, 4-5; XVIII, 11; Luke XXII, 53; John XIII, 30-32.

[5] Matt. IX, 36; XIV, 14; XV, 32; XX, 34; Acts X, 38, etc.

[6] Tit. III, 4.

[7] Matt. IX, 36.

to their true pasture, in God's own Kingdom. The liking he showed for the poor and the lowly was no mere feeling of social solidarity: it was rather a striking sign of the new values he had established by upsetting the whole scale of earthly values, as he proclaims in the Beatitudes. This is proved by the declaration of Jesus that he works miracles to fulfill the sayings of the Prophets. For example, St. John the Baptist sent two of his disciples to question him: "Are you he who is to come, or wait we for another?" They came upon Jesus at the very time that "he was curing many ills, casting out devils, and giving sight unto the blind." In his answer, Jesus placed his own wondrous works in the tradition of the messianic prophecies, and he plainly claimed for them the value which is proper to divine signs: "He answered and said: Go and tell John what you have seen and heard; the blind see, the lame walk, lepers are cleansed, the deaf hear, the dead arise, and the poor have the Gospel preached to them. Blessed is he who is not scandalized in me." [8] In his discussion with the Pharisees, Jesus never ceased to point to his miraculous powers in order that he might establish the truth of his divine mission: "The works which the Father has appointed me to do are the very works that I do: they prove that the Father has sent me." [9] Before raising Lazarus from the dead, Jesus prayed: "Father, I give Thee thanks that Thou hast heard me. Well do I know that You always hear me; but it is for the sake of the men who throng about me that I speak, so that they may believe that Thou has sent me." [10] When he was curing the paralytic who had been brought down through the roof, the Master relied upon his miracles to establish his divine power and his messianic mission: "That you may know that the Son of Man has power on earth to forgive sin, he declared to the paralytic, I say to you, arise, take up your bed and go to your house." [11] And

[8] Luke VII, 18-23 (cf. Matt. XI, 2-6). The reply of Jesus is given in the words of Isaiah (XXIX, 18ff., XXXV, 5ff., and LXI, 1). According to the narrative of Luke (IV, 16ff.) Jesus had already, at the very opening of his public life, read, in his discourse to the Synagogue, a text of Isaiah (LXI, 1-2) and had addded to it, by way of commentary: "Today, this portion of Scripture is verified unto you." Later on, the Gospel of Matthew (XII, 15ff.) cites another text from Isaiah (XLII, 1).

[9] John V, 36; see also John X, 25; XV, 24.

[10] John XI, 41-42.

[11] Luke V, 24.

Matthew records how, one day, "He reproached those cities which had seen so many miracles and had not done penance: Woe to you, Corozain! Woe to you, Bethsaida! Had such miracles as you have seen been done in Tyre and Sidon, they would early have done penance in sackcloth and ashes." [12]

These miracles have more than an extrinsic relationship to the message of Jesus; they are no mere manifestations from without certifying to the truth of what he teaches: they are *integral* parts of his teaching, and to an even greater extent, of his divinely *redemptive work*. To those Jews who reproached him, one day, for having cured the paralytic near the spring of Bethsaida on the Sabbath, he made this strange reply: "My Father ever worketh; and I also work." [13] His miracles form a part of the redemptive plan which God initiated at the dawn of time, pursues unremittingly, and completes in his own Person.

Even the *external aspects* of his miraculous works demonstrate a deep underlying link with the divine mission of the Saviour. When the Gospel speaks from Our Lord's viewpoint, it calls his miracles "mighty deeds," "works" (*virtutes, opera*); when it adopts the viewpoint of those who saw these wonders or of those who benefited from them, it uses the term "signs." They are, accordingly, the significant expressions of a divine activity, a supernatural kind of speech, a salvific or saving word, which is directed to us in meaningful actions. The main themes of the Gospel—freedom from the thralldom of sin, friendship with God through the sacrament of his Incarnate Word, the redemptive meaning of Christ's Cross and death, the means of grace and the hope of glory—every one of these themes is translated into action in the miracles of Jesus. They become lived images, symbols impregnated with meaning.

St. John's Gospel emphasizes the symbolic character of miracles. It makes frequent allusions (sometimes open, but more often veiled) depicting the acts and doings of Jesus as prefiguring symbols of his sacramental plan; and some modern exegetes think that they have discerned in this the key to the whole Gospel in its author's besetting care to bridge the gap between the Lord Christ of

[12] Matt. XI, 20-21.
[13] John V, 17.

the liturgy, and the historic Jesus of synoptic tradition.[14] According to the mind of Jesus, the curing of physical ills always presupposes a call to conversion and prepares the way for the soul's deliverance: all temporal favors are symbolic of the grace he showers upon his Church; every act of bodily healing or of resurrection to the life of this time is a prelude to and a pledge of the glory which awaits soul as well as body. For example, the multiplication of the loaves is to be taken, first of all, as prefiguring the action of Christ in offering himself as the Bread of Life and in giving us the Eucharistic Bread, when his hour would come. Jesus himself, in what he had to say on the occasion of that miracle, expressly applies this meaning to it.[15] Likewise, at Cana it was he who, by a veiled allusion, linked that miracle to the hour of his Passion, and his gift of his own blood.[16] The resurrection of Lazarus is given its meaning by the words of Jesus to Mary and Martha: "I am the resurrection and the life. Whoever believes in me shall live, even though he were dead; and whoever lives and believes in me shall not die." [17] Following upon the curing of the man born blind, he definitely pointed to the deep meaning of that event: "It is in judgment that I am come into this world, in order that those who are blind may have sight, and that those who see may become blind." [18] Augustine very properly comments: "What Our Lord had wrought in the body he wishes to have understood in the spirit. He wrought no miracles for their own sake, but rather that what he did might be strikingly wonderful to the viewer and charged with meaning for the discerning." [19]

[14] O. Cullmann: *Urchristentum und Gottesdienst* (Zurich, 1944). In a slightly revised form, this brochure has been published in English as *Early Christian Worship* (London, 1953). See also X. Léon-Dufour: "Actualité du quatrième évangile," *Nouv. Rev. Théol.*, 76 (1954), 499-468, and especially pp. 456ff: B. Vawter: "The Johannine Sacramentary," *Theological Studies*, 17 (1956), 151-166.

[15] John VI.

[16] John II, 1-11; Cf. O. Cullmann: *Early Christian Worship*, pp. 66-69. See also R. Schnackenburg: *Das Erste Wunder Jesu* (Freiburg i. Br., 1951); H. Van den Bussche: "Het wijnwonder te Cana," *Collat. Gandav.*, 2 (1952), 193-225; P. Schoonenberg: "De epiphanie van Kana," *Ned. Kath. Stemmen*, 52 (1956), 359-363; M. E. Boismard: *Du baptême à Cana* (In. I, 19–II, 11) (Paris, 1956), pp. 133-159; J. P. Charlier: *Le signe de Cana* (Brussels, 1959).

[17] John XI, 25-26.

[18] John IX, 39.

[19] St. Augustine: *Sermo* 98, c. 3, ML, XXXVIII, c. 592: *"Dominus enim*

Although the allegorical exegesis of the Fathers often wanders from the literal text, it is, nevertheless, close to the mind of Jesus in beholding in the sick man crying for deliverance a type of all mankind, groaning under original sin and in great need of redemption. Thus Rupert of Deutz thinks he hears in the anguished cry of the man born blind the plaint "of the whole human race, that blind creation whose reasoning faculty, a shadow of its Creator's glory, one day gazed with brilliant eyes on the magnificence of the Maker, but lost the power of sight when the first man turned toward the Prince of Darkness." [20] And, in like vein, Peter Chrysologus speaks of the man with the withered hand: "This is a very old illness; we were smitten with it at the very beginning of time. The cure of this man does no more than herald our own: our full cure is hidden in Christ; for our hands are truly cured of their aridity when we plunge them into the blood of Christ in his Passion." [21]

The *synoptic* Gospels also emphasize, even if less forcefully, the *symbolic* character of the miracles. The account of the miraculous draught of fishes is an example; it takes place in connection with Our Lord's prophecy to Peter: "Fear not, for you shall be a fisher of men." [22] The symbolic intention is equally evident in the accounts of the stilled tempest and of Our Lord's walking on the waters, if we link them to the frequent predictions of his passion, bearing in

---

noster Jesus Christus ea quae faciebat corporaliter, etiam spiritualiter volebat intelligi. Neque enim tantum miracula propter miracula faciebat, sed ut illa quae faciebat, mira essent videntibus, vera intelligentibus."

[20] Rupertus: *De divinis officiis,* I, 4. c. 21, ML, CLXX, c. 114: "*Genus humanum, magnum utique caecum, qui pulchros oculos ad videndum Creatorem menti, ubi fulget imago Factoris, inditos, in primo parente principem tenebrarum respiciente, perdidit.*" The same idea is found in Leo the Great, ML, LIV, c. 399; Caesarius of Arles, *Sermo* 172, n. 3; Gregory the Great: ML, LXXVI, c. 1082, etc.

[21] Peter Chrysologus: *Sermo* 32, ML, LII, c. 290 (the complete text of this homily is given in the Roman Breviary, in the Third Nocturn of the Office of St. John Damascene, whose feast is kept on March 27): "*Antiqua ista nimis erat, et quae in ipso mundi principio contigerat aegritudo; nec arte hominis aut beneficio poterat haec curari, quae Dei fuerat indignatione contracta . . . In hoc homine nostrae tantum geritur umbra sanitatis; perfecta autem salus nobis reservatur in Christo; quia tunc ariditas nostrae manus miseranda dissolvitur, cum cruore perfunditur Dominicae passionis . . .*"

[22] Luke V, 10.

mind the way in which the teaching of Jesus was designed to prepare his disciples to bear the scandal of that time. It is only in the symbolic sense that certain miracles have any meaning at all. From this point of view, the anathema which Jesus called down on the sterile fig tree is typical. Between his words and the discovery on the following day that the tree had withered, the Evangelist puts the episode of the vendors being cast out of the Temple: the miraculous curse is thus a parable in action.[23] The Transfiguration of Jesus on Mount Tabor, that sudden manifestation of his divine glory in the midst of his human state was a declaration of the coming glory of Easter and it strengthened the faith of the apostles against the dark hours of the Passion. What Jesus said, in coming down from the mountain, is a plain indication of this.[24]

Even when the words of the Master do not explicitly define the meaning of the miracles, the *total context* suggests the symbolism. This applies, especially, to the cures and the calling to life of the dead. The whole frame of reference of Old and New Testament literature, the behavior and the teaching of Jesus, plainly emphasize the *link* between *sin, suffering* and *death*. By suffering and death the ransom of sin is paid.[25] Behind all bodily ill is concealed the power of Evil, "a murderer from the beginning." [26] Jesus points out this relationship not alone in his many exorcisms, but also in his curing of ordinary illness: "Go," he says to the lame man whom he healed at Bethsaida, "Go and sin no more";[27] and to the other paralytic who had been let down from the roof, he declares: "Be of good heart; thy sins are forgiven." [28] Of the woman who has walked with a stoop for eighteen years, he himself said that she "was bound by Satan." [29] How eloquent a symbol of slavery and of deliverance is this! In what sense are we to take the deliverance of the two possessed Gadarenes whose evil spirits took refuge, after leaving them, in a herd of swine who straightway drowned them-

[23] Mark XI, 13-24.
[24] Matt. XVII, 2ff.; Mark IX, 1ff.
[25] Rom. V, 12.
[26] John VIII, 44; cf. also I John III, 8ff.
[27] John V, 14.
[28] Matt. IX, 2.
[29] Luke XIII, 16.

selves in the lake, unless it be as a revelation of the destructive power of sin and of God's sovereignty in bringing to naught the strength of Satan? [30]

Frequently, the context which surrounds the miracle includes another element which brings out its symbolic character: this is *faith*, exacted as a preliminary condition and marked as the result of the miracle. The faith here spoken of by the Gospel is not merely faith in the miraculous power of Christ but rather readiness to accept that whole redemptive plan which finds its expression in the person and in the act of Our Lord. From the beginning, this faith must be present, at least as a disposition, so that the miracle be not shorn of its meaning: this faith will grow in the event and will be confirmed by the accomplishment of the miracle. "This beginning of his signs did Jesus at Cana of Galilee; and he manifested his glory. And his disciples believed in him." [31] Such are the words with which John concludes his account of what took place at Cana.[32]

The Gospel narrative of the centurion of whom Jesus said, as Matthew reports, that he had not found such great faith in Israel, is taken up by St. John Chrysostom in a significant commentary: "He came to ask the bodily cure of his servant; when he returned, it was the Kingdom of God that he brought with him." [33]

The miracles wrought by Jesus are not, therefore, simple manifestations of God's power. They are signs through which God voices his saving message in a tongue which speaks to us. Rather than just being narrated in the Gospels, they are themselves Gospel-tidings, joyous messages of salvation given in living lessons. With Augustine, we can reach the conclusion: "We can ask of every miracle what it is that it has to say to us of Christ: to him

[30] Matt. VIII, 28ff.

[31] John II, 11.

[32] At first blush, it might be thought that this insistence upon faith contradicts my former proposition about the role of natural reason in the discernment of the miraculous. Actually, the Gospel does not profess to offer a theological analysis of faith, but takes the facts in their concrete and total reality; and I have already pointed out that, *as a matter of fact*, the miraculous occurrence is always set into a context wherein the initiative of grace appeals to reason and to faith alike. On this point, see G. Söhngen: *Die Einheit in der Theologie*, pp. 275-280.

[33] St. John Chrysostom: *Comm. in Matt.*, VIII, 5-13; MG, LVII, c. 338.

who understands, the miracle speaks with its own tongue. For, since Christ is the Word of God, every act of that Word is also a word addressed to us." [34]

II · HOW THE MIRACLE IS WROUGHT

The way in which Jesus accomplished his miracles is in complete consonance with their religious meaning and purpose.

Basically, there is no indication of any *self-seeking* in the Saviour as he brings into play his miraculous powers. He never worked a miracle in order to win favor or to avert embarrassment. He was a man like his fellows; he ate, drank, walked until wearied; he slept, and he awoke, just like his brethren; he crossed the lake of Genesareth in a boat, he hid from his enemies, he paid taxes, he gave into the hands of Judas a purse from which to purchase daily necessities.[35] Above all, during his Passion—despite the ironic indictment of his enemies, *You would save others; now save yourself!*—he put aside the least outward show of his power and did not spare himself from drinking his chalice to its dregs. This contrast has been developed by the patristic writers with what is very often a moving degree of eloquence. He who was Master of the winds and waves, who could command the forces of Nature, was yet obedient to the slightest precepts of the Mosaic Law; he who fed thousands from a few paltry loaves, fasted and felt hunger; he who restored withered limbs and gave them back their strength, he who promised to give rest to all, sat down in weariness by the side of Jacob's well and fell asleep in Peter's bark. Once his Passion had begun, he who had so often made the tongue of the dumb to sing suffered himself to be

[34] St. Augustine: *In Joannem*, tract. 24, 6; ML, XXXV, c. 1593: "*Interrogemus ipsa miracula, quid nobis loquantur de Christo; habent enim, si intelligantur, linguam suam. Nam quia ipse Christus Verbum Dei est, etiam factum Verbi verbum nobis est.*" I am using this phrase out of context, for Augustine's immediate contextual allusion is bound up with a highly debatable allegorism.

[35] Some of Christ's miracles might seem, at first glance, to contradict the notion of his total unselfishness so, for example, his walking on the waters or his payment of the tithe with the coin taken out of the mouth of a fish. But, under closer scrutiny, it is evident that the accomplishment of these miracles by Christ was not at all dictated by his personal convenience, but was for the purpose of giving some symbolic teaching to his disciples in the form of a striking object lesson. Cf., e.g., Matt. XVII, 24-27.

led to the slaughter, silent as a lamb. By one word, he had put the demons to flight; yet without a word, he delivers himself into the hands of the powers of darkness. With his own spittle he had cured the man born blind; yet he allowed himself to be blindfolded and spat upon. He who had made lepers whole became himself, as Isaiah had foretold, despised and rejected. That face which on Tabor had shone like the sun was now to be disfigured and distorted without let or hindrance. The Master who had changed water into wine let himself be given vinegar to quench his thirst. The Lord who had summoned Lazarus forth from the tomb, and who had given back her son, alive, to the widow of Naim, went himself alone to his death, and left behind him his own Mother to bear alone sorrow's heavy burden.[36]

We are in another atmosphere than that of the pagan wonder-workers like Aesculapius or Apollonius of Tyana. They drew to themselves plenteous honors in reward of their prodigious doings; they were little concerned with the spiritual betterment of men and seem to have been spurred only by a desire for lucre or for fame.[37] Their seeming prodigies resemble the miracles of Jesus as little as an advertisement in a pulp magazine resembles the starkly simple style of the Gospel. Moreover, Jesus had himself set his own disinterestedness as a mark of the authenticity of his message, in opposition to the attitude of false prophets; he spoke of them as "ravening wolves," and he laid upon his apostles the precept: "Freely you have received; freely give." [38] Peter, in his Second Epistle, and Paul, in his pastoral letters, denounced greed for gold as the scandalous badge of the false prophet.[39]

Even more characteristic of his deep unselfishness is his refusal to employ those punitive prodigies which are so frequent a feature

[36] Gregory Nazianzen, *Oratio* 29, MG, XXXVI, cc. 100-101, fully develops this theme. See also Cyril of Jerusalem: *Catechetical Lectures,* XIII, 13, MG, XXXIII, c. 789; Tertullian: *Adversus Praxeam,* ML, II, cc. 174-175; St. Leo the Great, ML, LIV, c. 769; St. Ephraem: *Hymni* XV, 1; Rouët de Journel, n. 716, etc. Many of the sayings of Jesus during the course of his Passion accentuate the voluntary nature of his renunciation of his miraculous powers (e.g., Matt. XXVI, 53).

[37] There is a meaningful passage in Origen's *Contra Celsum,* I, 68, MG, XI, c. 787.

[38] Matt. VII, 15; Matt. X, 8.

[39] II Peter II, 3; I Tim. VI, 5-10.

of pagan legend and even of Old Testament lore. Most wonder-workers have willingly made use of such things in order to keep up their prestige or to exploit the fear of the superstitious masses. The only striking analogy with this sort of thing is all that we know of Jesus concerns the barren fig tree, and it is wholly symbolic. When his disciples desired to call down fire from Heaven upon the inhospitable Samaritans, he rebuked them: "You do not know of whose spirit you are. The Son of Man has not come to lose souls but rather to save them." [40]

This complete lack of self-seeking in the Master is brought to perfection by a *restraint* which is in harmony with the religious meaning of his miracles. There is a total absence of all that would savor of worldliness, or which would pander to a taste for anything sensational or modeled on the spirit of the circus. If one would appreciate the simplicity, the sobriety, and that authoritative dignity which belonged to Jesus, one has only to consider his behavior by the side of that of those magicians, workers of marvels, and adepts in the occult sciences who have ever drawn the credulous about them.

Workers of marvels set themselves up with a great fanfare. Their whole behavior is carefully calculated to impress crowds who have already been subjected to suggestion. On the contrary, the miracles of Jesus take place quietly, often in silence, and afar off from the crowd; sometimes quite simply, just as he is passing by. He hides himself from the multitude whenever he can, because crowds tend to a blind reliance upon the sensational aspect while ignoring the true significance of a miracle. He wishes, too, to avoid their enthusiasm which would have crowned him as a political Messiah. "Amen, amen," he reproached the crowd after the multiplication of the loaves, "You seek me not because you have seen signs, but because you ate of the loaves and were filled." [41] St. Mark tells us the story of a leper who talked, in so many places, of his cure "that Jesus could no longer enter a town openly, but remained without, in the desert places; and they came to him from all sides." [42] The Gospel shows him sending the crowds away, so that he may go off

[40] Luke IX, 51-56.
[41] John VI, 26.
[42] Mark I, 45.

apart and pray.[43] Often he forbade those whom he had cured to tell of their healing, as though he dreaded always to attract the multitude to him by the outward glory of his miracles.[44]

Nor does Jesus use techniques and tricks to increase his hold on others. At the period, the charlatans were customarily accompanied by confederates—this is certain in the case of Apollonius of Tyana[45] —or else they would fall into trances, acting as would a medium, making use of suggestion and hypnosis in the midst of a complicated ceremonial, or even seeking by their phantasmagoria to distract the attention of the spectators from the trickery being practiced upon them. Often enough, in order the better to hold their votaries spellbound, they gave themselves over to dionysiac orgies, employing philters or narcotics or even abandoning the working of wonders for the practice of magic. It is by no means unusual to find the charlatan finally laid low by exhaustion, or the prey to the depression which is the inevitable consequence of artificial exaltation.

Jesus, on the other hand, remained always calm, well balanced, and master of himself. He accomplished his miracles alone, and without shouting or incantatory posturing; he scorned artifice: there would be a word or two, a simple symbolic gesture, or a brief command, *Volo*, "I will," and the wonder was wrought, at once, and sometimes even in a place afar off.[46] *Tacita potestate et sola voluntate*, as Tertullian puts it,—by his modest use of power, by the might of his will alone." [47] What restraint he showed, for example, at Cana; and how serene and rural is the atmosphere at the multiplication of the loaves! Even when he calls the dead to life again there is a wholesome recollectedness about it all! He did not

[43] E.g., John VI, 14-15; Matt. VIII, 16-18; XIV, 22-23; Luke V, 15-16, etc.

[44] See, e.g., Matt. VIII, 2; IX, 30; Mark I, 25-34; 44-45; III, 11-12; V, 43; VII, 36; VIII, 26, 30; Luke VIII, 56, etc. The apparent exceptions in Mark V, 19 and John IV, 39-42, rather serve to confirm my contention; for these concern miracles done to Samaritans among whom the danger of the political prostitution of messianic hope and the consequent deorientation of the miracle toward worldly objects was less to be feared.

[45] Philostratos: *Vita Apollonii*, II; 7; see in Fridrichsen: *op. cit.*, pp. 61-63, a whole series of patristic texts insisting on the difference between the miracles of Jesus and the wonders wrought by the pagan thaumaturges.

[46] E.g., Mark I, 41; IV, 39; V, 41; John V, 8, etc.

[47] Tertullian: *Adversus Marcionem*, IV, 35, ML, II, c. 446.

give vent to any exaggerated gestures when he met the widow of Naim; and it was with a gracious playfulness that he set at their ease those who were mourning the daughter of Jairus, when he said *talita koumi,* and aroused the girl. Even the resurrection of Lazarus, which took place in the sight of a crowd of partly hostile people, was accomplished in the most quiet and simple spirit of recollection and sobriety.

The gaze of Jesus as the Gospel depicts him for us when he turned his eyes upon the sick or the possessed, shows nothing of that magnetic force, nothing of that fixed glare of the seer or the medium. The eyes of Jesus were the serene eyes of God who searches and knows all reins and hearts, the eyes of him who had come to save and to judge, the eyes which put demons to flight but which drew children to him. Although *Jesus knew in himself that power had gone forth from him,*[48] he never experienced the psychical exhaustion of the charlatan or mind healer. He had a serene mastery of natural forces, an almost unconscious majesty: they obeyed him without stress or tension: he was assured in his mission, as became the Son of his Father; he was certain that even the least of his wishes would be carried out at once. Spontaneously, the comparison sprang from the lips of the centurion: "For I also am a man under authority, with soldiers under myself; and if to this man I say 'Go,' then he goes, and if to another, 'Come,' he comes, and if to my servant, 'Do this,' he does it." [49]

In the case of Jesus, restraint characterized not only the behavior of the thaumaturge but also the *kind* of wonders wrought and the *choice* of those whom he cured. He did not work every possible miracle; he did not cure all the sick. He did not visit all distress with solace: his choice would seem to have been dictated almost by chance; but, for all that, the context allows us to unveil the motivation of what he did, as he "worked" always with the intent to build up the Kingdom of God. It is for this reason that he generally displayed his miraculous power in cases where the sick person, his relations, or his friends implored it and were thus led, first of all, to an expression of their confident faith in him. In the case of casting out unclean spirits, however, it was otherwise: here he took

[48] Mark V, 30-32.
[49] Matt. VIII, 8-9 (cf. Luke VII, 8).

the initiative in the face of the Enemy, the Lord of this world, with whom he was ever at war. In such cases, he waited not for a request or a prayer: he proceeded at once to attack and vanquish the demon. Yet, at all other times, the employment of his power implies a context of prayer and a bending, on his part, to the confidence of his hearers. Often indeed, the account of what he did terminates by his words: "Thy faith has made thee whole." [50] It was enough that a petitioner show that he had faith in order that a miracle be done in favor of some third party.[51] The stammering faith which implored his help would appear to have been, in the eyes of Christ, the minimum requirement for the granting of a miraculous cure. Matthew, in telling us of the unbelief and the mockery which greeted Jesus at Nazareth, concluded: "He wrought few miracles there because of their want of faith," while Mark, in his account, makes use of a language which is even more direct: "And he wrought no miracles there, except that by the laying on of his hands, he cured a few sick people; for he was taken aback by their want of faith." [52] If we compare the two texts, it becomes clear that Jesus refused the miracle not because he was without power to grant it, but because the absence of faith would have made it meaningless. Jesus made use of his power only to show himself as the Holy One, the Saviour.

For the same reason, there was one *category of miracles* which he roundly repudiated—those namely which might, because of their spectacular nature, obscure their true significance or relegate it to second place. He knew that human pride is prone to ask for signs which are all too flashy. Men seek to escape the commitment of faith by continually imposing new demands on God or else to draw personal advantage from divine signs by turning them into instruments of propaganda or of worldly success.

In the hour of his temptation by Satan in the desert, Christ set his face firmly against this kind of miracle. When the Demon suggested that he cast himself down from the highest tower of the Temple that he might be borne in safety by the ministry of angels,

[50] Matt. IX, 22, 29; XV, 28; Mark VII, 26-30; X, 52; Luke VII, 50; XVII, 9, etc.

[51] Matt. VIII, 5-13; Mark II, 5; V, 36; IX, 22-24; Luke VII, 9, etc.

[52] Matt. XIII, 58; Mark VI, 5.

he replied in the words of Holy Writ: "Thou shalt not tempt the Lord thy God." [53] Yahweh is the God of wonders; but he wants them to further his kingdom. His power can never become the plaything which satisfies the whims or the pride of man. In the view of the exegetes, the temptations suffered by Our Lord in the desert were essentially directed against him as the Messiah. Christ refused to relegate the redemptive economy of the Father to a second place in order to achieve a political triumph in Israel. The second temptation and his reply express the firmness of his will to use his power only in the Father's service.

During his public life, he adhered to this position everywhere and against all comers. He had to contend primarily against this attempt to degrade his mission. All around him, all the Jews, and even his own disciples, yielded to the temptation. The Masters in Israel, the Pharisees, and the Doctors of the Law insistently demanded a "sign from heaven." With inflexibility Our Lord repulsed them: "An evil and adulterous generation seeks a sign, and the only sign that shall be given unto it is the sign of the prophet Jonah." [54] In the terminology of the Bible "adultery" symbolized unfaithfulness to Yahweh and to his Covenant; it is also indicative of a retrogression into paganism. To demand "a sign from heaven" therefore revealed the temerity and the impious pride of his hearers.

Was it not, ultimately, because he would not abase his messianic mission by making his miraculous power the mere instrument of a political scheme that Jesus was condemned and crucified? This catastrophe casts into bold relief his refusal to grant some spectacular prodigy to Herod, as well as "the silence of God" when his enemies tauntingly called upon him to come down from the Cross that they might receive him as "their" Messiah.

[53] Matt. IV, 7; Luke IV, 12.

[54] Matt. XII, 38-39; XVI, 4; John VI, 30; John II, 18-22. "Deep within their hearts, everyone of them awaited, desired, and wished for the Sign which would bring them to their knees with the cry: *Behold the Messiah!* This is the Sign sought by Judas and by Peter, as the one betrayed and the other denied him. This also is the Sign sought by the populace who cried out: *Crucify him!* I say that every one, each in his own fashion, sought to force Jesus to work a miracle by pushing him into a last, desperate state in which he would be so destitute of all human force that he would have to appear before the world, openly, as its Saviour. Perhaps not all of them realized this; but it is what they were hoping for" (D. Fabbri: *Procès à Jésus* [Paris, 1958], p. 17).

III • THE FUNCTION OF MIRACLES IN THE CONTEXT OF THE GOSPEL

What was the place which Christ assigned to miracles in the whole context of his redemptive work; did they fit into his total message? At some times, it seems that he accorded them an important place, at others, he allowed them to give way to other more essential elements.

First and foremost, the miracle arouses and strengthens *faith*. Witness the phrase with which Mark closes his Gospel and which we find again (in a form which, although most expressive, is not easy to translate) in the Epistle to the Hebrews: *συνεπιμαρτυροῦντος τοῦ Θεοῦ.*[55] Literally, this means: by these miracles God gave confirmation "with and in addition to." Faith is, in effect, man's self-abandonment in response to the divine testimony. According to the Scriptures, this testimony is a dual thing; on the one hand, it is an interior light and heavenly call—"No man," says Jesus, "can come to me unless the Father, who has sent me, draw him" [56]—; on the other hand, it is a human speech, uttered in God's name. The miracle is part of this external testimony: it is the seal, the divine guaranty, which authenticates the human message. The word *συνεπιμαρτυροῦντος* means that this testimony of God, immediate but created, is indissolubly linked to the testimony of the apostle (*συν* is equivalent to *with*) and gives to it a new persuasive force (*επι* = besides, furthermore). More than once Jesus emphasizes this divine witness: "I myself give testimony, in my own behalf; but I have another witness, who is my Father, who has sent me." [57] And later: "If I glorify myself, my glory is worth nothing; it is my Father who glorifies me." [58] And again, even more plainly: "The works which I do in my Father's name, these are my witness." [59]

It is also in order to stir up faith that the Master often appeals to

[55] In the Westminster version, the Markan text is as follows: "But they went forth and preached everywhere, *the Lord working with them and confirming the word by the signs that followed thereupon*" (Mark XVI, 20), while the words of the author of the Epistle to the Hebrews are thus rendered: "*God adding testimony by signs and wonders, and manifested deeds of power . . .*" (Heb. II, 4) [—Transl.].

[56] John VI, 44.

[57] John VIII, 18; see also John V, 31-32.

[58] John VIII, 54.

[59] John X, 25; see also John V, 36.

his "works," and he gives his miracles prime place among them: "If I do not the works of my Father, then do not believe me; but if I do them, then even though you believe not in me, believe in these works." [60] A miracle does not, automatically, give rise to faith, but it does provoke a religious wonderment and it opens the eye of man to supernatural reality: the divine call comes to a head and soon takes possession of a right conscience, winning man to make a choice: "Had I not done among them works which no man has done, they would not be guilty of sin," said Jesus in regard to the Jews who had rejected his Gospel, "but, now, they have seen my works and yet have hated both me and my Father." [61]

The Johannine Gospel forcefully underlines this effect of the miracle by its characteristic use of the verbs "to see" and "to believe." One may be in the presence of a miracle and not "see" it, if one has done no more than remain in the world of outward feeling, concentrated on the material good achieved, without even seeking to penetrate the inner meaning of what has taken place. Such was the state of the multitude who were satisfied "not because they had *seen* the sign, but because they had eaten bread and been filled." [62] To *see* a miracle means that one has beheld it and has then gone on to perceive its salvific meaning, that one feels the interior call and is conscious of his personal responsibility. Often do we read in the Gospel: he saw and he believed. But one can also resist the divine call; one can "see" and refuse to believe: "Despite all the signs Jesus had performed before them, they would not believe in him." [63] Jesus attributed the refusal of the Jews, who had seen his works, to believe in him, to their rejection of the grace offered to them: "You are not God's children, and that is why you do not hear." [64] The eyes of the believer open progressively to a new "view"; even while still earth-bound, his faith pierces the veils of this present time and attains to the sight of God's glory, revealed in Christ. It is in this sense that the prologue to John's Gospel speaks of the Incarnation: "We have seen his glory, such glory as befits

[60] John X, 37-38.

[61] John XV, 24. Cf. A. Oepke: article "Ἰάομαι," in *Theol. Wört z. N.T.*, III, 205-211.

[62] John VI, 26.

[63] John XII, 37.

[64] John VIII, 47; X, 26; XVIII, 37-38.

God's only Son, full of grace and truth." Jesus, himself, in his farewell discourse, said to Philip: "Whoever has seen me, has seen my Father." [65]

The account of miracles by the Synoptists as well as by St. John emphasizes the role of the miraculous in faith's growth. From the very beginning, the reaction is not mere worldly astonishment; it is marked by a religious attitude. "They were struck with fear" is often the closing phrase in these accounts; and then there follows: "they glorified God who had given such power to men." [66] This transition from fright to praise is characteristic of the feeling of one who is confronted by the holy; for he knows himself to be nothing worthy and in weakness, impure and sinful: he would flee; yet, irresistibly, he is drawn by the holiness and the fascination of the Presence wherein he stands. When Jesus sent the demons from a possessed man into a herd of swines who forthwith cast themselves into the waters, "the Gadarenes all besought him to leave their place; for they were gripped by great fear." [67] After the miraculous draught of fishes, Peter fell to his knees at the Master's feet and said, "Depart from me, O Lord; for I am a sinful man." [68]

There are some in whom, after their initial astonishment, the seed of faith cannot grow or bear fruit, for their hearts are already filled with worldly interests and material cares. Thus, at the multiplication of the loaves, the multitude prostituted the religious meaning of the miracle; they found the promise of the Eucharist

[65] John I, 14; XIV, 9; see also III, 3; XI, 40, and XII, 45. On the connection between "seeing" and "believing," cf. L. Cerfaux: *loc. cit.*, and O. Cullmann: "*Eiden kai episteusen*, La vie de Jésus objet de la 'vue' et de la 'foi' d'après le quatrième évangile" in *Aux Sources de la Tradition*, Mélanges Goguel (Neuchâtel, 1950). The "seeing" of the glory of Christ as a result of a miracle and the faith which it stirs up is expressly noted by St. John; this is true of both the first and the last miracle which he records. "Such was the first of the signs wrought by Jesus. He did this at Cana in Galilee. He manifested his glory and his disciples believed in him" (John II, 11). "This sickness will not end in death; it has come for God's glory, and to bring glory to God's son" (John XI, 4). "Have I not told you, said Jesus, that if you believe, you will see God's glory?" (John XI, 40).

[66] Matt. VIII, 27; VIII, 34; IX, 8; XV, 31; Mark IV, 41; Luke XIX, 37, etc.

[67] Luke VIII, 37.

[68] Luke V, 8.

shocking, and they clung to the mirage of material handouts.[69] The ten lepers joined in rejoicing over the recovery of their health; only one of them believed in the miracle and returned to Jesus.[70] There was a like absence of faith in those who sought to make him king: his miracles did no more for them than arouse their dream of political aggrandizement.

A second class receive the seed of faith in stony soil, where it is unable to take root nor to stand in strength against the assaults of opposition and persecution. Such were those of whom John declared "They believed in him, but, out of fear of the Pharisees, they would not show it, lest they be cast out of the Synagogue." [71] Such again was Nicodemus who came to Jesus under cover of night and freely declared: "No man could do the signs which you have wrought were God not with him," but it cost him a good deal to make the transition from "seeing" to that of "believing." [72] Or again, there were some "who believed in his Name when they had seen the signs he had wrought" but their belief was like the vague and flickering faith of the unnamed man lost in the crowd, so that Jesus "would not trust himself to them, because he knew them all so well that he had no need of the evidence of others; for he himself could read the inner man." [73]

A third class clearly apprehend the meaning of the miracle but fail to respond to the divine call. Even more guilty are those who, because of cowardice, pride, or bad will, do not wish to understand. The seed has fallen on their path; but the devil comes and snatches it away.[74] Such were the Pharisees and the Doctors of the Law, who for political reasons or clerical ambition, looked upon these miracles as a menace to their own status, and declared that Jesus was "a seducer of the people," [75] that "he was not of God, because he did not keep the Sabbath, and even healed men on that holy day";[76]

[69] John VI, 26.
[70] Luke XVII, 11-19.
[71] John XII, 42.
[72] John III, 2; III, 9-12.
[73] John II, 24-25.
[74] Cf. Luke VIII, 12.
[75] John VII, 12.
[76] Mark III, 1-6; Luke XIII, 10-16; John V, 10; IX, 16, etc.

they claimed, moreover, that he "cast out devils with the connivance of Beelzebub, the prince of darkness." [77] This reaction was so powerful that, following upon the resurrection of Lazarus, the Jews made use of this miracle as a pretext in order to arrange a conspiracy to destroy Jesus: "What are we to do? This man has wrought many signs. If we suffer him to go on like this, all the people will believe in him, and then the Romans will come and sweep away our Holy Place and our nation . . . From this time forward they resolved to destroy him." [78] Surely Jesus could say of them: "These are blind leaders of the blind." [79] It may be that they were truly blinded and, in the final analysis, unable to grasp the meaning of a miracle. Nevertheless, even such blindness was blameworthy; for it was the fruit of an obstinate rejection of grace, often offered to them in his signs. Is not this the very reproach which Jesus addressed to them after he had healed the man born blind: "Were you really blind, you would be guiltless; but because you say 'We see,' your guilt stands." [80] St. Paul also frequently reminds us that the repeated rejection of the grace of faith, offered with each sign, ends in a true spiritual blindness. This incapacity to grasp the meaning of divine signs becomes real and actual, not feigned, but nonetheless blameworthy (e.g. II Cor. IV, 4-5; IV, 15; II Thess. II, 10-12; II Tim. II, 13; Rom. I, 17; Eph. IV, 18; Hebr. III, 13). In his commentary on the text of John III, 18-21, St. Augustine says of men of such blindness of spirit; "It was their sin that darkened their sight." For them, as well as for others, the Light of the World had come, but "they loved darkness more than light, for their works were evil; and all that do evil hate the light, lest it reveal the evil that they do." [81] No matter what the sign, howsoever convincing or captivating, it would be useless in the face of their hardness of heart. Christ so declared in his parable of Dives: "Even if someone should rise from the dead, they would not believe." [82]

Finally, there are those who receive the seed in fertile soil; and in

[77] Matt. XII, 24-28.
[78] John XI, 48. 53.
[79] Matt. XV, 14.
[80] John IX, 41.
[81] John III, 19-20.
[82] Luke XVI, 31.

accordance with their generosity of spirit and their righteousness, they bear fruit, some thirty-fold, some sixty-fold, some even a hundred-fold. From the beginning, the apostles and disciples were wholly devoted to the Master. So was the man born blind who defended him in the face of the attacks of his enemies: "Were he not of God, he could have done nothing." [83] Such also were all those—often enough foreigners—who, even before the miracle was wrought, showed such faith that the Lord marveled; such were the Canaanite woman, the paralytic who had been let down through the roof, the centurion, and the father of the epileptic, whose touching prayer was "Lord, I believe; help thou my unbelief." [84] The centurion at the foot of the Cross was struck by the signs which marked the death of Jesus, and he declared: "Truly, this man was the Son of God." [85] Thanks to the signs of Jesus and to their own openhearted reception of them, all these came to a new "vision" of faith, to the inner seeing of God's glory, in his Son who is Our Lord: "Whoever believes in me, believes rather in him who has sent me than in me; and in seeing me, he sees him who sent me." [86]

For all of this, the miracle is *not*, according to the mind of Jesus, *the only road to faith*. When he said to the multitude: "Unless you see signs and wonders, you will not believe," [87] he intended this as a reproach to them. But for the ordinary sort of man who is a prisoner of his passing fancies, the miracle is that salutary and almost indispensable flash of light which draws his attention to the supernatural. He is not disposed to be touched by the inner core of Christ's message, in order to taste its inherent worth directly. The miracle is like "the hem of his garment," and it is often enough to brush against it for strength to come forth from him to heal both body and soul.[88]

But those who yield to the attraction of the Master's words and person penetrate directly to the very heart of love and faith. Even

[83] John IX, 33.
[84] Matt. XV, 21-28; Matt. IX, 2; John IV, 53; Mark IX, 23.
[85] Mark XV, 39.
[86] John XII, 44-45.
[87] John IV, 48.
[88] Matt. XIV, 36; Matt. IX, 20.

before Cana, John tells us, with deep insight, of the calling of the first disciples: they were convinced by the Baptist's witness and fascinated by the irresistible personality of the God-Man, they determined to follow him and to cleave to him. Like them, Mary Magdalene was converted all at once; Matthew left his counting table; Zacchaeus heard the call to the feast in God's Kingdom. Even prior to his public life, Jesus had faithful followers who believed in him: the Baptist, Anna the prophetess, the old man Simeon whose eyes had "seen" the salvation of the Lord, although he had not "seen" any sign; so also were the Shepherds on the first Christmas and St. Joseph. They needed no miraculous sign to believe with all their hearts. Mary, above all others, offered herself in the most complete and fervent faith, without having had any sign; she was greeted by Elisabeth as "blessed is she who has had faith." [89] This beatitude, placed at the very beginning of the Gospel, perfectly anticipates that which was later said to Thomas: "Blessed are they who have not seen and yet have believed." [90] These words of praise once again set forth the opposition between the terms "to see" and "to believe." "To see" is to be bent upon the sign; "to believe" is to grasp the reality it signifies. Thomas "saw" the signs of the wounds of Our Lord's glorified body; but it was in something else that he believed, and he expressed it when he cried out: "My Lord and my God." This beatitude is spoken of all who so hunger and thirst after justice that they have no need of the light of a miracle in order to attune their ears to the voice of God; from the moment of their initial confrontation with Christ, it is he in his own person who convinces them that it is "he alone who has the words of life."

The miracle serves not only to arouse faith; it *nourishes* it as well, and due to its suggestive symbolism it serves as a means of elementary instruction. Jesus freely employed miracles to bring his disciples to familiarity with the supernatural world when they were as yet enmeshed in worldly concerns. Does not St. Mark tell us

[89] Luke I, 45.

[90] John XX, 28-29. "*Videbat, tangebatque hominem, et confitebatur Deum quem non videbat neque tangebat, sed per hoc quod videbat atque tangebat, illud jam remota dubitatione credebat*" (St. Augustine: *In Jo. ev. tract.*, 121, n. 5; ML, XXXV, c. 1958).

how when Jesus came to them, walking on the waters, "they were completely dumbfounded, for they had not understood the miracle of the multiplication of the loaves, their hearts being yet untouched"; but when Peter, at the Master's word, went to him upon the waters, their minds were wonderfully enlightened, and they glimpsed the new heaven and the new earth to which faith had given them access? [91] The reckless Peter, seized by doubt, was again about to sink and to revert to his worldly sense of values; but the Master's hand grasped him and led him toward God's Kingdom. It was such lessons, ceaselessly repeated, that caused faith to become deeply rooted in the disciples' hearts.

Jesus also made use of miracles to strengthen their *hope* and their *love:* the Transfiguration prepared them for the dark days of his Passion, while the resurrection of Lazarus, the Lord's friend, gave them a glimpse of the marvels promised by the loving friendship of God their Saviour.

Before closing this chapter devoted to Jesus, the Wonderworker, it will be in order to say a word of those whom he associated in his own powers; his apostles who were to reveal him to the Gentiles. He irrevocably confided that power which surged forth from his physical body to his mystical body. During his preaching of his Gospel, when sending the disciples on their mission, he granted them "power to cast out evil spirits and to heal the sick and the ailing." [92] After the resurrection, as he was about to ascend into heaven, he sent his disciples forth and told them that "faith will bring miracles in its train." [93] In the infant Church, whose history Paul and Luke have written for us,[94] there was exhibited a miraculous strength which it would never lose and which would make it "a sign among the nations," throughout the centuries.[95]

The miracles of Jesus were signs of his redemptive presence

[91] Mark VI, 52; Matt. XIV, 22-23.

[92] Matt. X, 1.

[93] Mark XVI, 17.

[94] Mark XVI, 20; Acts III, 1-8, V, 12; IX, 32-42; XIV, 3, 8-10, etc.; Rom. XV, 19; II Cor. XII, 12; Gal. III, 5, etc.

[95] Is. XI, 12, appropriated to the Church by the First Vatican Council (ΔSch 3014).

amongst us. Likewise, miracles in the Church are the visible signs of the abiding presence of the same Saviour who promised, long ago, to his Church: "Behold, I am with you, always, even to the end of time." [96]

[96] Matt. XXVIII, 18. See also H. Van den Bussche: *Jesus' woorden aan het afscheidsmaal*, pp. 93-95.

7 · MIRACLES OUTSIDE THE CHURCH AND DEMONIC PSEUDO-MIRACLES

I have kept for consideration in this final chapter two important questions: (1) Is a true miracle possible outside the Catholic Church? (2) Can the devil work pseudo-miracles? In consonance with the point of view I have already chosen, these questions will be examined solely from the standpoint of faith. A chapter in the second part of this book will be given over to the study of the historical existence of such prodigies.

A few brief considerations will suffice for the question of the possibility of pagan miracles, but it will be necessary to devote more attention to the matter of the demonic pseudo-miracle, in view of the great number of problems which are linked to it.

I · THE POSSIBILITY OF AUTHENTIC MIRACLES OUTSIDE THE TRUE CHURCH

In the light of the psychology of religion, the expectation of the prodigies, which thrives in nearly all religions, is not an outlandish or unworthy thing, much less a sickly depravity of the religious spirit; far from being a mere accessory of religion, it is a genuine and *essential* aspect of it.[1]

In religious experience, the divine shows itself as the "wholly other," as the inaccessible and irrevocable absolute which transcends all that is created. R. Otto pointed out this fact in his phenomenology of the sacred: all religious experience necessarily comprises a moment made up less of admiration and respect than of a kind of stupefaction, a basic feeling of total otherness; if it would manifest or confront the divine, the worldly must yield. Yet, this astonishment or stupefaction does not, of itself, suffice to explain the expectation, the readiness, for the prodigious. But experience with the holy knows a second stage: the inaccessible sanctity of the divine reveals itself as being salvific. The deist's notion of the divine as immovably enthroned above all worldly things is no more than a rationalistic fiction; it has never been the basis of any living religion, for it goes against man's most elementary religious experience. Every true religion is a religion of salvation: full of pity and grace to men, the Inaccessible bends in man's direction and calls him to a fellowship in the holy, a wholly gratuitous fellowship which delivers man from his wretchedness, his impurity, and his misery, invading his nature by a Presence which gives blessedness. In all religion there is something which groans in undeniable expectation of a certain incarnation of the divine.

At the point where inaccessible transcendence and beatifying presence come to confrontation there arises, by reason of their complementary action, the expectation of the prodigy. This expectation is, at bottom, the hope that the divine, becoming present in man and yet retaining its total otherness, will manifest the transcendence of its coming by a transfiguration of earthly things. If the divine, always consistent in itself, should make itself perceptible by man, it is not surprising that earthly things should become, in turn, mysterious, divine, "wholly other" than they usually are.

It is only in the light of theology that these data of religious psychology take on their full meaning.[2]

[1] See, for example, A. Brunner: *Die Religion* (Freiburg i. Br., 1956), pp. 219-226. Père Pouget has boldly declared: "If you deny the miraculous, you mutilate religion" (G. Pouget: *Logia* [Paris, 1955], p. 3).

[2] Cf. T. Ohm: *Die Stellung der Heiden zu Natur und Uebernatur nach*

The revelation of God our Saviour occurs in a dual manner. On the one hand, there is the historic, prophetic, and public message culminating in Christ and handed on by his Church. On the other hand, there is the interior illumination of the human spirit, that divine attraction which, under the impulsion of the Holy Spirit, impels man to accept the external message. Inasmuch as all men are called to salvation in Christ, to friendship with the Father, the Son, and the Holy Spirit, that interior trust in God is universal and embedded also within the core of paganism as a kind of instinctive premonition, a latent desire for the incarnation of the divine. So long as this has not encountered revelation in its Catholic form, or remains, in good faith, apart from it, nothing is expressed in clear consciousness. It takes the form of an absolute openness of the soul, a total readiness to the call of God, which is as yet unknown or only vaguely suspected. This basic attitude is like the leaven in the dough: it obscurely permeates a religious life compounded of ideas and pre-conceptions, of dreams and yearnings.

In this light one can appreciate the myths of paganism at their true value: they strive to express, in imaginative forms which are often gross or childish, the desire—unconscious, but nevertheless real and inspired by divine grace—for a redeeming incarnation of the divine. Does not even the religious psychology of a non-believer describe the pagan myths as "not merely a story told, but a reality lived"? [3] An interior expectation and readiness, a confused certainty which is buoyed up by desire, sets off the inventive faculty and makes it concern itself with an object not yet encountered. The desire can be directed to a reality which is quite true, even though the story which seeks to express it be fictitious.

---

dem hl. Thomas von Aquin (Münster, 1927); L. Capéran: *Le problème du salut des infidèles* (Paris, 1934); H. de Lubac: *Catholicism, A Study of Dogma in Relation to the Corporate Destiny of Mankind* (New York, 1950), ch. VIII, "Predestination of the Church," pp. 126-143; K. Steur: *Het christendom en de andere godsdiensten* (Bussum, 1946); E. Lesimple: *Le pressentiment chrétien dans les religions anciennes* (Paris, 1942); ID.: *Religions antiques et spiritualité chrétienne* (Paris, 1947); H. R. Schlette: *Die Religionen als Thema der Theologie* (Quaestiones Disputatae 22) (Freiburg i. B., 1964).

[3] B. Malinowski: *Myth in Primitive Psychology* (London, 1926), p. 21. On the religious values of myths see also G. Van der Leeuw: "Primordial Time and Final Time," *Man and Time:* Papers from the Eranos Yearbooks (New York, 1957), pp. 324-350.

Nevertheless, the inner truth of the myth is never actually lived in its pure state. Inevitably, the divine transcendence is swallowed up in immanence, and is lost in the wretchedness, the weakness, and the narrowness of human conceptions. The divine is absorbed in the finite order and nothing is left but the shadowy outline of an obscure mystery. The concept of salvation ends always by being more or less degraded; material advantage and interest, freedom from stress and from strife, a worldly happiness wanting in consecration or eternal horizon, snuff out interior liberation and holiness, and earthly satisfaction is made king over the joys of heaven.[4]

It is only in the light of the Incarnation that the myth can reveal its inner core of truth; this historic fact allows us to disentangle the deep yearnings overlaid by mythical embroidery. In some remarkable passages, Chesterton has shown us how Christian orthodoxy has replied to the great yearnings of the human soul as that soul has expressed its longings in terms ranging from the myth down to the most gossamer-like of fairy-tales. But he notes also that man's story-telling propensity has never succeeded in evoking or establishing a link with the inaccessible God as envisioned by the highest pagan philosophy. For this to occur, man had to wait for that moment in history which saw the Living God, and no mythical figure, cradled in a manger, that moment with which, in the effulgence of historic light rather than in the mists of legendary lore, God's temporal existence really begins.[5]

In the light of the close relationship between the Incarnation and the Christian miracle, it is not surprising to find in paganism an equally close affinity between myth and the expectation of prodigious occurrences.

The Gospel miracles partake of the truth of the Incarnation; in paganism, however, the desire for the prodigy is, like the myth, a product of man's imagination. As in the case of the myth, the inner reality of what is awaited inevitably appears in an adulterated form because of the intrusion of worldly elements; the expectation of the prodigy degenerates into a sickly seeking after marvels, mani-

[4] Cfr. R. Guardini: *Der Heilbringer* (Zurich, 1946); A. Snoeck: "Mythus en geloof," *Streven* (1940), 1-10.

[5] G. K. Chesterton: *Orthodoxy* (London, 1908), pp. 63-86; ID.: *The Everlasting Man* (New York, 1926), ch. V: "Man and Mythologies," and VI: "Demons and Philosophers," pp. 108-157.

fested by imaginative elaborations built upon uncertain or non-existent elements; the prodigy is engulfed by earthly preoccupations, hopes of temporal advantage, by magic and diabolism; in a word, the divine is made the plaything of impious curiosity and the seedbed of the basest human passions.[6] Nevertheless, even in its most revolting deviations, this yearning for prodigies can never become a merely parasitic manifestation: it will always be the degradation of an authentically religious desire for the miraculous. But this passionate yearning does not appear in its true nature as a longing for divine salvation except in the light of the Christian miracle by which it is fulfilled.

On the basis of such consideration of pagan mythology, it is a simple matter to deduce the unanimous, but variously formulated, doctrine of Catholic theologians.[7] On the whole, the resemblance between pagan and Christian miracles will be found to be wholly *external:* the relationship is identical with that which links pagan mythology and Christian revelation. Just as myths differ from mysteries, so the pagan prodigy differs from the Christian by the same unbridgeable gulf which marks off the play of imagination from reality, fiction from history, the dream of man from the truth of God.

Nevertheless, God's prevenient grace is at work in paganism: there is no salvation outside the visible Church, but we cannot identify that Church with the Church as we see it. There are pagans who, by reason of their openness to the inner call of God's grace, are members *in voto* of the Church of Christ. There is no reason why, in the case of the Christians by desire, God may not, at times, will to snap the fibers of their enmeshing errors and their myths and to manifest himself to them by private revelations or

[6] Cf. A. Léonard: "La métamorphose du sacré dans la superstition," *Supplément* to *Vie Spirituelle*, 7 (1954), 5-29.

[7] Ordinarily, the patristic writers attributed pagan marvels either to artifice or to the intervention of the Devil (e.g., Tatian: *Oratio adversus graecos*, 14-19, PG, VI, cc. 836ff.; Tertullian: *Apologeticum*, 22, PL, I, cc. 406-11, etc.); however they explicitly held to the possibility of an authentic miracle (e.g., St. Augustine: *De diversis quaestionibus*, 83, q. 79, n. 4, PL, XL, c. 92). So also St. Thomas: *De potentia*, q. VI, a. 5, ad 5. See also: H. Fassbinder: "Wunder ausserhalb der wahren Kirche," *Pastor Bonus*, 27 (1914-15), 392-400, 449-456, 513-520; L. de Grandmaison: "Le Sadhu Sundar Singh et le problème de la sainteté hors de l'Église catholique," *Rech. de sc. rel.*, 12 (1922), 1-29.

mystical graces.[8] For the same reason, Christians have no grounds for denying that, under exceptional circumstances, God may will to offer to them, in visible fashion and in the shape of the miraculous, a sign of his presence and of his salvific purposes.

Theologically, therefore, it is quite possible that *true* miracles may be encountered in paganism, in spite of all its superstition, its legendary lore, or its magical leaning. Yet these are like the rare bits of gold dust which glimmer in a vast mass of baser minerals.

Can we possibly determine the conditions which properly surround such miracles? The theological principle which governs the case is a very simple one: any miracle which is lacking in Christian salvific signification is an impossibility. We must therefore, reject, out of hand, any miracle sought or "obtained" to confirm heresy or to buttress an heterodox creed. And likewise to be rejected is any prodigy which, whether or not directly sought or obtained to confirm error, would by its context suggest or confirm such an interpretation.

In the light of these principles, let us now consider the different contexts in which, as we have seen, miracles ordinarily occur.

It seems to me highly improbable that a miracle would confirm a divine *mission* outside the true Church, even were the preacher in question to be the vessel of mystical election or of truly prophetical power. Such signs are, in actuality, so closely linked to the whole context of the message in question that they would inevitably be interpreted as a confirmation of elements in the message which are purely human, incomplete, or false.

From such a point of view, the context of personal *sanctity* seems to me a more favorable one; yet the whole matter nevertheless remains problematical. That sanctity which has become recognized as the visible sign of God's presence in his Church, alone appears essentially linked to the miraculous. Consequently, we may ask if sanctity, existing as a moral miracle, has any meaning and can stand at all in default of a context of the full revelation of the

[8] On the possibility of the mystical experience outside the borders of Catholicism, see, *inter alia:* J. Maréchal: *Studies in the Psychology of the Mystics* (New York, 1927), pp. 239-344; L. Gardet: *Expériences mystiques en terres non-chrétiennes* (Paris, 1953); J. A. Cuttat: *The Encounter of Religions* (New York, 1960), esp. pp. 35-53; J. Daniélou: "Le Yogi et le Saint," *Études,* 250 (1948), 289-305.

Catholic Church. Should such a state of affairs be deemed impossible, then the miracle which springs up in its shadow would also be impossible. Doubtless, one can think of an exceptional case: the divine ascendancy over a pagan might cause him so to overstep the limitations of his own religious context that he would be directing himself in accord with a mystical ideal of perfection which would, as a matter of fact, be specifically Christian. The case remains doubtful. There is a great gulf fixed between the "holy man" and the "saint" in the full Catholic sense of the word. One may doubt whether this chasm can be bridged by one who is unable to participate in the full life of the Church.

Every true pagan miracle must, then, be situated in a context of *prayer*. What has been previously laid down in this regard allows us to look on this possibility optimistically. In actual fact, partial religious truth can give rise to prayer, in spite of false or incomplete doctrine, or faulty conceptualization. In moments of prayer, man's supernatural rectitude may instinctively outpace, more readily than in any other times, imperfections of doctrine and expression.[9] No doubt, it would be unusual to find, within the bosom of paganism, the kind of prayer that is addressed directly to the transcendent God; it would have had to halt at the half-way houses of every kind of human or celestial intermediaries; it would have become befogged in the cloud-land of magic and superstition, both incompatible with the authentically miraculous. However, it might nevertheless be that, in spite of this ambiguity—an ambiguity from which the piety of many Catholics also suffers—the desire for true salvation could, as it seems, beat out a path to Him and plead for a miracle. Here above all, we must respect the all-pervading mystery of God's uncovenanted salvific will; and we will be well-advised if we refrain from trying to shut up his loving kindness within the necessarily narrow fortresses of our personal theological views.

All the same, we may still ask if the miracles which might be vouchsafed in answer to the prayers of a pagan would not be likely to be confined to certain determined types.

Certain providential facts, certain answers to prayer, are of a sort which might arise in natural circumstances: it is only from the

[9] From this point of view phenomena like kathenotheism are symptomatic.

whole context of what has occurred that the believer is enabled to discern that they are true divine signs. There is no difficulty in admitting that prodigies of such an order might be found in a context of paganism. But there are other prodigies which display so flagrant an unlikeness to the natural course of things that they cannot fail to impress themselves on every spectator who views them with an unprejudiced eye as indubitable signs from God; their very nature forces one to recognize in them an apologetic significance.

Is it not theologically likely that such miracles, which spontaneously lend themselves to be used as apologetic arguments, will remain a monopoly of the true Church? Were such to be produced in paganism, they would create an insurmountable ambiguity for the mind searching for truth. The importance of this distinction will be carefully appraised in the apologetic section (part II) of the present work.

What has been said about non-Christian religions has even greater validity in respect to non-Catholic *Christian confessions*. In these groups it is not only the interior drawing-power of grace which is at work; they possess, moreover, a large measure of the treasures of Revelation. A good many of them recognize in Christ the God-Man, the Great Sign which touches the universe with its sacramental reality and thus gives to miracles all their real plausibility. Far better than the pagans, the followers of these confessions are prepared to see the divine sign in the prodigy; better than any non-Christian piety, their devotion provides a context which pleads for a miracle.

It is true that some of these Churches do not follow the logic of the Incarnation in their teaching on the sacraments and on the nature of the ecclesiastical community, and that, in consequence, they reject miracles. Yet the members of these Churches, because their devotion is deeply impregnated by the spirit of Christianity may—more easily than any non-Christians—surmount the deficiencies of their official doctrines. In the existential authenticity of their prayer-life they may regain that expectation of the miraculous which their credal formularies exclude.

In principle, however, the limitations which would apply to miracles in the non-Catholic Christian confessions are the same as those which I have noted in respect to the non-Christian religions.

God cannot give his sanction to error nor can he accord unconditional approval to partial truth. Once again, it is in the context of prayer that the Protestant or Orthodox miracle will take place rather than in the context of testimony or even of sanctity. And the occurrence of any major miracle which would, of its nature, suggest an apologetic use, remains, in the theological view, unlikely.

To sum up, I may say that miracles, like sanctity or catholicity, are a distinctive note of Christ's Church. There is no doubt that religious truth exists outside Christianity; but essentially, it is Christian truth; for the source of all revelation is Christ, and it is his Church alone which transmits it in its fulness. Holiness is to be found outside Christianity; but, essentially, it is Christian holiness; for it is Christ who is the source of all sanctification; and the fulness of that holiness is the distinctive sign of Christ's true Church. Likewise, miracles can take place outside Christianity; but, essentially, they are Christian miracles, for all signs of salvation are signs of Christ; and the miraculous sign, in all its fulness, is also a distinctive mark which makes the Church of Christ recognizable as such.

II · THE POSSIBILITY OF DIABOLICAL PSEUDO-MIRACLES

We are now faced with the second of the questions posed at the beginning of the present chapter: Is a counterfeit miracle possible?[10] To state the question more precisely, I may say that I am not

[10] On the problem of the Devil see: M. Garçon and J. Vinchon: *Le diable*, Étude historique, critique, et médicale (Paris, 1925); S. Lyonnet, J. Daniélou, A. and C. Guillaumont, F. Vandenbroucke: article "Démon," *Dict. de Spiritualité*, III, cc. 141-238; *Satan* in Études Carmélitaines (1948); C. Moeller: "Réflexions en marge du 'Satan' des Études Carmélitaines," *Collectanea Mechliniensia*, 19 (1949), 191-203; L. Cristiani: *Actualité de Satan* (Paris, 1954); N. Corté: *Who is the Devil?* (New York, 1958); M. de la Bigne de Villeneuve: *Satan dans la cité* (Paris, 1951); A. Roets: "De duivel en de stichting van het Godsrijk," *Collat. Brugenses et Gandavenses*, 2 (1956), 145-162, and 300-321; H. Hirschmann: "Der Teufel in unseren Versuchungen," *Geist und Leben*, 27 (1954), 16-20; A. Boehm: *Le temps des ténèbres* (Paris, 1958); E. von Petersdorff: *Daemonologie*, I: Dämonen im Weltenplan (Munich, 1956); D. Zaehringer: "Von der Macht des Teufels über den Menschen," *Bened. Monatsschr*, 34 (1958), 230-240, 315-322, 398-405, and 488-499; P. de Letter: "The Powers of Darkness," *The Clergy Monthly*, 24 (1960), 321-331. [As regards the publication *Satan* cited in the present footnote, it should be noted that twenty-six of the thirty-two contributions to this

seeking to know whether a diabolic prodigy has ever actually occurred; still less to discover whether the origin of such an occurrence could be discerned beyond peradventure. What I am here concerned with is to enquire if such prodigies can be fitted into the framework of the redemptive economy. From the theological viewpoint, does the marvel of demonic origin have any real plausibility?

A reply to this question must be preceded by a brief theological enquiry into the personal existence of Satan and his role in the plan of man's redemption.

Actually, contemporary thought is prone to understand all mention of the diabolical in a figurative sense, and to look upon the Demon as a personification of the powers of evil. This personification of whatever symbolizes evil, found in the Old and New Testament literature, seems to them to be a part of that mythological garb in which God's entire message comes to us. In this matter, as in others, the existentialist theology of our day seeks to extract the marrow of Christian preaching from every myth, to free that preaching from outmoded conceptual schemes, and to translate it into a more authentic religious expression.

However, if one reads the Scriptures with an open mind, not bound by preconceived notions, it is easy to see that one cannot eliminate the demon as a personal entity without changing the Christian message in its very essence. As far as the authors of the New Testament were concerned—even beyond that, in the thought of Christ himself—evil is, first of all, not some *thing* but some *one*. The struggle against "the Evil One" is of a strikingly personal character; and it is exactly for this reason that the battle on behalf of the Kingdom of God, like the battle which marks our own work-a-day lives, takes on an earnestness, an inexorable dramatic tension, which is the very touchstone of a true Christian life. The custom adopted by Christians, since the last century, of "demythologizing" Satan often, therefore, takes on the nature of a flight from the serious exactions of the Christian situation.[11]

---

volume appear in the English translation published by Sheed and Ward (New York, 1952). In subsequent references to this book, it will be cited as *Satan* where the selection exists in English. Otherwise it is cited as *Satan*, Études Carmélitaines (1948).—Transl.]

[11] H. Marrou: *Satan*, p. 68, writes: "The motives behind this defensive

a · Satan in Holy Writ

The Scriptures do not present him whom they call "Satan" or "the devil" or "the Evil One" [12] as a kind of anti-god of evil, an independent principle opposed to the divine principle. This dualistic view, one after the Manichean mode of thought, is totally foreign to Holy Writ. Satan there appears as being dependent upon God, a creature like others, one created, moreover, in the beginning as an angel of light. However, in a mysterious revolt of which St. John gives us a sketch in the Apocalypse,[13] he became the chief of the rebel angels "who forsook their own abode." [14] These backsliding spirits "were not spared by God, who consigned them to the dark pits of hell where they are held to await judgment"; [15] for "he has bound them in a lasting place, in the midst of darkness, where they await the judgment of the last day." [16] And Jesus himself declared: "I saw Satan falling, like lightning, from heaven." [17]

---

attitude, for defensive it certainly is, must be looked into very carefully. It is a sore point—the conscience hates to be questioned about it and does its best to let the problem slide." See, in the same sense: R. Guardini: *The Lord* (Chicago, 1954), Part Two, ch. VII: "The Enemy," pp. 115-121, and his *The Faith and Modern Man* (New York, 1952), pp. 139-154.

[12] On the Devil in the Old Testament, cf. J. Guillet: *Themes of the Bible* (Notre Dame, 1960), ch. V: "The Satanic Powers," pp. 137-147; R. Schaerf: *Die Gestalt des Satans im Alten Testament* (Zurich, 1948), with full critical bibliography. On the Devil in the New Testament, cf. W. Foerster: article "Daimon" in *Theol. Wört. zum N.T.*, II, 1-21; G. von Rad and W. Foerster: article "Diabolos," *ibid.*, 68-81; F. Prat: *The Theology of St. Paul* (Westminster, Md., 1952), II, pp. 413-416; J. Bonsirven: *Les enseignements de J.-C.* (Paris, 1946), pp. 88-123; S. Lyonnet: "Le démon dans l'Écriture," *Dict. de spiritualité*, III, pp. 142-152; L. Bouyer: "Le problème du mal dans le christianisme antique," *Dieu vivant*, n. 6; O. Koch: *Engel und Dämonen in der Hl. Schrift* (Wuppertal, 1951); G. Philips: "De angelis et daemonibus in Evangeliis," *Revue Eccl. de Liège* (1939-40), 172-179, 358-363; H. Schlier: *Principalities and Powers in the New Testament*, Quaestiones disputatae, 3 (New York, 1961). On the episode of the Temptation in the Desert, cf. E. Fascher: *Jesus und der Satan.* Eine Studie zur Auslegung der Versuchungsgeschichte (Halle, 1949); H. Thielicke: *Zwischen Gott und Satan* (Tübingen, 1946).

[13] Apoc. XII.

[14] Jude, v. 6.

[15] II Peter II, 4.

[16] Jude, v. 6.

[17] Luke X, 18.

Scripture does not specify what sin these angels committed. However, the entire corpus of New Testament texts supplies a solid foundation for the theological opinion of many patristic writers and theologians,[18] which was stated in systematic form by Scheeben during the last century. Together with their elevation to a supernatural state, the angels were told of God's salvific plan. He revealed to them the Incarnation and the mission which they themselves were to fulfill. Christ is actually the "first-born of Creation," the "chief of all Principalities and Powers." [19] When it appeared that the Word of God was prepared to take up his abode among men—for, "it is not angels, mark you, that he takes unto himself, but rather the children of Abraham" [20]—then it followed that the angels were to be made the servants of creatures which, unlike them, were not pure spirits. This humiliation proved too much for the pride of the rebels; for were not they all appointed to be "ministering spirits sent out to serve those who are destined to inherit salvation?" [21]

Thus, by origin, as in all his intentions and acts, Satan is seen to be, by definition, an *antichrist*. This hypothesis alone explains why St. John, in his Apocalypse, has explicitly associated the revolt of the angels with *the sign of the Woman*, a symbol of humanity in Christ of whom Mary is the archtype. Hence we can understand St. John's anathema against the Devil, "a murderer from the beginning." For it is he who, from the very inception of things, has sought to destroy the Son of Man, and it is solely to achieve this that his pride allows him to concern himself, at all, with the wretched crew of humans. Finally, this theory explains why St. John gives Satan the title, "Father of lies." [22] In his mind Truth is not an abstract concept but rather Christ in his own person; and, for this reason, Satan, the antichrist, is at the origin of every lie.

[18] For example, Cyprian and Tertullian point to their jealousy of man as being a determining motive of the revolt of the evil angels; cf. also St. Thomas: IIa IIae, q. 2, a. 7, ad 1. See also M. J. Scheeben: *The Mysteries of Christianity* (St. Louis, 1946), pp. 263ff.

[19] Col. I, 15; II, 9.

[20] Heb. II, 16.

[21] Heb. I, 14.

[22] From this point of view it is interesting to reread chapter XII of the Apocalypse; cf. J. Bonsirven: *L'Apocalypse* (Paris, 1951), pp. 213-221. The other two texts which are cited are found in John VIII, 44, and I John V, 20.

In this way, the whole mystery of salvation displays itself not simply on two planes, but on three which are distinct but complementary: one is eternal—that of the divine decisions; another, spiritual—that of angelic entities; the third, temporal—that of those occurrences which make up the whole history of mankind. Whether as ministrants or as rebels, the angels were to be part of the salvific mystery of the Incarnation and to cooperate in its historical accomplishment. Therefore, the incursion of the demon into human affairs is not a power which God has granted him, despite his sin. On the contrary, it is a *necessary projection* into human history of his refusal to serve and his spiritual revolt in opposition to the mystery of salvation. The compactness of angelic duration brings the drama to a head in a flash; but in the long prism of history, God's salvific act and the spiritual act of Satan are refracted in all the vicissitudes of an age-long battle, whose final result is, however, already inexorably determined.

Holy Writ records the decisive points in this battle.

Genesis describes its first stage: the fall of our first parents gave to Satan an ascendancy over mankind, over that "flesh and blood" which "would, one day, be shared" by the God-Man.[23] With all his grisly train—proneness to sin or concupiscence, sin itself, suffering, and death—Satan took his place, from the very beginning of human history on the throne of glory set apart for Christ. So he becomes "Lord of this world," "prince of darkness," as Christ calls him, "god of this world," in St. Paul's strong language.[24] From the beginning, then God's salvific plan was apparently brought to naught: but Yahweh nevertheless offered redemption to man in exchange for the supernatural elevation he had lost. In the very declaration of this first promise, he already indicated the whole argument of redemptive history. It was to be a pitiless personal conflict between Christ and Satan: "I will establish enmity between you and the woman. Her seed shall crush your head." [25] From this time, "the dragon, that serpent of old whose name is Satan," [26] has never ceased "to stand in front of the woman

[23] Hebr. II, 14.
[24] John XII, 31; XIV, 30; XVI, 11; II Cor. IV, 4; Ephes. IV, 11.
[25] Gen. III, 15.
[26] Apoc. XII, 9.

about to give birth, so that he might devour her child when it would be born."

With the historic occurrence of the Incarnation, there opens the decisive stage of the battle. Scarcely had the voice of the Father recognized Christ, then on the threshold of his public life, as his chosen servant and his well-beloved Son, when Satan attempted, in the desert, to bring him into subjection to himself. He aimed to reduce the Messiah to the status of an earthly potentate, enmeshed in this fallen world, by appealing to his sense of self-importance, to a desire for success and spectacular accomplishments: "All the kingdoms of this world will I give you, if, falling down, you will adore me." [27] The reply of Christ is the theandric echo of that *Quis ut Deus* which cast the rebel angel from the heights of heaven: "The Lord thy God alone shalt thou adore, and him only shalt thou serve." But, even though Satan was thus defeated and forced to retire, he did not accept his defeat as final: he left Jesus "for a time." [28]

The entire public life of the Messiah was dominated by his knowledge that he must conduct a personal battle. His frequent encounters with those possessed by demons are examples of violent confrontations with the enemy; but these were not his only moments of warfare: in his polemical discussions with the blinded and obstinate Pharisees, he recognized that behind them was the personal resistance of Satan: "Were God your Father, you would love me; but you have the devil for your father, and it is the will of your father that you seek to do." [29] He knew that Satan would exert control over one of his own apostles: "Have I not chosen you, all twelve? Yet, one of you is a devil." [30] And even of those who were faithful he knew that "Satan has asked for [them] that he might sift [them] as wheat." [31] Hard upon Peter's confession of faith at Caesarea Philippi of *Jesus as the Messiah, the Son of the Living God,* and Christ's promise to Peter that He would build His Church upon him as upon a rock, even poor Peter, in his simple-mindedness, became himself a tempter who would turn the Master

[27] Matt. IV, 8-9; Luke IV, 6.
[28] Luke IV, 13.
[29] John VIII, 42, 44.
[30] John VI, 71.
[31] Luke XXII, 31.

aside from his path of suffering; but Jesus, looking through and behind the Apostle, addressed himself to the Enemy to whose sentiments Peter was, unwittingly, giving voice, and he said: "Away with you Satan! You would stand in my path because your thoughts are the thoughts of men, not the thoughts of God!" [32]

Nonetheless, Jesus pressed onward, with full assurance, toward victory. He knew himself to be the stronger. His miracles and his casting out of evil spirits were the prophetic symbol of his triumph: "If by the finger of God I cast out devils, know then that the Kingdom of God is already come upon you. When a strong man is armed and keeping guard over his castle, then all that is his is safe; but when there comes upon him one who is stronger than he, he overpowers him, he takes from him the armor in which he trusted, and distributes the spoils." [33] Satan's favorite weapon is death; and, from the first, it had been his hope to bring the Son of Man to his death. But by his free acceptance of that death, Christ expressed his absolute love for his Father and himself took possession of the armor in which Satan had trusted. He knew that that hour which seemed, in a particular sense, to be Satan's own hour—did he not say to those who were come to take him: "This is your hour, the hour of the powers of darkness"? [34]—he knew, that, in the mystery of the divine will, it was his Hour, as well: "It is for this hour that I have come." [35] And, on a note of triumph, he added: "Now is the hour of this world's judgment; now shall the Prince of this world be driven out." In a striking phrase with two levels of meaning Christ prophetically summed up the whole of that great duel between Life and Death, of which the Paschal Sequence sings, as he said: "And I, when I shall be lifted up."—*exaltatus*, "raised up," applies both to his being *hoisted* upon the Cross and *glorified* in his Resurrection—"I shall draw all things unto me." [36]

As the decisive hour approached, the personal note of the con-

[32] Matt. XVI, 23.

[33] Luke XI, 20-22.

[34] Luke XXII, 53.

[35] John XII, 27. The French translation of Canon Osty seems preferable on this point to that of the Bible de Jérusalem, since it seems in better agreement with the other texts in which Jesus speaks of his "hour." [The Jerusalem Bible, like most of the English versions, translates, "but this is why I have come to this hour"—i.e., to carry out the Father's mission.—Transl.]

[36] John XII, 31.

frontation became even more evident: "The Prince of this world has come," said the Master, as he went forth to his Passion, "and against me he can do nothing; but it is needful that the world know that I love the Father and that I do the work which the Father has given me to do." [37] In the agony at Gethsemane lies the paroxysm of that conflict. Jesus fought alone, without the help of the "twelve legion of angels" whom the Father would have sent him, had he wished for them.[38] The Evil One assailed him with such fury that he was covered with a bloody sweat. But in his agonizing murmur: "My Father, not my will, but Thine, be done," Jesus proved that Satan "could do nothing against him."

The glorious resurrection is the seal set by the Father upon his victory: "If Christ be not risen from the dead, then vain is your faith, you are still in your sins . . . but the truth is that Christ has risen from the dead, the first fruits of them that sleep . . . Thanks be to God who gives us the victory through Our Lord Jesus Christ." [39]

On the first Pentecost, the Spirit came down upon the apostles "to confute the world and to show where right and wrong in judgment lie . . . because the Prince of this world stands condemned." [40]

This is the judgment that still awaits its execution. As long as the timeless mystery of salvation is unfolding in history, Satan's timeless revolt will continue to express itself. The demon ever roves about "like a lion seeking whom he may devour." [41] Although he can no longer prey upon the Head of the human race, he can yet mutilate him in his members and "make war upon the other children (of the Woman), upon all those who keep God's commandments and give their witness unto Jesus." [42]

In one last great effort, Satan will strive to raise up against the divine Incarnation an Antichrist who will likewise be incarnate in

[37] John XIV, 30-31.
[38] Matt. XXVI, 53.
[39] I Cor. XV, 17. 20. 57.
[40] John XVI, 9-11.
[41] I Peter V, 8.
[42] Apoc. XII, 17.

human history. The mystical Christ will then reach a final testing ground, the hour of its Gethsemane.[43]

But the last judgment will come. The sentence of Christ will go forth. He will send Satan and those who have succumbed to his seductions "into the fire prepared for the devil and his angels," [44] "and their punishment shall be through night and day, for all eternity." [45]

In the meanwhile, it is the Royalty of Christ that slowly brings mankind to unity with itself "until that time when he shall have placed all his enemies under his feet . . . and when all things are thus subject to him, then shall the Son submit himself to him who made all things subject to himself, and God shall be all in all." [46]

All our existence is deployed between the first and the second coming of Christ, in that "brief moment" [47] wherein the vanquished demon appears to have been the victor, in that time during which each of us must choose his captain. Our victory, like Christ's, will be achieved through the apparent defeat of death and the Cross; this defeat will be foreshadowed, as that of Satan, in the apparent victory of the threefold concupiscence.

The Scripture does not portray the choice made at each moment of our lives as being a selective act of human reason moved by abstract considerations: this choice consists rather in a vital relation to personal entities, in an existential commitment of love or hatred, leading to fellowship with either God or Satan. Unless we sacrifice the very essence of the Gospel message, it is impossible to reduce the texts to a merely symbolic use of language or a mythical personification of abstract concepts. Christ came "to bring out peace but the sword" in the fullest sense of the word. As "a Sign set up in contradiction," he confronts us with a radical choice.[48]

This is clear if we listen to the Master: it is the Devil who strives to snatch the seed of his message from the hearts of men.[49] He it is

[43] I John II, 18, 22; IV, 3; II John, 7.
[44] Matt. XXV, 41.
[45] Apoc. XX, 10.
[46] I Cor. XV, 25. 28.
[47] Apoc. XII, 12.
[48] Matt. X, 34; Luke II, 34.
[49] Luke VIII, 12.

again who is the enemy who sows cockle in the midst of the good grain; Jesus himself has told us this.[50] For the sake of his disciples he besought his Father: "I have not prayed the Father that they be taken from the world, but that they be saved from the Evil One." [51] And is not the closing petition of the prayer which he taught his apostles and all Christians: "But deliver us from evil"? [52]

Nor is there any equivocation in the thought of St. John or of St. Paul. Whenever St. John makes use of the words light, way, truth, and life, he is not using them in an abstract or purely ethical sense, but he gives them a metaphysical meaning which finds personal existence in Christ: Christ is the Way, the Truth, the Life, the Light. These values are mightily opposed by their contraries: darkness, lying, corruption, and death, personalized in Satan as an existential "nothingness" rising up against Christ. Especially in his First Epistle, St. John lays stress in lapidary language upon the personal note of the opposition. For example, when he says "the darkness has fled and now the true light shines," he is using these words in the sense of the saying of Jesus: "Now is the world judged; now is the Prince of this world cast out." [53] It is only in the light of this kind of understanding that the word "still" in what follows becomes intelligible: "Whoever pretends to walk in the light and yet hates his brother, is *still* in darkness." [54] Even more explicit are the texts which set against each other those "born of God" (a key-concept in Johannine theology) and those "born of the Devil." "We know that whoever is born of God does not sin; for he that is born of God keeps himself, and the Evil One cannot touch him"; [55] while "he who sins is of the Devil, for the Devil was a sinner from the first"; [56] and "we know that we are of God although

[50] Matt. XIII, 39.

[51] John XVII, 15.

[52] Matt. VI, 13. All the best commentators interpret this text, just as they do Matt. V, 37 and John XVII, 15, in the personal sense and not in the weakened meaning of "evil." This interpretation is confirmed by the parallelism of Matt. XIII, 19, "the Evil One," with Mark IV, 15, where we read "Satan," and Luke VII, 12, where we find "the Devil."

[53] I John II, 8, referring to John XII, 31.

[54] I John II, 9.

[55] I John V, 18.

[56] I John III, 8.

the whole world lies in the power of the Evil One." [57] According to John, every man bears, of necessity, either "the sign of Christ" or "the sign of the Beast." [58] For his Christians are simply those who, with Christ, "have vanquished the Evil One.[59] The whole of his theology may be summed up in a word: "Little children, you are of God and have overcome the Evil One; for he that is in you is greater than he that is in the world." [60]

The testimony of Paul is the same. He sees the obstacles to his apostolate as having been set up by Satan; [61] he attributes to the "Evil One" or to the "Tempter" [62] all the tribulations of Christians; even more, he urges them not to underestimate the evil against which they must fight, and he underlines its personal character: "For we wrestle not against flesh and blood, but against the principalities, against the powers, against the Rulers of this world of darkness." [63] He describes, in terms very close to those used by St. John, the opposition of Christ and Satan under the aspect of two kingdoms between which a man must make his choice. For him Satan is "the god of this world"; [64] he "blinds the heart of the unbeliever"; he sets himself against him "who has said: 'Out of darkness let light shine' "; against that God who "has made his light to shine in our hearts that we may know the bright knowledge of the glory of God in the face of Jesus Christ." [65] In the face of him "who has power over death," [66] God sets him "who calls us into his Kingdom and glory"; [67] into which "neither sin nor injustice, nor flesh and blood, can come." [68] He is the Father "who has delivered us from the powers of darkness and has brought us into the Kingdom of his well-beloved Son." [69]

[57] I John V, 20.
[58] Apoc. VII, 3; IX, 4; XIII, 17.
[59] I John II, 13-14.
[60] I John IV, 4.
[61] I Thess. II, 18; II Cor. XII, 7.
[62] I Thess. III, 5.
[63] Eph. VI, 11.
[64] II Cor. IV, 4.
[65] II Cor. IV, 6.
[66] Heb. II, 14.
[67] I Thess. II, 12.
[68] I Cor., VI, 9ff.; Gal. V, 21; I Cor. XV, 50.
[69] Col. I, 13. The self-same opposition, "light and darkness," which we

The terminology and doctrine concerning what would later be called "the Mystical Body" are inserted in the same perspectives. When Paul speaks to the Romans[70] of "the body of Sin" he is not far from thinking of it as a sort of anti-mystical body, fostered of Satan; and he sets alongside the unity of the mystical Christ, "that new man created in Christ Jesus," [71] another unity, that of "our old man," in which the descendants of Adam in the flesh are reassembled in a praeternatural community under subjection to sin. This is the City of those who live under subjection to "the Prince of the spiritual powers of the air, the Spirit now at work among God's rebellious subjects." [72] The Christian dies, with Christ, to the Old Man; in Christ he is become the New Man in a new creation. To the Christian who actually lives this personal mystical unity in its highest reality, by partaking of the eucharistic body of Christ, Paul addresses a warning not to relapse into his previous familiarity with Satan: "I would not have you enter the fellowship of demons . . . you cannot partake of the Table of the Lord and the table of demons." [73]

b · Diabolical Pseudo-Prodigies

Holy Writ tells us quite plainly that God's salvific plan for man is opposed by the contradictory plan of Satan.

Diabolical prodigies, like authentic miracles, are not theologically likely except within a definite context. Satan makes use of

---

find so often in St. John, is encountered in I Pet. II, 9: "He who has called you out of darkness into his wondrous light," and in Acts XXVI, 18. This seems to indicate not only that this coupling in opposition was in current usage in the Jewish world of the time (as the Dead Sea Scrolls indicate) but also that their application to the Kingdom of God and to Satan must have been of frequent occurrence in the preaching of Jesus himself.

[70] Rom. VI, 6; VII, 24. This interpretation is that of A. Frank-Duquesne, "Réflexions sur Satan en marge de la tradition judéo-chrétienne," *Satan*, Études Carmélitaines (1948), pp. 255-258. On the "corpus mysticum diaboli" as understood by the Latin Fathers and the authors of the Middle Ages, see S. Tromp: *Corpus Christi, quod est ecclesia* (Rome, 1946), pp. 160-166.

[71] Eph. II, 10.

[72] Eph. II, 2. Another characteristic text is that of Col. III, 5, where the word "membra"—that is, the terrestrial members or members of sin—does not refer (at least, in the Greek text) to "us" as members, but rather to the varying species of sin which all together make up a great "body of sin."

[73] I Cor. X, 20-21.

such prodigies to further his own plan and to thwart the plan of Christ. In its essence, the authentic miracle is a sign of salvation, while the Satanic prodigy is at the antipodes of this in being, of necessity, a sign of perdition for man. Behind the immediate desire to destroy man by deceiving an individual or a group one can detect the all-pervading intention of destroying the whole divine plan of salvation, the will to strike at Christ, to destroy his kingdom, and to snatch from him what he has ransomed.

This thought clarifies the problem of the Satanic prodigy. As a sign it leads to perdition; but it must not appear to do so, for then it would defeat its own purpose and be in check. In order to deceive, it therefore takes on the vesture of a sign of good intent and it becomes a *pseudo-salvific* prodigy.

It follows that the pseudo-miracle, if it exists at all, will then be even more infrequent than the miracle which comes from the hand of God.

As we have seen, God's providential plan for man is normally hidden behind the network of natural causality; only the eye of faith can discern it in the natural course of events. It is only on rare occasions that God himself directly interferes with Nature and gives a clear sign of his plan.

Satan has even stronger motives to mask his doings, hiding them behind the screen of human passions, natural drives, and psychological influences. God draws man from the deceitful show of terrestrial things and leads him to discover Himself, the only reality worthwhile; the miracle thus serves as a liberating force to this end. On the other hand, the demon shuts man up within the appearance of things, imprisoning him in terrestrial concerns as though they constituted his final home and ultimate happiness. Why then should Satan seek to divert men's minds from earthly things, even by wondrous signs, causing man to turn his gaze elsewhere? He is careful not to underestimate that need for God which lies deep within man's heart; he knows that yearning for grace which always tends to lead the race of Adam to the Source of their pristine dignity. He takes care not to fight openly against Christ. He shuffles the cards so as to make a plain choice an impossibility. Essentially, Satan is, as the Scripture says, the Spirit of darkness who works secretly in the dark, sowing the cockle stealthily, underhandedly arousing base passions, asserting easy platitudes and giving them the appearance of being common-sense arguments. Man ends by falling a victim to these wiles, and is led astray.

But precisely here we find an initial field for diabolical prodigies. The prodigy itself can serve as a *mask* for playing this game—a mask even more effective than the merely human or natural appearance of things. If he borrows God's own ways of acting, transforming himself, as St. Paul says, into an angel of light,[74] what astuteness and force does he show! He then plays to perfection his role as "diabolos," being at once the sower of discord and the ever ambiguous; for he bores into the very center of man's religious life in order to break and corrupt his union with God in its vital core.

This intention can be effected thanks to the inherent ambiguity of all signs. Satan's tactics never vary. His external sign will always be a faithful copy of the divine miracle. However, its meaning will be falsified with meticulous care, and the center of its gravity shifts from what is divine to what is of earth. Instead of attracting and fixing man's attention upon God, the sign will become an end in itself. Instead of arousing man's desire for redemption and that life that is lived on the Farther Shore, it will make him satisfied with the terrestrial good of an imaginary paradise; it will dull the spirit of sacrifice and love of the Cross by guiding men in the paths of self-love; it will put pride in the place of humility and will dethrone God in order to set man in his place.

The prodigies which Satan offered to do for Christ in the desert are the prototypes of all this kind of thing. Looked at from without, all of them seem stamped with the divine seal in origin and in context; would they not appear to be fulfillments of the divine promises by the Word Incarnate himself? Yet, in truth, they would, piecemeal, have turned Jesus aside from the messianic task willed by the Father and would have subordinated his miraculous powers to temporal success and private advantage. "Had Jesus yielded," one writer pertinently notes, "he would have become the Master of this World; he would have surpassed Caesar and Alexander, but remained like them both; he would have become like all other men who are vassals of Satan, a sinner ruling over other sin-

[74] II Cor. XI, 14.

ners, and the real master of men, still unconquered, would be Satan."[75]

The Beast of the Apocalypse, seen of John, wears the same ambiguous guise as does Satan: "it had two horns like a lamb but spoke like a dragon . . . it wrought great miracles, even to the making of fire come down from heaven before the eyes of all."[76] In his turn, Paul states on the subject of that Antichrist who is to embody in the latter days all the anti-Christian activity of Satan: "the coming of the Man of Sin shall be marked, through Satan's work, by all kinds of manifestations of power, signs and lying prodigies."[77] Jesus had himself foretold that the Antichrist and his satellites "will display great signs and wonders so as to mislead, if possible, even the elect."[78] Will the Antichrist deceive us by a false incarnation, by a caricature of God's human face? Will he attempt, in his turn, that most extraordinary miracle of all that God has ever wrought? St. John has warned us: "He that has understanding, let him count the number of the Beast; for it is the number of a man."[79]

It is only through the "discernment of spirits," delicately undertaken that the clear eye of faith can pierce the ambiguity of these signs and uncover the treacherous gifts of Satan.

It must be added that ambiguity burgeons forth in every aspect of the self-styled miracle; and this is, first of all, true of its *pseudo-transcendency.*

From the theological point of view a truly transcendent domination by the demon over natural things would be held to be impossible. No doubt, a pure spirit, such as he is, unlike the incarnate spirit, such as man is, is dowered with a relative degree of transcendency: in the abstract the influence of such a spirit upon matter and upon man excels any form of specifically human influence. But we have already seen that the transcendent ascendency over nature which is characteristic of the miracle is meaningless

[75] O. Koch: *op. cit.,* p. 43.

[76] Apoc. XIII, 11. 13.

[77] II Thess. II, 9; cfr. B. Rigaux: *L'Antichrist et l'opposition au Royaume messianique dans l'Ancien et le Nouveau Testament* (Gembloux, 1932).

[78] Matt. XXIV, 24.

[79] Apoc. XIII, 18.

except in the context of a supernatural plan. Satan, therefore, cannot exercise a transcendent influence apart from his role in the redemptive economy. And, moreover, even on the supernatural plane, the miracle is not the usual form of salvific relationship between God and his creatures: it is something which takes place by way of exception. Neither good nor evil angels can therefore employ it in the economy of salvation as the normal manner of initiating contact with man: it does not appertain to their designated roles in the historic development of the redemptive plan. When pure spirits are employed or chosen to act as instrumentalities in a miraculous occurrence, this can only be because they have been so designated in respect of some special divine mission, and this exceptional duty takes them away from their normal occupations.

We may apply these principles to Satan. He is concerned with the events of the Redemption only because he has taken his stand as being Antichrist: his role in respect to salvation is no more than the historical projection of the decision which he made before time began.[80] His service as a faithful angel would have allowed him habitual contact with human realities, and he has kept this advantage even though in his revolt he makes use of it in the wrong way. However, in order for him to accomplish a miracle, a *special* mission from God would have had to have been confided to him, and this is nonsensical; for it is absolutely unthinkable that God would instigate the deceit of his own chosen instrument.

The demon does indeed possess a certain ascendency over the sensible world and over the human spirit; but it rests, exclusively, in his power of suggestion, in his power to tempt; in other words, it is dependent upon man's free participation, through an act of his will, in Satan's revolt, that is to say by sin and by its vital attachments in man's psychic apparatus and in the material universe. The demon makes use of many auxiliaries: concupiscence, suffering, sickness, death—all the consequences of original sin and personal sin. He likewise exploits all that impersonal residue which

[80] Cf. St. Thomas: *De Potentia*, q. VI, a. 5 in c.: "*dicendum, quod sicut Angeli boni per gratiam aliquid possunt ultra naturalem virtutem, ita Angeli mali minus possunt ex divina providentia eos reprimente quam possint secundum naturalem virtutem: quia, ut Augustinus dicit* (3 de Trin. c. 9 a med.), *quaedem quae Angeli mali possent si permitterentur, ideo facere non possunt quia non permittuntur.*"

free acts bring in their train, which goes by the name of "evil." All this he uses to tempt man and to set his snares. But evil does not enter into the nature of things; the devil cannot take them over, because his power is limited to his normal role in regard to them on the supernatural plane. His refusal to serve drives him to oppose the divine plan, but keeps him within the limits of his appointed service.

As a messenger of salvation, an angel can exercise a transcendent influence upon things, for he is God's instrument; but the Devil cannot do this. It is not in his power either to cause an accident or an organic malady or to deliver a man from them at his pleasure. Even should a sinner freely put himself under his tutelage, Satan's evil influence may be either normal or paranormal, but it remains, in all cases, within human limits. Satan, nevertheless, can make thorough-going use of his influence on a man's sinful will; he can exacerbate the passions and those psychic mechanisms rooted in the personality; thanks to them, indeed, he can successfully subdue true freedom of will; he is able, moreover, to whip up these psychic manifestations to such a point that the effect upon a careless or inattentive onlooker will be similar to what is excited by the real transcendency of a divine miracle. All the success of the diabolical pseudo-prodigy is rooted in this ambiguity.

The *context* which surrounds the demonic prodigy displays the same ambiguity. A true miracle will often show itself in correlation with personal *holiness*. The demonic miracle stems from the hypocrisy of its performers rather than from their unworthiness or their corruption. Once men are persuaded of the reality of the prodigy, it will often betray its corrupting purpose. Once the duped spectator sees how he has been taken in, he then becomes suspicious of even the most authentic holiness and miraculous power. In this way, what was, in its inception, credulity draws the victim into an incurable skepticism.

The true miracle is often the confirmation and the guarantee of a *divine mission*. The Satanic prodigy does not come to the aid of atheism, nor is it made an instrument of propaganda for gross materialism. It is more apt to flourish as a seeming warranty for heresy, error, rebellion, disguised as "purity of doctrine," the "simplicity of the Gospel," or as virtuous opposition to the all too human elements in the Church. Satan is the expert intriguer who can kill the spirit by means of the letter and substitute the conformism beloved by the white sepulcher for the true assent of the heart. The possibilities of deceit and error grow apace because of the argument to which false miracles give rise: "The Church condemns us, but the miracle proves that God is on our side." The appearance of false miracles, in a more general sense, offers a prized foothold to relativism and a false ecumenicism. When prodigies arise in religious contexts of an indifferent sort, even in those which are least authentic or most absurd, they lose all value as guarantees of the truth of revelation.

Finally, the true miracle is closely linked with *prayer*. The Satanic miracle does not unfold itself in an atmosphere of blasphemy or of revolt, but, by preference, it will be surrounded by a kind of piety which has lost its interior vitality. Although linked to a Christian context, it will be a context in which Christianity has been watered down by superstitious practices, by magical rites, and by yearnings after marvels. As always, the cockle is carefully sown into the midst of the good seed. It seems indeed that, by a kind of general law, the Satanic miracle flourishes, by choice, alongside the authentic miracle; it will even seek to so enmesh itself with the latter that the two cannot be pried apart. Apparitions which have been approved by the Church have been almost always doubled in the same place or at least in the neighborhood of it, by counterfeits which are no more than caricatures. Satan wishes to lead astray the critical sense of the spectator; he discredits the true miracle by means of the false; he makes religious feeling ridiculous by confusing it with bigotry; he discourages Christian expectation of the miraculous by making it the partner of a frenzied thirst for marvels. Such were the tactics of the Pharisees who were scandalized by the miracles of Jesus and declared "that he casts out devils by the power of Beelzebub." [81] Satan banks on the lack of discernment which marks a faith not yet mature; and by a theatrical stroke he

[81] Luke XI, 15. P. Samain in his "L'accusation de magie contre le Christ dans les évangiles," *Eph. Theol. Lov.*, 15 (1938), 449-490, has shown that this was no casual insult but rather the habitual theme of an accusation brought against Jesus by his adversaries.

displays falsity and truth as mixed in an inextricable imbroglio, thus seeking to put everything in confusion.

There is a like ambiguity in the external manifestation of the Satanic prodigy. Its prime characteristic is its *exorbitance*, in striking contrast to the restraint characteristic of the true miracle. It glimmers with a false and fictitious glare; although it attracts and absorbs attention, there is a lack of any deep meaning behind it. Instead of opening eyes to the supernatural light which it ought let shine through it, the demonic prodigy blinds the spectator with its flashiness and it intoxicates him with its marvelous qualities. A second characteristic of the diabolic prodigy is its *unsuitability*. It does not fit into the scheme of Christianity: it pretends to make plain what must be mysterious in faith, and easy whatever is hard to bear in the Cross. Instead of buttressing up our expectations and helping us to bear the Cross, it suggests, in its false glory, a Crossless paradise fulfilled in this world. This scenery actually masks from our sight the true kingdom of Satan to which it belongs. Even Peter himself was tempted to rest forever in the shadow of the true miracle he had witnessed on Tabor, and he later strove to prevent Jesus from going forth to his Cross, for which Jesus rebuked him.[82] With how precious an opportunity does the false prodigy furnish Satan so that he may deceive the *profanum vulgus* with the dream of an earthly paradise!

The final characteristic of the demonic miracle is the *disturbing*, sensualistic, and perverse climate which surrounds it. However, let us not deceive ourselves: immorality is not the best sign by which to recognize the handiwork of Satan. He is a spirit, and it is in the self-pride of the human spirit in rebellion that he achieves his true victories. The weakness of the flesh is no more than a springboard to him: it opens the door to his true object. Or can it be that the demon seeks above all else the pleasure of befouling the image of the Word made flesh?

[82] Luke IX, 33. It is not in this sense that we are to understand the Evangelist's reflection: "He knew not what he was saying"? Is not this inadvertency the same thing as that with which Christ had reproached him at Caesarea Philippi: "Your thoughts are not the thoughts of God, but those of men"? (Matt. XVI, 23).

c · *Possession and Hauntings*

The pseudo-miracle caricatures the divine sign. But does Satan sometimes show himself for what he is? Does the demonic ever appear unveiled as a manifest sign?

We might be inclined to reply affirmatively to this question in view of phenomena frequently attested to in the course of history as being cases of diabolic possession, hauntings, Satanism, black magic, and the rest, and in view of the Gospel accounts of possession and the casting out of devils.

But experimental science—medicine and especially psychology—would refuse to subscribe to such an affirmation. Psychopathology describes a series of crises linked to psychical or somatic disturbances of which the symptoms are very close to those displayed in cases of diabolic possession. Furthermore, in recent years parapsychology has made definite progress, and is inclined to attribute to natural causes almost all cases of haunting.

Despite the scanty details supplied by the Gospel accounts, modern medicine recognizes, in the majority of the possessed, patients suffering from known and officially catalogued maladies.

If we keep to the viewpoint of faith, we must recognize in possession, at least, a diabolical manifestation. For to reject the ascendency of Satan over the possessed in the Gospels would be to make inexplicable *Christ's attitude towards them.*[83] We will not make the matter any clearer by taking refuge in the explanation

[83] On the possessed in the Gospels, see F. M. Catherinet: "Demoniacs in the Gospel," *Satan*, pp. 163-177; J. Smit: *De daemoniacis in historia evangelica* (Rome, 1913); G. J. Waffelaert: article "Possession diabolique," *Dict. Apol.*, IV, cc. 53-81; W. Foerster: article "Daimon," *Theol. Wört. z. N.T.*, II, 1-21: R. Kugelman and J. de Fraine: article "Diabolical Possession," *Ency. Dict. of the Bible*, cc. 565-567; A. Rodewyk: "Die Beurteilung der Bessenheit. Ein geschichtlicher Ueberblick," *Zeitschr. f. Kath. Theologie* (1950), 460-480. Protestant literature on the subject includes: J. Weiss: article "Dämonische," *Realenc. für prot. Theol. u. Kirche*, IV, 410-419; G. Sulzer: *Die Besessenheitsheilungen Jesu* (1921); A Titius: "Ueber die Heilungen vom Dämonischen im N.T.," *Theol. Festshrift für N. Bouwetsch* (1918), pp. 31ff. On demonology and possession from the standpoint of the history of religion, see T. K. Oesterreich: *Die Besessenheit* (Langensalza, 1921), pub. in French as *Les Possédés* (Paris, 1927); E. Langton: *Essentials of Demonology*. A Study of Jewish and Christian Doctrine: its Origin and Development (London, 1949), published in French as *La démonologie*. Étude de la doctrine juive et chrétienne. Origine et développement (Paris, 1951).

that He wished to adapt himself to the ideas or to the mental outlook of his contemporaries. Everything is, however, very clear if we take account of the plain difference between Christ's attitude towards and way of healing ordinary illness from that he adopted in the case of the possessed. He looked upon illness as being a *thing*, and he treated it as such; at times he explicitly denied that it was the result of hereditary or personal sin. On the contrary, exorcisms as practised by Christ are like the attack upon an enemy: a dialogue takes place between Christ and the patient, but, through the patient, he speaks to someone else who has taken his place. The replies of the possessed come not from himself but from another who, through his mouth, vomits forth his hatred, as though he felt personally in danger: "What have you to do with us, Jesus of Nazareth? Have you come to destroy us? I know who you are—the Holy One of God. I charge you, by God, not to trouble me." These, and similar expressions are repeated in all the exorcisms.[84] Jesus was accustomed to touch a sick person in a way which symbolized his pity; in the presence of the possessed, he stood at a distance as though to repudiate someone unworthy of his presence, a being whom he did not wish to touch. He spoke in command, but briefly and mordantly: "Be still, and go out of this man." He exercised absolute dominion without mercy or discussion. He would not even allow the demon "to tell what he knew." Only after the deliverance would he speak to the man or take him by the hand.[85] No purely psychological explanation of possession can justify this radical difference in the attitude of Jesus.

[84] E.g., Luke IV, 33-35; Mark III, 11; I, 34; V, 7; Matt. VIII, 16, etc.

[85] E.g., Mark V, 15; VIII, 26. It would seem, at first sight, that Jesus made an exception of the woman who had been crippled for eighteen years; he laid his hands upon her and made her straight again. Actually, this seems to me to prove that this woman was not possessed, and that when Christ called her "this daughter of Abraham whom Satan has enchained these eighteen years," he was not alluding to demonic possession. The fact that Christ uses the word "Satan" in connection with a disease is not enough to justify our attributing it to demonic possession. It may be that he was here simply making use of the language of his day, just as the evangelists do frequently in mentioning a "spirit of evil" without having in mind any direct ascendency of Satan. It is rather the whole bearing of Christ which would alone justify us in a decision in any particular case as to whether we are dealing with a simple illness or with a case of possession. On this point see the excellent remarks of A. Roets, *loc. cit.*

Accepting the facts narrated in the Gospels in the spirit of faith, we may examine how such an intrusion of the devil is possible and what can be its meaning. I shall then set this view from the standpoint of faith alongside the findings of science and attempt to reconcile the theological conclusions and the scientific findings.

According to theology, Satan manifests his presence in the human soul in three ways.

The human *will* can, in the depths of man's spiritual freedom of choice, give itself over to Satan. Every sin partakes of something of this kind: "he who sins is of the devil," just as he who lives in grace "is of God." The man who lives in God possesses the secret of a giving of self to him in a fuller sense than is true of particular actions placed under the impulsion of grace. Such a man responds to the indelible character which marks him as a member of the Body of Christ by a definite consecration of all his being. By an act which he wills to be everlasting and irrevocable, he anticipates that final fellowship in Christ which the act of dying alone can complete. Of his own choice, his life is thus consecrated to God forever, in at least whatever measure human mutability makes such a decision possible.

Now, it is conceivable that, on the other hand, a man long given over to evil-doing, may become obsessed by a wish to remain in this path of life by a basic act of choice. This would be a hardening of the human heart, a consecration in reverse, a vow made unto Satan. Let us not be too quick to equate this perversion with those "bargains with the devil" or "sales" of the soul to Satan; for in such cases psychological derangement often plays a greater role than a perverse will. The perverse act here in question will rather be the lucid choice of a Satanic pride, a fundamental option, deliberately enmeshing itself in its own autonomy and terrestrial immanence.

Is it not to Satan's advantage if, in such a case, he cast aside his anonymity and show his agreement to the explicit offering of his client by a sensible sign? Does it not increase his status as anti-God if he then, in a kind of caricature of the sacraments, *deconsecrate* the man in question as his vassal, his instrument, his ambassador, his priest? Soloviev, in his well known *Legend of the Antichrist,* describes how the spirit of Satan takes possession of the Antichrist, deliberately caricaturing the giving of the Holy Spirit to the apostles after the Resurrection.[86]

Such a manifestation is not, of necessity, linked to that kind of Satanism associated with devil-worship or those Black Masses of which we read, everywhere and in every age, in scandalous tales and in the legends of folklore.[87] No doubt, the demonic is no stranger to such abominations, but the greater part of them arise from more superficial layers of the human consciousness, and from pathological perversions of quite natural instincts. I am thinking, here, rather of a more secret involvement of the will, an involvement of which the possessed and perhaps he alone has had real experience. Is not this to take at face value what St. John has said of Judas who, at the Last Supper ate the bread which Jesus offered him—"Satan entered into Him"? [88] Did not Jesus foresee this moment

[86] W. Solowjew: *Uebermensch und Antichrist.* Ueber das Ende der Weltgeschichte (Freiburg i. B., 1958). In a commentary on this legend by A. Maceina [*Das Geheimnis der Bosheit.* Versuch einer Geschichtstheologie der Widersachers Christi als Deutung der "Erzählung vom Antichrist" Solowjews (Freiburg, 1955)], the critic offers one of the most penetrating analyses of the spirit of antichrist and of the demonic designs of which I am aware. See the English translation of the "legend" by S. Graham in V. Solovyof: *War and Christianity from the Russian Point of View:* Three Conversations (followed by a Short Narrative about Antichrist), (New York, 1915).

[87] See on this subject: A. Romeo: article "Satanismo," *Enciclopedia Cattolica,* X, cc. 1953-1961 (with full bibliography); "La sorcellerie dans les pays de mission," Semaine missiologique 1936 (Louvain, 1937); E. Bossard: *Gilles de Rais, maréchal de France, dit Barbe-Bleue, 1404-1440, d'après des documents inédits* (Paris, 1885); F. Funck-Brentano: *Le drame des poisons* (Paris, 1900), on the notorious business during the reign of Louis XIV which centered about a sorceress, Catherine Deshayes, known as "La Voisin," and in which were involved many of the great names among the noble houses, and even among families connected with the Royal Court. There is a summary of the facts in L. Cristiani: *Actualité de Satan* (Paris, 1954), pp. 120-123; E. Delcambre: *Les jeteurs de sort notamment dans l'ancienne Lorraine* (Nancy, 1950); E. Brouette: "The Sixteenth Century and Satanism," *Satan,* pp. 310-350; P. Villette: "La sorcellerie dans le Nord de la France du milieu du XVe siècle à la fin du XVIIe s.," *Mélanges de Science rel.,* 13 (1956), 39-62 and 129-156; Père Bruno de Jésus-Marie, O.C.D.: "The Confession of Boullan," *Satan,* pp. 262-267; H. R. Philippeau: article "Culte du démon," *Catholicisme,* III, c. 603; M. Bouteiller: *Sorciers et jeteurs de sort* (Paris, 1958).

[88] The expression "for it was night," in v. 30, has, when read in its context, a meaning which unquestionably concerns more than a mere indication of the hour. Would it be an exaggeration to think St. John wished to express, by making use here of the light and darkness terminology so much a part of his style of writing, that Satanic atmosphere which he had observed at this mo-

when, at the very time when he told them of the Eucharist, he declared: "One of you is a devil." [89]

Satan can also, it seems, exercise his influence in a second fashion. He here concerns himself not with man's free will, but enmeshes himself in that zone subject to determinism which we call the psychism, whence he threatens the personality and alters its free development by substituting for it a demonic pseudo-personality.

Here, it would seem, we are back with the evangelical cases of possession. Jesus did not speak personally to the demoniacs. There is not one word of the Master which would justify us in considering that he looked on possession as an indication of personal culpability. During the exorcism he acted as though the patient's own personality were in abeyance; after the devil had been cast out, and when he was face to face with the normal personality of the man, his attitude became benevolent and encouraging.

It seems, however, that there is a relationship between diabolic possession and a kind of moral weakness or imbalance. On one occasion Jesus actually refused to accept among his disciples one who had been possessed, despite the man's ardent wish to join the fellowship.[90] Furthermore, the Master warned one of the possessed whom he had delivered against the danger of a more serious relapse if he did not take possession "of his own house" by making a serious effort on the moral and religious levels.[91] The regulations of the Church continue those established by Our Lord; Cassian, for example, states that the Eucharist is not to be denied to one possessed; but Canon Law prohibits the admission to priestly ordination of one who has been so afflicted.[92]

How, then, are we to conceive of diabolic possession? I have stated that the demon has no more than a limited ascendency over

---

ment? On this subject see H. Van den Bussche: *op. cit.*, p. 58; M. Meinertz: "Die 'Nacht' im Johannesevangelium," *Theol. Quartalschr.*, 133 (1953), 400-407.

[89] John VI, 71.

[90] Mark V, 18-19.

[91] Matt. XII, 43-45.

[92] Cassian: *Collationes*, VII, 30, *CSEL*, XIII, p. 208; *Codex Juris Canonici*, n. 984, 3.

things and over the minds of men; his only access to human reality is through the gate opened by sin. Like the other consequences of sin, psychic disturbances—even though they may be rooted in natural causes and not due, directly, to personal sin—can be used by the Devil in tempting man. Yet he is not able to make himself master of the human soul at choice unless it be surrendered to him in one way or another by a free act of man's will.

This seems to me possible in two ways. One is by Satan's direct grasp of a man who, by repeated acts of his own choice, has been brought to such psychological weakness, to such total susceptibility to suggestions of evil that his soul is transformed into a completely subservient instrument, fit to be led and directed at the whim of whosoever grasps his hand. Indirectly, the Satanic dominance can be attained in the case of a soul which is weak by nature or as a result of sin, when another man who has surrendered to Satan exerts psychological pressure and communicates his own will to him.

In both cases, the demonic activity lies in the psychic forces of which it makes use. The symptoms of such possession do not fundamentally differ from other normal or paranormal human actions. The influence of Satan is to be found in the total persistency of outlook, always oriented toward a single, well-defined object. The careful student will discern that the deep motivations from which the manifestations in question stem are rooted in something quite beyond the drives of the distraught personality.

Occasionally, and in a flash, they will reveal their demonic origin. The paranormal and psychopathological derangements may exhibit such an origin through the waves of agony which they often generate. In the case of true possession they display an intent different from even the unconscious motivations of the possessed person.

Rarely, if ever, is it possible by a purely clinical diagnosis to discern true from false possession. Even the *Rituale Romanum*, in enumerating the characteristic notes of demonic possession, restricts itself to approximations which have only relative validity; [93]

[93] Cf. *Rituale Romanum*, Titulus XII, "De exorcizandis obsessis a daemonio"; the entirely relative character of the symptoms enumerated in chapter 1, no. 3 is indicated by the words: "*signa autem obsidentis daemonis esse* possunt . . .", and is found already suggested by Benedict XIV in his

and Canon Law insists that exorcisms be performed only by ecclesiastics who are both prudent and wise.[94]

In order to distinguish between psychopathological demonopathy and actual demonic possession, one must recourse to that "discernment of spirits" which the Church has practised throughout the centuries with unexampled spiritual care and a quiet tactfulness.[95] This is the only spiritual measuring rod which can estimate the Satanic potential in those apparent symptoms which would, at first blush, appear to coincide with those of well-known maladies. The same principles are valid, in the reverse, for the accessory phenomena of the mystical state.

It is evident that man's capacity to discern spirits can never attain to the clarity of knowledge possessed by Christ who, in one glance, could discover the presence of an evil spirit concealing itself behind psychological phenomena. Even if an exorcist be endowed with prudence and act with unremitting caution, he is always in danger of mistaking some natural psychological deformity for a case of possession or, on the contrary, of overlooking what is an authentic case of possession. In many of the cases of pseudo-possession of which history gives an account, the regulations of the Church went unobserved, something which afforded the Demon an unhoped for triumph. He has gained far more from the naïveté and vanity of exorcists and from the sickly curiosity of the masses than from the psychic influence of the wretched victims of hysteria

---

De servorum Dei beatificatione et beatorum canonizatione, lib. IV, c. 29, n. 5: "*Thyraeus monet, ex obsessorum signis nonnulla esse certa, nonnulla incerta, nonnulla vero probabilia.*" Also on this subject see: F. Claeys-Boúúaert, article "Exorcisme" and article "Exorciste," *Dict. de Droit Can.*, IV, cc. 668-671 and 671-678; H. R. Philippeau, article "Exorcisme," *Catholicisme*, IV, c. 941-945; F. X. Maquart: "Exorcism and Diabolical Manifestation," *Satan*, pp. 178-203.

[94] *CJC*, n. 1151, par. 2.

[95] The classic work on the subject is still Scaramelli: *Discernimento degli spiriti* (Venice, 1753); French translation, *Le discernement des esprits* (Paris, 1893). See, as well, A. Chollet: article "Discernement," *Dict. de Théol. cath.*, V, cc. 1375-1415; R. Brouillard: article "Discernement des esprits," *Catholicisme*, III, cc. 874-877; J. de Guibert: *The Theology of the Spiritual Life* (New York, 1953), pp. 129-144; J. Guillet, G. Bardy, *inter alia:* article "Discernement des esprits," *Dict. de Spirit.*, IV, cc. 1222-1291; H. Madinger: "Die Unterscheidung der Geister," *Mystische Theologie*, Jahrbuch, 1958, pp. 169-198.

whose mythomaniac and mythoplastic tendencies here displayed themselves.[96]

In order to determine the plausibility of demonic possession, we must, in the final analysis, reply to a question: What interest can the devil have in thus revealing his mastery over man and in making his own activity clear?

According to the doctrine of the discernment of spirits, anxiety, uneasiness, and confusion are Satan's favorite weapons. On the other hand, we know very well that abnormal psychological behavior begets a kind of epidemic, a contagious anxiety which brings in its train dizziness and the paralysis of all resistance. Is it not likely that Satan, in his own chosen time, may make use of these contagious effects to unleash upon his victims and their companions a

[96] On the possibility of clinical discernment between true possession and demonopathy, see J. de Tonquédec: *Les maladies nerveuses ou mentales et les manifestations diaboliques* (Paris, 1938); J. Lhermitte: *True and False Possession* (New York, 1963); ID.: *Mystiques et faux mystiques* (Paris, 1952), pp. 165-224; see also the articles by the same writers in *Satan*, pp. 40-51 and 280-299, and also: J. Vinchon: "Aspects of Possession," *ibid.*, pp. 204-212; V. White: "Devils and Complexes," *God and the Unconscious* (London, 1952), ch. X., pp. 175-189.

The reader will find information upon some of the best-known cases of pseudo-possession in the following works: on the Ursulines of Loudun, H. Bremond: *Histoire littéraire du sentiment religieux en France,* V (Paris, 1920); A. Huxley: *The Devils of Loudun* (London, 1952), summarized in J. Lhermitte: *op. cit.*, pp. 40-46, and in L. Cristiani: *op. cit.*, pp. 116-120. On the role of Père Surin in this affair, see the articles of Olphe-Gaillard, J. de Guibert, E. De Greeff, in *Sainteté et folie,* Études Carmélitaines (1938); and also Gelma: "La psychopathie mélancolique du Père Surin," *Cahiers de Psychiatrie* (1951), n. 1. On Anne de Chantraine, and Jeanne Ferry, see *Satan,* pp. 340-348, and 223-261, respectively; on Marie-Thérèse Noblet, see P. Giscard: *Mystique ou Hystérie* (Paris, 1953), and the articles devoted to her case by Roland-Dalbiez, Achille-Delmas, and J. Lhermitte in *La nuit mystique,* Études Carmélitaines (1938); the controversy stirred up by these articles in *Le risque chrétien,* Études Carmélitaines (1939), pp. 180-194; summary of the case in J. Lhermitte: *op. cit.*, pp. 31-40. On Marthe Brossier, see P. Bruno de Jésus-Marie, O.C.D.: *La belle Acarie* (Paris, 1941), pp. 433-447; J. Lhermitte: *op. cit.*, pp. 46-52. On Magdeleine de la Croix of Cordova (the diabolic Abbess) see M. Garçon: *Magdeleine de la Croix, Abbesse diabolique* (Sorlot, 1939); J. Lhermitte: *op. cit.*, pp. 52-61. On A. Gay, see J. H. Gruninger: *Le possédé qui glorifia la Sainte Vierge* (Lyons, 1954) and J. Lhermitte: *op. cit.*, pp. 102-107. The case of the "convulsionaries of Saint-Médard" will be treated in detail in Part II, chapter III. For bibliographical details on other cases see *Satan,* Études Carmélitaines (1948), pp. 660-664.

demonstration of his power and his seeming invincibility? This tactic may not always be successful. But, under fitting circumstances—when, for example, all Satan's forces are united for an offensive against the Kingdom of God, when a pseudo-religious excitement allows him to stir up a general anti-Christian hysteria—Satan forsakes his anonymous role and, as "the Prince of this world" seduces and threatens distraught souls.

If such be the incursions of Satan, it is only to be expected that the hour of Christ should be, at the same time, the hour of darkness,[97] and that in the great crises in the history of the Church Satan's presence should be keenly felt.

Yet a third form of Satanic influence is possible. This is not brought into play against weak and sinful man, but rather against one in whom grace has succeeded in welding all natural forces in unity to such a degree that the subject no longer seems exposed to ordinary forms of temptation, and this plenitude of grace is conveyed to all who have contact with him. It is a common tradition in the Church, among the Fathers, spiritual masters, and ascetical writers,[98] that in such cases Satan, driven by impotent rage, often reveals himself: he tries, although in vain, by means of *persecution* and agonizing suggestions to snatch such a man away from divine contemplation and to destroy his apostolic zeal through intimidation. That such demonic attacks take the form of bodily and psychical torture is a proof, according to good judges, that the demon has already lost the battle of the spirit.

Nevertheless, Satan is not able directly to cause a physical incapacity or an organic malady. He can never manifest himself without the help of enemies or of men who are already bound to him. It is only by making use of the normal and paranormal means in Nature that he can distress and plague his victims.

Such diabolic persecutions are not essentially different in their

[97] There are some writers who think that cases of diabolic possession are not now as numerous as they were during the time of Our Lord's public life; and they justify this idea by pointing to the significance of the preaching of Christ as a soteriological moment in the history of the world; see, e.g., R. Kugelman and J. de Fraine: article "Diabolical Possession," *Ency. Dict. of the Bible*, c. 567.

[98] See, e.g., *Vita Antonii*, PG, XXVI, c. 849; Evagrius Ponticus: *Antirrhéticos* (Frankenberg's edition), II, 55 (p. 492), IV, 22ff. (p. 504ff.), etc.

manifestations—which are often called demonic haunting—from what we find in ghost stories. All these extravagant doings can be plausibly explained as being due to the subconscious of the interested parties rather than to any real external force. Once again, it is by their context that simple natural phenomena can be distinguished from diabolical undertakings. Not infrequently, such violent doings cluster about important religious occurrences, or choose as their object some saintly character in order to upset his apostolic work. Without attempting to discuss the reality of diabolic interference in the life of the Curé of Ars, we may observe, as does that Saint himself, that the more violent of these manifestations always came before extraordinary conversions, to the extent that the Curé of Ars could predict them by reason of the intensity of the devil's persecution.[99] Also, during the course of the apparitions at Lourdes, an outcry was suddenly heard from confused and savage voices which died away in an anguished wail at a frown from the Lady.[100]

As this chapter comes to its term, the theological portion of the present work has been completed, and I wish to return to the Temptation in the desert in order to express the contrast which obtains between the Christian miracle and its diabolic counterfeit.

When, in the twilight, the stones in the desert seemed to the eyes of the fasting Jesus like loaves of bread, Satan intensified the illusion: he suggested that Christ cause appearance to turn into reality; under the pretext of proving his divine origin, he would be able to satisfy his gnawing hunger. "If Thou art the Son of God, turn these stones into bread." In his reply, Jesus plainly stated the meaning of the Christian miracle: "It is written: man does not live by bread alone, but by every word which comes forth from the mouth of God."

These words of Holy Writ are appreciated in their full force when taken in their context in the Old Testament Book of Deuteronomy.[101] Moses is calling on the people to trust in Yahweh. His speech to them outlines Israel's providential history and dwells es-

[99] On this subject see H. Lunshof: *De duivel in het wondere leven van J. M. Vianney, Pastoor van Ars* (Amsterdam, 1953).

[100] H. Rothoff: *Bernadette*, p. 55.

[101] Deut. VIII, 3.

pecially on the miracle of the manna in the desert: "He gave thee manna for thy food, which neither thou nor thy fathers knew: to show that *not* in bread alone does man live, but in every word that proceeds from the mouth of God." God thus miraculously appeased their bodily hunger, but only in order to arouse a hunger for deliverance and salvation, with confidence that that hunger would likewise be, one day, appeased by him. The manna is regarded by Christians as a figure of the eucharistic bread; and Jesus himself multiplied the loaves to symbolize his Eucharist. From this ancient text, cited by Our Lord to confound the Enemy, there emerges a world of meaning amounting to a splendid definition of the Christian miracle and its salvific value. And it is a definition which cannot be improved upon; for it was given to us by God and made incarnate in his Word.

PART 2

The Apologetics of the Miraculous

INTRODUCTORY NOTE

In the first part of the book we have dealt with the miraculous as seen through the eyes of faith. Analysis of its structure and its function in the Christian economy of salvation has helped to underline its apologetic value. We have said that it serves to prove the credibility of revelation to natural reason not yet enlightened by faith.

It is time now to set aside the light of faith and focus our attention, from a purely apologetic viewpoint, upon the following question: Do miracles really happen, and can we recognize them as divine signs with certainty? Or are they merely mythical expressions of religious emotions and desires, the "favorite children of credulity—*des Glaubens liebstes Kind*," as Goethe calls them?

The purpose of Part Two of this book will be to furnish a satisfactory answer to these questions. Obviously, the data of faith as gathered and presented in the previous chapters may not be called upon here as proofs. At the most we could build on them a working hypothesis, and the point will be precisely to show the actual validity of such a hypothesis.

The outline of our apologetic reasoning will be as follows.

As pointed out previously, if Christianity is what it claims to be, that is, the one true religion revealed by God, then within the fold of this religion the emergence of certain facts called miracles, which we have analyzed in detail, is by no means impossible, but highly probable. On the other hand, if Christianity is nothing more than subjective religious experience, and revelation merely an illusion, the existence of those facts is devoid of meaning and is itself illusory.

Now, in the following chapters we expect to demonstrate by strict reasoning that the existence of a number of facts fitting exactly the description of miracles is a matter of experience beyond any possibility of illusion. All of these facts appear within the religious context of Christianity, more exactly within the fold of the Catholic Church which seems to have a monopoly on them.

If we accept these facts for miracles, that is, if with the Church we recognize their value as divine signs, their explanation immediately becomes obvious and fully satisfactory. If we reject this interpretation, no other satisfactory explanation can possibly be found; in fact, we will not even know along what lines a search for an explanation should be carried on, and the facts will remain absolutely enigmatic and frustrating.

A wise and unbiased mind, faced with the choice between accepting a satisfactory explanation and giving up all hope of solving the riddle, cannot hesitate for one instant. Secure in its moral certitude, it will admit that these facts are truly signs produced by God, hence Christianity as it is professed and lived by the Catholic Church may and should be accepted as the one true religion signified by God through these events.

The argument thus sketched will be developed in the following chapters, the plan of which is already clear.

Chapter One will settle some preliminary questions pertaining to the nature of the facts and the attitude of the man who is to apply to them his critical judgment.

Chapters Two and Three demonstrate the reality and monopoly of "major miracles" in the Catholic Church as opposed to non-Christian religions and to other Christian denominations.

Chapter Four offers proof that no explanation is actually valid outside of interpreting these facts as divine signs, nor can we hope to find even a tentative road toward a different explanation. After examining the full impact of the conclusions resulting from these premises, we shall point out the demonstrative value of the miraculous for Christian revelation as transmitted and offered by the Catholic Church.

1 · PRELIMINARY QUESTIONS

Prior to the actual study of the events themselves two questions must be settled. One concerns the *selecting* of the facts as we present them. Does a miraculous event have apologetical value merely because a man, on the strength of his faith, considers it miraculous? The other concerns the person who *interprets* the facts. Since he is expected to be free of bias, it will be useful, before going any further, to scrutinize the types of attitude that are particularly detrimental to the objective nature of the quest.

I · THE KIND OF MIRACLE SUITED TO APOLOGETICS, OR "MAJOR PRODIGY"

Our theological analysis has shown that a miracle is not only a warrant of the credibility of revelation but also an instance of intimate union between the God-Man and his creature. Hence, not every fact accepted through faith as miraculous will necessarily acquire an apologetic value.

Moreover, theologically, the miraculous never becomes a formal motive of faith. It is one of those external signs whose purpose is to establish an accord between faith and reason. Man's need for these signs and the probative force he desires to find in them vary indefinitely with his disposition, maturity, intellectual level, social conditions, and his readiness to accept the supernatural. As a result, personal recognition of the miraculous nature of an event does not necessarily make such recognition universally binding. Furthermore, a proof may be universally binding and yet not necessarily communicable to all as a rational or apodictic argument. In other words, apologetics as a science does not extend to all of the motives of faith but only to those that have a universal value and may also be expressed as decisive arguments accessible to all.[1]

Those events which faith accepts as miracles will be, therefore, subject to selection. Some miracles are suited for use in apologetics, others are not.

First, we must eliminate those which only *individual experience* can perceive as signs. In the eyes of faith these might very well be true miracles, while having no application in the science of apologetics. Personal faith, in fact, often relies upon spontaneous arguments which, while being incomplete, may nevertheless be effective for a particular person in a particular set of circumstances, making the intimate calling of grace tangible for him and creating a practical obligation of assent. Moreover, many of the arguments faith wishes to lean upon are themselves very personal in nature. However great their objective validity may be otherwise, they are incommunicable by their very nature which includes an element of immediate experience and intuition. Hence they cannot be fitted into a rational outline for the sake of presenting it to others.

What is true of the rational foundations of faith in general is true in particular for the divine signs called miracles. At one time or another in his life, every man has experienced events that revealed to him in a tangible manner the love and providence of God. A sense of modesty makes him to shroud these experiences in silence. Their sharing with others might make their meaning ambiguous, and offered as proofs they might only provoke a somewhat contemptuous refusal. Also, with the passing of time the living context in which these experiences were inscribed will slowly fade and slide into the realm of memory; we ourselves will no longer be sure of their real meaning, although in their original context we

[1] See J. H. Walgrave: "Geloofwaardigheid en apologetica," pp. 23-24.

have recognized them as divine signs with objective certitude amounting to evidence.

An example, often encountered in the lives of saints, might serve here to clarify the point. An honest person incurs heavy debts in his endeavor to do the will of God and serve him. Payment is almost due, and he will need a large sum to meet his obligations, but the chest is empty. The man does not panic; he begins to pray, worried no more than the lilies of the field and the birds of the sky. In full confidence he places the future in the hands of God. A stranger knocks at the door, says a few trivialities and leaves a donation that turns out to be the exact amount needed. No one would construe such an event as an apodictic proof of divine intervention. Chance and coincidence cannot be excluded; circumstances may have alerted the benefactor to the gravity of the situation; who knows but that we have on our hands a phenomenon of suggestion or telepathy? Yet the one who is personally involved is not a fanatic or a dupe if he holds with unmistakable certitude that his explanation is the only true one, for the incommunicable context of the concrete data he experienced compels him to admit that God has spoken.[2]

Similar experiences often occur at the natural level. Although our strongest certitudes cannot be shared, this does not make them less valid. A trite word, seemingly no more than a polite commonplace, may very truly and beyond any romantic fiction communicate to two persons the certitude that their lives are linked forever. A glance that for a bystander has no particular meaning may spell final separation. Likewise, a moment of silence may be a more eloquent proof of the basic insincerity of a person than the best lie detector. The very nature of such certitudes makes it impossible to impart them to others in the form of an argument. At the most one could attest to their existence, or use them as a code to remind others of analogous experiences and intuitions of their own.

[2] Concerning the connection between miracle proper and "providential events" see J. Levie: *Sous les yeux de l'incroyant*, p. 43; C. S. Lewis: *Miracles*, appendix B on "Special Providences," pp. 208-216; J. Guitton: *Jésus* (Paris, 1956), p. 176.

Strictly personal experiences are not the only ones to be useless for an apologetic purpose. Here belong also facts that are outside the ordinary but are, by their very nature, susceptible of two interpretations, natural or supernatural. This *ambivalence* makes them unsuited or less suited for apologetic reasoning, for the criteria upon which a choice between the two interpretations could be based are too subtle and delicate to be incorporated into a rational demonstration binding for all.

We are speaking of phenomena that do not occur exclusively in the religious domain but may have their counterpart in a purely natural psychological or parapsychological context. We find in this class all of the secondary, physical or clinical manifestations of mystical experience: visions, inner voices, levitation, trance and ecstasy; more particularly still, apparitions and stigmata; finally, all manifestation related to parapsychological powers, such as premonitory dreams, mind-reading, prophesying, and the like.[3]

[3] Those wishing to study these problems in greater detail may consult the following publications:

On *paramystical* phenomena: J. Maréchal: *Studies in the Psychology of the Mystics,* transl. Algar Thorold (New York, 1927), sec. 1, "Empirical Science and Religious Psychology" and sec. 2, "Reflections on the Comparative Study of Mysticism"; A. Poulain: *Graces of Interior Prayer,* transl. L. Yorke Smith (London, 1950); J. Bernhart: "Heiligkeit und Krankheit," *Geist und Leben,* 23 (1950), pp. 172-195; G. Wunderle: *Arzt und Mystik* (Würzburg, 1949); H. Thurston: *The Physical Phenomena of Mysticism* (London, 1952) and *Surprising Mystics* (London, 1955); *Limites de l'humain,* Etudes Carmélitaines (1953); H. Thurn: "Aussergewöhnliche religiöse Erfahrungen im Lichte der Psychologie," *Geist und Leben,* 21 (1948), 170-178.

On *private apparitions and revelations:* Eus. Amort: *De revelationibus, visionibus et apparitionibus privatis regulae tutae ex Scriptura, conciliis, SS. Patribus, aliisque optimis auctoribus collectae, explicatae et exemplis illustratae* (Augsburg, 1744); H. Lais: *Eusebius Amort und seine Lehre über die Privatoffenbarungen* (Freiburg i. Br., 1941); K. Rahner: *Visions and Prophecies,* transl. C. Henkey and R. Strachen (New York, 1964); C. M. Staehlin: *Apariciones* (Madrid, 1954); "Les révélations privées," special issue of *Supplément* to *Vie Spirituelle,* 25 (1953), 121-175; E. Stakemeier: "Über Privatoffenbarungen," *Theologie und Glaube,* 44 (1954), 39-50; A. Knockaert: "Verschijningen en private openbaringen," *Bijdragen,* 16 (1955), 53-68; H. M. Schillebeeckx: *Maria, Christus mooiste wonderschepping* (Antwerp, 1954), ch. 3: "Betekenis en waarde van de Mariaverschijningen"; L. Lochet: "Apparitions," *Nouvelle Revue Théologique,* 76 (1954), 949-964, and 1009-1027; ID.: *Apparitions* (Bruges, 1957); E. Dhanis: "Bij de verschijningen en het geheim van Fatima," *Critische Bijdrage* (Bruges, 1945); H. Thurston: *Beauraing and Other Ap-*

All of these may well result from supernatural causes, but are open to a purely natural interpretation as well. It takes a very keen eye to discover which is the case; and most of the time this discernment must be based on criteria borrowed from religious psychology and will not be very convincing to the unbeliever. The Konnersreuth[4] controversy, still being waged among professionals, is a good example of how difficult it is in similar situations to isolate the supernatural completely and prove its authenticity. All of these manifestations are outside the category of apologetic miracles. Significantly, the Church has never accepted them as such.

This point deserves careful attention. In contemporary drama and novel the plot sometimes contains a miracle. Often the purpose is to reject it or make it doubtful, but through ignorance or

---

paritions (London, 1934); Gabriel de Ste-Marie-Madeleine: *Visions et vie mystique* (Paris, 1955); L. E. Halkin: "Les apparitions et la critique historique," *La revue nouvelle* (1956), 113-124; M. J. Congar: "*La crédibilité des révélations privées*," *Supplément* to *Vie Spirituelle*, 53 (Oct. 1937), [27]-[48]; J. Beumer: "Grundsätzliches zur Privatoffenbarung," *Theologie und Glaube*, 48 (1958) 175-185; P. Leitner: "Privatoffenbarungen," *Theol.-prakt. Quartelschrift*, 106 (1958), 209-214; R. Ernst: "Y a-t-il encore des révélations?", *Etudes religieuses*, 734 (Brussels, 1958); H. Lais and L. Monden: article "Erscheinung," *Lexikon für Theologie und Kirche* (1959), III, cc. 1047-1050; L. Volken: *Visions, Revelations and the Church*, transl. E. Gallagher (New York, 1963).

On *stigmatization:* A. Imbert-Gourbeyre: *La stigmatisation, l'extase divine et les miracles de Lourdes* (Paris, 1894): *Douleurs et stigmatisation*, Études Carmélitaines (1936); M. Waldmann: "Stigmatisation," *Lexikon für Theologie und Kirche*, IX, cc. 829-831; G. Wunderle: *Zur Psychologie der Stigmatisation* (Paderborn, 1938); L. Schleyer: *Die Stigmatisation mit den Blutmalen* (Bonn, 1949); W. Schamoni: *Stigmata, Hysterie oder Gnade?* (Wiesbaden, 1951); R. Biot: *L'énigme des stigmatisés* (Paris, 1955); J. Lhermitte: *Mystiques et faux mystiques* (Paris, 1952), pp. 65-130; M. Brändle: "Stigmatisationen, Rätsel oder Wunder?" *Orientierung*, 20 (1956), 31-33. See also our Part Two, ch. 3, p. 283 n. 71, bibliography on metapsychic phenomena.

[4] Among the countless articles, pamphlets and books published for, against, or about Therese Neumann, we call the reader's attention to some of the most recent and thorough studies: P. Siwek: *Une stigmatisée de nos jours* (Paris, 1950), and *The Riddle of Konnersreuth* (London, 1954); H. Graef: *The Case of Therese Neumann* (Cork, 1950); L. Rinser: *Die Wahrheit über Konnersreuth* (Zurich, 1954); J. H. Van der Veldt: "An Evaluation of the Konnersreuth Controversy, *American Ecclesiastical Review*, 128 (1953), 401-420 and 129 (1953), 38-57; L. De Munter: *De strijd om Thérèse Neumann* (Malines, 1956); P. Goemaere: *Thérèse Neumann, Visionnaire? Stigmatisée?* (Paris, 1957).

deliberate policy the choice is invariably restricted to this type of facts. As a result, the whole perspective of the Catholic apologetics of the miraculous is misrepresented.

G. Walschap, e.g., speaks in *Zuster Virgilia* of certain allegedly miraculous facts. Now, none of these would ever be accepted as such by a canonical committee of the Church; in fact, none would even be retained for eventual further inquiry. This is what the writer says through the spiritual director of the monastery: "What is happening to you, Sister Virgilia, is very little compared to what patients in mental hospitals would see every day, or to certain prodigies executed by some Indian fakirs and yogis who do not even have the true faith. I do not wish to discourage you but it is my duty to keep you from giving too much weight to things of this sort." These words, applied to the facts they concern, are words of considerable wisdom, but they could not be the basis of any conclusion whatever concerning the reality and probative force of the Catholic miracle.[5]

The same is true of the miracles vividly described in Sartre's *Le diable et le bon Dieu*, Bernhard Shaw's *Joan of Arc*, and even Cronin's *The Keys of the Kingdom* or Lavery's *The First Legion*. There is in all of these writings a great deal of discussion of the Christian miracles. Abundant as these discussions may be, they are irrelevant, for the facts themselves, whether presented as true or as imaginary, are beside the point, outside the domain of the apologetic miracle. They are, perhaps, interesting in other respects, but they cannot retain our attention as we try to establish our present line of reasoning.

Only those facts will be accepted as having an apologetic application whose extraordinary character suggests *beyond a doubt* a religious signification because identical or similar facts *never* appear in the purely secular domain. The characteristics of "major prodigy" as described by E. Dhanis, from whom we borrow the very expression,[6] are the following. "The ordinary course of natural

[5] G. Walschap: *Zuster Virgilia*[2] (Antwerp, 1958) p. 208; see also the rest of the chapter from which our quotation is taken.

[6] E. Dhanis: "Un chaînon de la preuve du miracle," *Problemi scelti di Teologia contemporanea* (Rome, 1954), pp. 63-86. The passage quoted is on p. 66. It should be made clear that we are speaking of "major miracles" in a

events from which these facts deviate has been observed many times and under a great variety of conditions; no man can recall a deviation of the same type and of comparable magnitude ever having occurred in secular circumstances; the prodigy must take place in a normal setting, that is, one excluding the suspicion that unusual conditions or means might be the cause." In the following we shall use the word "major prodigy" or "major miracle" in the precise sense of events meeting the conditions listed in this paragraph.

What facts, then, are to be included in this category? In what appears an order of increasing importance, we include certain cosmic manifestations; multiplications of matter, such as food or fuel; and finally, raising of the dead and the instantaneous or extremely rapid healing of properly diagnosed organic diseases.

If a raging storm were calmed on the instant, or an empty barn, securely bolted from the outside, were suddenly filled with grain, everyone would readily agree that never in the memory of mankind have such events occurred in a purely secular context. The difficulty arising here is this: these and similar manifestations must be accepted on testimony; outside of a perhaps abundant number of reliable witnesses, no tangible proof of the miraculous event can be offered as a rule. The one who clings to his doubt will always find it possible to challenge even the most dependable witness and thus avoid assenting to the reality of the miracle.

The conditions accompanying an instantaneous healing are altogether different. Characteristically, a disease is subject to every kind of scientific testing, objective diagnosis and measuring. Social progress makes the task even easier by establishing, in ever greater numbers, mutual aid societies, clinics and laboratories. The fact of a sudden miraculous cure does not have to be accepted on human testimony alone, or upon the personal diagnosis of one physician; a host of material, tangible and measurable proofs are normally available, showing the condition of the body both before and after the cure.

For practical purposes, therefore, miraculous cure is the best kind of apologetic proof. This being so, we should determine more

---

sense altogether different from that given by Benedict XIV to the words "prodigium maius."

accurately under what conditions a cure may be placed in the category of "major prodigies." To do this, we must first classify the various diseases according to their degree of incompatibility with instantaneous healing. We hope that our presentation, sketchy and simplified as it is, will nevertheless reflect the discoveries of contemporary medicine in their essential lines.

First, the practitioner recognizes *organic* lesions, when the anatomical or histological integrity of an organ is affected by an internal or external cause (hernia, cancer, toxication, parasites, and the like), or the organ shows a congenital malformation, or again it is in a state of degeneration or gradual disintegration. In any event it will show an anatomical or histological irregularity subject to precise examination. As for the healing of such organic lesions, medical science has established certain constants that vary with the gravity and the nature of the lesion but are statistically invariable when applied to a large number of cases. It has been found, e.g., that at the present state of medication some processes of tissue degeneration are irreversible and therefore incurable, while the healing of some other lesions requires a set time that is invariable or at the most varies only within clearly defined limits.

Other disorders are merely *functional*, resulting not from any physical lesion but from a dynamic disturbance of the functioning of an organ or system.[7] Such troubles are sometimes reactions to a lesion affecting some other organ, but just as often they can be traced to psychological causes and will be called "psychogenic." With the disappearance of the psychological cause the functional disorder will also disappear, and in certain cases this disappearance may take place on the instant. Also, some pseudo-organic hysterical disorders, despite their appearance, are really functional troubles; in these cases symptoms of an organic disease disappear without actual lesion. Pseudoperitonitis, e.g., is very similar to tubercular peritonitis, the symptoms are the same, although no bacilli are

[7] Some authors hold the difference between functional and organic to be one of quantity rather than quality. It must be pointed out, however, that the cases in which a predominantly functional phenomenon would change into an equivalent but predominantly organic phenomenon are extremely rare (such as the transition of a colitis of a mucous membrane into cancer). At any rate, these theoretical discussions in no way invalidate the practical distinction existing between functional and organic.

found and laparotomy will reveal no true inflammation of the peritoneum. Such pseudo-organic disorders stem in actual fact from psychogenic causes; they may disappear suddenly, following a radical change in the psychic contexture.

Finally, a third category of diseases occupies a middle position between functional and organic troubles. Modern medical science calls them *psychosomatic* disorders.[8] As they combine functional disturbance with organic lesion, they may appear in two forms. In some cases we find a psychosomatic situation with the psychic element dominating: psychic tensions, conscious or unconscious conflicts are the direct cause of organic troubles and irritations (called organic neuroses, among which we count a great many types of dermatitis and certain intestinal disorders), or the cause of frequent functional disturbances which eventually induce a deterioration of the organ itself (colitis of mucous membranes, ulcers, certain heart troubles of psychogenic origin). In other cases the dominating factor may be the organic, and we have a somatopsychic situation. As a general rule such diseases will be clearly organic in nature, originating, e.g., with bacillary infection, but the body's resistance to them varies according to the psychic, particularly the emotional, state of the patient. It is common knowledge, e.g., that the course of as clearly an infectious disease as tuberculosis depends to a great extent upon the psychic, especially the emotional, disposition of the patient; these factors either heighten or impair the resistance of the whole body and create an either favorable or unfavorable ground for the disease.

Organic neuroses may disappear in a very short time and without a trace either as a result of radical changes in the psychic contexture, e.g., when the target of the patient's emotive charge is suddenly shifted, or because a subconscious psychic tension is abruptly and totally eliminated. But real organic lesions, if they are incurable, merely become stationary or at best slow down their course,

[8] R. Pierloot: *Problèmes généraux de psychosomatique clinique* (Louvain, 1956); F. Alexander: *Psychosomatic Medicine* (London, 1952). See also a dissertation by L. Forno: *Le Miracle dans la perspective de la Médecine psychosomatique* (Marseille, 1952); J. Sarano: *La guérison* (collection *Que sais-je?* Paris, 1956), ch. 6: "Guérison et miracle," pp. 80-89; M. Sendrail: "Les guérisons inexpliquées," *Médecine et merveilleux* (collection *Convergences*, Paris, 1956), pp. 193-220.

while curable lesions disappear according to the usual laws of organic recovery, within a normal span of time, even if conditions are exceptionally favorable.

As a result, neither psychotherapy nor psychic influence of any other kind ever have an immediate effect upon organic lesions, even if the particular medical case presents some psychogenic components. An outside psychic force may eliminate the conscious or unconscious block erected by the psyche and hindering recovery, in which case it merely puts the patient back into the category of normal subjects and sometimes speeds up his cure considerably. The recovery of the organs themselves will always be slow, gradual, and complex, which is typical of organic restoration in general.

There exists, therefore, a domain where no psychological influence can ever reach: the realm of the organic as such. Official psychotherapy must be resigned to this fact, and so must be all other psychotherapeutic activities aimed at subjects suffering from an organic disease, whether carried on by a healer, a radiaesthetist, or anybody else. After a very thorough study of "healing" an observer[9] has arrived at this conclusion: "So far I have not been able to find a single case in which a demonstrably organic condition would have been cured (or even improved) by a healer, in instances where good medical treatment had failed."

Recovery from a functional disorder, even if instantaneous, will never have an extra-medical meaning, for one could never establish with absolute certainty that the cause was not some psychic experience or shock. On the other hand, the curing of a clearly diagnosed organic lesion considered incurable in contemporary medicine is quite a different matter, as is likewise the curing of an organic lesion, curable but grave, when the healing takes place in such a record time, compared to the normal span, that the recovery can be con-

[9] Dr. L. Rose: *Revue Métapsychique,* n. 29-30. On this problem of "healing," besides M. Oraison: *Médecine et guérisseurs* (previously cited) see especially the following publications: W. H. C. Tenhaeff: *Magnetiseurs, somnambulen en gebedsgenezers* (The Hague, 1951); N. Bayon: *Miracles chez les guérisseurs* (Paris, 1952); L. Beirnaert: "Le problème des guérisseurs," *Médecine et guérison* (Paris, 1955), pp. 179-197; J. Lhermitte: "Miracle et guérisseurs," *Le problème des miracles* (Paris, 1956), pp. 213-232; "Malades et guérisseurs," *Présence* (Revue du monde des malades), special issue (Spring 1955), with extensive bibliography; A. Mellor: *Le problème des guérisseurs* (Paris, 1958).

sidered instantaneous. In cases like these, despite the possible presence of psychogenic components, we can legitimately speak of extra-medical events, never observed in a secular setting. Without a doubt, such cures belong in the category of "major prodigies."[10]

II · ANALYSIS OF PREJUDICES

Do "major miracles" really occur? Not a few of those who hear the question will give to it a negative answer before examining the alleged facts. A priori notions and prejudices prompt them to consider the question already settled. Such preconceptions must be weeded out before we can proceed to a study of the facts.

The reason a man would reject the miraculous out of hand is that he holds it impossible. This impossibility is supported either by a particular philosophical system or some scientific consideration of a more positive nature. Even if our man admits a theoretical possibility he may still deny that historians could establish a strictly reliable witness to the alleged events.

Let us examine one by one the philosophical, scientific and historical prejudices.

An a priori approach in philosophy and natural science would consist in consciously treating a particular sector of human knowledge as an absolute and declaring it to be the only valid one.

Philosophical *rationalism* claims that the human mind is the only criterion of reality. Anything that reason cannot strictly, or at least in some fashion, deduce from its own essence, powers and aspirations, remains worthless and irrelevant as far as man's existence is concerned. Rationalism, therefore, refuses outright to study any reality, or accept any obligation, that does not show an evident "conformity with man." The very idea of a supernatural revelation, that is, the fact that God may communicate realities inaccessible to unaided reason, appears so absurd to a man sealed in his anthropomorphic views that he refuses to pay any attention to it. "I am not going to touch upon the question of revelation and of the miracu-

[10] See the fortunate comparison used by P. Teilhard de Chardin: "Les miracles de Lourdes et les enquêtes canoniques," *Etudes*, 118 (1909), 167-169, to illustrate the difference between organic and functional.

lous," says Renan in the preface of one of his books, "for in independent science that question has been antecedently resolved." [11]

As we have said in the first part of this writing, the miraculous has no meaning at all outside the context of supernatural revelation. Both are rejected a priori by the rationalist to whom any explanation, even the most involved and least coherent, will always be better than the acceptance of a miraculous event as a historical fact. Renan states in the same preface that "the first principle (of independent study of the Gospel) is that the miraculous has no more place in the texture of human destiny than in the succession of natural events; a critical study . . . must proclaim at the outset that everything in history has a human explanation." [12]

Our confutation of the rationalist prejudice will be brief. The relationship of all of us with a personal God, our tending toward him as our final end, is one of the structural laws that constitute the human mind. Why, then, hold it impossible that God would impart new knowledge to this mind oriented toward him, and call it to a new, more intimate friendship; that he would shower his grace upon reason, elevating it and making it capable of seeking and grasping his message?

Assuredly, the believer is aware that revelation transcends the natural powers of man. But that is no reason for him to consider it altogether foreign, for the self-revealing God confers upon the human mind the tremendous capacity of making this transcendence its own. If it is true that when we enter this new relationship with God the whole manner of our human existence and our attitude toward life are transformed, why should we be reluctant to see the miraculous as a symbol of this transformation?

When rationalism is pressed to its logical conclusion it makes man the norm of God and rejects God as the norm of man. Deliberately, or unwittingly, man in the end will declare himself God. "Rationalism, or want of faith, which has in the first place invented a spurious gospel, next looks complacently on its own offspring, and pronounces it to be the very image of that notion of the Divine Providence, according to which it was originally modeled; a

[11] E. Renan: *Etudes d'histoire religieuse* (Paris, 1859), p. XI.
[12] *Ibid.*, p. VII.

procedure, which, besides more serious objections, incurs the logical absurdity of arguing in a circle."[12a]

Modern philosophy has well recovered from this overestimation of human reason, so typical of the nineteenth century. Contemporary thinking follows an almost opposite path. But by practical attitude many a mind is still a prisoner of rationalism, having retained its anthropomorphic mentality. Man or human community have remained the gravitational center; man is absorbed by the immediate and the material and is depersonalized through his contact with a pragmatist society and technical bureaucracy; his readiness for the spiritual and his every chance of paying a however scant attention to the supernatural world are lost. This unconscious rationalist bias puts a man beyond the reach of any proof. The prisoner ought to be set free. Reasoning will not be of as much help in this gradual liberation as will the anxieties and fears arising in a world where man claims to be the regulating power; tragic events of which he is a witness will teach him how weak his shoulders are for carrying burden of divinity.

Similar to the philosophical prejudice and closely related to it in its origin we find the a priori attitude of the positive sciences.

The nineteenth century witnesses some giant forward steps in the sciences of nature. The vision of a scientific universe opens out before the eyes, a vision capable of explaining everything and shedding light into every corner. The champions of positive science acquire a boundless confidence in the value of their methods and techniques; they are convinced that the inevitability of natural events, among which many of them include human conduct and history, may no longer be looked upon as a mere scientific postulate but has become an established scientific fact, the exact replica of natural reality. *Determinism* in the realm of nature is upgraded into a hermetic *conception of the world*, and positive science proclaims itself the only and all-powerful instrument to ensure man's dominion over reality.[13]

[12a] ["The Introduction of Rationalistic Principles into Revealed Religion" in Card. Newman: *Essay Critical and Historical*[8] (London, 1888), I, p. 48.—Transl.]

[13] See M. Pareau: "De l'attribution à la 'méthode' du caractère de 'doctrine'," *Le Spectateur* (1911), pp. 73ff.

The miraculous which Catholic apologists describe as an exception to the laws of nature, a breach in determinism, induced by divine intervention, is rejected emphatically as impossible and contrary to scientific progress. A study of the facts would be a waste of time; there is no miracle because there could and should be none. Marcuse, a physician, wrote in 1912: "The healing of Pierre De Rudder *cannot* be true, for such an event would be a slap in the face of every law of biology and pathology." [14]

The very way in which this prejudice is expressed indicates the best manner of its confutation. Science, in fact, cannot be the foundation of a valid view of the world; it covers a very small and relatively unimportant segment of total reality, human or divine; its method of approach can only reach so far, suited as it is to its particular object and aim but having no grip upon other realities. Duty, art, love, freedom, faith, all of the great values of human existence, are beyond the boundaries of science and elude its methods.

A scientist, hoping to find happiness through conjugal life, does not enter marriage with the scientific certitude of finding what he seeks; when after a day of hard work he sits down to listen to a concert, what holds him spellbound is not the sound frequency modulations; if in the course of his scientific work he decides to try upon his own person some dangerous experiment, or if he declines a blissfully secure but sterile offer in order to continue his personal research in poverty but in freedom, he finds inspiration in something quite else than cold mathematical probability to support his hope for a distant success.

Every realm of human experience calls for a manner of knowing and evaluating that is proper to that realm. If we were to establish a hierarchy of values we would doubtless assign the highest ranks to nonscientific values, for these are the ones that stem from the deepest and most primordial layers of human existence. The best proof of this is the utopian nature of the idea of strictly objective and uncommitted scientific observation. A scientist is a human being before he is a scientist; his position concerning the essential

[14] Dr. J. Marcuse: *Berliner Tageblatt* (Oct. 13, 1912). J. Guitton: *Jésus*, p. 58, quotes from Renan a statement to the same effect: "If there is any truth in the miraculous, my book is nothing but a list of errors."

questions and values of his existence has already been defined; unavoidably, his scientific activity unfolds against the background of these nonscientific decisions and judgments which determine, at least in part, the researcher's field of vision and restrict his thinking, even though he may be unaware of this restriction.[15]

There is only one way of understanding science properly and determining its value: by placing it within the live complexity of the human person. Only from an all-embracing humanistic perspective may an answer be derived to the following question: Is the exceptional, appearing in the miraculous, a shocking irregularity, a grimace that distorts the face of nature, or is it rather the mark of a genius whose inspiration in creating a masterpiece is found in a unity deriving from sources far beyond some superficial uniformity? By placing ourselves in all firmness at the very center of total reality, divine or human, we shall be able to decide whether the scientist who clings to the law of science as the ultimate norm of things behaves like the schoolboy who has just learned the rules of prosody: a spondee he comes across in Virgil makes him reject the poet as a bungler who does not know the first thing about versification.[16]

But why bother to confute this scientific prejudice, at least as it is a systematic postulate? In the wake of its own progress, science has begun in the early nineteen hundreds to achieve a more accurate view of its own methods. Today the postulate of determinism is being very carefully qualified, and science recognizes far more

[15] See, e.g., E. Spranger: "Der Sinn der Voraussetzungslosigkeit in den Geisteswissenschaften," *Sitzungberichte der preuss. Akademie der Wiss., phil.-hist. Klasse* (1929), pp. 6 and 28; J. Maréchal: *Studies in the Psychology of the Mystics*, "Empirical Science and Religious Psychology," pp. 8-11; C. G. Jung: *Seelenprobleme der Gegenwart*[5] (Zurich, 1950), p. 86: "Preconceived ideas will inevitably be present, and because they will, one should not pretend to be free of them." See also J. Peters: "Wetenschap en vooroordeel," *Geloof en Wetenschap* (Utrecht, 1950).

[16] C. S. Lewis, from whom we have borrowed this comparison, says in *Miracles*, p. 116: ". . . there are rules behind the rules, and a unity which is deeper than uniformity. A supreme workman will never break by one note or one syllable or one stroke of the brush the living and inward law of the work he is producing. But he will break without scruple any number of those superficial regularities and orthodoxies which little, unimaginative critics mistake for its laws."

clearly its ineluctable dependence upon prejudice and its limits as merely one of the many branches of human knowledge.[17] In a recent work, W. Heisenberg writes: "The space in which man develops as a spiritual being has more dimensions than the single one which it [life] has occupied during the last centuries." [18]

And yet scientific bias is more persistent than philosophical rationalism. It appears as a mentality, a bent of mind, found not only among scientists but intellectuals and semi-intellectuals in general whom it reaches through the thousand and one channels of popularization. The theoretical possibility of the supernatural and the miraculous is not being denied, but the minds are so completely cast under the powerful spell of the exact methods of science, their habit of thinking and reasoning along those lines is so deeply rooted, that they are impervious to any other kind of certitude. All that is "ascientific" is labeled "a product of emotions, prejudice, education, or psychological predisposition," in other words, lacking all objectivity susceptible of verification. A serious study of the Catholic miracle is not even attempted, for mind and sensibility are totally absorbed by exact science and technology. However credible and serious the information on a miraculous event may be, it clashes against a spontaneous attitude thus expressed by Hume: "When anyone tells me that he saw a dead man restored to life, I immediately consider with myself whether it be more probable that this person should either deceive or be deceived, or that the fact which he relates should really have happened." [19] For Hume and others the problem has been settled long beforehand, not by ex-

[17] See on this matter H. Dolch: *Theologie und Physik.* Der Wandel in der Strukturauffassung naturwissenschaftlicher Erkenntnisse und seine theologische Bedeutung (Freiburg i. Br., 1951); the compatibility of modern physical science with a concept of the miraculous that would not be "*Sinnzerstörend, sondern sinnaufschliessend* (would not confuse but rather help unfold the true meaning)" is discussed on pp. 96-103. See also P. Jordan: *Das Bild der modernen Physik*[2] (Hamburg, 1947), e.g., pp. 61ff.; W. Heisenberg: *Die Physik der Atomkerne* (Braunschweig, 1947); C. F. von Weizsaecker: *Zum Weltbild der Physik* (Leipzig, 1944), pp. 83ff, etc. (*World View of Physics,* transl. M. Green, Chicago, 1952).

[18] W. Heisenberg: *The Physicist's Conception of Nature,* transl. A. J. Pomerans (New York, 1958), p. 31.

[19] D. Hume: *Essay on Miracles,* end of Part One.

plicit reasoning or in bad faith, but by an instinctive preference for the monopoly of science which may not, under any circumstances, yield to the mysticism of a questionable fact.[20]

One could doubtless attempt to crush this frame of mind by an "ad hominem" argument showing that dogmatism, upheld in the name of science, is a very unscientific principle. Science considers its own conclusions provisional and forever subject to revision. Therefore, it views with great respect every new fact, however strange and unexpected. True science will examine every new datum with a sharp critical eye but also with unbiased honesty. The man of science will be on his guard against boundless self-confidence, this professional deformity that would make him a prisoner of his own scientific conquests. On the strength of these considerations and within the strictly scientific domain, we may point out one of the lessons of the history of science: most great discoveries, when first proposed, met with the resistance of outstanding scientists who would a priori stand by an alleged scientific conclusion, rather than listening to the facts. Some men of science seem to display the same kind of attitude when confronted with the miraculous. Their refusal is well summed up in this ironical remark we quote from an Anglican apologist: " 'We know' (that is, 'I and several other people think') 'that such an event as the Resurrection is impossible.' " [21]

In actual fact, however, any "ad hominem" reasoning would

[20] The problem of scientific outlook vs. Christian faith has been in the recent past a major topic of research and discussion. See e.g., G. Söhngen: "Der Geist des Glaubens und der Geist der Wissenschaft," *Die Einheit in der Theologie*, pp. 393-404; P. Tiberghien: "Esprit scientifique et esprit de foi," *La science mène-t-elle à Dieu*, pp. 169-182; K. Rahner: "Wissenschaft als Konfession?" *Wort und Wahrheit*, 9 (1954), 809-819; J. Daniélou: "Foi et mentalité contemporaine," *Etudes*, 283 (1954), pp. 289-301; D. Dubarle: "Spiritualité de la science et spiritualité de la foi," *La vie intellectuelle*, 25 (Oct. 1954), 23-40; (Nov.), 6-28; P. Cremer: "Savant et croyant," *Etudes religieuses*, 707 (Liège, 1955); "Pensée scientifique et foi chrétienne," *Recherches et débats du centre catholique des intellectuels français* (Paris, 1954); P. Teilhard de Chardin: "La mystique de la science," *Etudes*, 238 (1939), 725-742, and *The Phenomenon of Man* (New York, 1959), pp. 283-285 and *passim*; *Geloof en wetenschap*, Levenbeschouwing en levenshouding van de academicus (Utrecht, 1950).

[21] J. V. L. Casserley: *The Retreat from Christianity in the Modern World* (London, 1952), p. 81.

clash against the wall of unconscious prejudices. Fighting this mentality with facts or a long recital of miracles would achieve very little; the very manner of vision ought to be changed. Its victims should be made to realize that they are accepting a great deal unwittingly, and they should be brought to facing their own responsibility. That is what C. S. Lewis attempts to do in a spirited paragraph: "If you have hitherto disbelieved in miracles, it is worth pausing a moment to consider whether this is not chiefly because you thought you had discovered what the story was really about—that atoms, and time and space and economics and politics were the main plot. And is it certain you were right? It is easy to make mistakes in such matters. A friend of mine wrote a play in which the main idea was that the hero had a pathological horror of trees and a mania for cutting them down. But naturally other things came in as well; there was some sort of love story mixed up with it. And the trees killed the man in the end. When my friend had written it, he sent it to an older man to criticize. It came back with the comment, 'Not bad. But I'd cut out those bits of *padding* about the trees.' To be sure, God might be expected to make a better story than my friend. But it is a very *long* story, with a complicated plot; and we are not, perhaps, very attentive readers." [22]

The third kind of prejudice, more widespread than the first two, consists in an invincible skepticism in regard to all miraculous events presented in apologetics. The reason why many find this particular bias so attractive is that apparently it is not based on preconceived ideas but on the very nature of the facts. The miraculous, being extraordinary and unexpected by definition, is beyond the reach of a systematic approach, and more important still, beyond experimentation. E. Le Roy has a valid reason to say that "the miraculous belongs no more in an observatory than in a laboratory." [23] Any certitude we may acquire concerning a miraculous event will essentially be a *historical* certitude, which is simply a convergence of probabilities. How is a fact established as histori-

[22] C. S. Lewis: *Miracles*, pp. 119-120.

[23] E. Le Roy: "Essai sur la notion du miracle," *Annales de philosophie chrétienne*, 153 (1906-1907), 172; on pp. 167-173 he develops a proof of the quasi-impossibility of scientifically establishing a miraculous event.

cally true? Precisely by a convergence of independent testimonies that constitute authority and display the greatest possible diversity of viewpoints and interests on the part of the witnesses; also by the coherence of some particular event with the framework of known and solidly established historical facts. Now, in the case of miraculous events, it is generally impossible to use the argument of convergence. These events are unpredictable, and the witnesses, through confessional preference, mass hysteria or religious exaltation, are too deeply involved in the trial to render reliable evidence. Also, setting the facts against the background of established historical events is a practically impossible task. For the miraculous, more often than not, involves ordinary people who go unnoticed in secular history. From the latter's standpoint the miraculous has no meaning of any kind; it is a marginal phenomenon beyond verification.

To the skeptic the ever recurring miraculous stories seem to be made up of fraud and human fancy; they are the fruits of repression, the spontaneous offspring of the subconscious mind; personal interest is partly responsible for them, together with psychic imbalance and superstition; all of which makes it impossible for us to draw a line of demarcation between "*Wahrheit und Dichtung*." It is definitely wiser to dismiss the whole realm than to risk being entrapped in every single case.

In our attempt to answer this problem we find an excellent takeoff point in an observation by C. S. Lewis. "Most stories about miraculous events are probably false; if it comes to that, most stories about natural events are false. Lies, exaggerations, misunderstandings and hearsay make up perhaps more than half of all that is said and written in the world. We must therefore find a criterion whereby to judge any particular story of the miraculous.[24] These criteria are no different from those used by critical history in establishing the authenticity of a past event, but they will be applied here with a more exacting care, since the research is being carried on in a domain where human fancy is more prone to error that in other areas and where we often encounter the devious manifestations of a primitive religious instinct.

Obviously, the critical researcher will not try, any more than he

[24] C. S. Lewis: *op. cit.*, p. 121.

would in the realm of political or scientific events, to gather his information from stories supplied by oral tradition, news agencies and press reports, or by pious literature more interested in the readers' edification than in historical truth.[25]

On the other hand, we may not reject a reliable witness who is free of prejudice and dishonest intent, any more than we may treat with complete distrust objective data and documents when data of the same kind would be promptly accepted as conclusive historical evidence if they happened to support a secular event. It may well be that a considerable number of Catholic miracles are not suited to this critical method of historical demonstration, but such demonstration may not be declared impossible for every miracle unless in every particular instance proof to this effect has been established with a sharp critical sense, no doubt, but also with great honesty and independence.

Otherwise we would be looking at the facts with the skeptic's bias. "Exceptions to a rule are always irritating," says Pascal. "In fact, we must be severe and reluctant in admitting them. Since, however, exceptions to the rule are certainly known to occur, they must be treated severely but justly." [26]

We hope to have thus answered the preliminary questions; we shall now turn our attention to the events themselves, submitting them to the critical and impartial judgment of the reader.

[25] See on pp. 119-120 of Leuret and Bon, *Modern Miraculous Cures*, a book already quoted, an edifying story concerning the off-handed attitude of a news reporter toward a pseudo-miracle.

[26] B. Pascal: *Pensées* (ed. Brunschvicg), n. 833.

2 · MAJOR MIRACLES IN THE CATHOLIC CHURCH

This chapter, we hope, will provide proof for the existence of major miracles within the fold of the Catholic Church. The witness of Alexis Carrel, a physiologist of world fame at the beginning of the twentieth century, would seem the most appropriate introduction to the chapter. His life and thought were deeply affected by the Catholic miracle, primarily by the miracles of Lourdes.

In 1902 Carrel is thirty years old. The young and brilliant physician, an unbeliever, is about to receive the title of "staff surgeon." That is when the story begins. One of his female patients is suffering of a tuberculous abscess of the loins. Despairing of the case he sends her to Lourdes and the woman returns cured. Shortly after the event several doctors are discussing the case at the dinner table. Carrel reports the complete recovery of his patient. "I am not making any statements," he says, "I am not discussing, interpreting, or supposing anything; I am simply stating the facts. As for the mechanics. . . ." At this point Professor C. interrupts him: "No need to go any further. I feel I have a right to say, Doctor, that with these ideas of yours you do not belong among us. The Lyons Medical School will never open its doors for you." Carrel replies:

"If that is the case, I am leaving. There are enough places where I will be welcome. . . ." This incident accounts for his transfer to the United States where his brilliant achievements at the Rockefeller Institute earned for him the Nobel Prize of Medicine in 1913.[1]

In 1903, the year following the incident, he is once again exposed to the miraculous, now in Lourdes itself. A young woman (tuberculous peritonitis) whom he has personally and carefully examined, arrives in Lourdes, in critical condition. Carrel says to a friend jokingly: "She may die at any moment right under my nose. If such a case as hers were cured, it would indeed be a miracle; I would never doubt again; I would become a monk!" [2] A few hours go by; now he is standing next to his patient and scribbles on his starched shirt cuffs the chronometry of the cure which is achieved in a matter of minutes. A vigorous account of his "Voyage to Lourdes" is published posthumously, fifty years after the event. Many years will go by from the date of this miracle to the time when Carrel draws from it the last conclusions.

From that day, however, the miraculous is uppermost in his thoughts; he is fascinated by it. On several occasions he is confronted again face to face with the miraculous. "I believe in miraculous cures," he writes in an article, "and I shall never forget the impact I felt watching with my own eyes how an enormous cancerous growth on the hand of a worker dissolved and changed into a light scar. I cannot understand, but I can even less doubt what I saw with my own eyes." [3]

R. H. Benson finishes a book on Lourdes in 1914, a few months before his death. He mentions a conversation with Carrel, and quotes him as saying: "No scientific hypothesis up to the present accounts satisfactorily for the phenomena." "Upon his saying this to me," continues Benson, "I breathed the word 'suggestion'; and

[1] The incident as told by one of Carrel's fellow students in *Science et Vie* is quoted by A. Vallet: *Mes Conférences,* pp. 21-22. See also an article by G. Siegmund: "A. Carrel als Zeuge für Lourdes," *Stimmen der Zeit,* 148 (1951), 270-277. Some passages in Carrel's diary, published posthumously, show that as early as in 1896 he was already concerned with the problem of miracles, particularly the events of Lourdes; see A. Carrel: *Jour après jour* (Paris, 1956), pp. 18-20.

[2] A. Carrel: *The Voyage to Lourdes* (New York, 1950), p. 22.

[3] In an article quoted by J. Hartmann: *Lourdes* (Zurich, 1939), p. 206.

his answer was to laugh in my face, and to tell me, practically, that this is the most ludicrous hypothesis of all."[4]

An initial summary and evaluation of Carrel's experiences may be found in his famous book, *Man, the Unknown*:

> In all countries, at all times, people have believed in the existence of miracles, in the more or less rapid healing of the sick at places of pilgrimage, at certain sanctuaries. But after the great impetus of science during the nineteenth century, such belief completely disappeared. It was generally admitted, not only that miracles did not exist, but that they could not exist. As the laws of thermodynamics make perpetual motion impossible, physiological laws oppose miracles. Such is still the attitude of most physiologists and physicians. However, in view of the facts observed in the last fifty years this attitude cannot be sustained. The most important cases of miraculous healing have been recorded by the Medical Bureau of Lourdes. Our present conception of the influence of prayer upon pathological lesions is based upon the observation of patients who have been cured almost instantaneously of various affections, such as peritoneal tuberculosis, cold abscesses, osteitis, suppurating wounds, lupus, cancer, etc. The process of healing changes little from one individual to another. Often, an acute pain. Then a sudden sensation of being cured. In a few seconds, a few minutes, at the most a few hours, wounds are cicatrized, pathological symptoms disappear, appetite returns. Sometimes functional disorders vanish before the anatomical lesions are repaired. The skeletal deformations of Pott's disease, the cancerous glands, may still persist two or three days after the healing of the main lesions. The miracle is chiefly characterized by an extreme acceleration of the processes of organic repair. There is no doubt that the rate of cicatrization of the anatomical defects is much greater than the normal one. The only condition indispensable to the occurrence of the phenomenon is prayer. But there is no need for the patient himself to pray, or even to have any religious faith. It is sufficient that some one around him be in a state of prayer. Such facts are of profound significance.[5]

[4] R. H. Benson: *Lourdes* (London, 1914), preface. See also the excellent article of H. Thurston: "Lourdes," *Hastings' Encyclopaedia of Religion and Ethics*, VIII (Edinburgh, 1916), pp. 148-151.

[5] A. Carrel: *Man, The Unknown* (New York, 1935), pp. 148-149.

At this stage of his personal evolution Carrel is still trying to find an explanation of the "relations, of still unknown nature, between psychological and organic processes." In his booklet on prayer, published in January 1944, he defines his idea a little more precisely: "However strange this may appear, we must consider as true that whosoever asks receives, and that the door is opened to him who knocks. To sum up, everything happens as if God listened to man and answered him." [6] In November 1944, only a few weeks before his death, Carrel finally reaches the end of his long search, recognizes the practical conclusions and receives the sacraments.[7]

We shall now attempt in turn to investigate this series of miraculous events, starting as he did with the events in Lourdes, for that is the shrine where the apparatus for checking the miraculous is the most complete and reliable we could find at the present time. A brief résumé of the history and organization of the Bureau of Medical Findings will be followed by an account of some of the striking cases on record, and by an account of other Christian miracles obtained at certain shrines or through the intercession of the saints.[8]

[6] A. Carrel: *Prayer* (New York, 1948), pp. 44-45. Carrel had written in 1941 an article in English for *Reader's Digest*. The publisher mutilated and modified his text so much that Carrel could not recognize his own ideas and decided to publish the genuine version as a brochure. Passages in his diary show that he had been thinking along these lines since 1927. See A. Carrel: *Jour après jour*, pp. 43, 86, 93, 95. Numerous comments on the Lourdes miracles have been culled from Carrel's letters for the years 1909-40 by J. T. Durkin in his *Hope for Our Time: Alexis Carrel on Man and Society* (New York, 1965), pp. 111-117.

[7] H. Mazerat: article "Carrel" in *Catholicisme*, II, cc. 594-595.

[8] A full bibliography on Lourdes would include about four thousand titles, which means that in this short account a great number of valuable contributions cannot even be mentioned.

On the *apparitions*, two of the older and very important works we would like to call attention to are G. Bertrin: *Lourdes: A History of Its Apparitions and Cures.* Transl. Mrs. Philip Gibbs (London, 1908), and especially L. Cros: *Histoire de N.D. de Lourdes d'après les documents et les témoins*[3] (Paris, 1925-6). Among the most important of the recent works are the six volumes of R. Laurentin: *Lourdes,* Documents authentiques (Paris, 1957-8) and a new edition by M. Olphe-Galliard of documentation gathered by L. M. Cros: *Lourdes 1858,* Témoins de l'évènement (Paris, 1957). The most interesting available information makes up the substance of a number of outstanding biographies of Bernadette, many of which are quite recent. See H. Rothoff: *Berna-*

I • LOURDES: THE APPARATUS OF CONTROL

The religious events that gave birth to the Lourdes miracles are commonly known. Between February 11 and July 16, 1858, only four years after the proclamation of the dogma of the Immaculate

---

dette[2] (Tilburg, 1934); M. de Saint-Pierre: *Bernadette et Lourdes* (Paris, 1953); F. Trochu: *Sainte Bernadette, la voyante de Lourdes* (Lyons, 1954); F. Trochu and L. von Matt: *Bernadette,* Une biographie en images (Paris, 1956); M. Auclair: *Bernadette* (New York, 1958); H. R. Williamson: *The Challenge of Bernadette* (London, 1958). The popular book of F. Werfel: *The Song of Bernadette,* is a fictional rather than strictly historical biography. For the history of the grotto, see J. B. Courtin: *Lourdes, le domaine de N.D. de 1858 à 1947* (Rennes, 1949). R. Laurentin: *Sens de Lourdes* (Paris, 1955) discusses the underlying religious meaning of the Lourdes apparitions. For full documentation see R. Laurentin's many-volumed *Lourdes: Histoire authentique des apparitions* (Paris, 1961ff.).

Accounts of the most important *miracles* are found in a sizable number of books and pamphlets. For the early miracles, the following works must still be consulted: G. Bertrin; *op. cit.;* Dr. Dozous: *La grotte de Lourdes, sa fontaine, ses guérisons* (Paris, 1870; we are quoting from the second edition, 1926); and especially Dr. Boissarie: *Lourdes, histoire médicale, 1858-1891* (Paris, 1891); ID.: *Les grandes guérisons de Lourdes* (Paris, 1900); ID.: *L'oeuvre de Lourdes* (Paris, 1909) [transl. *Heaven's Recent Wonders,* New York, 1909]; ID.: *Lourdes, les guérisons,* 4 series (Paris, 1911-1922). For the more recent cases, our documentation is mostly taken from books published by the successive presidents of the Bureau of Medical Findings, such as A. Vallet: *Mes conférences sur les guérisons miraculeuses de Lourdes* (Paris, 1939; quoted as Vallet I); ID.: *La vérité sur Lourdes et ses guérisons miraculeuses* (Paris, 1944; quoted as Vallet II); R. Le Bec: *Raisons médicales de croire au miracle* (9th ed., completely revised by F. Leuret, Paris, 1950); F. Leuret and H. Bon: *Modern Miraculous Cures* (New York, 1957). See also a publication undertaken by Dr. Leuret but eventually finished and published by P. Miest: *Les 54 miracles de Lourdes au jugement du droit canonique* (Paris, 1958).

Critical discussion of the facts, especially from the medical viewpoint, gave birth to an abundant literature. Let us mention first the numerous doctoral dissertations in medicine on Lourdes; Leuret and Bon, *op. cit.,* pp. 203-204, and A. Deroo (whom we shall quote later), pp. 15-22, give a more or less complete list of these dissertations. Other books on the matter are F. de Grandmaison de Bruno: *Vingt guérisons à Lourdes discutées médicalement* (Paris, 1912); R. Vander Elst: *Vraies et fausses guérisons miraculeuses* (Paris, 1924); "Les guérisons de Lourdes," *Cahiers Laënnec,* 8 (1948), n. 2 and 3 [Transl. in P. Flood (ed.), *New Problems in Medical Ethics,* I (Westminster, Md., 1953), pp. 173-259]; L. Schleyer: *Die Heilungen von Lourdes,* Eine kritische Untersuchung (Bonn, 1949); S. Koster: *Genezing van organische ziekten door gebed* (Amsterdam, 1953); R. Biot: *Lourdes et le miracle,* Dialogues de médecins (Paris, 1958); A. Deroo: *Lourdes, cité des miracles ou marché d'illusions* (Paris, 1956). Among the opponents of Lourdes are, on medical grounds: R. Ferron: *Etudes sur les guérisons dites miraculeuses* (Paris, 1939); H. Roger:

Conception, a poor and somewhat physically retarded little girl, Bernadette Soubirous, sees eighteen consecutive apparitions of a beautiful lady near the Massabielle grotto. On March 25, at the seventeenth apparition, Bernadette asks the beautiful lady her name and is answered in the local dialect: "Que soy era Immaculade Councepsiou." On the way to town where she is to report the answer to the parish priest, she keeps repeating these difficult words; not understanding, she is afraid she might forget them; in fact, to her last day she will have difficulty in pronouncing the words. The event has just happened; as Bernadette gives her report she is interrupted by Mademoiselle Estrade. Bernadette, confused and apprehensive, stops, turns toward the woman and asks her timidly: "Mademoiselle, what does it mean: Immaculade Councepsiou?" [9]

At the February 25 apparition the lady gives Bernadette a strange order: "Drink and wash at the spring, and eat of the grass that you find there." There is no water nearby other than the

---

Les miracles (Paris, 1934); T. and G. Valot: *Lourdes et l'illusion* (Paris, 1956); D. J. West: *Eleven Lourdes Miracles* (London, 1957); on the side of Protestant theology: P. Petit: *Lourdes, les Protestants et la Tradition chrétienne* (Paris, 1958); *Réforme,* Feb. 15, 1958. For further details on the medical controversy see n. 28 below. The following *popularizing literature* ought to be mentioned: J. M. Tauriac: *Miracles à Lourdes* (Paris, 1956); P. Claudel: *Mystère de Lourdes* (Paris, 1958); and especially a remarkable report by an American Protestant woman, R. Cranston: *The Miracle of Lourdes* (New York, 1955). *Lourdes et ses miracles,* a documentary film by Georges Rouquier, also deserves mentioning. Let us finally indicate some of the best *articles* on Lourdes. P. Teilhard de Chardin: "Les miracles de Lourdes et les enquêtes canoniques," *Etudes,* 118 (1909), 161-183; R. Biot: "L'apologétique de Lourdes et les miracles du Christ," *Revue apologétique,* 52, 1931), 432-440; G. Siegmund: "Wunderheilungen im Lichte der modernen Heilkunde," *Stimmen der Zeit,* 148 (1951), 366-374. A number of articles by the same author have been published in a book, G. Siegmund: *Wunder,* Eine Untersuchung über ihren Wirklichkeitswert (Berlin, 1959). *See also* J. J. McGreevy: "The Lourdes Miracles," *Irish Eccl. Record,* 89 (1958), 106-123; M. Olphe-Galliard: "Le fait de Lourdes; son histoire—sa théologie," *Revue d'Ascétique et de Mystique,* 34 (1958), 27-46; a special issue of *La Vie Spirituelle,* 98, Feb. 1958; of *Table Ronde,* May, 1958; both of which were published at the occasion of the centenary of Lourdes. The proceedings of the International Mariological Academy held at Lourdes in 1950 are published in *Maria et Ecclesia,* XIII (1960): *De miraculis et sanctionibus Lourdensibus.*—For a more detailed bibliography, see *Katholiek Archief,* 1958, cc. 73-136.

[9] L. Cros, I, pp. 451-463.

Gave, so Bernadette starts toward that creek. Now, under the eyes of a watchful crowd, she abruptly stops, turns around, listens, and nods that she understands. She takes two steps toward the grotto, stops again, asks a wordless question; finally she bends down and scratches the ground where some muddy water begins to appear; she straightens up, her face covered with mud. The crowd lets out a bewildered cry. Would the poor child have lost her mind? Around noon on the same day, however, passersby discover a rillet flowing toward the Gave. The flow swells by the hour, and toward the evening a real stream is headed toward the river. Soon the water will be led through a pool; by that time the yield is close to 30,000 gallons a day.[10] After a new apparition on March 2, Bernadette again visits the pastor, the Rev. Peyramale, and repeats to him a command of the lady who requests the building of a chapel on the Massabielle rock, adding that "I wish the people to come here in procession."

At the outset every one concerned with the apparitions is distrustful; a flood of skepticism, calumnies and insults swells and hits Lourdes from all over France which refuses to believe. As a result, all of the first witnesses assume a very critical attitude and thus the data collected by them have a great probative value from the very beginning. Long before anybody thought of a bureau of medical findings, three points are submitted to strict critical tests.

First of all, an examination of *Bernadette* herself. The family physician, Dr. Dozous, an unbeliever who goes to church only for funerals, accompanies Bernadette to the grotto on February 20. In his own words, he is entertaining "the hope to destroy in the name of science this whole childish fabrication of a sickly, mystical mind." All through the apparition he keeps his finger on the radial artery of the child's arm, and later reports that "the pulse was quiet and regular, breathing was easy; there was in the girl no indication whatever of nervous overexcitement acting in any particular way upon the body." [11] Two days later, Monsieur Estrade, a Lourdes tax collector and leading citizen, decides to visit the grotto. On the way he is still joking about the visions. On the return trip he seems

[10] L. Cros, I, pp. 255-288; G. Bertrin, pp. 25-27; M. de Saint-Pierre, pp. 63-65.

[11] L. Cros, I, pp. 187-188; G. Bertrin, p. 19; M. de Saint-Pierre, p. 50.

completely changed. He and Doctor Dozous are asked: "You did not see anything, did you?" The answer is simple and leaves no doubt: "Oh yes, I saw Bernadette's face." [12] Finally, on March 25, the chief administrator of the department of Tarbes, Baron Massy, has Bernadette examined by three psychiatrists in the hope of finding a reason to commit her to an institution. The three practitioners, Balancie, Lacrampe and Peyrus, examine the girl at length; in their conclusion they attribute the apparitions to what they call an "ecstatic state," while stating that otherwise Bernadette is sound of mind and her good faith is beyond doubt.[13]

In the meantime a series of new events demand the attention of Doctor Dozous; he starts a new investigation. Ever since the new spring began to flow, rumors of extraordinary *cures* are being spread. A quarrier by the name of Louis Bouriette lost his vision of the right eye twenty years ago when a stone fragment lodged in it at an explosion in the quarry. In the morning of February 26 he asks his daughter to bring him water from the new spring. He bathes his bad eye. The following day he meets Doctor Dozous who had been treating him and shouts: I am cured. The physician shrugs his shoulder, scribbles a few words on a piece of paper, covers the man's left eye with the palm of his hand and tells him to read the note with the right eye. The quarrier reads without hesitation: "Bouriette is suffering of an incurable amaurosis; he cannot see and will never see again." [14] Dozous is deeply upset by the case and within a few days begins an examination of all of those miraculously cured. He calls on Professor Verges of the Montpellier Medical School. On July 28 Bishop Laurence of Tarbes establishes a commission with Professor Vergès as chairman and Doctor Dozous, Professor Chrétien of Montpellier and Doctor Bermond, a surgeon from Bordeaux, as members. The commission will study well over a hundred cases, finally retaining eight as being medically

[12] M. de Saint-Pierre, p. 62; see also L. Cros, I, pp. 228-229; and a report by M. Estrade in *Univers*, Aug. 28, 1858.

[13] L. Cros, I, pp. 464-472; G. Bertrin, p. 37; F. Leuret and H. Bon, p. 99. F. de Grandmaison de Bruno published two articles in *Revue pratique d'Apologétique*, 16 (1913): "Bernadette Soubirous n'était pas une hystérique," 33-52, and "Bernadette Soubirous n'était pas hallucinée," 321-338.

[14] Dr. Dozous, *op. cit.*, p. 108-118; Leuret and Bon, pp. 94-96. See a critical discussion of this cure in L. Schleyer, p. 147.

unexplainable. Seven of these the bishop proclaims as miraculous.[15]

In a third study the *water of the spring* is tested. The Lourdes town council, interested in the cures, attributes them to the healing qualities of the water and entertains the hope of turning Lourdes into a famous spa. Professor Filhol of Toulouse analyzes the water and on August 7, 1958, submits a detailed report with the following conclusion: "This water contains no active ingredients that would lend it special therapeutic properties. It is safe to drink." [16]

However, no permanent system of control will be established until 1882, despite the commotion caused in 1863 by a publication entitled *L'histoire de Notre-Dame de Lourdes,* by Henri Lasserre, a newspaper columnist personally cured at Lourdes. In 1882 Doctor Dunot de Saint-Maclou organizes a "Bureau de Constatations Médicales" [Bureau of Medical Findings, B.M.F.]. This office, first located in wooden barracks, proposes to gather serious and critical material permitting a competent handling of all cases of miraculous cure. From 1891 the Bureau is headed by Doctor Boissarie, de Saint-Maclou's assistant since 1886. In the same year of 1891 he publishes a "Medical History of Lourdes" which awakens a lively interest in the medical community and draws a great number of physicians to Lourdes. By the time of his death in June 1917, Boissarie, the great Boissarie, has put the seal of his powerful personality upon the activities of the B.M.F. His successors, Le Bec, Marchand, Vallet, and other physicians, who carry on his work, will remain faithful to his methods.

The B.M.F. welcomes any physician, regardless of nationality or philosophical opinions, to participate in its activities. Cases brought to its attention are tested twice. The first test concerns the existence of the disease and the alleged cure; the second seeks to determine whether the cure is extramedical or not. Until quite recently patients were not examined at their arrival in Lourdes. The Bureau requested, studied, and eventually completed the medical history of a patient only if the latter claimed to be cured.

The subject of an alleged miraculous cure is examined on the

[15] G. Bertrin, pp. 77-82.
[16] See the full text of the report in Vallet II, pp. 175-179.

spot and any physician who cares to do so may participate in the examination. The preliminary records of the case are signed by all participating physicians one of whom is assigned the task of completing the record a year later when the patient is requested to return to Lourdes. Since 1925 an "Association Médicale Internationale de Notre-Dame de Lourdes," established by Doctor Vallet, facilitates regular checking and the completion of case histories at the patients' own place of residence. Members of the Association, which is a truly international body, take care without charge of all analyses, laboratory work and photographic documentation.[17] The patient is requested to return to Lourdes after a year; his history is reopened and studied again; the physicians present may ask any questions, raise any objections, or reexamine the patient. The main purpose now is to determine whether the cure was permanent, without reoccurrence of any kind. The B.M.F. sometimes postpones its final statement a year or two, upon the request of a participating physician. If, however, the facts themselves are established beyond a doubt, the Bureau proceeds to the discussion of the second point: Is the cure, now a matter of record, susceptible of a natural explanation?[18]

The B.M.F. makes no statement concerning the miraculous or non-miraculous nature of a cure. In this domain the only competent agency will be a canonical commission appointed specially and separately for each case by the authorities of the Church. Cures that the B.M.F. finds beyond medical explanation are far from being automatically accepted as miraculous by the Church. Between 1938 and 1948, e.g., the B.M.F. found twelve extramedical cases. By the end of 1949 only four of these have been eventually declared miraculous by the various commissions.[19]

The whole manner in which this checking is handled excludes any deliberate fraud and confutes in advance any charge of partiality or preconceived opinion concerning the cures. As all unbiased

[17] See Vallet II, pp. 45-48.

[18] On the procedures of the Bureau of Medical Findings, see Vallet II, pp. 42-45; Leuret and Bon, pp. 147-152. On the history of the Bureau, see F. Boissarie de l'Epine: *Lourdes, médicine et guérisons* (Paris, 1952); A. Valette: *Le grand inconnu du Centenaire de Lourdes: Le Bureau des Constatations Médicales* (Paris, 1958).

[19] Cf. R. Le Bec, p. xix in the introduction by F. Leuret.

researchers will agree the material gathered by the B.M.F. may be accepted without reservation as being entirely honest and excluding all possibility of doubt. The question remains, however, whether the material thus gathered has been in every case sufficiently complete and decisive, allowing us to draw an absolutely clear picture of the history of the disease and the cure. The reason why doubt may remain in this respect is the fact that for many years the scientific equipment of the Bureau was inadequate by the standards of a constantly progressing medical science. In the absence of previous examinations any subsequent inquiry had to be based upon fragmented, vague, and insufficiently verified indications supplied by practitioners; there was always a possibility of the diagnosis being wrong or at least doubtful. The practitioner, in fact, does not make of his patient an object of scientific study; he wishes to make him well. His examination will be conditioned by this practical intention. And since the Bureau lacked the proper technical equipment, it was unable to make on the spot the necessary scientific diagnoses which in many cases would have dispelled any doubt concerning the extramedical nature of a cure.

> A description of the B.M.F. by Doctor Leuret is worth reading: There was one room where all the activities of the medical staff took place: examination of the sick, medical conferences and, when the necessity arose, announcement of the findings of investigations. There were no facilities for technical investigations, no proper examination couch and when a patient was to be examined it was necessary to stretch him out on the table at which the secretary was writing and on which the case notes were piled. No facilities for a reliable scientific examination existed either, no X-ray apparatus, only the simplest auscultatory equipment.[20]

There is a point in the witty remark by E. Le Roy who called the B.M.F. "an agency not for the studying but the policing of miracles." [21]

We do possess exhaustive and conclusive proofs concerning many older cases, but these were established not so much through

[20] Leuret and Bon, p. 104.

[21] E. Le Roy: "Essai sur la notion du miracle," *Annales de philosophie chrétienne*, 153 (1906-1907), 171.

the organizational and operational methods of the B.M.F. as through the experience, incredible industry and professional competency of Boissarie and his colleagues.

It was, therefore, a welcome decision on the part of Bishop Théas of Lourdes to call upon Doctor Leuret (died in 1954) for a thorough reorganization of the Lourdes medical office in 1947. The agency of control is henceforth called the Medical Bureau of Lourdes (M.B.L.). The former premises now house a museum, the archives, and a first aid station. The "Bureau of Scientific Studies" (B.S.S.) provides far more adequate space for a library, X-ray laboratory, examination room and the basic equipment for endoscopy, ophthalmology, otorhinolaryngology, microscopes for biopsy, electrocardiograph, and so forth.

Space and equipment now make prior examinations feasible. By 1959 the files contained the records of 3,000 patients. In 1949 a three-year-old girl from Birmingham, England, was cured of infantile cerebral diplegia; she had been examined at the Bureau three days before the cure.[22]

At the same time a "National Medical Committee" is established, to act as a liaison between the Medical Bureau and the canonical commissions appointed by the bishop for the purpose of making pronouncements concerning the miraculous nature of cures. This agency is soon enlarged into an "International Medical Committee." In the future, the Medical Bureau may not forward a case file to the canonical commission before the properly scientific aspects of the case are reviewed and approved by the International Committee which meets once a year. The Committee is made up of distinguished specialists associated with the various medical schools of France; a number of specialists from the major European countries assist them in their task.[23]

The following figures will help to evaluate the significance of this agency of control. In 1948 some 15,800 patients visited Lourdes; in 1949, 20,000; in 1950, 30,000; and in 1958, 50,000. On October 15,

[22] Leuret-Bon, pp. 104-111 (cf. French edition [Paris, 1950], pp. 114-126, 206).

[23] See, e.g., in Leuret-Bon, p. 103, a list of members of the National Medical Commission as of 1950. More recent listings of the membership are given in A. Deroo, pp. 212-213 and P. Miest, pp. 258-260. Dr. A. Olivieri became chairman in 1960, suceeding Dr. J. Pellissier.

1949 the Medical Bureau registers the 25,000th physician participating in its activities since the beginning; 750 physicians are registered in 1947; in 1948, the number is 1,000; in 1950, 1,400; and in 1957, 1,453.[24] The long list contains the names of physicians of every description: unbelievers, Protestants, Masons, Jews, Moslems, Buddhists, Confucianists, Eastern Orthodox, etc. In 1947 we find among them 47 university professors from London, Glasgow, Dublin, Liège, Padua, Geneva, Lyons, Paris, Lille, etc., representing all of the major fields of specialization.[25]

As for the cases, a first selection in 1946 retains 26 files; in the following year, 14 of these files are reexamined but only four pass the second trial. Corresponding figures for 1947: 75, 11 and 6; for 1948: 83, 15 and 9.[26] Out of the 1,047 cases studied by the B.M.F. between 1918 and 1956, 216 are retained and 831 rejected. All other factors being equal, the percentage of cures is approximately the same for males and females but is considerably higher for children.[27]

II • LOURDES: THE EVENTS

It is an obvious impossibility to present in a few pages a complete report on the medical aspects of the Lourdes cures, even limiting the report to the most outstanding cases. We must be satisfied with a few typical examples. Each category will be followed by a list of similar cases with the pertinent references for the benefit of the reader who might wish to consult them at his leisure. Unfortunately, no full scale comparative study encompassing all of the cases, based on primary sources of information and conducted from a strictly medico-critical viewpoint, has been published so far, although several worthy attempts have been made.[28] We will turn for

[24] Leuret-Bon, pp. 103 and 107; Le Bec, p. xiii, note.

[25] Leuret-Bon, p. 107.

[26] *Ibid.*, p. 151.

[27] Leuret-Bon, French ed., p. 205, based on statistical data from 1920 to 1950. P. Miest, p. 30, gives precise figures for 1953: 156,342 female users of the pool as compared with 53,500 males. Of the 54 miracles accepted by the end of 1957, eight concern children (three boys and five girls). These data answer the criticism of L. Schleyer, *op. cit.*, pp. 191-192 (see following note).

[28] Only three of the recent publications undertake a comprehensive study

information to those authors who present the records in a more or less complete manner and whose indications will be mutually enlightening. In making this necessary choice we shall disregard as

---

of the Lourdes facts. There are first the two special issues of *Cahiers Laënnec*, 8 (1948, nos. 3 and 4) [E.T. in Flood, *op. cit.*, above, n. 8], which contain a series of lectures delivered at the Société Saint-Luc du Sud-Est and a conclusion by Dr. Béhague; then a book by L. Schleyer: *Die Heilungen von Lourdes*, Eine kritische Untersuchung (Bonn, 1949); finally a doctoral dissertation by T. Valot: *Lourdes et l'illusion en thérapeutique* (Paris, 1956). All three writings follow a policy of classifying the cases according to the medical specialty they pertain to. Their qualities are widely different, but none of the three works seems to fulfill what one might expect from a truly comprehensive scientific study of the problems of Lourdes.

The essays published in the two issues of *Cahiers Laënnec* were written during the Second World War when the Lourdes archives were not accessible. They are thus based on very incomplete material gathered at random, which the authors themselves admit quite freely (see Flood, pp. 174, 177, 227, etc.)

Schleyer's book, on the other hand, has the appearance of a complete critical study and contains a great number of valuable observations, especially from the strictly medical viewpoint. In actual fact, however, it has some serious deficiencies which rule out its acceptance as a final and satisfactory critical study. The main deficiencies are the following:

1) Schleyer undertook his work during the war and was thus barred, like his French colleagues, from the original files. He never went to Lourdes and had no contact with the physician members of the Bureau of Medical Findings. His exclusive source is previously published material treated most of the time in an apologetic manner and meant for the general public, not for specialists. Furthermore, this literature is often content with a very summary rendering of the original information. Thus Schleyer did not always have a way of checking whether missing elements were contained or not in the files, and in case of doubt he could not consult the original sources. In several instances he throws out or questions cases because of insufficient data or the alleged absence of conclusive evidence. As it happens, this evidence is quoted by more recent authors, sometimes with ample detail. (See, e.g., the Traynor case, pp. 108-110, excluded because of the absence of any sure data on the disappearance of the epileptic attacks. Now, these data are listed explicitly in Le Bec, pp. 149-154, and Vallet II, pp. 98-108. Also the case of Lydia Le Hérice, p. 172, which Schleyer puts in the category of "Hysterical Reactions." He is forced to modify his verdict while correcting the proofs, because in the meantime he has discovered additional data on the case in Vallet II, pp. 222ff. Also the Decreton case, p. 61—he is not familiar with the name—, the data on which are available in Le Bec, pp. 179ff., even though very incomplete, especially the data on verification. Again, the case of Abbé Fiamma, p. 128—he does not know this name either—, a clear-cut case which Schleyer discards without a verdict, apparently because of the absence of sufficient historical data; see Le Bec, p. 197ff.)

2) Although the book was published in 1949, it deals only with cases prior to 1936 (and not 1944, as the author seems to suggest). Assuredly, some

much as possible the elements of personal evaluation by the diagnostician in case, which always remain controversial. Of the older cases we shall retain only those that could be diagnosed unmistaka-

---

more recent cases are mentioned in an appendix, but they do not enter the critical and statistical discussions in the body of the book. Thus the majority of the cases studied by Schleyer go back to a time when the technical means of verification were less refined than today and the subjective elements weighed more heavily in the medical diagnosis.

3) The third and perhaps most significant deficiency of Schleyer's book is an all-too-evident lack of delicacy of judgment, a quality no one can afford to lack in dealing with such a sensitive subject. Professor Renon's rule: "A physician has no right to question the diagnosis of a colleague if he himself did not examine the patient either before or after the cure," was altogether ignored by Schleyer, not only in the material sense, which was inevitable, but also as a basic attitude, which is an even more dangerous mistake. W. Schamoni has some valid reasons to write to G. Siegmund, *art. cit.*, note 2: "It is routine procedure with Schleyer to point out the abstract possibility of a natural explanation which is excluded by the concrete explanation derived from the diagnosis in case. Elements that do not suit him are treated casually and are often underestimated. In this manner he is left with many question marks which prompt him to conclude that this or that 'could not possibly' be true." By a simple "unwahrscheinlich," in fact, he often disposes summarily of a diagnosis explicitly supported not only by the family doctor but by outstanding specialists, although he himself has never seen or examined the patient. Now, no one claims that diagnoses are infallible, and in several cases Schleyer is perfectly justified in discounting some vague and largely unsupported conclusions by overzealous doctors. But he pushes casualness a little too far, as in the Vion-Dury case, p. 157 (see the conclusions of Dr. Merlin in Flood, *op. cit.*, pp. 186-187); the reader is invited to compare his summary and opinion of the cure of Gilbert Clot (3 years), p. 82, with the detailed report of the family doctor quoted by Vallet I, pp. 65-69; or to see how he treats the case of Marie Baillie, apparently not suspecting that he is criticizing a diagnosis by A. Carrel (see *Voyage to Lourdes*, pp. 24, 36ff.) and indulging in patently gratuitous suppositions. We might also point out that several cases in which Schleyer criticizes the diagnosis of a colleague have turned out to be quite valid through analogy with other, more recent cases of the same kind, in which the diagnosis was supported by objective laboratory tests.

4) All of this shows that his conclusions quite often are mere extrapolations from his basic material. Thus, e.g., he quotes in absolute numbers the proportion of men and women among the subjects of miracles, but forgets to compare this with their proportion among the total number of Lourdes pilgrims. Also, he finds—and eagerly points out—an abundance of "psychogenic" patterns in the majority of miraculous cases, but fails to ask if these alleged patterns are anything more than normal accompanying symptoms of a chronic organic disease which has a depressing and weakening effect on the psyche and thus accounts for the symptoms indirectly. If the number of cures attributed to psychogenic causes were as great as Schleyer claims, the percentage of cases recognized as medically unexplainable by the Bureau of Medical Findings should

bly through the medical means available at the time, or whose nature is such as to exclude all uncertainty. As for the more recent cases, we shall select the ones the diagnosis of which is based on objective proof established through technical means.

---

have been constantly diminishing with the progressive refinement of modern laboratory techniques utilized in diagnostics; but the fact is that the proportions have remained fairly stable through the last few decades (see Vallet II, p. 59.). The facts contradict even more manifestly another statement by Schleyer (p. 191) to the effect that there is an increasing lack of variety in the types of diseases cured in Lourdes. He insists, e.g., that during the years his research is concerned with, that is, the period after the death of Boissarie, there has been no mention of a single case of cancer, a single case pertaining to otorhinolaryngology, a single cure of an eye disease, etc. As it happens, however, *all* of these instances turn up again in the Lourdes literature dealing with more recent cases. Moreover, Schleyer expresses surprise in his conclusion that among all the Lourdes cases there is not a single cure of a circulatory disease (e.g., he says, arteriosclerosis) or heart disease, but he overlooks the fact that he himself has mentioned in his introduction, and quoted again in an appendix as cases he did not intend to utilize in his appraisal although they had been accepted by the Bureau of Medical Findings for 1937, one case of coronary sclerosis and one of malignant myocarditis, the two exact diseases whose "total" absence from the Lourdes files he finds so surprising.

The recently published work of G. and T. Valot: *Lourdes et l'illusion en thérapeutique* (Paris, 1956) is a doctoral dissertation presented at the medical school of the University of Paris, with introduction by G. Valot, husband of the author and himself a physician. The dissertation claims to be a strictly scientific study, but in actual fact it is no more than a propaganda pamphlet which completely and arbitrarily neglects all firsthand information and is full of inaccuracies, mutilated quotations and unsupported insinuations. These deficiencies are demonstrated in detail by A. Deroo: *Lourdes, cité des miracles ou marché d'illusions* (Paris, 1956). The following statement, repeated twice by the authors (pp. 10 and 105): "There were no archives kept, no documentation in Lourdes," is enough for anyone even vaguely familiar with the Lourdes files to conclude that the book has no scientific value whatever. For all the reports of the Bureau of Medical Findings since 1888 are on file; from 1913 the files contain all documentation and factual evidence; since 1947 the reports of the International Committee are added. Any physician, believer or unbeliever, is welcome to consult and study the files. A scientific study of Lourdes conducted in complete ignorance of this material is a contradiction.

Finally, a few words ought to be said about Dr. D. J. West: *Eleven Lourdes Miracles* (London, 1957), which does not claim to cover all of the Lourdes facts but concentrates in detail on eleven more recent cases, not dealt with by Schleyer. The author's information concerning these eleven cases is generally accurate and complete. The manner, however, in which he uses this information in discussing the facts, betrays such a high degree of apriorism and carelessness that one often finds it hard to suppose in him the good faith which he is so eager to question in others. At any rate, what we said of Schleyer applies even more to West. Moreover, the introductory and con-

Our account of the illnesses and their cures will be made in a style of almost telegraphic brevity. Such style, while favoring both concision and completeness, should also help us in presenting the data objectively and in a manner free of the kind of apologetic romanticism and rhetorical effects that so often mars apologetic treatments of miraculous events.

We begin with three cases of recovery from cancer. The first is an early case; the second occurred thirty-six years ago, and the third is recent.

1. René CLÉMÉNT, 80, retired gendarme domiciled at Anglet (province of Basses-Pyrénées). Epithelioma of the face located at the right nasolabial groove. Treated by Doctor Gentilhe. Two years of treatment followed in 1907 by surgery by Doctor Moynac of Bayonne. Another two years go by when in 1909 a recurrence is found on the scar left by the surgery. Rapid growth of the tumor. In 1912 Doctor Gentilhe finds "a thriving, protruding tumor almost the size of an egg, with a base almost 4 centimeters long. It extends from the bridge of the nose and the lower eyelid, which is pulled downward, to the upper lip, which is stretched upward and is itself attacked. The nostril is obstructed on this side and the tear duct is closed." The patient refuses to submit to a second operation because the first one was too painful. At the beginning of 1913 he is reexamined by Doctor Moynac who now rules out an operation because of the man's age and the advanced stage of the disease. Clement's daughters suggest a trip to Lourdes. Upon his refusal they start a novena, also applying Lourdes water to the daily changes of dressing. On the morning of the second day of the novena, three weeks after the last medical examination, one of the daughters notices upon returning from Mass that the dressing is no longer tight. She removes it; the tumor has disappeared; no pus or

---

cluding chapters are very poorly documented and appear to have been largely copied from Valot. One cannot help to feel that their only purpose is to present the eleven cases to previously prejudiced and skeptical readers. See our review of West's book in *Bijdragen*, 18 (1957), 428-429, and an article by A. Deroo: "Les miracles de Lourdes; Observations sur les problèmes posés par le livre du Dr. D. J. West: Eleven Lourdes Miracles," *La Tour Saint Jacques*, nos. 11-12, pp. 248-261. See *ibid.*, nos. 13-14, pp. 202-205, a reply by Dr. West and further by A. Deroo.

gangrenous secretion is found on the dressing. The patient was unaware of the cure which must have occurred in his sleep. The following day Doctor Gentilhe finds that the tumor has disappeared except for a clearly defined mass on the upper lip, the size of a hazelnut. This mass also disappears in another twenty-four hours. "The skin is as healthy and flexible on the side where the tumor has been as on the side that had not been affected." The nasal passage is completely free, and so is the tear duct. Only the surgery scar is visible. His findings are corroborated by Doctor Moynac who examines the patient two weeks later, and by Doctor Pineau who examines him a little less than a year later, in August, 1913. Several subsequent examinations by Doctor Gentilhe show no recurrence.[29]

2. Elisabeth DELOT, 49, teacher, Boulogne-sur-Mer. In November, 1924, she is examined by the school physician, Doctor Wallois, for the first time. She complains of abdominal disturbances: pain after meals, loss of appetite, loss of weight. Diagnosis: hyperchlorhydria. Treatment ineffective. In December, X-rays reveal "an enlarged, sagging stomach; slow digestion; no indication of ulcer or tumor." Tonics cause no return of appetite; constant pain unrelieved by the application of a corset; weight loss of 13 kilograms [28.6 pounds] between October, 1924 and August, 1925. From then on, tarry stools, daily vomiting. In November, 1925 X-rayed by Doctor Cherfils of Boulogne: "Clearly defined dark area on the lesser curvature of the stomach. By the end of the day still no bismuth enters the duodenum." On November 28, 1925 surgery by Doctor Houzel at the Boulogne hospital; he finds "cancer of the pylorus, susceptible of immobilization," performs only gastroenterostomy (linking the intestine with an unaffected area of the stomach). The patient improves temporarily; no vomiting, weight gain, but still no appetite. Three months later, recurrence with vomiting. Doctor Wallois finds in April, 1926 "a large mass integrated

[29] A. Olivieri, "Difficultés contre le caractère extra-naturel des guérisons de Lourdes," *Maria et Ecclesia*, 13, (1960), pp. 247-270. Also see Le Bec, pp. 160-165. Pp. 163-165 discuss a differential diagnosis; L. Schleyer with all his critical attitude is satisfied with this brief comment on the case: "Little could be said in opposition to some extramedical process (*Gegen einen extramedikalen Vorgang lässt sich wenig éinbringen*)" (p. 143). He is, incidentally, mistaken about the date of the event which is 1913 and not 1912.

with the old surgical scar," also "the liver protrudes 2 to 3 centimeters beyond the floating ribs and shows nodulation typical of cancerous metastasis." Diagnosis: secondary cancer of the liver. In July, all nutrition stops; patient does not tolerate even water.

On July 30 Mademoiselle Delot arrives at Lourdes with the diocesan pilgrimage of Arras. She is so completely exhausted that she is taken to the pool before registering at the Shelter. Terrible pains while bathing; burning, grinding sensations in the stomach, the liver, and the intestines, as if "I were held under a pile hammer." Upon leaving the pool, sensation of well-being and health. She is able to dress without aid; violent sensation of hunger. Tolerates soup and mash; normal stool.

Examination at the B.M.F. on August 1. X-rayed on August 20 and 21 by Doctor Cherfils: "Atonic stomach, very much elongated; strong ptosis of the transverse colon. Slight delay in stomachic evacuation." Otherwise all is normal. "The tests conducted today do not allow to conclude to the presence of gastroenterostomy." On August 26, examination by Doctor Wallois: nutrition is normal; result of auscultation completely negative. On February 14, 1927 Doctor Houzel's findings are the same. New examination at the B.M.F. on August 2, 1927: gain of 9 kilograms, perfect health. The former patient writes in 1936: "Since that day of July 30, 1926, ten years ago, I have completely forgotten what stomach pain means. I can digest anything." Her weight is between 87 and 89 kilograms [between 191 and 196 pounds] (at her arrival in Lourdes she weighed 60 kilograms [132 pounds]).

The objection has been raised that it is normal for a still existing gastroenterostomy not to appear on X-ray, for a section of the small intestines was sacrificed in the operation and thus could not fill with barium. But an observation made by the radiologist in case contradicts this supposition: "the peristaltic wave runs through the entire length of the large curvature without interruption, and palpation dissociates the gastric wall completely from any neighboring intestinal ansa; not a drop of barium passes through anywhere but the pylorus."

Mademoiselle Delot consented to autopsy and the biopsy of the stomach wall. Circumstances of her death, however, made an autopsy impossible: she was killed in 1944 in an aerial bombardment at Boulogne-sur-Mer. She had never suffered a recurrence of cancer.[30]

3. Rose MARTIN, 45, born in Nice. In November, 1945 symptoms of cancer of the cervix (metrorrhagia, menorrhagia; at vaginal palpation: hardening of the cervix which bleeds at the slightest touch). Surgery on February 19, 1946, by Doctor Fay of the Pasteur Hospital in Nice: extended hysterectomy; anatomopathological test of the excised tumor; cylindrical glandular epithelioma of the cervix. Postoperative complication: rupture. Second operation on October 4, 1946: repair of the wall and radical cure of a parietal fistula caused by an infected hair root. On April 25, 1947, new examination following gastric disturbances; no stool without enema; the stool contains fetid fragments; extreme rectal pains radiating into the lower limbs. Rectal examination reveals "a tumor the size of a tangerine, located on the anterior wall at the junction of the rectum with the sigmoid. Tumor palpable at abdominal examination." General condition extremely poor: bedridden for months; advanced cachexia; abundant and fetid vaginal discharge. Diagnosis: metastasis to the rectum. The surgeon decides that a biopsy would serve no purpose, which is regrettable for our case. Condition of patient critical; morphine injections four times a day (8 centigrams) to relieve the terrible pains in the rectum.

On June 30, 1947 arrival in Lourdes; total cachexia, constant subcomatose state, numerous camphor injections. After a third bath in the pool (July 3), the patient who for months had been unable to stand asks to be bathed without a stretcher frame. In the evening she stands up unaided, drags herself to the toilet where for the first time she has a normal stool without enema. There is no discharge of pus or any other gathering, either at this time or in the following; the pain has disappeared; ravenous appetite.

Return to Nice, examination by Doctor Fay: not only have the

[30] Vallet II, pp. 139-144; L. Schleyer, pp. 90-91; Flood, *op. cit.*, pp. 218-220. The different viewpoints entering the discussion of the radiological data are listed in Schleyer, *loc. cit.*, and Flood, pp. 223-224. The absolutely gratuitous theory of Valot, p. 65 (adopted by West, p. 113) according to which Dr. Houzel committed an error in saying that he had performed a gastro-enterostomy on Mlle Delot, is too easy a way out and only serves to show the embarrassment this case has caused among the opponents of Lourdes.—The circumstances of Mlle Delot's death are described in detail in A. Deroo, *loc. cit.*, p. 123.

functional troubles disappeared, but so did the very rectal tumor. No pains, daily stool, no vaginal discharge, appetite better than normal. Morphine withdrawal achieved in a short time; in January 1948 the drug is no longer needed. The patient is examined regularly for a year. She gains 17 kilograms [37 pounds] in ten months, despite hard work as housekeeper. On March 10, 1948, barium enema; vagina is normal and flexible. On July 6, 1948, a year after the cure, reexamination at the B.M.F.: condition excellent, gained 25 kilograms [55 pounds]. Rectoscopy by Doctor Leuret, chairman: rectum is perfectly normal. On February 4, 1949, examination by Doctor Fay: perfect health.

The National Medical Committee, acting upon a report by Doctor Merlin, states the extramedical nature of the cure. Bishop Rémond of Nice proclaims the case as miraculous on May 3, 1949.[31]

Readers seeking information on other cures of cancerous diseases in Lourdes will find the case of Catherine LAPEYRE interesting. At 50 years of age, after recurrence of cancer of the tongue, she is cured without any medication on July 22, 1889, the last day of a novena to Our Lady of Lourdes; she merely rinses her mouth with Lourdes water. There are in her file photographs taken at the time of her first cancer, and after the cure.[32] Another interesting case is that of Constance PIQUET, 42, cancer of the breast, cured at the third bathing in the pool on August 24, 1893.[33]

There are many cures of tubercular patients, doubtless because this infirmity allows a trip to Lourdes more generally than other diseases. It has always been at the top of the percentage list of chronic cases registered at Lourdes.[34] We are quoting here three

[31] Leuret-Bon, pp. 138-140; P. Miest, 172-176.

[32] R. Le Bec, pp. 165-168; photographs on page facing p. 117; see also F. de Grandmaison, pp. 171-172; L. Schleyer, p. 130.

[33] G. Boissarie: *Les grandes guérisons de Lourdes*, pp. 153-158; F. de Grandmaison, pp. 173-178; L. Schleyer, p. 130.

[34] Schleyer, p. 190, who tendentiously emphasizes the high percentage of tubercular patients among those cured in Lourdes, does not reckon with these data. Yet he could have read in Vallet II, p. 12, that the majority of the sick who visit Lourdes belong to those definite categories of chronic patients which are more easily approached by the various "Lourdes Committees" and other religious organizations. In all probability the percentage of tubercular patients is substantially the same among all the visitors as among those cured. Since

typical cures, adding some references for an eventual study of other interesting cases.

1. Paulette MARGERIE, 22 years of age, Aix-en-Provence. Raised in poverty and want. A sister has died of meningitis; a small brother has died very young of unknown causes. As for the patient herself, from the age of a few months: serious enteritis, measles, whooping cough, bronchitis, conjunctivitis. At 5 years of age: typhoid fever followed by chronic enteritis; the child is a mere "small walking corpse." Living in Marseilles at the age of 7, she has pains in the vertebrae; examination at La Conception hospital, complete rest. From 7 to 14 she never leaves the house; lack of hygiene and care; undernourished. A court orders her removal from home "because of insufficient care"; hospitalized in Aix. Treated for enteritis and general condition of health; in 1925 surgery by Doctor Latil for inguinal hernia. Stay at the La Rose preventorium, Marseilles, from August, 1925 to April, 1926; general condition extremely weak. After this rest she works as a maid for a few months in Aix. In August, 1926, readmitted to the Aix hospital; violent vertebral pains; put in cast (Doctor Guillomon). In April, 1927 sent back to preventorium for convalescence; cast removed, but complete immobility, sunbathing, cutaneous cauterization. In April, 1928 return to the Aix hospital; enteritis, treated by Doctor Martin for a month. Works for a month, then relapses; examining Doctor Charpin finds a pronounced edema of the right knee. His statement: "clinically, every sign points to bacillary infection, but I have no facilities for X-ray or bacteriological testing." On November 8, 1928, patient enters the Santa Maria hospital in Cannes. Prognosis improves; but in May, 1929 double bronchitis sets in with high temperatures. Diagnosis: bacillosis, which cannot be confirmed, however, since there is no expectoration. X-rays after recovery from the bronchitis show normal lungs.

Then suddenly, at the beginning of July, 1929, shivering, accompanied by symptoms of a meningitic attack. Kernig's signs very strong; clonus; pupillary contraction; strong photophobia; rapid pulse, temperature 38.8 C. [102 F.]. Lumbar tap and L.C.R. test

---

antibiotics have dramatically reduced the cases of tuberculosis, the incidence of their cure in Lourdes has also been reduced. In recent years only a very few isolated instances have been mentioned.

by Doctor Maubert, on July 3. Results: 150 lymphocites per cubic millimeter; glucose 0.69 grams per L (the normal being 0.24 mg %); albumin 0.40 grams per L; culture negative; Gram-negative, but Ziehl positive, and in the whole preparation five medium homogeneous type Koch's bacilli are found. Diagnosis: tubercular meningitis with normal course. Treatment: ice applied to abdomen; syntholic vaporization on skull, forehead, nape, spine. Day and night, violent headaches, delirium, vomiting, hallucinations, muscular contractions in neck and thighs, jaws locked. Extreme unction on July 25. Around noon July 27, 1929, terrible attack: convulsions, screaming. Calmed with morphine. In the afternoon, patient is unconscious or at the most semiconscious. Immobility, amaurosis. At 11 P.M. the end seems near; eyes staring, face livid, rattle. Prayers of the dying.

At this moment the attending nurse picks up a jar filled with Lourdes water; pours a few drops in the open mouth of the dying patient; the latter suddenly sits up in the bed, shakes her head violently while her body is shaking with convulsions. She reaches for a small picture of Our Lady of Lourdes that the sisters had placed there the same morning; she gets out of bed, kisses the picture, lies down again and asks for more water; then she takes a glass of milk with some crackers. The next day she gets up and dresses unaided, goes to Mass. Weight: 43 kilograms [95 pounds]. "From then on she follows the common routine."

Doctors Castelnau and Bertrand examine her and provisionally conclude to a state of perfect health: "All I can discover is a somewhat strong knee reflex and some dilatation of the pupils which otherwise contract at light." On August 5 (nine days after the cure) spinal tap by Doctor Coeurderoy; L.C.R. is "absolutely clear and transparent without a trace of pathological elements." Paulette Margerie comes to Lourdes on August 21 on a pilgrimage of thanksgiving and is examined by the B.M.F. Apart from a mild mydriasis no neurological anomaly is found. Weight 48.5 kilograms [107 pounds]. Another examination on August 22, 1930; the 25 physicians present declare her perfectly healthy.[35]

2. Charles McDONALD, 31, carpenter, Dublin. Childhood

[35] Vallet I, pp. 41-59; L. Schleyer, p. 80; presentation and detailed discussion of the case by Dr. Béhague in Flood, *op. cit.*, pp. 203-210.

normal; no tuberculosis in family. Married at 19; has three healthy children. In October, 1924 he begins to feel tired and nervous, perspires at night, coughs. Examining Doctor Young (Dublin) finds Koch's bacilli in the expectoration; X-rays reveal tuberculosis of the lungs. Six weeks in a sanitarium, then hospitalized in Dublin. Spits blood twice. By June, 1925 he has lost 16 kilograms. Despite medical advice he travels to South Africa, leaving on July 3, 1925. He seems well from 1926 to 1931. In January, 1931, after a hard soccer game, he feels pain in the hips and the nape. Soon steady pain sets in at the back (lumbar region) and the sides, especially when getting on a bicycle. X-rays in October, 1931 reveal tubercular infection of the twelfth vertebra. Metal corset, which he takes off for daily sunbathing. By December, 1931 very little progress; doctors suggest bone graft; patient refuses and returns to Ireland; discards the corset which he finds uncomfortable. By March, 1932 incapacitated for work because of constant pains in his sides and the lumbar region. Three months of rest at home. In June, 1932 examining Doctor Lane (Dublin) finds tuberculosis of the spine and refers the patient to Doctor Lynch (Dublin) to determine whether the condition of the lungs permits surgery. Doctor Lynch is against the operation because of the alarming state of the lungs. The patient begins to use the corset again. In September, 1932 large abscesses appear in the lumbar region and on the left shoulder. The one on the shoulder is aspirated, but the one in the loins must be excised because the pus is too thick. By the summer of 1933 the fistulas suppurate abundantly. General condition stationary. In June, 1933 sudden downward turn; violent vomiting followed by fainting; a week later edema covers the entire body. Diagnosis by Doctor O'Connell (Dublin): acute nephritis. 13 weeks at the Meath clinic. Urinalysis: blood, albumine, pus. Pains necessitate frequent sedation. In November, 1935 Doctor Boxwell wishes to place him in a hospital for the incurably ill; the patient refuses and goes home instead. In June, 1936 Doctor O'Connell states that there is nothing he can do for him. The patient has been bedridden for 15 months.

On September 5, 1936, the patient arrives at Lourdes, carried on a stretcher. He shows a certificate by Doctor O'Connell: Pott's disease of the third thoracic vertebra; nephritis; tubercular arthritis of the left shoulder. All of these are confirmed by 15 X-ray pictures taken at the Meath clinic. Disease is in full course when this testimony is given. Doctor Hannigan, physician accompanying the group of pilgrims to Lourdes, examines him during the trip; three fistulas on the left shoulder and two at the lumbar region, all of them suppurating; symptoms of tubercular infection of the urinary tract. "I have personally cleaned the abscesses during the trip. On the way over they all suppurated abundantly."

Morning of September 6: first bath; shivering at leaving the water; no improvement. On the 7th, second bath; euphoria upon leaving. The next day the patient gets up and dresses unaided. Taken to the grotto on wheelchair. On September 9, third bath; he enters and leaves the pool unassisted; dresses alone. Leaves Lourdes during the night of September 9 to 10; is not examined at the B.M.F. because the improvement is believed to be merely functional. During the Paris stopover, however, the nurses who change the bandages find all of the abscesses cicatrized, except one fistula at the lumbar region which still shows a light serous emission. Conditions ascertained immediately; examination by Doctor Hannigan. Reexamination at the B.M.F. on September 17 and 18, 1937. Chairman of the examining committee is Dr. Smiley Blanton of the Rockefeller Institute of New York. Results: all wounds completely cicatrized; on the left side, convex scoliosis of the thorax; normal movement of vertebral column; ankylosis of left shoulder. X-rays: head of humerus and of articular cavity have completely disappeared. Conclusion: unequivocal signs of the previous existence and complete disappearance of tubercular infection of the left shoulder, the spine and the kidneys. In 1954 the patient was still in perfect health.[36]

3. Jeanne FRETEL, 34, nurse, from Rennes. Always of frail health. Childhood: measles, scarlet fever, diphtheria. In January, 1938: appendicitis, surgery. In August she returns to the clinic; intestinal pains, abdomen inflated, hard and doughy to the touch. Treatment with ultraviolet rays cause some improvement. In Janu-

[36] Vallet II, pp. 267-277; L. Schleyer, p. 187; R. Cranston, pp. 67-74. Dr. Smiley Blanton presented a report on this case at a joint meeting of the American Psychoanalytic and American Psychiatric Associations. The subject himself gave an account of his illness and cure: C. McDonald: *Miracle at Lourdes* (Dublin, 1953).

ary, 1939 Doctor Maruelle operates to remove a tubercular cyst of the ovaries with adhesions; cut heals rapidly. In September, pains start again and increase gradually. On March 18 patient returns to the Hôtel-Dieu hospital in Rennes. Diagnosis: tubercular peritonitis. Laparotomy results merely in causing a stercoral fistula which is finally closed at the fifth attempt (November, 1944). Abdomen remains inflated and hard. In January, 1946 patient enters the Pessac sanitarium (Gironde); in April she is transferred to La Benne-Océan (Landes). On July 16, operation for suppuration attributed to osteitis of the upper jaw; she loses her teeth except for three in the upper and six in the lower jaw. General condition worse. On December 3 she is transferred to the Pontchaillou hospital where she receives the last rites for the second time. She has been bedridden for a year. Average daily temperature: about 39,5 C. [103 F.] in the morning and 36,5 C. [97 F.] in the evening; pains in the abdomen which is doughy to the touch and resounds loudly at percussion; 6 centigrams of morphine per day. In April, 1948 streptomycin is administered for 25 days by Doctor Pellé; pains subside but vomiting (often tarry) continues. Fever first diminishes, but soon rises again to 40 C. [104 F.] mornings and 36 C. [97 F.] evenings (file contains 18 monthly temperature charts). Patient weakens between August and October; tolerates only some liquid. Symptoms of meningitis; stools mixed with much pus; frequent heart failures endanger her life. On September 29 she receives, for the third time, the last rites.

On October 4 she arrives in Lourdes. Critical state of cachexia. Patient is not even conscious of being in Lourdes. On October 5, bathing in the pool causes no improvement. On October 8, after the Mass of the sick, she is placed, dying, at the foot of the altar of St. Bernadette. The priest hesitates to give her communion because of repeated vomitings; he only gives her a fragment. The following is a part of her statement made to the canonical commission: "That is when I suddenly began to feel very well and became aware of being in Lourdes. Asked how I felt I said that I felt very well. My abdomen was still hard and inflated, but I had no pains. I was given a cup of coffee with milk which I drank eagerly and kept. After the Mass I was taken to the grotto, still on a stretcher. A few minutes after I got there I felt as if someone had reached under my arms to help me sit up. I found myself sitting. I turned around to see who could have helped me, but I saw nobody. Sitting down immediately I again felt as if the same hands that had helped me to sit up took my hands and placed them on my abdomen. I was at first wondering what was happening to me, whether I was cured or merely awakening from a dream. I noticed that my abdomen had become normal. Then I felt extremely hungry." Upon returning to the hospital, she eats with great appetite; gets up in the afternoon, dresses unaided, returns to the pool and takes a bath standing up and without any difficulty. In the evening she eats again with good appetite; wakes up at 11 P.M., complaining of hunger; eats again and goes back to sleep.

The next day five physicians examine her at the B.S.S. Waist size reduced from 1 meter to 0.70 meter [from 40 to 30 inches]; abdomen normal and soft; no pain at all at palpation. Apart from some muscular atrophy everything is normal. Travels home by train, standing up during almost the entire trip. Morphine is withdrawn without any adjustment or disintoxication. Immediately upon her return to Rennes examining Doctor Pelle declares her complete recovery. Gains 14 kilograms [31 pounds] between October 9 and 25 (during the first eight days, 1,350 kilograms a day); after that, weight remains stationary. She begins to work immediately, getting up at 5:30 A.M. and retiring at 11:30 P.M. No fever on any day (files contain 12 temperature charts after the cure). Excellent appetite and sleep. A year later, on October 5, 1949, second examination at the B.S.S. The record is signed by 28 physicians and concludes to a case of extramedical cure. Cardinal Rogues, archbishop of Rennes, declares the cure miraculous on November 20, 1950.[37]

[37] G. Siegmund: "Wunderheilungen im Lichte modernen Heilkunde," *Stimmen der Zeit*, 148 (1951), 366-374; P. Miest, pp. 185-193. With D. J. West, p. 89ff., we may regret that no bacteriological tests have been performed, for they could have reinforced the theoretical certitude of the diagnosis in this case. We agree emphatically, however, with the physicians in charge who are non-Catholics, with the physicians of the Bureau of Medical Findings and with B. G. Sandhurst: *Miracles Still Happen*, pp. 52-53, that the absence of bacteriological data does in no way weaken the conclusions of a prolonged clinical examination performed by specialists in very favorable circumstances created by repeated surgery. Incidentally, none of the substitute diagnoses suggested by West accounts for all the clinical symptoms. As for the supposition

Other cases of various forms of tuberculosis could also be quoted. Marie BAILLIE, 22 (the Marie Ferrand of Carrel's *Voyage to Lourdes*), cured in 1902 of tubercular peritonitis; Aurélie HUPRELLE, 27, cured instantly in 1895 of pulmonary tuberculosis in its last stage; Amélie HÉBERT, 42, cured suddenly in 1900 of cavernous pulmonary tuberculosis; Amata ALOPPÉ, 38, cured in 1909 of five suppurating fistulas originating from tuberculous gums; Jeanne TULASNE, 20, cured suddenly in 1897, also of Pott's disease of the dorso-lumbar region with gibbus; Emilie CAILLEUX, 26, cured instantly in 1921 of a Pott's gibbus of the ninth thoracic vertebra; Marie BOREL, 27, cured in 1907 of six stercoral fistulas of tubercular origin; Lydia BROSSE, 41, sudden cure in 1930 of a recidivous abscess and repeated phlegmons of the buttock region and the lower part of the abdominal wall; Louise JAMAIN, 23, sudden cure in 1937 of tuberculosis of the lungs, intestines and peritoneum; Odette RIVIÈRE, 27, sudden cure in 1936 of progressive ileocecal tuberculosis.[38]

Some cures of blind persons have a distinguished place in the annals of Lourdes, first because of the absolutely incurable nature

---

he is trying to smuggle in through the back door at the end of his commentary: "Or simply gross hysteria?", this is so far beyond the limits of the most elementary probability that it only serves to demonstrate the author's aprioristic attitude.

[38] On Marie Baillie, see A. Carrel: *The Voyage to Lourdes*; L. Schleyer, pp. 59-60; on Aurélie Huprelle, see G. Boissarie: *Les grandes guérisons de Lourdes*, pp. 67ff.; L. Schleyer, p. 20; on Amélie Hébert, see G. Boissarie: *L'oeuvre de Lourdes*, p. 292; L. Schleyer, pp. 21-22; R. Le Bec, pp. 192-196; on Aimée Allopé, see J. Rumeau: *Jugement canonique sur le cas de Mlle Allopé* (Paris); L. Schleyer, p. 64; P. Miest, pp. 126-130; on Jeanne Tulasne, see G. Bertrin: *Un miracle contemporain* (Paris, 1910); F. de Grandmaison, pp. 197-200; L. Schleyer, p. 39; P. Miest, pp. 48-50; on Emilie Cailleux, see P. Goret: *Une observation médicale presque en forme d'expérience, faite à Lourdes en 1920-1921 par un ancien interne des Hôpitaux de Paris* (Paris, 1922); L. Schleyer, pp. 41-42; on Marie Borel, see G. Boissarie: *L'oeuvre de Lourdes*, pp. 233-245 (with photographs); R. Le Bec, pp. 188-189 (photographs); F. de Grandmaison, pp. 97-110; L. Schleyer, pp. 63-64; P. Miest, pp. 141-145; on Lydia Brosse, see Vallet I, pp. 132-137; Vallet II, pp. 201-207; L. Schleyer, p. 144; on Louise Jamain, see Vallet II, pp. 108-122; L. Schleyer, p. 188, P. Miest, p. 198-200; on Odette Rivière, see Vallet II, pp. 251-266; L. Schleyer, pp. 187-188.

of their forms of blindness, and secondly because of the anomaly observed in the process of recovery: functional recovery precedes the organic. We list here some of the most typical cases.

1. Marie BIRÉ, 42, from Saint-Gemme. Precarious health since 1904; much disturbed by the death of two of her children and afraid of losing a third. In February, 1908, according to the testimony of Doctor Hibert of Luçon, her condition suddenly worsens; following an emesis of red blood, violent headaches that make her scream; afterwards, abundant and frequent vomitings with greenish contents. Five days in coma; on February 25 patient is completely blind as a result of pupillary atrophy. For several months physicians try to eradicate the disease. In July there is a new crisis. The patient who lives in Vendée insists on going to Lourdes over the opposition of her family which is afraid that she would not survive the trip. On August 3 she is transferred to Luçon and from there leaves for Lourdes; the trip is very painful. After arriving in Lourdes on August 4 she assists at the benediction of the Blessed Sacrament and at the following prayers, but is exhausted and must be carried back to the hospital. Has a bad night; long period of unconsciousness which seems to herald the worst. In the morning of August 5, Mass and communion at the grotto, followed by an unsuccessful attempt at bathing at the pool: too many visitors. At 10:15 she is carried back to the grotto on a stretcher; the last Mass is over and the Blessed Sacrament is being taken back to the basilica of the Rosary. As the priest passes by her, Madame Biré sits up and whispers: "Oh, I see the Blessed Virgin." She faints and falls back in her carriage; a trickle of blood appears at the corner of her mouth. She regains consciousness and sees perfectly.

In the afternoon, examination at the B.M.F. in the presence of a large number of physicians, among them Boissarie and Doctor Lainey, a well-known ophthalmologist from Rouen. The latter, at his great surprise, finds the following: "Right eye: white nacreous pupil; almost imperceptible central veins, the rest of the bottom of the eye is normal. Left eye: white nacreous pupil, center veins very small, although about twice the size of those in the right eye; still they are about one third of the normal size. Madame Biré suffers of white atrophy of the pupils, cerebral in origin. All authors consider this disease absolutely incurable." Thus the organic lesion remained, and yet Madame Biré sees; she can read the smallest print in the newspaper; distant vision is also perfect. The next day she is examined again at the B.M.F. Condition the same; further checking and extensive tests put the whole problem in a fresh light, for now it appears altogether insoluble. Another examination in the afternoon, with the same results. On August 7 and 8 no change is observed in the condition of the eyes. General condition is rapidly improving. A month later Madame Biré is at Poitiers; Doctor Lainey, Doctor Creuzy of Poitiers, and Doctor Rubbrecht of Bruges examine her. Doctor Rubbrecht's report: "We found no trace of the atrophy of the optical nerve mentioned by Doctor Lainey. The pupil of both eyes is of a healthy rosy color; blood veins are of normal size. Pupil reacts adequately to light and accommodation. In other words, everything is normal." From the organic standpoint Madame Biré is now "entitled to see." A year later she is reexamined at the B.M.F.: "Madame Biré returns in perfect health; gained 52 pounds; vision excellent . . . bottom of eye normal, vision perfect." Doctor Vallet testifies that he saw Madame Biré again in Lourdes, in 1933; her eyes were in good condition, and her vision at that time was normal for a 69-year-old woman. The bishop of Luçon declares in 1910 that the cure was miraculous in nature.[39]

[39] Vallet II, 150-156; L. Schleyer, p. 152; P. Miest, pp. 123-126. The critical remarks on this case by J. Lhermitte: *Le problème des miracles,* pp. 101-102, contradict the data on file and seem to indicate a lack of information on the part of the author.

Let us quote as a counterexample a recent case rejected by the authorities of the Church. The subject is Gérard Baillie, four and a half years, Saint-Pol-sur-Mer. At the age of three he is stricken with choroiditis and bilateral optical atrophy as a result of general anesthesia induced for surgery. With his right eye he can count his fingers at a distance of 20 inches, whereas the vision in the left eye is reduced to the perception of light only. He visits Lourdes after a two-year treatment in an institute for the young blind in Arras where he has been admitted on the basis of a statement by Dr. Biziaut, an ophthalmologist: "Bilateral optical atrophy. *Incurable blindness*" (underlined by Dr. Biziaut). The same diagnosis is added to his file by D. Viton, an Arras ophthalmologist who examined him during his stay at the institution. The patient arrives in Lourdes on September 26, 1947. He is examined by several physicians who concur in the same diagnosis. On the fourth day he visits the Stations of the Cross with his mother who must lead him by the hand. At the fourth station the child suddenly exclaims: "Mommy, you have a pretty dress." He now sees as if through keyholes, without peripheral vision

Other interesting cures of blind persons: François VION-DURY, 30, soldier, cured instantly (like a rifle shot) of bilateral retinal detachment; little François PASCAL, 4, of Beaucaire, cured in 1938 of quadriplegia and total blindness resulting from an aseptic lymphocytic meningitis.[40]

In conclusion we quote a few cases from other sectors of the medical domain, referring those interested to the numerous cases they could find in a great many different fields of medical specialization.

---

or perception of perspective. The next day he is jumping from bed to bed in the dormitory. He is taken to Dr. Camps, a Tarbes ophthalmologist; on the way he is commenting on all the things he sees. Diagnosis: "Bilateral chorioretinitis with bilateral optical atrophy; he cannot and must not see." Leaves Lourdes the following day. Transfers from the Arras institution to a regular school for normal children; he walks three kilometers every day, crossing several heavily traveled main highways. He can read the blackboard, follows the classes without trouble and his notebooks are properly kept. He is examined in July and again in September, 1948, in Glasgow, by the ophthalmologist Dr. Smith among others. Diagnosis: "Bilateral chorioretinitis. He should not see." Files are sent to the National Medical Committee which orders further tests by specialists. The patient is examined by Dr. Lescaut, an ophthalmologist at the Hôpitaux de Lille. Conclusion of this latest examination in 1949: "There seems to be no doubt that Gérard Baillie had in the past a bilateral chorioretinitis with bilateral optical atrophy. He no longer suffers from this disease. Now, I have never seen a case of recovery from chorioretinitis with optical atrophy." Vision, however, is only 0.2 and 0.3. The canonical commission did not accept the case as miraculous because the blindness was not complete, the recovery was not complete, and the possibility of psychic influences in the cure (suggested by Dr. Deloge of Nice and M. Krudewig, a psychologist) is not excluded absolutely beyond doubt. The commission, however, does not deny that "God has answered the prayers of mother and child and this grace was obtained through the all-powerful intercession of Our Lady of Lourdes." Literature on the case: Leuret-Bon, pp. 152-156; A. Deroo, pp. 167-170. Psychological explanations offered by M. Krudewig: "Die Wunderheilung des Knaben G. Baillie im Lichte neueren Wahrnehmungstheorie," *Jahrbuch für Psychologie und Psychotherapie* (1953), pp. 321-330; rebuttal by G. Siegmund: "Zu der in Lourdes erfolgten Heilung des blinden Knaben G. Baillie," *Stimmen der Zeit*, 156 (1955), pp. 151-152, reprinted in *Jahrbuch f. Psych. und Psychoth* (1955), p. 305.

[40] On Vion-Dury, see Flood, *op. cit.*, pp. 186-187; L. Schleyer, p. 157; the case was presented by Dr. Dor at the May 1, 1893 meeting of the Société française d'Ophthalmologie, *Annales d'Ocul.*, 109 (1893), 419. On Francis Pascal, see Leuret-Bon, pp. 123-124 (French ed., pp. 143-161) (complete files); R. Le Bec, p. xxi (in Leuret's introduction, short summary of the facts).

1. Abbé FIAMMA, 51, diocese of Paris. At 35 swelling of the arteries of the leg; difficulty in walking. At 42, abscesses; Doctor Roesch of Marlotte (Seine-et-Marne) finds six on the right leg, and eight on the left. Suppuration resists several attempted treatments; pains are so disturbing that the patient's ministry suffers as a result; he is sent for a rest in the neighborhood of the Fontainebleau forest. Practically no improvement. Doctor Roesch thinks the disease incurable. At 49, sudden fainting; the examining physician concludes to a heart attack. At the age of 51, in 1908, his superior asks him to go to Lourdes on a pilgrimage. The abbé confidentially tells Doctor Le Bec: "My archbishop wants me to go to Lourdes. I obey, but I go without any hope of being cured." He has his legs examined: "Both legs are covered with huge varices involving both the length of the saphenous veins and most of the collaterals. On the inside face of the knees varicose knots were observed, called 'Medusa heads.' Both of the inner saphenous veins showed twists and bends, ascending to the root of the thighs. Along their length ampullar dilatations were found, typical of old varices. On the left leg, above the inner malleolus, there was a small elongated mass, very painful when touched. It was a clot lodged in a limited section of the inner saphenous vein." The first contact with the pool water causes a very sharp pain, "as if a red-hot iron penetrated under my skin." Upon leaving the water, the abbé finds that varices and tumors have disappeared. Examination by Doctor Le Bec, president of the B.M.F.: "Right leg: skin white, with a layer of fat underneath; bluish veins of normal dimensions and without varicose dilatation. In the rear, below the terminal point of the twin muscles: seven small spots of faint rosy color, covered with smooth skin; no depression at this place, and no adhesion. Left leg: same general appearance. About the middle of the inner face, eight small spots similar to those on the right leg." Seven years later, on September 24, 1915, new examination: veins on both legs normal in volume, almost straight, without any elongation, tortuosity, or ampullar dilatation. Skin of flat white color; some very small and inconsequential cutaneous varices; the painful knottiness of the left leg has disappeared. The place of the former ulcers is marked by very small spots of a somewhat yellowish color different from the brown spots usually remaining at the place of an

ulcer cured in the ordinary way." Patient experiences no difficulty in walking; no more heart trouble. Abbé Fiamma eventually died of pneumonia in 1917.[41]

2. John TRAYNOR, 40, driver in the British Marines. In October, 1914 wounded on the head by shrapnel at Wilrijk (Antwerp); unconscious for five weeks; surgery. Leaves hospital end of December in apparent state of recovery. In January 1915 he rejoins his unit. In February, superficial wound on right knee by rifle bullet near Ismaila (Egypt). In May, 1915, during bayonet attack at the Dardanelles, wounded by three machine gun bullets; two pass through the chest, the third hits the right arm at the height of the inside end of the biceps. The third bullet is found and extracted only after a few days, at the height of the corresponding clavicle. Evacuated by way of Alexandria; at sea, considerable hemorrhage of the chest wound. At hospital no. 15 Doctor Treves makes a first and unsuccessful attempt at resewing the nerve. Traynor is shipped home on the hospital ship Gurka where Major Ross tries again to reconnect the nerve; that is when Traynor has his first epileptiform attack. At the naval hospital in Haslar, still another and unsuccessful attempt at mending the nerve. A committee, among the members of which we find Gen. Davies and A. Sanders, surgeons, recommends amputation of the arm. Traynor refuses; he is discharged with an 80 per cent disability pension which the next year is raised to 100 per cent. Traynor settles down in Liverpool; visits Doctors Warrington and Nelson, neurologists; they refer him to Doctor McMurray, a surgeon who on November 27, 1916 makes still another attempt, the fourth one, at reconnecting the nerve. From 1917 the epileptic attacks become more frequent; in 1918 Traynor spends ten months at Mendell Home, a hospital for epileptics, whence he is transferred to Northern Hospital in Liverpool. In April, 1919 amputation is again recommended; the doctors decide to try electrotherapy first, and the patient is transferred to the Alder Hay hospital where he remains until January 1920. No results. One attack after the other; transferred to Knotty Ash hospital in Springfields where in April, 1920 trepanation by Doctor Monsarrat: removal of bone splinters. After the operation, partial paralysis of the legs, vertigo, lapses of memory, constant cephalea;

[41] R. Le Bec, pp. 197-201; L. Schleyer, p. 128.

epileptiform convulsions become a rule and make the patient fall out of bed; during the attacks, pronounced cyanosis, face livid, eyes glassy, bites on lips and tongue. At the end of 1920 the patient loses control of the sphincters of bladder and anus. The arm is completely paralyzed, "wrist swings, hands tightened in a grip," atrophy of muscles. By August, 1922 two attacks per day on the average, resulting in numerous cuts and bruises.

Arrival in Lourdes on July 22, 1923; numerous attacks on the way. Physicians Azurdia (London), Marley (London) and Finn (Liverpool) who accompany the pilgrims, make a thorough examination the result of which is a report confirming all of the data listed above. In addition, the doctors find a trepanation opening of 2 by 5 centimeters, through which brain pulsations are visible; patient must be protected by a metal disc.

At the second bathing in the pool, abundant bleeding through the mouth, followed by epileptic attack. He is refused permission to enter the pool a third time, but upon his insistence the permission is eventually granted. The attacks stop, but everything else remains the same. At the ninth bathing, violent convulsions of the legs—the arm remains inert—most of the water is kicked out of the pool. He attempts to stand but is so exhausted that he falls back on his wheelchair. Carried to the procession of the Blessed Sacrament; at benediction, his arm shakes with the same kind of convulsions. He takes off the bandage, frees his arm, wishes to get up but is made to remain seated until the procession is over. Wheeled back to the hospital; allowed to get up and walk; he takes seven steps and falls, completely exhausted.

Examination on the same day by the three physicians of the pilgrimage. Findings: "recovered use of legs; nervous reflexes reestablished. Venous congestion in both feet which hurt very much. Walking with some difficulty." Pain in every part of the body. A morphine injection fails to have any effect. Sleepless night until 5:30 A.M. when the patient hears the three strikes of the bell sounding the Angelus; jumps out of bed, kneels down to finish his rosary which he has started in the evening; runs barefooted to the grotto; having finished his prayers, returns to the hospital where he puts on his shoes and clothes unaided. Must leave immediately and thus cannot be checked at the B.M.F.

On the following day, July 27, 1923 he is examined by the same three physicians. Report: "Traynor walks perfectly. Recovered full use and functioning of right arm. Sensitivity of the legs has also disappeared. Trepanation opening considerably reduced. Brain pulsation no longer perceptible. Patient has removed the protective disc." The trepanation hole will disappear completely in a week.

The three doctors keep the patient under observation. In 1924 he goes back to Lourdes, volunteers as a stretcher-bearer and will periodically reassume these duties for many years. Report by Doctor McConnell: "Since July, 1923 not a single epileptic attack" (July 23, 1924). The B.M.F. waits two years before issuing a final report. On July 7, 1926, Traynor returns with the three physicians who have examined him at the time of his cure. They testify that "Traynor has remained under our observation for three years. He had no epileptic attacks. The trepanation hole is reduced to a small bony depression on the cranium. Slight atrophy of the muscles of the hand which is still slightly crooked." Testimony by the beneficiary of the miracle: "I sell coal; I have four trucks and a dozen men working for me. I work with them. I can lift a two hundred-pound bag as easily as the best of them; my performance is that of a good solid worker. Every year I go to Lourdes to act as a stretcher-bearer." Died of hernia in 1943.[42]

3. Evasio GANORA, 37, Casale (Italy). Since 1949, Hodgkin's disease (malignant lymphogranulomatosis; at the present stage of medical science the disease takes as a rule four to five years to reach its fatal climax). Large ganglions in the left armpit; swelling of liver and spleen; pruritus; from 1950, persistent fever, 37 C. [98.6 F.] mornings, and 40 C. [105 F.] evenings. Three tests by Professors Storti (Pavia), Fillibaldi (Alexandria) and Gianfulmo (Genoa) reveal the presence of Sternberg-Reed cells. Antibiotics have no effect whatsoever. On January 23, 1950 he enters the Ca-

[42] Vallet II, pp. 98-108; R. Le Bec, pp. 149-154; the conclusions of L. Schleyer, pp. 108-110, are founded on incomplete data. The above details show also that the critical remarks on the case by J. Lhermitte: *Le problème des miracles*, p. 142, note, are without foundation. The beneficiary of the miracles himself tells the story of his illness and recovery in P. O'Connor: *I Met a Miracle*, Catholic Truth Society (London, 1951). See also in G. B. Sandhurst: *Miracles Still Happen*, p. 183, the testimony of Dr. Azurdia stating that the trepanation is completely closed in less than a week.

sale hospital; on March 25 returns home; 22 blood transfusions fail to induce any improvement. Arrives at Lourdes on May 31, 1950, in critical condition; at the Shelter, long and dangerous fainting spells upon leaving his bed. On June 2, first bathing in the pool; impression of a strong wave of heat throughout the body, followed by euphoria. Walks back to the Shelter. Doctor Vizetti examines him immediately: "Fever and ganglions have disappeared; swellings at the seat of the lymphatic ganglions and of the tumor of the spleen; liver not palpable." The next day the patient makes the Way of the Cross; the day after he is helping in the transportation of the sick. In Milan he is found completely cured and remains so in the following years. Doctor Vizetti testifies in 1953: the patient is very well; capable of the heaviest physical work without fatigue. Reexamination in Lourdes on August 16, 1954: general condition excellent; liver and spleen normal; two small ganglions in the armpit. The Bureau asks for still another examination which eventually takes place on September 18, 1954: no trace of the small ganglions; excellent general health.

The files are forwarded to the International Committee. Professor Sendrail (Toulouse), in reporting the case, asks his Italian colleague for the tissues that had been preserved after the various analyses. The tissues are sent by Doctor Vittadini and are examined by two well-known pathologists, Professors Fabre and Nanta of Toulouse. Both confirm the presence of properties characteristic of Hodgkin's disease. At its February 13, 1955 meeting the Committee declares the extramedical nature of the cure: "The history of medicine knows of no instance of a Hodgkin's disease being cured while in full evolutive course, in a matter of hours, and without any medication" (Prof. Mauriac). On May 31, 1955 the cure is declared miraculous by the bishop of Casale-Monferrato. Evasio Ganora, an active farmer, was crushed by his tractor and died in December, 1957.[43]

4. Edeltraud FULDA, 36, ballet dancer in Vienna. In 1937, following a period of gastric disturbances, she has a violent attack on stage during a ballet performance in Milan; perforation of the intestine and acute peritonitis. Surgery, following which the patient is between life and death for months; her condition improves a

[43] P. Miest, pp. 212-225.

little and she is transferred to Vienna by airplane. Soon nephritis sets in, followed by symptoms of Addison's disease (insufficiency of suprarenal glands) discovered through meticulous examination of the patient's metabolism at Child Hospital in Vienna. Another surgery (kidneys and bladder); no results. Patient is kept alive by substitutive treatment (addition of lacking organic products without cure of the causes of the insufficiency): extensive hormone, therapy by Professor Siedeck (Vienna).

Arrives in Lourdes in August, 1950; cachectic condition; grave digestive disturbances, established anemia (only two million red corpuscles), tension very low (8 to 10), characteristic brownish pigmentation of the skin. Moved about on wheelchair. On August 10, after the first bathing, insists that she is cured and refuses to accept further hormonal injections. On August 16, examination at the Medical Bureau; all of the symptoms have disappeared, including pigmentation of the skin.

Professor Siedeck examines the patient upon her return to Austria; on August 28, 1950, he confirms her complete recovery. Testimony of Doctor Kline: "It is a cause of great joy even for me, who in no way share the convictions of my former patient, to know that such a very grave and critical case of Addison's disease could be cured in Lourdes so thoroughly that all further medication could be stopped and the patient could resume a full-time professional career." Miss Fulda is too old now to start a retraining in choreography; she works on a knitting machine and does her job standing up.

On August 22, 1952, examination by Doctor Blanc of Lyons who confirms once again the patient's complete recovery. Her health has been perfect ever since. The International Committee, at a meeting on February 13, 1955, hears a report by Professor Langeron (Lille) and recognizes the extramedical nature of the cure which Cardinal Innitzer of Vienna proclaims miraculous in April, 1955.[44]

Other cases: In 1878, Joachime DEHAUT, 29, is cured suddenly of a gangrenous wound on the leg (32 by 15 centimeters): Yvonne

[44] P. Miest, pp. 225-231; A. Deroo, pp. 136-139. Miss Fulda tells the story of her illness and recovery in a series of articles in *La Croix de Paris,* August 19, 20, 21 and 22, 1955.

AUMAÎTRE, 22 months, sudden cure in 1896 of double congenital clubfoot; Léonie LEVÊQUE, 29, teacher, sudden cure in 1908 of double frontal sinusitis with osteitis of the frontal bone; Madeleine LOYER, 28, sudden cure in 1937 of the consequences of a chronic myelitis, (syringomyelitis and syringobulbia); Madame QUARTIER, 43, wife of a physician, instantaneous cure in 1937 of angina pectoris resulting from coronary atheroma found through electrocardiogram by Professor Lian; Guy LEYDET, 3½, sudden cure in 1946 of total postencephalitic idiocy and paralysis of all four limbs; Ernestine GIBAULT, 41, suddenly cured in 1947 of labyrinthic syndrome with deafness, resulting from fracture of cranium in an epileptic attack; Gabrielle CLAUZEL, sudden cure in 1943, in the Palissy parish church through the intervention of Our Lady of Lourdes, of rheumatic spondylosis with compression of the rachitic roots; Marie-Louise BIGOT, sudden cure in 1953 of right hemiplegia and in 1954 of total deafness and blindness resulting from arachnoiditis of the posterior channel with adhesions.[45]

Since the appearance of the original edition of this book, several other cures have been held medically inexplicable by the International Medical Committee and proclaimed miraculous by the competent bishops. For example: Leo SCHWAGER, suddenly cured, in 1952, of a very advanced state of multiple sclerosis; Juliette TAMBURINI; aged 23, suddenly cured on June 16, 1959 of osteomyelitis of the left femur.

[45] On Joachime Dehaut, see G. Boissarie: *Les grandes guérisons de Lourdes*, pp. 162-169; F. de Grandmaison, pp. 165-169; R. Le Bec, pp. 168-172; L. Schleyer, p. 138; on Yvonne Aumaître, see R. Le Bec, pp. 202-205; G. Boissarie: *Les grandes guérisons de Lourdes*, pp. 374-377; L. Schleyer, p. 117; see also *Annales des sciences psychiques* (1907), pp. 858ff.; on Léonie Lévêque, see G. Boissarie: *L'oeuvre de Lourdes*, pp. 10-22; F. de Grandmaison, pp. 59-75; L. Schleyer, pp. 145-146; on Madeleine Loyer, see Vallet II, pp. 285-298; L. Schleyer, p. 189; on Mme Quartier, see Vallet II, pp. 278-285; L. Schleyer, pp. 189-190; on Guy Leydet, see Leuret-Bon, French ed., pp. 205-207; on Ernestine Gibault, see *ibid.*, pp. 208-215; on Gabrielle Clauzel, see *ibid.*, pp. 161-184 (with photographs) (Eng. transl., pp. 134-138); P. Miest, pp. 167-172; on Marie-Louise Bigot, see G. Debroise: *Un miracle à Lourdes* (Rennes, 1957); P. Miest, pp. 236-241.

III · LOURDES: ANALYSIS OF THE EVENTS

The problem of deriving an apologetic argument from these events through explicit linking of the miraculous facts with their characteristic value as divine signs, will be dealt with in a subsequent chapter. Here we wish only to ascertain that the facts constitute a solid ground to build on. Two questions arise in this connection:

1. Do the facts reflect the Catholic concept of the miraculous? In other words, does the manner of their manifestation fit the characteristics discussed in Part One?

2. Is their historicity firmly established, and do these events belong in the category of "major miracles," that is, are equivalent phenomena ever observed also in purely secular medicine?

As to the first question, the Lourdes facts unquestionably show the properties of what a Catholic would call a "miracle." They show this, first, by the *religious context* surrounding them.

The apparitions and the message attached to them account for the thorough immersion of the Lourdes miracles in the atmosphere of devotion to Mary as practiced by the Roman Catholic Church; they arise in a climate of boundless confidence in the maternal intercession of the Immaculate Heart of Mary; more precisely, the spirit of the pilgrimages that bring the sick to Lourdes, the atmosphere of faith, confidence and prayer which characterizes them, create a context that automatically lends to the miracles a religious meaning. Assuredly, the unbridled commercialism raging around the shrine, together with a shameless exploitation of religious feelings, often committed by unscrupulous individuals who lack all faith, are far from conducing to the creation of a prayerful climate. Worse still, the advertising of Lourdes as a tourist attraction makes of it an object of purely secular curiosity, a place where the prodigious and the sensational unfold against a background of unspoiled natural beauty. The enormous proportions this propaganda has assumed in recent years have even created in some observers the fear of an almost complete extinction of the religious climate, which would make the occurrence of miracles as impossible as it was in Christ's native town and in Herod's court.[46] One thing, however,

[46] Upon his return in 1939 from a long stay in the United States, A.

is evident and beyond controversy: in actual fact, the great miracles, as well as the devotion of the true pilgrims, are free of all sensationalism and commercialization. Most of the miracles, says Vallet, occur not in the clatter of publicity and agitation, but in silence. The sick who rise on their stretcher during a procession with the Blessed Sacrament and loudly announce their cure, are a priori subject to suspicion. Such cures are often mere illusions, resulting from some violent autosuggestive effort, burning up the last ounce of energy of a poor patient who might even die a few days later.

The real cures in Lourdes never lack the spiritual element which is their dominant feature. Nothing shows this better than the great number of religious vocations among the subjects of these miracles. According to Vallet there were about twenty such vocations between 1926 and 1944.[47] Conversions among the subjects, the eyewitnesses, or among simple pilgrims, prove the same point. All of the authors writing on Lourdes emphasize this one characteristic aspect: a great number of miracles suggest by their very context a comparison with the Gospel accounts[48]; furthermore, Lourdes seems to show a divine preference for the poor (*pauperes evangelizantur*) in the miracles, as it did in the apparitions, and cures of the rich are the exception.[49]

Let us add that in the accounts of all the cures one word keeps recurring almost as a refrain: the word "prayer." On the preceding pages the facts were reported only from the medical viewpoint, and few details were mentioned besides the technical. Every event, however, is deeply embedded in a concrete context which is often very impressive[50]; prayer, which we invariably find as a main com-

---

Carrel: *Prayer*, p. 43, writes: "At Lourdes miracles are much less frequent than they were forty or fifty years ago. For the sick no longer find there the atmosphere of profound contemplation which formerly reigned there. The pilgrims have become tourists and their prayers are inefficacious."

[47] Vallet II, p. 17.

[48] See, e.g., Vallet II, p. 153; R. Le Bec, p. 165; Leuret-Bon, French ed., p. 197; Dr. Béhague in Flood, *op. cit.*, pp. 243-44; etc., J. Guitton: *The Virgin Mary*, transl. A. G. Smith (New York, 1952), p. 103: "What is no less recognizable is the relationship between the experience of Lourdes and a typical scene in the Gospels."

[49] R. Le Bec, p. 122.

[50] G. Boissarie is a real master in the art of evoking this religious atmos-

ponent, is constantly mentioned. This prayer may be full of confidence, or weakened by doubting and vacillation; it may be simple as that of a child, or virile and direct as the prayer of a grown man; hesitant upon the lips of the atheist or unbeliever,[51] but piercing when uttered by a mother who is prepared to reap the gift of heaven by violence; it may be the calm or submissive prayer of a soul already cleansed by suffering, or the heroic prayer of the patient who offers himself up as a sacrifice for the benefit of someone else. Not only is prayer the most remarkable constant in the miraculous contexture of Lourdes, it is the only such constant. The diseases cured in Lourdes are very diversified; the sick are not alike; the circumstances surrounding the cures do not suggest any uniformity of process. The event may occur in the pool or outside of it; during a procession or in the solitude of private prayer at the grotto, or at Mass; before arrival in Lourdes, or after leaving the shrine; in the isolation of a room or in the corner of a ward. As Carrel has pointed out in the text quoted at the beginning of this chapter, prayer is the only invariable factor present in all of the miraculous cures.

Another feature of the Lourdes miracles, a close kin to prayer, is *discretion.* It has been pointed out that this element is typical of every authentic miracle; now, it is invariably found in connection with the Lourdes events; thus the latter truly represent the miraculous as understood by the Catholic Church.

There are no mass cures in Lourdes; a miracle is always a relatively exceptional event. It resists all human calculation; no consideration or angle of vision can lead to foreseeing and anticipating, with any degree of statistical probability, a miracle in any particular case. The extramedical cures seem to depend upon motives and aims altogether different from mere medical efficiency or a sort of human pity.

The very manner in which the miracles occur is marked by the greatest discretion. No instance, ever, of "new creation"; no new limb to replace a lost one; no fabulous or fantastic display of power

---

phere. See also P. Teilhard de Chardin, *art. cit.*, pp. 181-182; R. Cranston, *op. cit., passim,* or a report in C. Fournier: *Miraculés de Lourdes* (Paris, 1957).

[51] Leuret-Bon, Eng. transl., p. 30: "Even unbelievers and atheists have been cured."

by some capricious fairy who would be playing with the laws of nature. These are "cures" in the full sense of the word, and they always retain their spiritual reference, underlined by their context. Specialists comparing the ways in which the various miraculous cures occur, agree that they follow the patterns of natural recovery. All of those who had studied the events are practically unanimous in stating that a cure always takes place as a natural process, only at an infinitely higher rate of speed. "If it were possible," says Teilhard de Chardin, "to observe the process of such a cure through a microscope, we would doubtless discover in it the known patterns of cellular multiplication." [52] In some cases, evidence to the same effect has been found even without technical facilities. Such was the cure of a fistula in the case of Marie Borel. One of the physicians said immediately after the event: "It seems like a spider at work; you could watch the skin coming back." [53] Many patients, at the moment of their cure, experience strong pain combined with violent sensations of hunger, the first sign of reconquered health; these again support the same conclusion.

The persistence of scars or, frequently, other traces of a former diseased condition, which continue to exist after evident occurrence of a miraculous cure, is one of the most relevant symbols of the discreet nature of the Lourdes events. These signs are, in fact, an open invitation for the observer to look for the real, profound meaning of the events at a different level. In relating certain cases of blindness we have called the reader's attention to the striking phenomenon of organic recovery following long after the restoration of functional integrity (which, incidentally, has been observed in several other cures as well). This phenomenon is indeed so common, even in diseases other than blindness, that some physicians were prompted to call it "the signature of the Blessed Virgin." [54]

•

[52] P. Teilhard de Chardin: *art. cit.*, p. 174. Some physicians conclude from this that miraculous recovery from a disease proves that that disease is not absolutely incurable even from the purely natural viewpoint. A cure of optical atrophy, e.g., would justify the hope that medical science will eventually discover the secret of the same natural process of recovery which occurs also in the event of a miracle, only at an infinitely accelerated rate, See, e.g., Dr. Merlin in Flood, *op. cit.*, pp. 191-193.

[53] G. Boissarie: *L'oeuvre de Lourdes*, p. 241.

[54] R. Le Bec, p. 166; Leuret-Bon, French ed., 198.

The second question was: Have the Lourdes events been proven to be perfectly authentic; do they belong in the category of major miracles; have they no equivalent in secular medicine?

The historical *authenticity* of the facts is absolutely certain, based as it is upon the testimony of dozens of physicians in each particular case, upon transcripts of clinical files, insurance company or laboratory records, and often upon official data kept in the files of civilian or military authorities. The physician testifying may be an unbeliever or a religious person. A great deal of data has been gathered, and to deny all of them obstinately one would have to invoke an improbable accumulation of error and dishonest intent. Thousands of persons would have to be accused of bad faith gratuitously, and such a fantastic conspiracy to fabricate a miracle would appear more unlikely than even the most unlikely cure.

Moreover, improvements in the techniques of medical examination, achieved through the invention of modern facilities and measuring devices that register the data with extreme accuracy, have cast no doubt upon Lourdes; on the contrary, they have contributed additional and incontrovertible confirmation of the facts. One may question the diagnosis of a colleague, but rejection of the witness of an X-ray picture or the results of a blood test would be very difficult. As appears in the cases studied in this chapter, objective clinical analysis often dissipates all doubt concerning the real nature of a disease. In fact, few of those specialists who take the trouble of pressing the facts closely would think of questioning their authenticity.

But could we not find similar cases in the domain of purely secular medicine? A correct understanding of this question is important. At this point we are not asking whether a natural explanation is possible; this problem will be dealt with separately. We merely wish to know whether the events, susceptible or not of a natural explanation, appear *exclusively* in a religious contexture, or medical science knows of identical or at least equivalent phenomena occurring in ordinary practice. The difference between these two problems appears clearly in a discussion at the B.S.S. The subject matter is the 1946 cure of Guy Leydet, a five-year-old child stricken with total idiocy and paralysis of all four limbs, resulting from encephalitis. The B.S.S. is the scene of an impassioned discussion. Can the cure be explained naturally, or can it not? Even Leuret admits that "the case could be argued indefinitely." One of the physicians, however, stands up and states: "If anyone here has ever seen a postencephalitic idiot recover his health in this way, I vow never to sign my name to another record at the Lourdes Medical Bureau." No one among the sixty physicians present takes up his challenge. All of them are in complete agreement that no such recovery has ever been observed in secular circumstances.[55]

We can state a fortiori that considering all the above reported cases together, nothing in any way comparable to them has ever been reported in the history of secular medicine.

Every instance, in fact, presents beyond a doubt a case of some specifically organic disease, the existence of which has been confirmed through objective proofs. According to the principles set forth above, the possible presence of psychogenetic features in the total picture of a disease supplies no valid explanation of a recovery from organic lesions, nor does the so-called "atmosphere of exaltation" explain anything, for a substantial number of cures occur elsewhere than in Lourdes.

Medical science at its present stage considers absolutely incurable several of the diseases cured, such as the three cancer cases and one case of blindness, mentioned above. The non-existence of analogous cases in secular medicine requires no proof; the facts themselves supply their own evidence. As for the other cases, the diseases involved normally call for intensive therapeutic treatment, and the process of recovery is a long one. In none of the Lourdes cases did such therapy take place, mainly because it was not yet known at the time (e.g., streptomycin in the case of Paulette Margerie, or surgical intervention for Abbé Fiamma); or medication has long been abandoned as ineffective; furthermore, the recovery takes place at such a speed that the element of time may be considered negligible, for in practically every case the cure is in-

[55] Leuret-Bon, French ed., p. 207. Leuret attributes this statement to Prof. Lelong, although in actual fact it was made by another physician, as Leuret himself recognizes in a later publication (*Bulletin de l'A.M.I.L.*, July, 1951).

stantaneous. Also, one would look in vain for the typical signs of convalescence which invariably follow recovery from any serious illness, obtained through medical means.

Attempts have been made in the past to attribute remedial properties to the Lourdes water and to bathing in the pool. We know that the water has no such properties. The latest analysis, undertaken with the object of finding any radioactivity that might be present, yielded completely negative results.[56] What is really strange is that this water, seldom changed and soiled as it is by the contact of the sick, many of whom are victims of contagious diseases, should not have caused some epidemic or contaminated other pilgrims.[57]

One of the favorite expressions used in the pseudo-scientific lingo of the late eighteen hundreds was "emotive shock caused by cold balneation." It is evident today that in most of the cases quoted above, bathing (if bathing it was, indeed, and not mere washing, or tasting of the water) was not at all an appropriate remedy. Rather, it is surprising that no accidents result from immersion in this cold water (48 degrees F.). Doctor Leuret, in an attempt to find out for himself what the experience was like, once stayed in the water fifteen seconds, the time usually spent by the sick in the pool. He called the experience "atrocious." [58]

•

[56] See the results of this second examination in Vallet II, pp. 184-190; R. Le Bec, p. 92.

[57] A great number of visitors use the pool before the water is changed periodically. Moreover, it is customary with some of the personnel to drink a glass of the soiled water after the sessions, as an expression of their faith. There are no known cases of disease caused by the drinking of this water. The results of several bacteriological tests (Bertrand laboratories, Antwerp; Provincial laboratory for bacteriological analysis, Ghent; board of health of the Hautes Pyrénées province, Tarbes) seemed to indicate a supersterilization of the Lourdes water which did not prove pathogenic for guinea pigs, whereas some other polluted waters, such as the Seine, quickly killed half of the experimental animals it had been injected into. (See Vallet II, pp. 190-199). Further tests, however, showed that bacillary concentration in the water of Lourdes was considerably lower than in the Seine. When bacillary concentration was increased in a centrifugal separator, the Lourdes water had the same effect on guinea pigs as the water of the Seine (see Tauriac, pp. 113-120.). One can thus accept without qualifications this statement of Leuret: "The Lourdes water is nothing but common, ordinary water."

[58] Leuret-Bon, p. 97 (French ed., pp. 104-105).

Doctor Béhague concludes his series of studies, published in the *Cahiers Laënnec* and quoted several times by us in the present work, with the following *ad hominem* appeal:

> You doctors, and you specialists in particular; you former and present students who work in the services which deal with the sick in their thousands, have you seen:
>
> (a) A case of two detached retinas originating in a shock suddenly cured seven and a half years afterwards, the sight returning 'like a shot from a gun'? (Vion-Dury).
>
> (b) White atrophy of the papillas of both eyes cured in such a way that the sight returned instantly and permanently while the papillary whiteness only disappeared as time went on? (Mme Biré).
>
> (c) A case of evolutive pulmonary tuberculosis calcify in a few days or a case of peritoneal tuberculosis rapidly disappearing? (Louise Jamain, Gabrielle Durand).
>
> (d) A case of tubercular meningitis (with Koch bacilli in the cerebrospinal fluid which contained 150 lymphocytes per mm^3) make a single leap from the final coma and possess, within a month after the previous lumbar puncture, a normal cerebrospinal fluid free from bacilli? (Mlle Margerie).
>
> (e) An open fracture of the leg with chronic osteomyelitis and pseudarthrosis heal instantly and spontaneously so as to permit of immediate walking? (De Rudder).
>
> (f) A cancer of the pylorus and the liver heal suddenly and the functioning of the gastroenterostomy (visible by X-rays) instantly disappear? (Mlle Delot).
>
> If you have seen any of these things please let us know. We ourselves have never seen them except in the cases mentioned . . .[59]

As every physician will agree, nothing of the sort has ever occurred in his practice; he knows that never in the memory of man have such rapid cures been reported in the annals of medicine.

IV • OTHER MIRACLES IN THE CATHOLIC CHURCH

We have given a lengthy account of the Lourdes facts, and found in them, as did many others before us, the Catholic idea of the

[59] Flood, *op. cit.*, p. 242.

miraculous in its clearest form, precisely because at this shrine the miraculous is an object of well organized, systematic checking. Yet it would be impossible to conclude that Lourdes has a monopoly on miracles, even on miracles within the Catholic Church.

There exist other *privileged places* where miraculous cures did and do occur under the same conditions of serious checking and verification. In Fatima we find a medical bureau for the examination of the sick. Some 15,000 patients have passed through this bureau between 1926 and 1937, and some 800 cures have been studied. There is, for instance, the case of Marguerite REBELO, 23, paralyzed through medullary compression resulting from a fracture of the second lumbar vertebra; suppurating cystitis with fistula; her cure is a miracle comparable in every way to those occurring in Lourdes.[60]

The Banneux and Beauraing shrines, while having no such medical office, have been the stages of miraculous cures that serious study will consider verified beyond a doubt. A bishop's commission, appointed for the study of the Beauraing apparitions, retained two cases the historical validity and extramedical nature of which are as solidly established as would be in Lourdes: Sister PUDENTIENNE (Mlle Van Laer), cured of osteomyelitis, and Mme ACAR, cured of uterine myoma (report on this case was submitted by Professor Renaer of the University of Louvain).[61] At Banneux, we find the case of little Joseph VAESSEN from Kadier-en-Keer (Limburg in Holland); age 9, near death as a result of acute crisis of leukemia. On January 21, 1946, as he takes some Banneux water, color returns to his face; within a few days he is completely cured (the facts are confirmed by his attending physician, Doctor Leit of the clinic of Maastricht.[62]

The cure of Pierre De Rudder at Oostakker, a Flanders shrine dedicated to Our Lady of Lourdes, appears to be one of the most striking miracles in recent centuries. None has provoked more literature or given rise to more passionate polemics. More than a hundred physicians have studied the events; the Medical Academy

[60] Leuret-Bon, pp. 37-43; M. Agnellet: *Miracles à Fatima* (Paris, 1958).

[61] See A. Monin: *Notre-Dame de Beauraing* (Bruges, 1949); his text is repeated word by word in Leuret-Bon, pp. 52-54.

[62] See Msgr. Kerkhofs: *Notre-Dame de Banneux* (Tournai, 1950), pp. 132-133.

of Milan has discussed it in a five-hour meeting; it has even been the proposed subject of a debate, prepared but never actually carried out, before a court of honor.[63] This event, therefore, could not be omitted from a study of major miracles within the fold of the Catholic Church. The following is a summary of the facts.

Pierre DE RUDDER, 53, gardener at Jabbeke. On February 16, 1867, has his left leg smashed by a falling tree; double fracture of tibia and fibula. Bone splinters removed by Doctor Affenaer of Oudenbourg, fracture set; limb put in cast. Because of unbearable pain, the cast is removed after a few weeks; a deep and suppurating wound appears at the back of the foot, with another deep and gangrenous lesion leading to the seat of the fracture. Not the slightest indication of improvement. Bedridden for a year; condition unchanged. In 1871 Doctor Van Hoestenberghe of Stalhille examines the patient for the first time, not as his family physician but on his own behalf and out of pity. Brownish and fetid pus trickles from the tumor which is the size of a large egg; holding the knee in the left hand and the heel in the right, one is able to turn around the foot so that the heel is where the toes should be, and can even be pushed to some distance past that position; bending of the injured leg exposes the four tips of broken bone; on these extremities there is no periosteum; when released, the leg dangles something like the hammer of a bell. From 1873 the patient is under the care of Doctor Verriest who, after several consultations with Doctor Van Hoestenberghe, concludes that the case is hope-

[63] The principal source on this case is evidently the records of the canonical investigation conducted between 1907 and 1908, thirty-two years after the event, and ten years after De Rudder's death. The investigation, initiated on the insistence of Dr. Boissarie at the fiftieth anniversary of Our Lady of Lourdes, did far more than merely list the detailed records of earlier inquests: the commission heard again the testimony of all the witnesses still alive and succeeded in locating still others who had not testified previously. The full text of these records has just been published on the centenary of Lourdes; see A. De Meester: *De wonderbare genezing van Pieter de Rudder*, Het kanoniek onderzoek 1907-1908 (Oostakker, 1958). A footnote on pp. 13-14 gives a bibliography of publications after the inquest. Earlier bibliography on the miracle is listed in a pamphlet by A. De Meester: *La guérison miraculeuse de Pierre De Rudder*, Relation des deux premières enquêtes faites en 1875 (Roulers, 1910), pp. 7-9 note. The difficulties the planned "honor debate" ran into are described in a series of articles by H. Bolsius: "Dr. Aigners wonderweerlegging," *Studiën*, 71 (1909), 403-420; 72 (1909), 580-610; 73 (1910) pp. 77-88.

less. Another treatment, completely unsuccessful. Patient refuses amputation of the leg. At the end of December, 1874 Doctor Van Hoestenberghe finds the patient's condition unchanged. The fractured bones stand 2 to 3 centimeters apart. After a last examination in the middle of January, 1875, Doctor Verriest decides to discontinue his treatment. About three weeks before the Oostakker pilgrimage, Doctor Van Hoestenberghe tests once again the abnormal movement of the leg, although without removing the bandages. Other witnesses make the same observation on April 2 and 5. On April 6, the day before the pilgrimage, three witnesses see Pierre take off the bandage; they verify the dangling of the leg and see how the patient is able to twist his leg around. Their testimonies concur in every detail. Many other witnesses also meet him during the pilgrimage, such as the trainmaster who helps him into the car; the coachman of the omnibus in which he rides from Dampoort to Oostakker notices the abnormal mobility of the leg.

The pilgrimage takes place on April 7, 1875. Pierre visits the grotto with the other pilgrims; he is greatly in pain and must be supported, then made to sit on a bench. Sudden uneasiness; he gets up, walks through the lines of pilgrims and kneels down before the statue of the Blessed Virgin. He realized instantly what is happening: "I am cured," he says. Rises again, walks about the grotto three times. Examined immediately at the chateau of marquise Courtebourne, owner of the estate: "Leg and foot, swollen and large a few seconds ago, now appear normal; the bandages have fallen off by themselves; both wounds have disappeared; the fractured bones are perfectly consolidated; a bluish scar marks the place of the fracture; walking as easy as before the accident." On the next day, examination by Doctor Affenaer whose findings are the same. Doctor Van Hoestenberghe concludes to complete recovery; notes this in his diary. The man does not limp; the bones feel solid and smooth to the touch; "there is not the slightest irregularity on the inner surface of the tibia, only a small depression on the crest where the fracture has been." (Royer)

De Rudder works in his former trade until his death 22 years later; he is known by all as a vigorous and brave worker. He dies in 1898 of pneumonia. Disinterment fourteen months after his death; tibia and fibula of both legs are examined, described and photographed. At the date of this writing the bones are still preserved at the residence of the bishop of Bruges.

Did the events really take place as reported? If so, their extra-medical nature is so evident that no physician could challenge this miracle in any way from a medico-surgical standpoint.[64] Objections, therefore, must be directed at the historical aspect; the events did not take place as reported, or at least it is impossible to verify with absolute certainty that conditions at the time of the pilgrimage were really such as the eyewitness accounts claim them to be.

In trying to question the historicity of the facts the opponents quote an opinion given in 1908, that is, thirty years after the event and ten years after De Rudder's death, by two talented young physicians. These two men appear before an episcopal committee; their good faith and competency are unquestionable. One is a Doctor Nelis, later a professor at the University of Louvain, and the other, Doctor Rubbrecht, a well-known Bruges practitioner. Doctor Nelis's report defends the theory that "the facts have not been established scientifically." Two other physicians, Doctor Van Coillie of Brussels and Surgeon Depla of Courtrai are also asked by the commission to give their opinion. They consider the proof established and refute the arguments of Nelis and Rubbrecht, whereupon the bishop declares the miraculous nature of the cure.

Even the ablest physician may sometimes overestimate the probative force of an experiment or may be the unwitting prisoner of some current prejudice. An actual reading of Doctor Nelis's report would confirm the suspicion that he was not free of either mistake. These are the three grounds upon which he felt compelled to say that the miracle has not been established as a fact:

a) The last medical examination took place three months before the cure; in matters of scientific observation all testimonies by laymen must be considered irrelevant;

b) It appears strange that De Rudder should have been able to twist his foot without pain, in the manner so often described; only

[64] A detailed medico-surgical analysis of the case is published by Prof. L. Elaut: "Mirakel en wetenschap; De beenderen van Petrus De Rudder," *Universitasschriften* n. I (Antwerp, 1951) pp. 93-103. There is an earlier, similar study by Prof. Reverchon of the Catholic University of Lille (see *Bulletin de l'A.M.I.L.*, 1929, pp. 114ff.).

a detailed report on his general state of health, particularly on his neurological condition, could eliminate the possibility of psychogenic insensitivity with all of the pertinent consequences for the evaluation of the case as a whole. The word "hysteria," while not used, is present in the whole context;

c) The medical findings of Doctor Van Hoestenberghe and his colleagues are evidently inexact, for experiments on a corpse have convinced the reporting physician that simultaneous protrusion of four broken bone tips through an open fracture is impossible.

Many answers have been offered to each of these statements, by the other two consulting physicians and others.

a) In the De Rudder case there was no need for professional competency to make useful observations. In a case like this the testimony of a layman is hardly less valid than that of a physician, and one must resort to prejudice to reject it as irrelevant. Doctor Tennesson expressed this truth very clearly some fifty years ago when he said that "it does not take a tailor to see that a coat is full of holes." Van Coillie's report states that "the lesion is so easy to diagnose that error is simply impossible." From the scientific viewpoint the only thing that counts here is the necessity of applying the rules of critical history in any attempt to establish the value of the testimonies given. Now, there is absolute unanimity among the witnesses; all of the authors agree that the depositions show every sign of reliability. The witnesses come from a variety of environments; their complete independence from one another excludes connivance, while concordance is proven even in minute details; in fact, on all points of some importance the accord is perfect.[65] Moreover, the supposition that a suppurating fracture that has resisted medical efforts for eight years and involves a 3-centimeter gap between the tips of the fractured bones should heal in three months without any treatment, is so fantastic as to be beyond all scientific probability; all the more as a physician verifies the abnormal mobility of the leg three weeks before the event, and this mobility, as demonstrated by the very experiments of Doctors Nelis

[65] See pp. 216ff. of the records for details of this demonstration, by the promoter of the case, Canon A. De Meester.

and Rubbrecht, would have substantially diminished in the event of gradual, partial consolidation.

b) To our knowledge, no one has ever spoken of the insensibility of De Rudder's leg, whereas all of the witnesses say that he suffered a great deal. But even if such insensitivity did exist, a more accurate conclusion would be to attribute it to organic causes rather than to hysteria. Doctor Depla mentions "considerable weakening and diminished resistance of the tissues." De Rudder's conduct after the cure makes the hypothesis of hysterical insensitivity worse than improbable.[66] Even if this relative insensitivity were found to be a psychogenic result of the organic lesion itself (falling timber can hardly be a product of hysteria), it would be completely irrelevant to the extramedical nature of sudden recovery from an irrefutably established organic lesion.

c) In his testimony, Doctor Depla, the Courtrai surgeon, counters the experiment of Doctors Nelis and Rubbrecht by his own findings; he states that "this phenomenon, the simultaneous appearance of both the upper and lower tips of broken bones, was observed by him several times in the course of surgical treatments at Doctor Lauwers's clinic." The impossibility stated by the two Bruges physicians is therefore accidental and may not be considered a scientific conclusion.[67]

[66] See, e.g., the testimony of Dr. Royer at the inquest: ". . . I challenge anyone to find in this vigorous old man the least trace of neurosis, or to find a single testimony that would lead to such a suspicion even remotely" (Records, p. 96). The testimony of the viscountess du Bus de Giségnies, Records, p. 71 states: "There is not a trace of intent to seek personal or monetary gain, either in De Rudder or members of his family. To prove this: I offered a very high price for their house where I would have liked to build a grotto and a shrine. These honest people refused to sell."

[67] On this whole question, see R. Deschamps and D. Le Bec: *Le cas Pierre De Rudder et les objections des médecins* (Paris, 1913) (report by Dr. Nelis, p. 228; discussion of the experiment attempted by him and Dr. Rubbrecht, pp. 150-154; reports of Dr. Van Coillie and Dr. Depla, pp. 230-233 and 234-237). All these reports are reproduced in the Records of the canonical inquest. See also R. Le Bec: *Raisons médicales de croire au miracle*, pp. 49-56; the ironical remarks on the validity of lay testimony in medical matters, pp. 124-126. One may check also G. Laffitte in Flood, *op. cit.*, pp. 212-215; L. Schleyer, pp. 115-116; B. G. Sandhurst: *Miracles Still Happen*, pp. 138-157. Objections voiced by many authors, e.g., J. Lhermitte: *Le problème des miracles*, pp. 106-107, are based on data which are very incomplete and taken out of context. It

We may thus conclude without any fear of error that the historicity of De Rudder's cure has been solidly established on incontrovertible grounds.

The Catholic miracle is not only a flower decorating certain religious shrines; it is also very closely linked with *personal holiness.* The Church is so fully aware of this connection that before beatifying or canonizing a servant of God who is not a martyr, she demands, in addition to an inquest on the heroic degree of virtues, several miracles as the signs of divine confirmation. The regulations governing this inquest on miracles are extremely severe; two miracles are required for beatification, and two more for canonization. The rules are codified in Canon Law and refer to a masterly work by Benedict XIV, published by him while still Cardinal Lambertini, under this title: *Doctrina de servorum Dei beatificatione et beatorum canonisatione.*[68]

A careful reading of the records of canonization trials, published officially in recent years, will convince anyone that an impressive

---

is perfectly true, e.g., that Dr. Van Hoestenberghe wrote in a letter to Boissarie: "By holding the leg by the heel, it was possible to twist it over a full turn around the axis of the limb" (Records, p. 44). But critics forget that Dr. Van Hoestenberghe, a Fleming, was translating very inadequately a Flemish expression meaning literally that it was possible to twist the limb "front side back." The records contain other explicit statements by Dr. Van Hoestenberghe to the effect that "one could twist the leg so that the heel would be in front and would even pass beyond the half circle by 3 to 4 centimeters (Records, pp. 35, 46, 48, and 55).—Incidentally, the "first report" which Lhermitte seems to question is not Dr. Van Hoestenberghe's alone. There exists a statement, recorded hardly a week after the miracle by all the leading citizens of the village (among them P. De Lorge, an atheist who was buried civilly); see the facsimile of this document in Records, facing p. 82. The Records contain also a report written on April 11, four days after the event, by A. Rommelaere, assistant pastor; pp. 79-82. Also, *Godsdienstige Week van Vlaanderen*, bulletin of the diocese of Ghent, contains a report on the miracle in the April 9 issue; it begins with the words "We received a communication from Oostakker" and must have been written on the very day of the event. Finally, the theory that the leg examined was the right leg instead of the injured left one lacks absolutely all foundation in light of the data on record.

[68] See *Codex Iuris Canonici*, can. 1999 to 2141. Chapter IV of Leuret-Bon (written by Msgr. Gardié) gives an interesting insight into the procedure of the Sacred Congregation of Rites in beatification and canonization trials, pp. 68-87. See also S. Romani, "I miracoli nelle cause di beatificazione e canonizzazione," *Maria et Ecclesia*, 13 (1960), 271-320.

number of facts have been established through the strictest historical criteria and appear clearly extramedical in nature.[69] Let us quote a recent example taken from the 1954 canonization trial of Pius X. Two miracles are retained: Francesco BELSANI, a Naples attorney, is cured suddenly on August 25, 1951 of a fetid abscess of the lung with a prognosis pointing to a proximate fatal end; Maria Ludovica SCORCIA, a Vincentian sister of Charity, cured instantly on February 24, 1952 of meningocephalomyelitis caused by a neurotropic virus. According to the commission, these two cures were complete and permanent. Two miracles were investigated in 1951, before the beatification: cure of an osteosarcoma on the left thigh, and sudden disappearance of a malignant tumor on the left side of the abdominal cavity.[70]

As a rule, the two miracles required are selected from among a large number of miracles obtained through the intercession of a servant of God. Saints are sometimes responsible for an abundance of miraculous deeds, as was St. Francis de Sales of whom Pope Alexander VII has said: "The records of the trial of the Saint of Geneva contain more miracles than would be needed for the elevation of fifty Blessed to the altar." [71] Everyone has heard of the flood

[69] The official reports of the Sacred Congregation of Rites are published in *Acta processuum beatificationis et canonisationis* where each trial is given a separate volume containing also the details of discussions on miraculous cases presented by the promoter of the case. Beatification and canonization decrees which are regularly published in *Acta Apostolicae Sedis (AAS)* always contain an abbreviated mention of the two miracles accepted by the Congregation. The reader will find a whole series of such cases, with references to *AAS*, in A. Seitz: "Neuzeitliche Wunder bei Heiligsprechungen," *Theologisch-praktische Quartalschrift*, 71 (1918), 77-92; a more recent collection of cases in F. Baumann: "Heilige und Wunder," *Theologisch-praktische Quartalschrift*, 104 (1956), 22-42. H. Bon: *Le miracle devant la science* (Paris, 1957) gives summary medical description of a good many miraculous cures, extracted from records of canonization trials.

[70] See *AAS*, 47 (1955), pp. 122-124. The same volume contains mention of the miracles accepted for the canonization of St. Joseph Pignatelli, pp. 192-194, and of St. Gaspar del Buffalo, pp. 181-182. Leuret-Bon, pp. 88-93 reports in more detail on two cases: St. Grignion de Montfort and St. Jeanne de Lestonnac. The reader might see also R. Le Bec: *Les deux miracles pour la canonisation de Sainte Jeanne d'Arc* (Paris, 1922) where he could follow in detail the procedure of the Congregation. An article by J. M. Berthau: "Un procès 'super miraculis' abandonné pour insuffisance de témoignages" *Revue apologétique*, 38 (1924), 727-740, will help to realize the severity of canonical inquests.

[71] See, e.g., F. Trochu: *Saint François de Sales* (Paris, 1942), II, p. 735.

of miracles, extending to all corners of the earth, which caused the early canonization of St. Thérèse of Lisieux, a very unusual thing in the Church. These prodigies are the fulfillment of a promise recorded in the Saint's diary. She hears the biography of a sick person read in the refectory; a shower of roses falling upon her bed assures her that her prayers have been answered; then she writes this short prophetical note: "After my death I will make a shower of roses fall upon the earth." [72] By 1925 (she died in 1897) the accounts of these blessings fill three thousand pages of the "Shower of Roses" which is a history of cures, conversions and various graces obtained through her intercession. Unfortunately, the whole collection has been gathered with such a complete lack of critical care as to make it altogether useless for our present purposes. The intercession of a servant of God, Charbel Makhlouf, causes in the Near East a multitude of extraordinary cures among Orthodox and Moslems, as well as among Catholics.[73]

God's approval is not always deferred until after the death of his servants who often possess the gift of miracles while still on this earth. This power does not belong merely in the Golden Legend of the Middle Ages; it stands unabated even with the searchlight of the most critical hagiography focused on it. To mention only the most recent past, the lives of the Curé of Ars and of Don Bosco contain certain facts that are verified on solid historical grounds

---

Detailed account of a number of miracles, but unfortunately without critical analysis of the sources, is contained in a booklet edited by the Sisters of Visitation of Annecy at the occasion of the canonization (1685): *Pouvoir de Saint François de Sales,* Miracles et guérisons opérées par le Saint Evêque[2] (Bourg, 1911).

[72] See St. Thérèse of Lisieux: *History of a Soul,* ch. XII. Similar predictions are found in other passages. In the same chapter, e.g., she is trying to express her idea of heaven: "To love, to be loved, and to come back on earth to make Love loved." Among her "Advice and Memories" we find the following answer: "You will look at us from heaven, will you not?—No, I shall come back." On the "Storm of Glory" following her death, see the very inspiring introduction of I. Goerres: *The Hidden Face* (London, 1959).

[73] See J. De Fraine: *Sjarbel Machloef, de moderne wonderdoener* (Bruges, 1953); P. Daher: *Vie, survie et prodiges de l'ermite Charbel Makhlouf* (Paris, 1953); Leuret-Bon, pp. 62-65. [At the beatification of Father Makhlouf on Dec. 5, 1965 both of the persons whose cures were accepted as miracles in the cause were actually present (see *Osservatore Romano,* Dec. 6-7, 1965).—Transl.]

and are without equivalent in any secular history.[74] Their miracles are not limited to cures of the sick. Both of them are credited, as are, incidentally, many other saints, with multiplications of food, fuel or money, and the witnesses testifying to the facts in precise detail may not be dismissed summarily.[75] The life of the Curé of Ars offers among other things a striking instance in which wheat was multiplied. His close associate, Abbé Tocanier, reports in these words an account by the Saint himself:

> I had many orphans to feed, and there was but a handful of corn left in the attic. I thought that St. Francis Regis, who during his life miraculously fed the destitute, would do likewise after his death. I had a relic of the Saint; I put it in the handful of grains that remained; the little ones prayed, and the attic was found to be full.

At the canonical trial Baroness de Belvey testifies of a conversation with Monsignor Devie who told her that, while visiting the Saint, he had gone with him to the barn and asked point blank: "Father, the grain was piled this high, was it not?" The curé said without hesitation: "No, Monsignor, it was higher, at about this level." [76]

[74] See, e.g., F. Trochu: *The Curé d'Ars* (Westminster, Md., 1949), ch. 27: "The miracles of the curé d'Ars"; A. Auffray: *Un grand Educateur. Le bienheureux Don Bosco* (Paris, 1929), ch. 11: "Le thaumaturge"; for Don Bosco see also the privately published fascicules: *Memorie biografice di Don Giovanni Bosco;* L. Ponelle and L. Bordet: *Saint Philippe Néri et la société romaine de son temps* (Paris, 1928), pp. 99-117. There seems to be no shortage of such miracles in our own twentieth century; with all the usual cautions let us mention H. P. Bergeron: *Le Frère André* (Paris, 1947), and Abbé Mouly: *Des miracles révolutionnent l'Amérique* (Paris, 1946); see also Leuret-Bon, pp. 58-62: A. Hatch: *Le miracle de la montagne. L'histoire de Frère André et de l'Oratoire Saint Joseph à Montréal* (Paris, 1960).

[75] Many such accounts, corroborated by serious testimony, are found in H. Thurston: "The Multiplication of Food," *The Month,* 162 (1933), 440-450; O. Leroy: "De la multiplication miraculeuse des biens," *La Vie Spirituelle —Etudes et documents,* 50 (1937), pp. (148) to (171) and 51 (1937), pp. (14) to (41); ID.: "Quelques faits récents de multiplication des biens," *ibid.,* 55 (1938), pp. (43) to (53); ID: *Miracles,* pp. 72-92.

[76] F. Trochu: *The Curé d'Ars,* pp. 203-204. "It is unquestionable that most of the miracles attributed, for example, to the Curé of Ars are veridical" (A. Carrel: *Prayer,* p. 44).

We believe that we may conclude this study with the statement that the presence of "major miracles" within the Catholic Church is an undeniable fact for everyone but the prejudiced. Furthermore, although exceptional, they occur with a regularity that excludes all possibility of error and fortuitous coincidence. If there were only one instance, doubt could be permissible. But it is against all reason not to accept as real events that occur in an impressive sequence, are supported by reliable testimony and objective findings, appear in the greatest variety of circumstances of time, place and cultural environment, and have for their only common denominator a specifically Catholic religious context which suggests that a definite sign value is attached to them. Thus there is no way to avoid dealing with the problem of their interpretation.

Before building the facts into an apologetic argument, another, no less important, aspect of the whole question must be pointed out and discussed. The "major prodigy" appears in the Catholic Church in an unpredictable and yet regular manner, which is in striking contrast with non-Christian religions and other Christian denominations, where its absence is glaring.

3 · THE ABSENCE OF MAJOR MIRACLES OUTSIDE THE CATHOLIC CHURCH

To head off any possible misunderstanding, the aim and scope of the following study on the existence of major miracles outside the Catholic Church must be defined clearly.

There is no doubt that certain events occurring outside the Catholic Church may be interpreted as divine signs. A review of the pertinent theological principles set forth in Part One would serve no purpose here, for the problem arising at this juncture has nothing to do with theological probability. It is a *purely historical* problem which could be expressed in the following terms. Prodigious events have definitely been observed within non-Christian religions and non-Catholic Christianity; the question is whether we can find among them some solidly established historical events that would qualify as "major prodigies."

The modern reader may find it difficult to repress a skeptical smile at the suggestion that the answer is, perhaps, negative. Comparative religious history reveals in fact that the desire and expectation of the miraculous are present in every religion. Very nearly all of them have their own sacred shrines, temples, curative springs, ex-votos, pilgrimages, saints and miracle-workers. Would it be surprising if in every instance the bale of straw of legends and tables turned out to contain the same proportion of good grain? Is it not a fact that even the true miracles of Catholicism are enshrouded in layer upon layer of legends, superstitions and popular stories beyond any possible verification? The occasional occurrence of true prodigies which diligent study could extricate from this mass of fictional and legendary accounts, should not this be just as probable in other religions?

In the name of religious science present currents of thought are rather susceptible of this mania of superficial comparison whereby all phenomena that happen to show some common exterior features are put on the same level. Cut glass resembles diamond but the real values are anything but identical. Wax figures displayed in some museums resemble their live models so closely that sometimes we feel tempted to shake hands with them. Imitation is supposed to resemble the original, and nothing could be more detrimental to truth than the drawing of hasty conclusions based on an incomplete study of the facts and on some superficial similarity.

Expectation and desire of the miraculous stem from man's primitive religious instincts. It is natural, therefore, that miraculous stories and legends should abound everywhere as manifestations of this basic tendency.

This expectation of the miraculous finds its expression in definite forms and symbols, such as springs, shrines, ex-votos, and the like. Because the archetype of these symbols is inscribed in the very psyche of man, the development of legendary miraculous accounts follows a constantly recurring set pattern. Indeed, these archetypical structures grow out of the very foundations of being. Divine power, in the achievement of a miraculous feat, will take account of these psychic frames, with the result that similar patterns will be discernible in the Christian miracle also. There will remain, however, a definite difference in the style of the symbolic language: human fiction betrays its own narrowness, entanglement, vanity and passions, whereas a truly divine feat exhibits properties characteristic of a divine act, such as infinity, holiness, simplicity, purity and majesty. The mere existence of a language of symbols in both the Christian and non-Christian miracle is not a valid basis in religious psychology for any conclusion whatever that would authorize either acceptance or rejection of the historicity of the prodigious event connected with this symbolism. The problem of historicity can be resolved only through strictly historical criteria.

We can now proceed to our study of the miraculous in the non-Christian world. Quite evidently the standards applied in this research will have to be less severe than in the case of Lourdes. Failing to make allowances would be, in fact, somewhat dishonest, for none of these religions can claim a system of supervision even remotely comparable to that existing in Lourdes. On the other hand, imposing draconian conditions upon the acceptance of the Christian miracle, while bowing one's head in naive credulity before every non-Christian prodigious feat, would be equally unreasonable. This attitude is more common than the uninitiated might be inclined to think. The Catholic miracle is approached with this silent question: "Could it not be that it does not really exist after all?" Before the non-Catholic prodigy, the question is worded like this: "Could it not be true after all?" Such frame of mind would be an indication, not of scientific concern for truth but of some morbid compulsion to doubt, apparently typical of our age. This bias must be eliminated if the facts are to be dealt with in full independence.

The very nature of the question excludes the possibility of establishing complete proof that events of this sort have never occurred. First of all, there exist no comprehensive studies offering a satisfactory synthesis of the non-Christian miracle;[1] the researcher must be satisfied with the available monographs and accept the risk of omissions inherent in any limited study of this sort. Moreover, even apart from the question of such risks, one might always ob-

[1] J. De Bonniot: *Le miracle et ses contrefaçons* (Paris, 1887) is completely outdated, but R. Vander Elst: *Vraies et fausses guérisons miraculeuses* (Paris, 1924) and J. A. McCulloch: "Miracles," *Hastings' Encyclopaedia of Religion and Ethics*, VIII (Edinburgh, 1916), pp. 677-679, still contain many valid elements. C. J. Wright: *Miracle in History and Modern Thought* (London, 1930) contains a good deal of information, which would be very interesting if the author had abstained from mixing exceptional and ordinary facts, historical data and legends haphazardly and without any critical discrimination; the bibliography offered on pp. 409-424 remains a useful guide in research. A recent book by G. Mensching: *Das Wunder im Glauben und Aberglauben der Völker* (Leiden, 1957), while containing a certain amount of factual data, interprets them from an a priori comparatist viewpoint rather than in the light of critical history.

ject: "Did you study all of the cases? Could not certain facts exist that chance and circumstances have concealed from your eyes?"

The alternative is to study those events which have already been dealt with in comparative religious history. If the results turn out to be negative, they will yield the following argument. Through progress achieved in the field of comparative religious science during the last fifty years, a material of immense proportions has been accumulated. Even though the research was often motivated by the avowed desire of refuting the Catholic claim to monopoly on major miracles, religious history has not disclosed further data. The scientifically best suited explanation of this lack is the actual nonexistence of such additional facts.

I · THE MIRACULOUS IN NON-CHRISTIAN RELIGIONS

For the sake of clarity we shall deal with the prodigies of ancient paganism and those of the contemporary non-Christian religions, in that order.

a · Ancient Paganism

Hellenism is the ground preferred by most scholars in their quest for a sequence of facts that could be aligned with the miracles of the Christian religion.[2] The sequence develops at the *Asclepieia* or sacred shrines of Aesculapius, the god of medicine. Let us study it as a typical example.

[2] On Greek miracles, see O. Weinreich: *Antike Heilungswunder;* Untersuchungen zum Wunderglauben der Griechen und Römer (Giessen, 1909); W. A. Jayne: *The Healing Gods of Ancient Civilizations* (New Haven, 1925); M. Delcourt; *Les grands sanctuaires de la Grèce* (Paris, 1947), particularly pp. 93-113; R. Reitzenstein: *Hellenistische Wundererzählungen* (Leipzig, 1906); R. Bultmann: *The History of the Synoptic Tradition* (Oxford, 1963), pp. 209-244; on these last two books, see the criticism by L. de Grandmaison: *Jesus Christ,* III, pp. 260-267; A. Oepke: "Ἰάομαι," *Theol. Wörterbuch z. N.T.,* III, pp. 205-211; O. Kern: *Die Religion der Griechen,* 3 vols. (Berlin, 1926-1938); K. Prümm: *Religionsgeschichtliches Handbuch für den Raum der altchristlichen Umwelt*[2] (Rome, 1954), pp. 442-464; B. Kötting: *Peregrinatio Antiqua;* Wallfahrten in der Antike und das Pilgerwesen in der Alten Kirche (Münster, 1950); R. Bloch: *Les prodiges dans l'Antiquité classique* (Paris, 1963); P. Fiebig: *Antike Wundergeschichten zum Studium der Wunder des Neuen Testamentes;* Kleine Texte für Vorlesungen und Übungen, n. 79 (Bonn, 1911), has gathered in a booklet the classical texts on the matter.

These shrines are found at Cos, Athens, Epidaurus, Alexandria and other places. Excavations at the end of the last century have brought to light the architecture of the Epidaurus Hieron.[3] A sacred fountain and a double colonnade have been found near the temple and in direct communication with it. The colonnade served as a dormitory (abaton) open to the pilgrims who came here hoping to be healed. That is where the incubation rites (εγκοίμησις) were performed; they consisted of the patients' assuming a motionless state of holy expectation preparing them for the reception of divine messages. The god appeared to the patients in their sleep, explaining to them how they would be cured. This dream was the coveted end of the pilgrimages. Those eventually visited by the god either found themselves cured in the morning or received instructions on the therapy that would make them well. Leaving their offerings in the temple, they would then return to their homes.[4]

As at our Christian shrines, the walls of the Epidaurus temple are covered with all kinds of ex-votos: rings and coins, but also silver hands, feet and eyes. No reproduction indicating a miraculous cure is found at Epidaurus.[5] All these objects supply no proof of the miraculous nature of the cures, any more than do the ex-votos of Catholic devotion.

There existed within the compound of the Epidaurus temple six commemorative tables of stone mentioned by Pausanias.[6] Excavations have uncovered three of them; one was intact, the second, legible for the most part, and the third, heavily damaged. Frag-

[3] On the Asclepieion at Epidaurus, see particularly R. Herzog: *Die Wunderheilungen von Epidauros* (Leipzig, 1931); useful data will also be found in comprehensive works on hellenistic miracles, in A. Defrasse and H. Lechat: *Epidaure* (Paris, 1895), and in the polemics on Epidaurus between E. Mangenot and G. Bertrin; see especially E. Mangenot: "Les miracles d'Esculape," *Revue du clergé français*, 91 (1917), 289-303, 424-505; answer by G. Bertrin: "Sur les guérisons attribuées à Esculape," *ibid.*, 94 (1918), 281-299; and a rejoinder by E. Mangenot: "Riposte de M. Magenot à M. Bertrin," *ibid.*, pp. 299-307.

[4] These incubation rites, tolerated rather than encouraged by the Church, have subsisted for centuries in Christian religious practices in greatly varying forms and mixed with all sorts of superstitions. On this subject see, besides the above quoted book by Kötting, also H. Leclercq: "Incubation," *Dictionn. d'Archéol. chrét. et de liturgie*, VII, cc. 511-517.

[5] See R. Herzog: *loc. cit.*, p. 55.

[6] Pausanias, II, 27, 3.

ments of a fourth slab have also been found. These tables are made of smooth sandstone, measure about 65 by 29 inches and contain in fourth century B.C. script the accounts of some outstanding cures.[7]

Precise evaluation of the historical validity of these accounts is a difficult task. The *Real-Encyclopädie* of Pauly-Wissowa[8] considers them mere legends, whereas R. Herzog who has studied the Epidaurus texts with extreme care arrives at a more carefully qualified conclusion which we have also adopted in its main lines.[9] He believes that "the basic contents of these accounts are real. They are, however, encumbered by an enormous proliferation of legendary stories born of popular fantasy, in a manner similar to the genesis of some literary traditions that develop under our own eyes, and by accounts of fictitious miracles, many of which actually originate elsewhere than in Epidaurus. Responsibility for the creation of these miraculous stories is not borne by the priests or regular visitors of the temple alone; the imagination of pilgrims who invented these fables to make the long wait more bearable or as a means of mutual encouragement to hope, must have been a contributing factor. While the leaders must have evidently asked the pilgrims to report to them any eventual miraculous cures, they were responsible for the actual writing of the reports to which they added stories of comminatory prodigies."

Such an indictment does not make the interpretation of these oneiric accounts any easier. Where does reality end and storytelling begin? Is the illness real or imaginary? Does the cure take place with or without medical aid? As for the dreams themselves, are they spontaneous, although prompted and prepared by the reading

[7] The Greek text whose mutilated passages have been reconstructed through patient and meticulous epigraphical and philological research is available in R. Herzog: *loc. cit.*, pp. 8-35, with an excellent German translation. Passages quoted here are borrowed from this text.

[8] Pauly-Wissowa: *Real-Encyclopädie der klass. Altertumwiss*, I, cc. 1686-1687.

[9] R. Herzog: *op. cit.*, pp. 57-58. The seven slabs found at the Asclepieion at Lebene in Crete are damaged almost beyond legibility. It has been possible, however, to decipher the information that the inscriptions on the slabs had been compiled from wooden ex-voto tablets of pilgrims. We may then suppose that the Epidaurus texts have also been composed, at least partly, from these "πίνακες."

of the inscriptions, or are they provoked by artificial means? All of these questions have been dealt with by numerous distinguished authors whose answers range from one extreme to the other. Let us gather, however, those indications which could be helpful in drawing the line between history and fiction.

First of all, are the descriptions and diagnoses of the various illnesses admissible as they stand? The reports use no technical terminology, not even the medical language of the age, but are worded, apparently on purpose, in popular style. Therefore, such words as "blind," "mute," "paralytic," must be interpreted in a very relative sense, and internal diseases are diagnosed from external symptoms evaluated by norms typical of popular imagination.[10]

Did the patients receive medical assistance, or did they not? It has been established beyond a doubt that in the second century A.D. the sick at the Asclepieia of Pergamus, Lebene and Epidaurus were looked after and treated by professional physicians. The Cos Asclepieion (founded, incidentally, by physicians) and the one in Athens were thus managed as early as in the fourth century B.C.[11] No similar information is available concerning Epidaurus at the date of the inscriptions containing the miraculous accounts. The texts themselves, however, reveal a considerable number of elements pointing to systematic treatment typical of contemporary medical practice: ointments, medicinal plants, thermal cures, gymnastics. It is therefore probable that in ancient Epidaurus also priest-physicians made up the personnel of the temple.[12]

Aristophanes draws a sharp caricature of the Asclepieia in his Plutos.[13] Some have concluded from his play that the apparitions and interventions attributed to Aesculapius and his assistants must have been nothing more than dishonest comedy performed by priests and physicians. In actual fact, the documents reveal nothing that would support a theory of conscious deception. Quite a number of the dreams resemble actual experience so closely that attributing them, as to their exclusive source, to painful sensations, somatic states or symbolizations of the subconscious, would be

[10] See R. Herzog: *op. cit.*, pp. 57 and 66.

[11] See R. Herzog: *op. cit.*, pp. 144-149.

[12] On this point we adopt the criticism of B. Kötting, *op. cit.*, p. 25, n. 127, against the position taken by Herzog.

[13] Aristophanes: *Plutos*, vs. 653-763.

difficult.[14] Thus even in the absence of any historical testimony we are tempted to accept, as a hypothesis strongly suggested by the text, that "after offering to the patient some somniferous medicine the physician-priests of Epidaurus took advantage of his sleep to administer some rapid and energetic treatment." [15] The elementary forms of surgery were well known in contemporary medicine which knew also the possibilities of hypnotic suggestion; the Homeric heroes were familiar with narcotic beverages.

The accounts of cures, read in this light, show that there is *not a single one* among the cases discussed that would not be liable to natural interpretation.

About sixty accounts of cures have been deciphered. Six of them report the cases of women who after an apparition of the god in their sleep or after having relations with him, gave birth to a child (W 1, 2, 31, 34, 39, 42). Whether this is a coincidence (six instances would not be too many among the thousands of hopeful pilgrims), or these were cases of an all too natural intervention on the part of the personnel of the temple, it would be difficult to call them miracles. At this point popular imagination takes over and exaggerates some of the cases to a grotesque extreme. For instance:

> W 1. Cleo had been pregnant for five years when she came to seek the god's help; she fell asleep in the abaton. She had hardly left the place and was outside the Hieron when she gave birth to a boy who the minute after he was born washed himself in the water of the spring and began to toddle along beside his mother.[16]

[14] Herzog: *op. cit., passim,* attempts (in our opinion unsuccessfully) to reduce everything to this single explanation.

[15] The quotation is from A. J. Festugière, in M. Gorce and R. Mortier: *Histoire générale des religions,* II, p. 136. Herzog's rejection of this hypothesis, *op. cit.,* p. 67: "Die durch nichts an die Hand gegebene Annahme von Rauschgiften oder Hypnose (the completely unwarranted assumption of narcotic poisons and hypnosis)" seems exaggerated.

[16] Long pseudo-pregnancy involving the absence of menstruation or the growth of a mole is not an infrequent phenomenon which was well known in the antiquity; see Herzog, pp. 71-72. It may be terminated by evacuation of the mole or by normal pregnancy. The alleged age of this infant is probably better explained by popular imagination than substitution of an older orphan by the personnel of the temple, as suggested by Vander Elst: *op. cit.,* p. 148.

Some ten cases (W 4, 9, 11, 18, 22, 32, 40, 55, 69) concern various eye diseases. Lack of hygiene in these southerly lands accounts for a great many of illnesses of this sort. The word "blind" is not used in the absolute sense. The majority of cases as reported would rather fall in the category of inflammation and abscess of the eyelids. These afflictions are sometimes so severe that the eye altogether disappears. In the opinion of Dr. Josionek there is not one among the cases of blindness in Epidaurus that could not have been relieved by a spontaneous bursting of the abscess or through simple disinfection. A few examples will confirm this opinion.

> W 9. A man turns to the god for help; he is blind of one eye; there remains only the eyelid which no longer covers anything but empty space. The people in the Hieron find his faith very naive, for he expects to recover his sight when nothing remains of his eye but its place; in his sleep he receives the privilege of a vision; it seems to him that the god prepares some medicine, lifts his eyelid and pours the medicine inside. When leaving at daybreak he sees with both eyes.
>
> W 40. Timon of X. is injured under the eye by a spear. He has a dream in his sleep; it seems to him that the god, who has pounded some herb, pours something in his eye. He is cured.
>
> W 65. A blind man. He loses his ointment at the pond; sleeps in the abaton; dreams that the god advises him to look for the ointment in the large shelter, to his left at the entrance. When daylight comes he is assisted in his search by the slave. He enters the shelter, sees his ointment and is cured.

The accounts report also three cures of muteness and seven cases of paralysis (W 5, 44, 41, and W 3, 15, 35, 37, 38, 57, 64). The description of both the illnesses and the manner of their cure makes it evident that the afflictions were simple psychogenic functional troubles with their corresponding cures. We take an example of each kind.

> W 44. A young girl, mute. She is walking about in the sanctuary; sees a snake sliding off a tree and heading toward the woods; terrified, she calls her father and mother; returns cured.
>
> W 37. Clemenes of Argus is paralyzed; he enters the abaton, falls asleep, has a dream; the god wraps him in a red blanket, takes him

to bathe outside the sacred compound in a pond with very cold water; he is shaking with fear, Aesculapius tells him that he does not heal the cowardly but only those who come with confidence; these he would not harm in any way but would dismiss them healed. Clemenes wakes up, takes a bath, returns in perfect state of health.

Two other cases (W 8 and 14) concern the evidently spontaneous evacuation of gallstones during sleep; in one account, the circumstances of the discharge are not mentioned; in the second, it is the result of a homosexual dream.

Five accounts (W 17, 45, 48, 61, 66) tell about abscesses bursting in the patient's sleep or following some accidental perforation. We quote an example, one that has doubtless been embellished by popular fantasy.

W 61. NN of X suffers of an abscess. He enters the shrine. He does not obtain his wish; the god does not appear to him in his sleep at the abaton; he feels neglected by the god and returns home. No longer capable of bearing the pains, he tries to kill himself by thrusting a dagger into the tumor. His daughter finds him in an unconscious state, takes him in her arms, extracts the dagger. Blood gushes forth from the tumor and the patient is healed.

Three cases of infected wounds (W 12, 30, 53) and one of an abdominal tumor (W 27) seem to involve elementary surgery under narcosis.

W 12. Evippus, wounded by a spear, has been carrying in his jaw a spearhead for six years. He falls asleep in the abaton; the god extracts the spearhead and places it in the patient's hand. At dawn the man leaves, healed, and carrying the spearhead in his hands.

W 53. NN of X is wounded in the chest. The wound is suppurating; he turns to the god for help. While sleeping in the abaton, he has a dream: the god washes his chest with fresh milk and applies some ointment to the wound. After wiping him, he orders him to take a bath in cold water. Upon awakening, the man takes a bath in running water and is healed.

W. 27. A man suffers of a tumor in the abdomen. He has a dream at the abaton; the god orders his assistants to hold him still and open his abdomen; he runs away but is caught and tied to the doorpost. Asclepius opens his abdomen, cuts out the abscess and resews the wound; the patient is untied. He returns home healed; the floor was covered with blood.

Five cases (W 13, 21, 23, 25, 41) involve persons afflicted with dropsy, intestinal ailments, or tapeworms. These patients are cured in their sleep by fantastic operations (decapitation, etc.) We quote here one case that is somewhat less fantastic and suggests medical intervention.

W 41. Erasippa of C. Her abdomen was swollen, she could not digest anything. She sleeps in the abaton, has a dream; the god massages her abdomen and embraces her; then he offers her a cupful of medicine, ordering her to drink it; he forces her to vomit; which she does, filling her dress. At daybreak she finds her dress all soiled by the vomiting; she feels cured.

To complete the list of wonders, we should mention the cure of a migraine (W 29), deliverance from an invasion of lice (W 28) and a cure of baldness (W 19), all three of which would be rather difficult to classify as major miracles. In three instances the god gave instructions leading to the recovery of missing persons or objects (W 24, 46, 63). We also note a cure of epilepsy (W 62); the problem is whether this was an actual healing or a temporary improvement. The latter is often the case with epileptic patients.

Some of the accounts (W 10, 33) are considered mere legends by all of the commentators, while others (W 6, 7, 11, 36, 47) appear suspicious for the very fact that they relate comminatory wonders. We have thus covered the whole list of cures achieved in the subjects' sleep. Although making every possible allowance for their historical validity, we fail to find a single case that could be classified as a "major prodigy."

Four cases, not yet mentioned, would seem more relevant, since they are not connected with dreams but occur in a state of full consciousness. Every one of these accounts contains the word "ὕπαρ" that is, state of wakefulness. The cases described deserve special consideration, not only because they are less suspect from the historical viewpoint, but also because their nature allows a more accurate comparison with the Christian miracle. The following are the actual accounts of these four wonders.

> W 16. Nicanor, paralytic. He is seated, fully awake. A street urchin grabs his walking stick and runs away with it. He gets up, runs after the boy, and from then on he is healthy.
>
> W 20. Lyson from Hermione is a blind child. While fully awake, he was treated by one of the sacred dogs that licked his eye; he goes home cured.
>
> W 26. A child from Aegina is cured by a dog. The child had a tumor on the neck. While fully awake, he was treated by one of the sacred dogs that licked the wound and healed it.
>
> W 43. NN from Chios, immobilized by gout. While fully awake, he was bitten by a goose; the wound caused by the bird bled abundantly; the patient was healed.

None of our readers will find in these cases anything but some purely natural phenomenon. It is a universally recognized fact that the saliva of an animal has a soothing effect on skin lesions; in fact, when combined with the pressure of the tongue, it might cause the bursting of a ripe abscess, or clean and free eyelids closed by pus. Moreover, it does not require much professional psychiatric knowledge today to recognize the possible effects of emotional shocks upon psychogenic paralysis.

In addition to these accounts of cures we also possess the definitely historical testimony of Aelius Aristides, a neurotic rhetorician and firm believer in Aesculapius.[17] For nine years he undergoes treatment after treatment at the most famous Asclepieia. Having gained some temporary improvement he faithfully pursues the treatments until his death, never giving up hope to regain his health. The diary he kept on his illness, amounting to some thirty thousand lines, gives us an accurate picture of everyday life at the Aesculapius shrines.

[17] See A. Boulanger: *Aelius Aristides—Discours sacrés* (Paris, 1923), pp. 163-210.

A long inscription by Julianus Apellas,[18] who seeks relief from his stomach ailment in Epidaurus and explains lengthily the cure prescribed for him by the god, presents the same picture. Both texts speak at great length of medical prescriptions and treatments, but there is nothing in them that would make the reader think of major miracles or even minor wonders.

This somewhat prolonged discussion should have prepared us for the proper appraisal of comments such as the one by Loisy, who unblushingly speaks of "cures that occur in Lourdes and have occurred in the past at the Asclepius temples," [19] or of this ironical remark by Pierre Janet, also concerning Lourdes: "We may state with satisfaction that twentieth-century miracles are not very much inferior in kind to those that have occurred at the Athens Asclepieion, several centuries before Christ." [20]

Wonders of this kind, abounding at *shrines*, tombs, fountains or caves, have been reported in the history of almost every religious group. An unbiased study of any of these accounts, excepting those reported in the Christian religion, leads to the same conclusion. If a report is found definitely unusual, critical history invariably finds that it is based on some legendary source or tradition. If, on the other hand, the story seems more realistic but is examined in the light of modern science, the miraculous element becomes so tenuous that one no longer may speak of major prodigies in the proper sense.

Trying to prove this point in detail and quoting examples from the various religions would be both monotonous and unprofitable. One typical example should suffice.

The warrior sect of the Sikhs in Punjab, India, founded by Baba Nanak in the 16th century, holds the successors of the founder in great honor. The history of these ten prophets, called "gurus" (a

[18] See the complete text with German translation in Herzog: *op. cit.*, pp. 43-44; French translation in Defrasse and Lechat: *op. cit.*, pp. 152-153.

[19] A. Loisy: *Quelques lettres sur des questions actuelles et sur des événements récents* (Ceffonds, 1908), pp. 60-61.

[20] P. Janet: *Les médications psychologiques* (Paris, 1925), I, p. 17 [transl. *Psychological Healing*, 2 vols. (New York, 1925)].

common name for masters of spiritual life), is so deformed by the most fantastic legends that it is now practically beyond recognition.[21] The Sikhs have at Amritsar a majestic temple, known to Westerners as the "Golden Temple." The sanctuary comprises a sacred pond called Amrita, i.e., "pond of immortality," excavated in 1574 by Ram Das, the fourth guru. The pond has been desecrated and filled in several times by Moslem invaders, to be, however, reconquered and purified by the Sikhs each time. The present temple was built at the beginning of the 19th century.[22]

The miracle that had originally prompted the construction of the pond is represented in a low relief. The story is told to the visitors of the temple in the following terms:

> In the time of the guru just named [Ram Das] there lived a man who had a beautiful daughter, devoted heart and soul to religion. Being for some reason or other angry with the girl, the father gave her in marriage to a man with maimed hands and feet, some say a leper, and the heartless parent scoffingly bid his daughter support herself and her helpless husband upon the bounty of God.
>
> In Indian fashion, the young wife performed her duty to herself and her crippled husband, by collecting alms from the people around, and in her begging tours she usually carried her lord in a basket on her head. One day she left her burden in the shade of some trees near a weed-covered pond, and went off to a neighboring village to beg for food. While she was away, her husband noticed with astonishment that a lame crow came and dipped its injured legs into the water, and by doing so, not only recovered the use of those limbs, but had its plumage miraculously bleached to a perfectly white color. The healing power of the water so strikingly manifested might, thought the cripple, benefit himself too, and so he crept to the edge of the pond, and entered the water, with the result that, to his infinite joy, he became whole again.
>
> When the dutiful wife returned to the spot she could not recognize her transformed husband, and did not believe that the sound man before her was the cripple she had left in the basket

[21] See J. C. Oman: *Cults, Customs and Superstitions of India* (London, 1908), pp. 83-84.

[22] See thorough description of the temple in J. C. Oman: *op. cit.*, pp. 85-103.

under the trees; but her very natural doubts were dispelled when the Guru Ram Das himself assured her that the man was indeed her own husband.[23]

Even if we should allow this account some historical truth, the cure cannot be characterized as a major miracle, for it concerns only a functional disorder. However, the legendary style of the whole story, and especially the artificial way in which themes borrowed from ancient Indian mythology are being used here, point beyond a doubt to an etiological legend, that is, a story invented after some event for the purpose of providing a sacred place with the halo of religious consecration.[24]

Thousands of pilgrims still seek today relief from their bodily ills in the waters of this pond. One would, therefore, expect to hear of more recent wonders occurring at the shrine; such accounts would be more reliable historically, as they would be recorded not several centuries but at the most a few years after the events. There are, in fact, two commemorative tables, the size of a man, at the main gate; they relate in Hindi and English the most striking wonder that has taken place since the building of the new temple. During a storm on April 30, 1877, a lightning bolt ran through the temple where four hundred people had gathered to pray: "miraculously," there were no deaths or injuries.[25] This is the greatest prodigy adorning in a whole century a temple and sacred pond maintained for the healing of all diseases.

The discrepancy between the low relief and the memorial tables at the Golden Temple of Amritsar is an eloquent symbol of the contrast between legend and history.

The accounts quoted on these pages have led us in several instances to the borderline separating prodigy from magic. In pagan rites this border is deliberately violated and the expectation of the miraculous is replaced by a deliberate *magic* treatment of things and events. As a first reaction one might expect to see under these

[23] See J. C. Oman: *The Brahmans, Theists and Muslims of India* (London, 1906), pp. 262-263.
[24] *Ibid.*, p. 263.
[25] See full text in J. C. Oman: *Cults, Customs, and . . .*, pp. 99-100.

conditions a proliferation of miracles which become increasingly fantastic. The actual result is precisely the opposite. It would seem that a constant recourse to magic in even the simplest matters of life neutralizes the expectation of miracles so completely that no room is left for anything beyond the ordinary and the habitual. If everything is magic then there is no natural order wherein the miraculous would constitute an exception. Quite typically, therefore, we find that an area such as ancient Egypt, where the practice of magic permeated all aspects of religious life, is also the one where the miraculous is hardly ever mentioned and the capacity for legendary narration seems to have dried up completely. Such an eminently scientific encyclopedia as the *Reallexicon der Aegyptischen Religionsgeschichte*[26], while presenting long articles under the headings "magician" and "magic," does not even contain the words "prodigy" or "miracle."

Beside wonders connected with some geographic place we find others linked to *persons*.

History records the names of many persons who achieved notoriety as magicians or *thaumaturgists*. Quite often the relationship between their activities on the one hand and their religion on the other is entirely superficial. Their wonders are more like theatrical performances or even tricks, not meant to confirm a particular mission or doctrine and not depending in any way upon the moral or religious stature of the thaumaturgists. On the contrary, their reputation as possessing superhuman powers is the direct result of the dramatic effect of their performance; this lends them a pseudo-religious prestige which they are eager to exploit.

The best known among them is Apollonius of Tyana whose pseudo-miracles have been used since the earliest times in attacks against the Christian miracle. His is, therefore, a typical case.

Apollonius of Tyana, a Pythagorean philosopher, lived in the

[26] H. Bonnet: *Reallexikon der Aegyptischen Religionsgeschichte* (Berlin, 1952); see also J. Sainte Fare Garnot: *La vie religieuse dans l'ancienne Egypte* (Paris, 1948), pp. 127-135; F. Lexa: *La magie dans l'Egypte ancienne*, 3 vols. (Paris, 1925). See a typical example of the prodigious being absorbed by magic in G. Maspero: *Etudes de mythologie et d'archéologie égyptiennes* (Paris, 1893), II, pp. 402-410, under this misleading title: "La Déesse Miritskro et ses guérisons miraculeuses."

first century A.D. Moiragenes, his first biographer (a fragment of this book is found among the writings of Origen) speaks of him as a magician involved in a controversy over his art with Euphrates, the Stoic.[27] In the second century he is again mentioned briefly by Lucian who describes him as a prestidigitator avidly seeking to exploit the credulousness of the people.

In the third century, however, or a century and a half after the events, the widow of the superstitious Emperor Septimus Severus, Julia Domna, hires Philostratus, a rhetorician, to write a new biography of Apollonius. The author draws upon the alleged memories of a certain Damis,[28] but his main contribution consists in lending considerable support to the anti-Christian controversy.[29]

His book relates an impressive number of extraordinary wonders clearly invented after the model of the miracles of the Gospel and the Acts of the Apostles. There is today unanimous agreement among all serious critics that the work is nothing more than a propaganda pamphlet whose author, while drawing on ancient sources, fictionalizes and edits his data in order to transform a notorious prestidigitator into a moralizing thaumaturgist. All critical history can salvage from his book amounts to hardly more than the name of Apollonius and, to a certain extent, the itinerary of his travels.[30]

[27] Origen: *Contra Celsum*, VI, 41.

[28] E. Meyer: "Apollonius von Tyane und Philostratus," *Hermes*, 52 (1917), 371-424 [reprinted in his *Kleine Schriften* (Halle, 1924), II, pp. 133-191], has attempted to prove that the "Memoirs of Damis" and the other so-called sources on Apollonius are mere literary fiction; Meyer's thesis was favorably received. On the same matter see also A. Wikenhauser: *Die Apostelgeschichte und ihr Geschichtswert* (Münster, 1921), p. 385.

[29] On the history of this fictional biography of Apollonius, see especially P. de Labriolle: *La réaction païenne*, Etude sur la polémique antichrétienne du Ier au VIe siècle (Paris, 1934), pp. 175ff. There is a thorough bibliography of critical works on Philostratus's book in L. de Grandmaison: *Jesus Christ*, II, pp. 365-369; K. Prümm: *Religionsgeschichtliches Handbuch*, pp. 458-460; M. J. Lagrange: "Les légendes Pythagoriciennes et l'Evangile, B. Le Neo-pythagorisme, Apollonius de Tyane," *Revue Biblique*, 46 (1937), 5-28. F. G. Conybeare has edited, with an English translation, Philostratus: *The Life of Apollonius of Tyana, The Epistles of Apollonius*, and the *Treatise of Eusebius I-II* (New York, 1912).

[30] On some other wonder-workers, such as Peregrinus Proteus and Alexander of Abonuteichos, see K. Prümm: *op. cit.*, pp. 460-462, who also has a bibliography on the subject.

The almost divine authority that was attributed to the *kings* and *emperors* of antiquity explains also their reputation as wonder-workers. One of the frequently quoted examples is the healing of two sick men by Vespasian. The facts have a certain historical validity. Tacitus himself, a conscientious and critical historian, vouches for their reliability. In actual fact, the details supplied by Tacitus eliminate at once the supposition of organic recovery. The physicians consulted by the emperor find that the afflictions are merely functional and could be cured by the appropriate treatment (disinfection by bathing the eyelids, and manual pressure to reset a dislocation). The following is Tacitus' account: [31]

> A plebeian from Alexandria, known as a blind person, throws himself at the emperor's feet, begging him to heal his blindness. He claims that he came to the emperor following an order by Serapis, the god of this superstitious people, and he pleads with the emperor to apply saliva to his cheeks and eyelids. Another man, whose hand is paralyzed, begs him in the name of this god to do him the favor of stepping on his hand. Vespasian first jokes with them and refuses to comply with their request. Their insistence, however, makes him to hesitate; he is reluctant to do something that would be interpreted as a sign of absurd vanity, but he is swayed by his visitors' insistence and the flattery of his own advisors. Finally he orders his physicians to determine whether the blind man and the one with the paralyzed hand could be cured by purely human means. After some consulting, the physicians give their opinion; the blind man's organ of vision is not destroyed and could function again if the stuff that obstructs it is removed; as for the other, his hand is dislocated and could be put back in place by some pressure; this might be, in fact, the very intention of the gods who have chosen the emperor as their instrument. Considering all the odds, if the treatment is successful, all the credit will be given to the emperor, whereas in case of failure only the unfortunate beggars would appear ridiculous. Vespasian, confident that his lucky star makes everything possible for him and that the feat he is asked to achieve is not altogether improbable, turns to the task with a relaxed air and does what he is asked

[31] Tacitus: *Historiae*, 1. IV, c. 81; see also Suetonius: *De vita Caesaris*, VII, 2ff. See on the matter S. Morenz: "Vespasian, Heiland der Kranken," *Würzburg. Jahrb. Alt.*, IV (1949), pp. 370-378.

to do before the eyes of an excited and curious mob. Instantly, the dislocated hand begins to function again, and the blind man regains his sight. To this day the double cure is corroborated by eyewitnesses who no longer could expect any benefit from lying.

Most prodigies, however, are attributed to great *religious figures*: mystics and saints, especially founders and reformers.

The biography of most founders of religion reveals that almost all of them either ignored the miraculous or at least disclaimed any credit for prodigious feats. This is particularly true of Buddha, Zoroaster, Confucius and Lao-Tse.[32] Subsequent centuries, however, credited them with all sorts of extravagant miracles, sometimes in the very writings in which they themselves express their dislike for the miraculous.

These legends are in no case supported by contemporary evidence and often appear only centuries after the events they intend to illustrate. Some of them, in fact, are so fantastic, immoral or childish as to contradict clearly the deep religious feelings of the man they claim to honor, and thus betray beyond a doubt their legendary nature. Even in those cases in which the limits of reality are not altogether ignored, a closer look almost invariably reveals the classic laws of the evolution of legends, as formulated by the masterly pen of H. Delehaye, the Bollandist who studied the development of legends in the Christian Middle Ages.[33]

There is hardly anything in this whole profusion of miraculous tales that would deserve our attention here. The titles "miracle" or "prodigy" in the indices of the standard works on comparative reli-

[32] On the miracles of Buddha, see note in L. de Grandmaison: *Jesus Christ*, III, pp. 239-242; also J. Przyluski: *Le Bouddhisme* (Paris, 1932); some typical texts in *Sacred Books of the East* (*SBE*), X, pp. 63ff.; on Confucius, see some texts in *SBE*, XXVIII, pp. 303ff.; A. Rygaloff: *Confucius* (Paris, 1946); on Zoroaster, some texts in *SBE*, XXXI, p. XXVI; E. Herzfeld: *Zoroaster and His World*, 2 vols. (Princeton, 1947). General survey of miracles by great founders of religions in McCulloch; "Miracles," *Hastings' Encyclopaedia of Religion and Ethics*, VIII, pp. 677-678. The author's conclusion: "As to these miracles as a whole, there is no evidence that they ever occurred"; his conclusion on pagan miracles in general is just as categorical: "on the whole, the miracles of ethnic religions do not possess an air of truth"; see also C. J. Wright: *op. cit.*, pp. 57-62.

[33] H. Delehaye: *The Legends of the Saints* (New York, 1962), especially pp. 12-85.

gious history contain no reference to the lives of the respective founders, or to miracles achieved within the religious body they have founded.

The case of Islam is an exception to the rule. The Koran states clearly that Mohammed never claimed to possess the gift of miracles. When doubters assail his prophecies as unreliable and demand to see actual miracles, he tells them that he is not a wonder-worker, that he does not know the future, and that the only and decisive divine sign he appeals to is the Koran itself.[34]

This in no way kept his first biographers from crediting him with a great variety of miracles, and his life, as well as those of the other prophets of Islam, eventually became surrounded by an abundant growth of legends.[35] Most of these fantasies are distorted replicas of Bible and Gospel miracles.[36]

Moreover, the expanding Islam soon faced the task of assimilating into its fold various ethnic groups, some pagan with deeply rooted desires for the prodigious, and some Christian, with their faith in miracles firmly established. It was quite natural that Mohammedanism should attempt to direct the aim of these movements and desires upon the martyrs, founders and Sufis of Islam.

Notwithstanding the explicit statements in the Koran, orthodox Moslem theology eventually came to contradict its own rigid monotheism, which excludes the concept of any mediation between God and man, and admitted both the possibility and the actual occurrence of miracles, which are achieved in support of the prophets' mission and the humiliation of their opponents (these prodigies are called "mu'jiza"), or as displays of divine goodwill toward a holy person (in which case the miracles are called "karâmah"). The theological explanation of the possibility of these

[34] See e.g. in the Koran, Surah VII, 188; XIII, 8, 27; XVII, 95; XXV, 8-11; see J. Houben: "De Islam," *Christus*. Handbook voor de geschiedenis der godsdiensten (Utrecht, 1950), p. 648. Also R. D. Smith: *Comparative Miracles* (St. Louis, 1965), pp. 106-123, 179-180.

[35] See H. Gottschalk: "Der Islam, seine Entstehung, Entwicklung und Lehre," in F. König: *Christus und die Religionen der Erde* (Vienna, 1951), III, p. 66; T. Andrae: *Mohammed: The Man and His Faith* (New York, 1936); R. D. Smith: *op. cit.*, pp. 124-137.

[36] Proof of this claim in D. Sidersky: *Les origines des légendes musulmanes dans le Coran et dans la vie des prophètes* (Paris, 1933).

miracles is based on the Mohammedan conception of natural events which is altogether different from our Western idea of the laws of nature. Allah is the only agent always and everywhere. Our "natural law" is simply the habitual manner in which events are governed by Allah. Whenever Allah chooses to modify this habitual pattern, a miracle results.[37] Later theologians, among them Al-Idji, eventually worked out a theory of the nature and apologetic value of the miraculous that is not too far from the Catholic view.[38]

This acceptance of the miraculous nonetheless contradicts the very core of Mohammedanism and amounts to a change in doctrine, an allowance to the popular thirst for the prodigious. In fact, violent movements have emerged periodically throughout the centuries, opposing in the name of Moslem orthodoxy any belief in miracles. Such reactions are still current in Islam.[39]

Even a quick glance of these miraculous stories will reveal to anyone the degree to which they owe their existence to popular fantasy. The atmosphere we find in them bears a closer resemblance to the world of the Thousand and One Nights than to religious experience. None of the books and articles we have been able to consult on the matter offered a single fact that would bear both the mark of historical validity, and some resemblance, close or remote, to our "major prodigy." [40]

There is only one important exception: the personality of al-

[37] See Houben, *op. cit.*, pp. 700 and 704; also A. J. Wensinck: *The Muslim Creed* (Cambridge, 1932), p. 224; I. Goldziher: *Le dogme et la loi de l'Islam* (Paris, 1958), pp. 107-109.

[38] See A. J. Wensinck: "Mu'djiza," *Handwörterbuch des Islam* (Leiden, 1941), pp. 517-518.

[39] See Houben, p. 704; let us only mention as an example the destruction of a great number of tombs of Moslem saints by the Wahabites in 1924.

[40] See, e.g., I. Goldziher: *Muhammedanische Studien* (Halle, 1890), II, pp. 275-378: "Die Heiligenverehrung im Islam" (particularly pp. 292-295); C. Trumelet: *Les saints de l'Islam.* Légendes hagiologiques et croyances algériennes (Paris, 1881); E. Montet: "Le culte des saints dans l'Islam au Maghreb," *Hibbert Journal,* 7 (1909), 844-863; also, in reference to this article, a discussion in "comparative religion" by A. Kampmeier: "Muhammedan Parallels to Christian Miracles," *The Open Court* (Chicago), 23 (1909), 698-701; C. de Foucauld: *Reconnaissance au Maroc* (Paris, 1888); L. B. Juredeini: "Miracles of Ali Dinar of Darfu," *The Moslem World* (October, 1916); D. MacDonald: *Religious Attitude and Life in Islam* (Chicago, 1909), pp. 135-153.

Hosayn-ibn-Mansoor, better known as "al Hallaj" (the wool-comber).[41] The case is exceptional, first because al Hallaj is one of the true mystics of the non-Christian world, and one of the highest caliber; he dies a martyr's death on March 26, 922, when he is executed as a heretic because of his mystical views.[42] But the main reason why he is an exception to the rule is the fact that his miracles are not events attributed to him by popular fantasy; he himself, at least in the latter part of his life, sees in them the authenticating sign of his mystical inspiration and divine misson.[43] The main charge brought against him at his trial is based precisely on these miracles which he never wished to hide, being as they were personal gifts of Allah (karâmahs), but talked about them openly as being the signs of his mission (mu'jiza), thus violating the monopoly of the prophets and sinning against the orthodox theological doctrine considering the Koran as the last of public miracles.[44] The prodigies achieved by him were thus freely discussed by friends and enemies alike as facts accepted by everyone.

The moral stature of al Hallaj, the lofty standards of his life and mystical teaching, rule out our following his enemies in considering these facts as common quackery, or questioning his good faith.[45] Nor can we accept the opinion of those of his time who supposed that he had assimilated the yoga technique in India; for the facts he was reproached with happened before he made his trip to India.[46] We have no choice but to admit that the life of this mystic contains some extraordinary facts belonging in an authentic religious context; they are indeed such in nature as to appear to him personally as confirmations of his teaching and create for him a reputation as a miracle-worker.

[41] See L. Massignon: *La passion d'al-Hosayn-ibn-Mansour, al-Hallaj, martyr mystique de l'Islam*, 2 vols. (Paris, 1922).

[42] See on this subject J. Maréchal: "The Problem of Mystical Grace in Islam," in his *Studies in the Psychology of the Mystics*, pp. 239-281. The most striking feature of al-Hallaj is his preference for inner holiness rather than legalistic attitudes, and therefore the preference his theology shows for Jesus over Mohammed (see particularly pp. 267-271).

[43] See Massignon: p. 133: "Cas unique dans l'hagiographie sunnite, il y a corrélation entre les miracles et la doctrine (as a unique instance in Sunnite hagiography, there is here a connection between miracles and doctrine)."

[44] *Ibid.*, pp. 132-134.

[45] *Ibid.*, pp. 106-111.

[46] *Ibid.*, pp. 80-90.

The question is whether we can find among them some that would qualify as major prodigies. This calls for a closer examination.

For the task of separating those rather few elements which offer a guarantee of historicity from the mass of legends surrounding his person, and from the one-sided testimony of his friends and enemies, is not an easy one.[47] Furthermore, no account of healings is available that would facilitate comparison with the major miracle in the Christian sense.[48] Those historically valid accounts that speak of truly prodigious facts are restricted to a number of multiplications of food. These are the reports which, at least in Massignon's opinion, we cannot simply throw into the category of legendary inventions.[49]

A careful reading of these accounts will show the following point, brought out by Massignon himself: the case is not so much one of actual multiplication of foodstuffs as of a phenomenon closely related to the "apport phenomena" mentioned non infrequently in parapsychology, especially in connection with certain mediums, a subject upon which we shall return later. What we witness is not an actual, physical presence of food, but rather an ecstatic psychic experience similar to that found among shamans and yogis. This psychic experience is so intensive that the subject himself takes it for material reality, while the intensive power of suggestion he enjoys when in this condition involves the onlookers so intimately in the experience that after it is over they retain the irresistible impression of having actually and objectively participated in the event. Some examples will be quoted later.

This interpretation has the advantage of fitting perfectly into the mystical experience of al Hallaj, as attested to by all the witnesses and by himself.[50] The Sufi's extended periods of fasting and the presence of the desert mirage may well have a favorable influence

[47] Evidently legendary elements, e.g., the story explaining the origin of his surname, pp. 18-19; the punitive miracle, p. 131; accounts reported on pp. 314-315 and 442-460.

[48] Massignon, pp. 110-111, quotes the testimony of only one of his accusers who blames him for having staged a so-called cure; the miracle on p. 128 is too vague and the setting is definitely legendary (the episode of the money purse would be enough to prove this point).

[49] See text in Massignon, pp. 100-106.

[50] See, e.g., a very typical utterance quoted in Massignon, p. 136.

upon such experiences. Let us quote the most typical one of these accounts for the reader's benefit, inviting him to compare it with the literal text of the Gospel account of the multiplication of loaves. Let us point out that the "halawah" mentioned here is a kind of honey cake which plays an important part in Sufistic mysticism.[51]

Ibrahim al Holwani said:

> I was accompanying al-Hosayn-ibn-Mansoor with three of his disciples, and we were between Wasit and Bagdad. He was speaking, and in the conversation he uttered the word 'halawah.' And we said: 'The sheik should provide some for us.' He raised his head and exclaimed: 'O Thou whom no conscience can attain and no thought or opinion can decipher, Thou art the One visible in all bodies and all forms without touching them or mixing with them. Thou art the One shining forth from every and all, the One shining in the eternity of past and future; Thou who allowest no one to find Thee until all seems lost, and who appearest only shrouded in the guise of a riddle . . . If Thou valuest at all my nearness to Thee and my isolation from other creatures, give us this halawah for the sake of my companions.' Then he walked away from the road to a distance of about a mile, and we noticed there a piece of halawah of lively color, and we ate it. He himself did not taste it. When we had finished eating and started again on the road, an evil suspicion crept on me and I could not take my eyes away from the spot which I analyzed the best I could (so as to be able to find it again). Then I left the road under the pretext of purification, while the others kept walking ahead. Then I went back to the spot where we had eaten, but I did not see anything; I prayed and made two prostrations, saying: 'Deliver me, O God, from this base suspicion.' And a voice said to me: 'You have eaten upon the mountain of marvels, and now you wish to see the halawah. Correct your thinking. This sheik is no other than the King of the world.'

b · *The Non-Christian World of Today*

Various groups of facts of a more or less religious nature are being quoted by the non-Christian world of today as comparing with the

[51] See text in Massignon, pp. 103-104; in reference to the function of "halawah" in sufi mysticism, see *ibid.*, n. 2.

Christian miracle. Historical paganism quotes the achievements of yogis and fakirs and the manifestations of shamanism; in Western neopaganism attention is mainly called to the spiritist phenomena. The claims of both groups warrant a closer study.

Yoga,[52] an important part of Hindu spirituality, consists essentially in a technique of asceticism and concentration. Through certain practices and exercises the mind frees itself of the multiplicity of thought bound to matter and prepares itself for a free union with the divinity. Its classic form was borrowed from the "yoga-sutras" or "sayings on concentration" of Patañjali, probably written in the fourth or fifth century A.D. Shortly after, a Buddhist yoga called Tantrism, doubtless originated in Asanga,[53] appears in history; after conquering China and Japan, it is still very much alive in Tibetan Lamaism.

The real purpose of Yoga is not the mastering of certain "powers," but an ever more perfect liberation of the soul. For this reason a true Yogi will beware of the satisfaction he derives from using his superhuman powers. If he were to yield to the temptation of complacency, he would no longer be advancing on the road to deliverance but would lose his chance to acquire further powers and would become a slave of the qualities he already possesses.[54]

The temptation is indeed a dangerous one, and many fall to it. If

[52] See M. Eliade: *Techniques du Yoga* (Paris, 1948); ID.: *Yoga: Immortality and Freedom* (New York, 1958); J. W. Hauer: *Der Yoga* (Suttgart, 1958); R. Schmidt: *Fakire und Fakirtum im alten und modernen Indien* (Berlin, 1908); A. David-Neel: *With mystics and magicians in Tibet* (London, 1931); P. Brunton: *A Search in Secret India* (New York, 1935); O. Lacombe: "Sur le Yoga Indien," *Illuminations et sécheresses*, Etudes Carmélitaines, 27 (1937), pp. 163-176; R. Godel: *Essais sur l'expérience libératrice* (Paris, 1952); J. Filliozat: "Limites des pouvoirs humains dans l'Inde," *Limites de l'humain*, Etudes Carmélitaines (1953), pp. 23-38; H. Harrer: *Sieben Jahre in Thibet* (Vienna, 1952) [Transl. *Seven Years in Tibet* (New York)]; O. Leroy: *Les hommes-salamandres*, Recherches et réflexions sur l'incorruptibilité du corps humain (Paris, 1931); L. Gardet and C. Baudouin: "Expérience du Yoga et christianisme," *Suppl.* to *Vie Spirituelle*, 10 (1957), 486-496.

[53] See M. Eliade: *Yoga*, pp. 200ff.

[54] See Eliade: *Yoga*, p. 100. In reference to the growing dissemination of Yoga techniques in the Western world and popularized translations of certain esoteric texts from India and Tibet, many authors constantly caution their readers against inconsiderate enthusiasm for doctrines and practices separated from their natural context. See, e.g., Hauer: *Der Yoga*, pp. 407ff.; W. Stählin: "Thibetisches Yoga," *Quatember Evangelische Jahresbriefe* (1955), pp. 220-222.

a Yogi uses his paranormal powers for wordly success or material advantage, he will be drawn into desiring to display them more and more and use trickery and prestidigitation, should his actual powers fail.

"Yogi" is a generic term (Mohammedan terminology speaks of fakirs and dervishes), comprising a great variety of followers of Yoga practices, from genuine mystics and ascetics down to common jugglers and charlatans.

The Yoga exercises of bodily mastery, such as concentration of vision, highly developed techniques for the control of breathing, and other similar practices, help the Yogi to acquire tremendous capacities for clairvoyance, telepathy, thought transmission, and an almost unlimited power of psychic, particularly hypnotic, influence over others. Some even achieve mastery over their conditioned reflexes and vegetative functions on a scale quite beyond the comprehension of the Western mind. In the state of trance the Yogi can stop his digestive processes or regulate his body temperature, exposing himself to severe cold for a considerable length of time, or walking barefooted on burning coals; some of them, in fact, are able to slow down the rhythm of their bodily reactions so drastically that they fall into a prolonged state of lethargy comparable to animal hibernation.

Some years ago Presidency College of the University of Calcutta conducted a test with a Yogi under exacting scientific conditions. Indian Nobel Prize winner professor C. V. Raman was present at the experiment. One of the laboratories of the University had carefully prepared a dose of potassium cyanide sufficient to kill an adult person in three minutes. This dose was then swallowed by the Yogi. Three hours later the entire amount was extracted from his stomach. He had been able to immobilize his vegetative apparatus at will; the poison could not act upon the body since the digestive functions remained suspended for several hours. This must be the correct interpretation, since the same Yogi in a similar experiment, unable to enter the state of trance in time, died of cyanide poisoning.[55]

[55] See H. Woltereck: *Das Tor zur Seele* (Seebruck am Chiemsee, 1951), p. 208. Further details in P. Brunton: *A Search in Secret India,* pp. 186-188.

These acts have nothing to do with the miraculous; they are extraordinary achievements by a human body and result from an unusual degree of skill in self-mastery, obtained through long and arduous training. In fact, serious Yoga literature carefully and quite openly derives all paranormal achievements from certain "powers" that are acquired through a long practice in which supernatural forces play no part.[56] The Indian Yoga Institute, established near Bombay in 1924, is engaged in a full-scale research of Yogi activities, applying Western scientific standards to the job. Similar and successful efforts have been made in the United States and France.[57]

Public performances by Yogis and fakirs in India and elsewhere are not based exclusively on these extraordinary powers. Trickery and prestidigitation often have a part in these demonstrations. Whenever the intention is to surpass the human realm and enter into the domain of unprecedented marvels, the performer resorts to magic tricks, or to hypnosis and suggestion. In this category belong some of the well-known Yogi "miracles," including the most sensational of all, the rope trick.

After a pompous introduction the fakir pulls out a 15 feet long rope from a basket. While he continues to talk to the audience, the rope suddenly straightens out like a pole. A little boy, the fakir's helper, climbs upon the rope, followed by the fakir who carries a knife. Both of them disappear as in a cloud. Suddenly, the blood-soaked limbs of the child begin to fall one by one from the cloud until the ground is littered with them. The fakir reappears, sliding down the rope and carrying the child's head on a string attached to his belt. Having reached the ground, he collects the limbs and throws them in the basket which he then covers with a piece of cloth. He recites some unintelligible formulas while twisting and turning his body in all directions. Suddenly the show is over: the

[56] See Eliade: *Yoga*, p. 99.

[57] About the Yale University experiments, see Woltereck: *op. cit.*, p. 200; for France, see a study by C. Laubry and T. Brosse: "Documents recueillis aux Indes sur les 'Yoguis' par l'enregistrement simultané du pouls, de la respiration et de l'électrocardiogramme," *Presse médicale*, 83 (Oct. 14, 1936); see also a special issue of *Psyche*, 70-71 (Aug.-Sept., 1952) and discussion of Yoga at the international convention of Royaumont in May, 1956. There exist, incidentally, in the Western world many methods of relaxation, asceticism and reeducation of reflexes, which are more or less admittedly applications of Yoga techniques.

rope is on the ground in a neat bundle and the child smiles and bows to the bewildered audience.

The mystery remained unsolved for the longest time, even despite Queen Victoria's promise of a two thousand-pound reward to anyone who would find the answer for her. Today it is evident that the whole performance is a skillful act of suggestion through mass hypnotism. The Englishman Carlson witnesses a performance in the spring of 1946 and sees the whole event exactly as dictated by the fakir. His companion, however, who is not familiar with the language used, insists that the child was peacefully squatting on the ground throughout the whole act. Photographs also prove decisively that nothing actually happens and the spectacle is an illusion produced through psychological means.[58]

The same is true of the "miracle" of the mango tree. In this act the fakir buries in the ground a seed which, in a matter of seconds and before the very eyes of the spectators, grows into a young mango tree; there are even fruits on the tree. A rather simple magic trick.[59]

Are there any true instances of telekinesis (making objects move about from a distance) or levitation (lifting and moving of the human body in space without support) produced through Yoga techniques? The question is still unresolved, also in areas other than Yoga.

All of the known Oriental wonders seem to be based in every case on trickery or illusion. One only has to read the reports of Paul Brunton. The Yogi he visits makes puppets move on a table without touching them, makes a (seemingly) dead bird clap with its wings, or causes a handkerchief to smell of the kind of perfume the spectators select. All of these are magic tricks, several of them commonly performed in Europe as well.[60]

There is the case of the Yogi who, supporting himself on his

[58] On the rope trick, see Eliade: *Yoga*, pp. 321-323; J. Filliozat: *art. cit.*, pp. 24-25; H. Woltereck, pp. 209-213 (with reproductions of trick photographs).

[59] P. Brunton: *op. cit.*, pp. 164-167, tells how with a few rupees he bribed a fakir into revealing the secret of this prodigy; see also Eliade: *Yoga*, p. 330; R. Tocquet: *Tout l'occultisme dévoilé* (Paris, 1952), p. 188, reveals still other techniques used in the performance of the same trick.

[60] P. Brunton: *op. cit.*, pp. 193-196. See explanations of several such tricks in R. Tocquet: *op. cit.*, p. 185.

fingertips which rest on the top of a stick, stays in a horizontal position for four minutes. The June 6, 1936 issue of the *Illustrated London News* carries a report on this act, described by Professor Filliozat. There are six photographs accompanying the article. But in this case also, the most likely explanation is trickery which has actually been unveiled in a number of analogous instances. Scheschal, a Brahmin, who featured a levitation act, was wearing under his clothing a steel corset connected with the stick and carefully concealed with pieces of cloth.[61]

We have not been able to discern in this whole literature a single genuine fact that could be categorized as a major miracle. In particular, the extraordinary healings present no demonstrable facts that would be any more noteworthy than those achieved as a matter of routine by European healers and bonesetters.

The following story of a "miraculous" healing as reported to J. C. Oman by a witness does not, in fact, warrant a conclusion to a miraculous event:

> A boy had been ill of fever for some time. All the usual remedies had been tried without success, when the mother had the sufferer carried into the presence of the yogi. The holy man touched him, and handing his mother a few *chillies,* directed her to give the patient one every morning. She did so, and in a very short time the boy was quite restored to health.[62]

The same author reports another event which he himself witnessed during a visit to northern India in 1893:

> It was given out during the heat of certain religious controversies in Lahore, between the orthodox and certain unorthodox sects of Hindus, that a worshipper of Kali had offered a slice of his tongue to the goddess as a sacrifice [voluntary mutilations for religious motives are not uncommon in certain sects], and that the gratified divinity had miraculously restored the mutilated organ to its original state. Five days after this incident, a procession in

[61] See J. Lhermitte: *Le problème des miracles* (Paris, 1956), pp. 191-197; description of performances by Scheschal in R. Tocquet: *op. cit.*, pp. 183-184.

[62] See J. C. Oman: *Cults, Customs and Superstitions of India* (London, 1908), pp. 5-6.

honour of the event paraded the city on the 31st March 1893. . . . Preceded by drummers and cymbal players who led the way, came a litter well filled with long necklaces of white strongly scented flowers. . . . Beside the litter walked the hero of the hour, but he declined to show the tongue which had been miraculously restored by the goddess. . . .

A native who had, at my request, visited the temple where the miraculous event occurred, told me that he found a vast crowd—mostly women—assembled there. On a tray he saw a piece of something very red indeed, and was assured by the attendants that it was the tongue of a man who had cut it off, and made an offering of it to the goddess. The man whose severed tongue was being exhibited was lying—wrapped up head and all—motionless on the floor of the temple, and the Pujaris (officiating priests) assured the visitors that before many hours would lapse the faithful devotee would have his tongue restored to a perfect condition.[63]

Not long ago there appeared in Angul (Orissa province) a miracle-worker, Nepal Baba, credited with a great number of miraculous healings. The Hindus proudly declared to Christians mixed among the tremendous crowds of pilgrims: "We, too, finally have our own Lourdes." It was not long before the miracle-worker became a victim of his own success. Epidemics of cholera and smallpox, spread by the crowds of the infected sick, killed hundreds of pilgrims until drastic measures had to be applied by the police; the miracle-worker's reputation crumbled pitifully.[64]

Shamanism is another phenomenon often connected with the idea of the miraculous.[65] We are not undertaking here a discussion of the problems of ethnology and religious history connected with

[63] See J. C. Oman: *The Brahmans, Theists and Muslims of India* (London, 1906), pp. 17-19.

[64] See *Nishkalanka* (Ranchi), January 1951, p. 14, and February 1951, p. 30.

[65] See M. Eliade: *Le Chamanisme et les techniques archaïques de l'extase* (Paris, 1951); ID.: "Le problème du chamanisme," *Revue de l'histoire des religions,* 131 (1946), pp. 1-52; Åke Ohlmarks: *Studien zum Problem des Chamanismus* (Lund-Copenhagen, 1939); G. W. Ksenofontow: *Legenden von Schamanen* (Irkutsk, 1928); M. Bouteiller: *Chamanisme et guérison magique* (Paris, 1950).

it, nor are we taking sides in the controversy concerning the origin of Shamanism and its affinity with Yoga and Tantrism. We deal only with the question whether these phenomena yield any facts we could call "major prodigies."

Shamanism is not so much a religion as a form of ecstatic experience, a technique designed to bring this experience about, and a well-defined theory of the utilization of powers obtained by these means. Similar powers, incidentally, are widely found among many other religious rites and cultures (in Indonesia and America, among the Mundas, in India, Iran, China and, according to some authors, in Assyria and among the old Germanic tribes).

Every shaman is a priest and healer, but not every healer is necessarily a shaman. According to M. Eliade, shamanism shows the following characteristics:

1) A candidate becomes shaman through an initiation rite that includes his dismemberment, death and symbolic resurrection, together with a descent into hell and ascension to heaven, among other things.

2) A shaman is capable of undertaking ecstatic journeys outside his own body and can thus fulfill his function as a healer by finding the patient's soul stolen by the demons, recapturing it and reuniting it with the body; he can also accompany the souls of the dead to the nether world, etc.

3) He is a "master of fire," being able to touch a hot iron without injury, or to walk on burning coals, etc.

4) He can take on animal forms (e.g., fly like a bird) and make himself invisible.[66]

Shamans are preferably chosen from among hereditary epileptics or others showing signs of serious psychic imbalance. Such conditions are favorable to the achievement of the ecstatic state characteristic of shamanism, a state of trance reached through listening to monotonous sounds of prolonged drumming, concentration on a fixed point for hours, ringing of bells, or wild dances often ending with complete exhaustion and unconsciousness.[67] Once the subject has reached this state he shows the same parapsychological disposi-

[66] See Eliade: *Yoga,* p. 320.
[67] See description of a similar dance in H. Harrer: *op. cit.,* pp. 194-198.

tions as the Yogi and acquires a great power of hypnotic suggestion over others.[68] The ecstatic travels and acts of bilocation of the shaman, his ability for metamorphosis and the recapturing of souls, while not being altogether fictitious, are not real in the ordinary sense of the word. The abundant data available on this subject prove that this ability is based upon psychological experiences of such hallucinatory intensity as to produce, in a state of trance, the impression of a real experience.[69] Furthermore, hypnotic suggestion may cause such an intensive involvement of witnesses in the experience that in all good faith they believe to have had an actual part in them. As is invariably the case with persons whose psychic balance is deficient, there will also be a conscious or unconscious exercise of trickery destined to enhance and reinforce the impression made upon the spectators. It is a known fact that many shamans are ventriloquists; they use this skill in making the spirits talk; also, they are often helped by accomplices in staging the various apparitions of spirits.

W. Bogoras's accounts of an expeditionary trip contain a report on a shaman in the Chuckchee who conjures up the explorer's spirit in a tent. The explorer can hear the spirit come closer and closer and eventually enter the tent; suddenly he feels that the spirit is talking directly into his ear and he instinctively makes a

[68] Some authors have the interesting opinion that the "rope trick" we have dealt with above is a laicized derivative of a shamanistic initiation ceremony representing the symbolic death and resurrection of the initiated person. See on this matter M. Eliade: *Yoga*, pp. 321ff.

[69] Analogous phenomena are known in Western history as well, e.g., in witchcraft: "States of hysterical exaltation were obtained through an abuse of narcotic drugs, through inhalation, drinking and questionable manual stimulation. When the air was saturated with toxins, the witches would apply to their entire body various ointments composed of the same poisons: aconite, mandragora, henbane, belladonna, opium, marijuana, and the like. All of this would induce a delirium after which they seemed to be convinced to have actually flown through the air for the sabbat, to have engaged there in all sorts of impure excesses and worshiped Satan. This explains why so many of them swore during their very trials that they had partaken in sabbats, surrendered to Satan and committed the most abominable crimes in his company. There have been witches who would confess to crimes of this sort at the very stake." (L. Cristiani: *Actualité de Satan*, p. 96). Modern neurology has found that similar experiences are not infrequent in connection with certain psychopathological conditions; see, e.g., E. Bozzano: *Les phénomènes de bilocation* (Paris, 1937); J. Lhermitte: *L'image de notre corps* (Paris, 1939); ID.: *Les hallucinations* (Paris, 1952); ID.: *Le cerveau et la pensée* (Paris, 1952).

defensive gesture in that direction. At the shaman's command the spirit withdraws and enters the ground whence his voice is heard more and more feebly.[70]

Diaries, letters and accounts of missionaries often mention events like this. The fact is, however, that the activities of shamans who are supposed to be professional medicine men and healers, have never resulted in a single event that could be categorized as a major miracle, such as a genuine and irrefutable case of healing an organic disease.

We now turn our attention to another group of phenomena, related to the ones we have just examined, and characteristic of the neopaganism prevailing in our dechristianized society. We are speaking of *spiritism*.[71] As in shamanism, here also mediumship is

[70] W. Bogoras: "The Chuckchee" (public. of the Jessup North Pacific Expedition), *Memoirs of the Amer. Museum of Nat. History,* XI (1909).

[71] As for material, the dissertations in metapsychology published before the Second World War contain reports on a great many experiments and offer many facts which are still very interesting; but from the viewpoint of critical examination and interpretation of the facts, these works are largely outdated. Among the most important publications, let us mention C. Richet: *Thirty Years of Psychical Research* (New York, 1923); E. and M. Osty: *Les pouvoirs inconnus de l'esprit sur la matière* (Paris, 1932); F. Moser: *Okkultismus, Täuschungen und Tatsachen* (Munich, 1935); M. Dessoir: *Von Jenseits der Seele,* Die Geheimwissenschaften in kritischer Betrachtung (Stuttgart, 1931). Among the countless works in parapsychology published after the Second World War, the following may serve as a guide for further research: R. Amadou: *La parapsychologie* (Paris, 1954); "Parapsychologie," special issue of *Kultuurleven* (May 1951) with rich bibliography; M. Dessoir: *Das Ich, Der Traum, Der Tod* (Stuttgart, 1947); R. Tischner: *Ergebnisse okkulter Forschung* (Stuttgart, 1950) (Fr. transl. *Introduction à la parapsychologie,* Paris, 1953); P. A. Dietz: *Verschijningen en Verschijnselen* (The Hague, 1948); ID.: *Wereldzicht der parapsychologie* (The Hague, 1954); F. A. Heyn and J. J. Mulckhuyse: *Vorderingen en problemen der parapsychologie* (Delft, 1950); W. H. C. Tenhaeff: *Het spiritisme* (The Hague, 1951); Y. Castellan: *Le spiritisme* (coll. *Que sais-je?*) (Paris, 1954); J. Marlet: *Paranormale verschijnselen* (Bilthoven, 1957). On Christian appraisal of spiritualism, see L. Roure: *Le merveilleux spirite* (Paris, 1922); H. Thurston: *The Church and Spiritualism* (London, 1935); M. Waldmann: "Spiritismus," *Lexikon für Theol. u. Kirche,* IX (1937), cc. 729-730; J. Feldmann: *Okkulte verschijnselen* (third edition completely revised by G. Steffens) (Antwerp, 1949); J. de Tonquédec: *Merveilleux métapsychique et miracle chrétien* (Paris, 1955); Réginald-Omez: *Peut-on communiquer avec les morts?* (Paris, 1955); ID.: *Psychical Phenomena* (London, 1959); *Médecine et merveilleux* (Groupe Lyonnais d'Etudes Médicales) (Paris, 1956).

required, according to the spiritists, for making contact with the souls of the dead. Actual contact with the nether world is revealed, we are told, through certain "supernatural" phenomena, such as raps, table turning, automatic writing, and primarily the so-called materialization in which a mysterious substance generally called ectoplasm is said to be secreted by the medium and appears in various shapes to the participants.

Mediums again are psychically unbalanced, hypersensitive, extremely impressionable individuals, susceptible of all manners of influencing. All of this creates a favorable disposition to experiencing paroxystic interludes in the medium's normal existence. The interludes are called states of trance or "secondary" states and result from a kind of autohypnosis. Normal consciousness is inhibited to give free play to impulsions originating from the subconscious. The state of trance is revealed by external signs, such as staring eyes, fluttering or closing of the eyelids, agitation of the hands and convulsive movements which sometimes resemble an epileptoid attack. In bringing about the trance mediums often resort to additional means, such as darkness, silence, staring at a crystal ball or a mirror; alcohol and narcotics also help create the necessary disposition for entering into trance. The state of trance heightens the intensity and frequency of such paranormal manifestations as double sight, telepathy and thought transmission; the medium himself becomes much more receptive of suggestion while his ability to influence others psychically is enhanced. Trance often brings about even a state of "psychic dissociation" in which the normal half of the medium's personality sincerely considers everything done in the state of trance as done by another person.[72] The medium's evident imbalance and his desire to perform what he is asked to perform, together with his moral weakness and uncontrolled instinctive makeup, will prompt him, despite his basic good faith, to resort to trickery and ruse to fill the lacunas in his paranormal powers.

These spiritistic phenomena cannot be properly evaluated before answering a twofold question. One concerns the reality of the

[72] Characteristic features recognized by all authors as typical of the psychology of mediums are summed up in J. de Tonquédec: *op. cit.*, pp. 25-43.

manifestations. Once this is more or less solidly established, another question will be raised concerning the probability of a spiritistic or "supernatural" explanation.

First of all, we can expect considerable trickery and fraud which seem to have put their stamp on spiritism from the outset. As is well known, the movement originated in a small town in upstate New York, Hydesville, where certain manifestations take place in 1848 in the home of a Quaker by the name of Fox. Through the mediumistic intervention of his two adolescent daughters, a series of phenomena are produced, such as raps and transportation of heavy physical objects. The manifestations are interpreted as coming from the soul of a recently murdered salesman. Stories of these happenings begin to spread, public reaction is aroused, and spiritism floods the United States and the rest of the Western world like a tidal wave. Forty years later the two sisters confess to fraud; they explain clearly how they have staged these events. All of this is to no avail; the spirits would not let go of their quarry and declare that the two women are the instruments of evil spirits who force them to make false confessions. Wherever spiritism survives today the two of them are still considered among the greatest of all mediums.[73]

The whole evolution of spiritism is obscured by the same climate of charlatanism and vaudeville. It is difficult to find even one medium who at one time or other has not been caught in an act of fraud. Flammarion is not afraid to make the following statement: "I can say that in the past forty years almost all of the famous mediums have visited my house on the Avenue de l'Observatoire in Paris; I caught nearly all of them cheating." [74] Some ten of these mediums have eventually published their memoirs; they admit not to have spared fraud and trickery. One such book, entitled *Revelations of a Spirit Medium,* was published anonymously in 1891; its author is probably a medium by the name of Donovan. In the same year the whole edition was bought up and shipped to the paper mill by an association of mediums and spiritists of America,

[73] See C. von Klinckowstroem: "Selbstbekenntnisse von Medien," *Stimmen der Zeit,* 157 (1955-56), 149-152.

[74] Quoted by B. Grasset: *L'Occultisme d'hier et d'aujourd'hui,* p. 75, n.2.

which was certainly not conducive to the quelling of skepticism about the great spiritist claims.[75] Some well-known scholars, keenly interested in occultism, such as Richet, Lombroso and Crookes, were repeatedly victimized, not even by some elaborate fraud but by primitive trickery. Committees of investigation now always have professional prestidigitators and illusionists among their members. All of this shows the extent of care one must take in accepting the spiritist claims for facts. Moreover, professional illusionists have been able to duplicate almost all of the spiritist phenomena, and they did this so convincingly that in numerous instances when they offered to explain the mechanics of the fraud the spectators strongly protested and refused to listen.[76]

Does this mean that all spiritist phenomena must be rejected as nonexistent and resulting from nothing but pure trickery? Or may it be supposed that among all the charlatanism there is an occasional manifestation of true paranormal activity? Science, which has been concerned with this problem for several decades, is still searching for a truly scientific answer solidly based on facts. Although no comprehensive light has yet been shed on the entire domain, some valid conclusions have been reached. They differ widely according as they concern the physical or the mental phenomena.

The physical manifestations comprise first of all certain psychokinetic phenomena (causing objects to move without physical contact), levitation (rising and maintaining of the human body in the air without support) and materialization (shapeless ectoplasm or ectoplasmic figures).

The practice of fraud is so frequent and widespread in the entire realm that it is impossible to accept some particular experiment as valid merely because no fraud has been detected in that instance. The probability of deft trickery greatly outweighs that of truth which remains very questionable. This is all the more true since for a long time, in cases where the absence of material fraud by the medium has been established, no consideration was given to the possibility of hypnotic suggestion suffered by the observers them-

[75] C. von Klinckowstroem: *art. cit.*, p. 149.

[76] See, e.g., H. Woltereck: *op. cit.*, pp. 147ff.; R. Tocquet: *op. cit.*, *passim.*

selves, or to errors of judgment such suggestions may have been responsible for. Today, however, studies on shamanism and fakirism, together with some recent discoveries in neurology and psychology, have made it abundantly clear that the phenomena must be interpreted with the greatest care and attention.

R. Amadou, who for many years has been the editor of the *Revue Métapsychique* and has collected data and records on a variety of first-rate experiments, concludes the pertinent chapter of his classic work on parapsychology with these words: "We must state that no proof of the real existence of these phenomena has ever been supplied." As for the phenomena of materialization, he thinks it unnecessary even to mention them.[77]

This opinion finds a decisive support in the fact that all of these physical phenomena have altogether disappeared from the picture ever since the invention of scientific devices capable of detecting and eliminating simulation and fraud with objective certainty. The events a widely circulated periodical still insists on referring to, are at least twenty years old. Whereas the events of Lourdes, e.g., have found unexpected confirmation through the progress of technology, this same progress has dealt a fatal blow to the posterity of the great original exponents of physical mediumship.[78]

Modern parapsychologists, a considerable number of whom still accept the existence of psychokinesis, no longer rely on mediumistic performances but base their conclusions on laboratory experi-

[77] R. Amadou: *op. cit.*, p. 71. In his recent book, the author furnishes detailed proof of this claim; see *Les grands médiums* (Paris, 1957). See also B. De Cressac: *La métapsychique devant la science* (Paris, 1948), p. 135, who expresses the same opinion; G. Steffens: "Het paranormale in zijn diverse vormen." *Parapsychologie*, special issue of *Kultuurleven* (May, 1951), 268, arrives at the same conclusion; J. B. Rhine says that he was led to undertake his famous experiments (summarized in text below) because he had found it "impossible to draw conclusive evidence of psychokinesis from previous experiments"; Réginald-Omez: *Psychical Phenomena*, pp. 101-106, also shares the opinion of Amadou. A verdict of the Belgian Committee for Scientific Investigation of Alleged Paranormal Phenomena (C.B.I.S.P.R.P.) is even more negative; see, e.g., Dr. Hougardy: *Archiva Medica Belgica* (1950), pp. 1 ff.

[78] One typical example should suffice: "In 1931 a prize of 50,000 francs (1931 value) has been officially offered in Paris to anyone who would move a pencil placed on a pane of glass, under observation. No one has attempted the experiment" (J. Tondriau: *Fakirisme physique*, p. 8, quoted in Réginald-Omez: *op. cit.*, p. 102).

ments of the type introduced by J. B. Rhine.[79] In this light psychokinesis is no longer a "supernatural" manifestation. If the so far very hypothetical conclusions of Rhine are ever confirmed, adequate explanation will be found in a purely natural psychic power within the reach of every man. Through a mysterious process yet to be defined, this power would change into physical energy, although never beyond the boundaries of a rather narrow field of experience.

The mental phenomena turn out to be less disappointing upon balance. Telepathy, double sight, thought transfer, and to some extent even precognition, or more exactly divination, of future events, seem beyond the possibility of outright skepticism. These phenomena are not at all restricted to spiritist seances and the practice of professional mediumship. J. B. Rhine has conducted strictly scientific experiments with individuals lacking any special mediumistic ability. His conclusion is that these manifestations are paranormal in appearance only, and are more or less within the reach of practically everybody. They may take on, however, some added importance due to special circumstances, pathological conditions or systematic training.[80] Explanation is to be sought not in

[79] J. B. Rhine: *New Frontiers of the Mind* (London, 1938); ID.: *Extra-Sensory Perception After Sixty Years* (London, 1940). The experiments consisted in the following: subjects without any special mediumistic abilities were asked to concentrate by thought and wish alone on guessing high and low figures. The average results, compared with the expected statistically normal results based on mathematical probability showed a certain gap which, while not being altogether conclusive, was significant enough to rule out an explanation by hazard alone. The size, weight, shape and material of the dice had no effect on the results, neither did it make any notable difference whether the dice were thrown mechanically or by hand. Alcohol and other stimulants heightened the performance, whereas fatigue and narcotics showed a tendency to reduce the statistical gap. Since the possibility of contributing factors other than the purely psychic had not been excluded with full certainty in these first experiments, Rhine himself endeavored to perfect the mechanics of his experiments, while other researchers were trying to refine similar and more sophisticated methods (see on this matter R. Amadou: *op. cit.*, pp. 274-287). As the conditions of observation became more and more rigorous, the gap kept shrinking to the point of losing all statistical significance. At the present stage of research no definitive conclusions can be drawn yet, although many researchers think that we have the final answer. See on this matter J. B. Rhine: *Reach of the Mind* (New York, 1947).

[80] See J. B. Rhine: *loc. cit.* The international parapsychological conventions of Utrecht (1953) and St-Paul de Vence (1954) had these psychic phenomena as the first order of their considerations; see *La science et le paranormal* (Utrecht and St-Paul de Vence, Paris, 1955). See also W. Büchel:

some power surpassing what is strictly human in man, but rather in those residual primitive instincts that have not been gradually absorbed by consciousness and intellect. These instincts, which animals possess in abundance, have not completely disappeared from man either, and may be suddenly awakened in favorable circumstances.[81]

The considerations offered here suggest an answer to the second question. Supposing that the facts are genuine, a supernatural interpretation would seem to violate the scientific principle of economy which forbids the seeking of extraordinary explanations when the simple explanation is the obvious one.[82]

The same phenomena, in fact, occur in domains other than spiritism and bear a striking resemblance to their counterparts in Oriental Yoga and shamanism. Also, they are produced through the services of a medium whose psychic makeup itself supplies a partial explanation. The phenomena are reinforced through technical dexterity or some pathological condition. As a final and very serious argument, they are so well marked with a patently human, sometimes altogether evil, character that rather than having anything to do with "another world" or spiritual beings, they appear to be intimately linked to the most banal aspirations and concerns of the subconscious human mind.[83]

At any rate, the golden age of spiritism is gone. In recent years

---

"Natürliches Vorauswissen zukünftiger Ereignisse, Ein Überblick." *Scholastik*, 30 (1955), 233-240; R. Amadou: *op. cit.*, pp. 157-273; A. Neuhäusler: *Telepathie, Hellschen, Präkognition* (Munich, 1957); R. Haynes: *The Hidden Springs. An Enquiry into Extra-Sensory Perception* (London, 1961).

[81] One should not, however, jump to the conclusion that these facts indicate a phenomenon of regression toward inferior life forms or a more primitive stage in the evolution of man. As other instinctive manifestations, they rather show a clear ambiguity and change their meaning with the changing of the psychological and spiritual setting in which they take place. This ambiguity would explain why these paramystical phenomena are both similar to, and different from, genuinely mediumistic performances.

[82] R. Dalbiez: "Miracle et logique," Etudes Carmélitaines (Oct. 1934), pp. 360-381, applies this "rule of economy" to spiritualism in the sense we have indicated. J. Guitton: *Jésus*, p. 72, formulates the same rule: "In searching for a cause it is necessary not to suppose that which it is not necessary to suppose."

[83] Several authors consider this argument conclusive; see, e.g., Woltereck: *op. cit.*, pp. 188-189; J. de Tonquédec: *op. cit.*, pp. 91-104, etc.

the phenomena of occultism have been transferred from the realm of mystery to that of a still young experimental science called parapsychology.[84] There is among its exponents a growing tendency to emphasize the "normal" nature of paranormal manifestations and to remand them within the domain of traditional experimental psychology.

Besides these experimental, that is purposely induced, phenomena encountered in spiritism, we are informed of a variety of spontaneous manifestations bearing a resemblance to the former but lacking, in the minds of many, any natural explanation. Let us comprise them under the general term of "*phenomena of haunting.*" Here belong poltergeists, raps (various noises, crackling of chairs and furniture), icy drafts in closed rooms, various apport phenomena (moving, dancing, even flying of heavy objects; rain of stones without apparent cause, etc.); finally the production of materializations in the form of phantoms which sometimes are rather shapeless, sometimes neatly cut out and identifiable.

A large portion of these stories, spread by publications of a certain type or by word of mouth, certainly do not deserve any credit. Some of the events appear very mysterious while being in fact the

[84] The term "parapsychology," first suggested by M. Dessoir, is now currently adopted even in France where specialists had long preferred "metapsychology." The Netherlands were the first country where a special university department (Utrecht) has been established for the study of parapsychology. In Belgium we have a "Belgian Committee for Scientific Investigation of Alleged Paranormal Phenomena" (Comité Belge pour l'Investigation Scientifique des Phénomènes Réputés Paranormaux); see present membership of this Committee in Réginald-Omez: *op. cit.*, pp. 36-37. In Germany there exists an "Institute for the Study of Border Regions between Psychology and Psychohygiene (Institut für Grenzgebiete der Psychologie and Psychohygiene)" in Freiburg, under the direction of H. Bender. In recent years several international parapsychological conventions have taken place (Utrecht, St.-Paul de Vence, Royaumont) the records of which are regularly published. The older associations, such as the British S.P.R. (Society for Psychical Research, founded in 1882), the French "Institut métapsychique international" (1920), and the "Studievereniging voor Psychical Research" (1920) in the Netherlands have been orienting their research in the same directions. To illustrate the present trends toward integrating parapsychological phenomena with normal psychology, let us quote this definition by R. Amadou: "In the strict sense, parapsychology is the unveiling and experimental study of psychic functions not yet incorporated in the system of scientific psychology in order to incorporate them in this system which will thus be enlarged and supplemented" (*op. cit.*, p. 45).

products of purposeful malice, insanity, vengeance, mystification, or misplaced practical joking, others are born of the need for the sensational, of popular imagination, credulousness, hallucination, hysterical affabulation or other mental disturbances; they may even be produced by certain types of intoxication, not only through alcohol but also carbon monoxide or mercury, a common ingredient in paints. These substances are responsible for the origin of a great many fantastic tales.

Some of the stories, however, are supported by witnesses testifying in such manner and with so great a precision that it would be difficult to discount them as mere products of the imagination.[85]

The scientific efforts of investigation, which have barely begun, are seriously hampered by the fact that the apparitions to be studied are spontaneous by definition. No truly certain explanation can be offered at the present time. Certain existing elements in parapsychology, however, point once again to a natural explanation. The following is a brief summary of these already established points:

1) All the events practically without exception are centered upon some particular individual who seems to act as a medium for all of the manifestations; even haunting linked with a definite place (haunted house, etc.) seems to exist only through the intermediary of a subject.

2) Such subjects are invariably persons with an unstable psychic constitution. Of these we know that they often develop paranormal powers, become very receptive of suggestion and acquire great capacity for acting upon others through suggestion. Frequently they are young persons (mostly girls) at the early stages of puberty, which is a favorite age for the appearance of psychic disturbances and temporary pathological conditions.[86]

3) In the light of a superficial psychology one often gathers the

[85] H. Thurston: *Ghosts and Poltergeists* (London, 1954) has gathered a great number of older cases; more recent accounts, based on police reports, are available in Cdt Tizané: *Sur la piste de l'homme inconnu* (Paris, 1951); the latter author makes the mistake of burdening the factual accounts with attempted interpretations which are not always borne out by the facts; see also F. Moser: *Der Spuk* (Zurich, 1950); P. Devaux: *Les fantômes devant la science* (Paris, 1954); G. N. M. Tyrell: *Apparitions* (London, 1953); some typical cases quoted in M. Dessoir: *Vom Jenseits der Seele*, pp. 291-293.

[86] M. Dessoir: *op. cit.*, pp. 291-292; E. Tizané, pp. 84ff.

impression that the facts are stupid and meaningless. By consulting, however, the subconscious of the subject who is their intermediary, we can detect their secret motivation without much trouble. The motives, which find their symbolic expression in the facts, appear quite human, often all too human, and supply a very simple and very plausible explanation of the external phenomena.[87]

4) If the subject who fulfills the functions of medium is taken away from the haunted place, the manifestations automatically stop. Sometimes they occur again at the new location of the subject, but in the event the environmental change reduces considerably the tensions created by subconscious motives, the phenomena altogether cease. The same results may be achieved through psychotherapy helping the subject to obtain sufficient abreaction of the psychic tension and thus restoring his psychic balance. If close observation puts the subject in such a state of embarrassment that the spontaneous play of unconscious forces becomes impossible or the unconscious activity can be carried on only through obsessive constraint upon the conscious personality, the subject is frequently caught redhanded in fraudulent manipulation, conscious or semiconscious, for that is how the subject tries to supplement the best he can an activity that has begun unconsciously and in perfect good faith.[88]

We are now ready to conclude. Most phenomena of haunting appear as if a psychologically unstable personality had suddenly split into two personalities: one, consisting of the sum total of instincts and subconscious motivations, performs in a state of trance a series of acts and produces the phenomena; the other is the normal, conscious personality which registers the events with great surprise, even as the participants do. The latter are evidently exposed to considerable suggestive influence by the medium. This

[87] See *Psychanalyse et parapsychologie*, Inst. Métaps. Intern. (Paris, 1954); see some typical examples in J. Feldmann—G. Steffens: *Okkulte Verschijnselen*, pp. 395-396; E. Tizané: *op. cit.*, pp. 106-110.

[88] Disappearance of phenomena through withdrawal of mediumistic subject, e.g., Tizané: *op. cit.*, pp. 32, 56, etc.; through psychotherapy, e.g., F. Moser: *Okkultismus*, II, pp. 844-846; Tizané: *op. cit.*, pp. 55-56, etc.; switch to simulation, e.g., Tizané, pp. 33-40; 52-58, etc.; effects of suggestion on environment, see F. Moser: *op. cit.*, p. 848, who explains these effects by "eine Art gemeinsames Unterbewusstseins auf telepathischer Grundlage (a kind of collective subconsciousness of telepathic origin)."

greatly hampers or even totally warps the objective perception of actual participants, incidental witnesses or official observers.

There remains one important question for us to deal with. Do ghost stories spring from an unconscious but otherwise normal psychic activity on the part of the subject, compounded by purely subjective psychic experiences on the part of spectators placed in a state of suggestion by a spontaneous medium, or are we forced to admit that the subject in trance draws not only on parapsychic, but also paraphysical forces? In other words, are poltergeists, the door that opens or closes by itself, etc., merely the effects of psychic suggestion, or of a psychokinetic power possessed by the medium? Are ghosts simply hallucinations shared by the participants under hypnotic suggestion by the medium, or genuine materializations emanating from a subject in trance? Are the stones or other accessories being manipulated by the medium, unconsciously to be sure, but through ordinary physical means, or are they moved through psychokinesis?

At the present state of science no certain answer can be given to these questions. The structure, however, of the events referred to on these pages, in addition to the existence of unconscious but normal physical activities, would seem to point toward an interpretation in terms of psychic powers alone. A number of additional data now available lend a very great degree of probability to this hypothesis.[89]

[89] See H. Woltereck: *op. cit.*, p. 194: "Nach allem, was wir heute über diese Dinge wissen, ist aber zum mindesten eine sehr grosse Wahrscheinlichkeit dafür vorhanden, dass wir in the Spukerscheinungen aller Art nichts anderes vor uns haben als besondere Leistungen des Unterbewusstseins (At the present stage of our knowledge of these things there is at least a very strong probability that all these ghost phenomena are merely special products of the subconscious)." Tizané quotes a considerable number of cases which support this opinion. He notices, e.g., that the rocks mostly seem to fall from very close, without great force and almost vertically, which supports the theory that they are actually thrown by one of the participants. A reading of the accounts on pp. 46-57 and 162-165 would convince anyone that all the reported facts can be explained by normal physical activity on the part of a mediumistic subject in trance. It is also rather strange that flying objects, sometimes of considerable weight, never hit any of the spectators, or if they do, they never hurt them; that fragile objects often fall over three feet without breaking; that heavy objects fall noiselessly, etc. (see, e.g., pp. 175, 177, 221, etc.; also Woltereck: *op. cit.*, p. 193). All of these data seem to suggest a psychic rather than physical cause. Tizané finds in his summary of the facts

•

Let us conclude our study of wonders in the contemporary non-Christian world with a summary of the findings, which amount to the following. Yoga and shamanism, together with all other occult phenomena, show in essence certain unusual achievements of the human mind; the manifestations occur in a wide variety of contexts, religious and otherwise; science has been able to detect with certainty their purely natural character and psychic origin, although the mechanics of these operations are not yet fully understood.

These phenomena, no doubt, have very great importance for any study of the Catholic miracle. They bear a striking resemblance to a number of secondary manifestations in Christian mysticism, such as ecstasies, visions, levitation, bilocation, apparitions and prophecies, and also to the signs of possession or infestation which Christians attribute to the devil. Because science compels us to look for the same cause in explaining the same effects, there arises the problem of the originality and discernment of genuine mysticism, together with the problem of diabolical manifestations in the history of the Christian religion.[90]

In any event, these phenomena have no common features with, or resemblance to, major prodigies. There is no common measure between the functional mastery of a Yogi and the Lourdes patient who is suddenly cured of an organic disease, or between some apport phenomenon in a ghost story and the genuine multiplication of food. The events not only differ in degree but belong to altogether different realms.

---

that the mysterious agent he sees in the phenomena of hauting behaves like "a fearful being, acting mostly by surprise, behind the participants' back," "is momentarily disturbed by any scrutiny" and generally behaves like "a stupid force." See also the data quoted in R. Amadou: *op. cit.*, pp. 52-57.

[90] See the bibliography given supra, Part II, ch. 1, n. 3. If our analysis is correct we must conclude that the opinions of some authors on paramystical phenomena (e.g., O. Leroy: *La lévitation, contribution historique à l'étude du merveilleux*, Paris, 1928) are scarcely valid.

II · THE MIRACULOUS IN NON-CATHOLIC CHRISTIANITY

Are the claims of non-Catholic Christian denominations to the major miracle better founded than those of the non-Christian religions? In order to find the answer to this question we must study the Protestant churches, the sects, the Russian Orthodox Church, and Jansenism.

a · The Miraculous in the Protestant Churches and the Sects

At first sight it would seem that *Protestantism* should not present any special problems here. Its principal exponents, in fact, have been from the very beginning opposed to the notion of non-biblical miracles. In Luther's opinion God permitted the occurrence of miracles at the beginning in order to strengthen the newly-born Christian faith. Once the Church had been established, however, there was no need for miracles; they are now replaced by a purely internal transformation obtained through the sacraments and the Word of God.[91] The majority of even those Protestant theologians whom rationalism has not contaminated and who support both the possibility of the miraculous and the historicity of the miracles of the Bible and the Gospels, have remained faithful to this restrictive theory.[92] The major schools of thought, representing the official Protestant views, are opposed to any expectation of miracles in our time and do not appeal to the miraculous as a guarantee of the genuineness of the Christian message.

Several outstanding exponents of Anglican theology maintain views rather closely resembling the Catholic theory of the miraculous and are considerably less influenced by rationalism than, e.g., many German Protestant theologians; yet Anglicanism also limits the miraculous to the Old Testament, the Gospel, and the early Church. The article on "miracle" in the *Encyclopaedia Britannica*

[91] Martin Luther: *Werke* (Erlanger Ausgabe), L, pp. 86-87; see also XVI, p. 190; LVIII, p. 95; LIX, p. 3.

[92] For a conservative Protestant position, cf. B. B. Warfield: *Counterfeit Miracles* (New York, 1918). Even authors close to the Catholic position on the nature of miracles remain faithful to the Protestant tradition on this point; e.g., A. Schlatter (on whose views cf. G. Marquardt, *op. cit.*, supra, Part I, Author's Preface, n. 4). Cf. also the works of O. Cullmann and P. H. Menoud cited in Part I, ch. 5, n. 1.

makes an interesting reading in this respect; its author, a faithful Anglican, speaks of the "belief of miracles through the Middle Ages and in modern times" as a typically Roman Catholic belief.[93]

In actual fact devout Protestants are far less reticent about the miraculous than their theological literature would suggest. This has been noted by Baumgarten who says that "faith in the miraculous as proposed in evangelical theology which, as a matter of principle, limits the miraculous to Christ's lifetime and the early Church and refuses to consider the possibility of miracles in personal life, is hardly ever found among the faithful." [94] The history of traditional Protestantism in the past fifty years shows certain efforts at reassessment, together with a resurgence of nostalgia for the miraculous. A discreet echo of these currents of thought can be detected in theological publications. But the concrete examples from which the various authors try to derive a proof for the existence of miracles in Protestantism turn out to be, at least when the facts are satisfactorily established, events that must be called providential but are definitely not major miracles.[95]

At any rate, when some truly prodigious facts seem to appear in the Protestant community, it is quite striking to see how enthusiastically they are received and utilized. One of the characteristic examples is the conversion of Sundar Singh, an Indian sâdhu (wise and holy man). The story, as told by himself, begins in December, 1904 with an apparition of Christ who invites him to become a Christian. After joining the Anglican Church he travels extensively in China, Japan, and later in America and Europe. He preaches a Christian spirituality of the liberal kind, emphasizing its mystical and visionary aspects and pointing out the kinship between Christian teachings and certain Hindu theories. He tells of the many prodigious experiences he encountered in his travels; these prodigies, even more than his preaching, earn for him the enthusiastic attention of the masses and for a time he is the great star of the religious

[93] A. E. Garvie: "Miracle," *Encyclopaedia Britannica*, XV (Chicago, 1964), pp. 585-587.

[94] D. Baumgarten: "Wunder," *Religion in Geschichte und Gegenwart* (1913), V, c. 2164.

[95] See, e.g., K. Heim: *The Transformation of the Scientific World View* (London, 1953), ch. 5, "The Problem of Miracles in the Light of Modern Natural Science," pp. 193-199.

world, not only in the East but soon on five continents. Outstanding Protestants, among them N. Söderblom, and especially F. Heiler who published several writings about him, held him in great respect, and many Catholic theologians, such as Delehaye, de Grandmaison, von Hügel, and K. Adam also praised him, at least at the earlier stages of his career. His prodigies never bore the earmarks of a major prodigy, but some of the more remarkable facts made a tremendous impression on the general public. He told, e.g., of fasting forty days after his conversion; in Tibet he met a Christian hermit who was over three hundred years old; a beggar, in order to deceive him, made believe that he was dead, only to die really as a punishment for having tried to deceive a man of God; he was once saved from a hermetically sealed well without finding the least trace of his rescuer.

Unfortunately, a sudden change developed in 1924-25 when both Protestants and Catholics began to ask serious and penetrating questions about the credibility of these events. The stories turned out to be full of exaggerations, impossibilities, falsifications and contradictions, and the Sadhu was compelled to fall back on the allegorical nature of the purported events, which in turn forced his admirers, both Protestant and Catholic, to reappraise entirely their opinion of him, at least in the matter of the miracles.[96]

[96] The numerous alleged miracles attributed to Sâdhu Sundar Singh are dealt with in his biographies, e.g. that of Mrs. A. Parker, *Sâdhu Sundar Singh, Called of God* (London, 1920); B. H. Streeter and A. J. Appasamy: *The Sâdhu,* A Study in Mysticism and Practical Religion (London, 1922); see also C. W. Emmet: "Miracles of Sâdhu Sundar Singh," *The Hibbert Journal,* 19 (Jan. 1921), 308-318; for the very favorable reception he enjoyed with some Catholic writers, see L. de Grandmaison: "Le Sâdhu Sundar Singh et le problème de la sainteté hors de l'Eglise catholique," *Rech. de science rel.,* 12 (1922), 1-29. The first critical studies on the Catholic side were published between 1923 and 1925 by H. Hosten in a series of articles in the *Catholic Herald of India;* his arguments were adopted and amplified by H. Sierp: "Sâdhu Sundar Singh," *Stimmen der Zeit,* 107 (1924), 415-425; ID.: "Religionswissenschaft oder Legendenbildung?" *ibid.,* 108 (1925), 109-120; ID.: "Friedrich Heiler und der Sâdhu," *ibid.,* 108 (1925), 270-282; then by G. Schulemann: "Christliche Sâdhus," *Hochland,* 21 (1924), II, pp. 287-300; ID.: "Zum Streit um den Sâdhu Sundar Singh," *Hochland,* 22 (1925), II, pp. 737-742. On the Protestant side the severest critic is P. Pfister, in a series of articles in *Zeitschrift für Missionskunde und Religionswissenschaft* (1924), fascicle 4, and in his book: *Die Legende Sundar Singhs* (1926).

Apart from the level of traditional theology and orthodox devotion, Protestantism offers a radically different picture.

As stated before, expectation of the miraculous is one of the common and constant manifestations of religious sentiment among men. Whenever official teachings lend no support to these desires, or even discourage them, the instinctive expectations will turn on a thousand devious paths in their search for fulfillment. This explains why revivalism, and *sectarianism* in general, finds the most vigorous response among Protestant ethnic groups, especially when prodigious elements are incorporated among the basic tenets of a particular sect. Sectarianism is as old as the Christian religion itself and almost invariably thrives on the fertile ground of revolt against some existing, all-to-easy or all-to-human compromise between the various facets of religious experience and religious ideals.[97] A survey of the various Protestant sects[98] will reveal that in many of these communities the suppressed desire for the miraculous breaks through the surface with the impetuous force of an elementary and unbridled instinct. Some of these sects, such as Christian Science and the Pentecostal churches, actually specialize in extraordinary healings. A brief study of these would be in order here.

The *Christian Science*[99] movement originates with Mary Baker, better known as Mrs. Eddy after her third husband (the first one

[97] The best monography on the psychology of the sects is by R. Knox: *Enthusiasm,* A chapter in the History of Religion, with special reference to the XVII and XVIII Centuries (Oxford, 1950). See also W. Nigg: *The Heretics* (New York, 1962).

[98] See a survey of some 120 sects by K. Hutten: *Seher, Grübler, Enthusiasten,* Sekten und religiöse Sondergemeinschaften der Gegenwart³ (Stuttgart, 1953). To be consulted also: H. C. Chéry: *L'offensive des sectes* (Paris, 1954); M. B. Lavaud: *Sectes modernes et foi catholique* (Paris, 1954); F. Blanke: *Kirche und Sekten,* Führer durch die religiösen Gruppen der Gegenwart (Zurich, 1955); M. Colinon: *Faux prophètes et Sectes d'aujourd'hui* (Paris, 1953); "Die Sekten," special issue of *Lebendige Seelsorge* (1955), pp. 153-183; T. Séguy: *Les sectes protestantes dans la France contemporaine* (Paris, 1956); W. J. Whalen: *Faiths for the Few* (Milwaukee, 1963).

[99] H. Thurston: "Christian Science," *The Month,* 115 (1910), 1-16, 132-147 and 241-258; these articles were published separately in pamphlet form by the Catholic Truth Society; L. Roure: *Au pays de l'occultisme* (Paris, 1925), pp. 85-126; A. Roozen: *Christian Science* (Hilversum, 1934); C. Braden: *Christian Science Today* (London, 1959). The comprehensive works quoted in the preceding note contain some pages on Christian Science.

died after one year of marriage; the second marriage ended in divorce). Born in 1821, she begins to display at a very early age strong symptoms of religious exaltation. She suffers recurring attacks of hysteria from her childhood. After the death of her first husband she abandons her child whom she is not to see again until thirty-five years later. Periods of complete apathy are followed by frantic traveling across the country. Although she is now an adult woman, she wants to be rocked to sleep like a small child; her second husband, an itinerant dentist, is forced to haul around his wife's crib in his wagon. At the time of her divorce she is already acquainted with a magnetizer by the name of Phineas Parkhurst Quimby who uses her in his experimenting with a hypnotic method known as "mind cure." In 1886, in a matter of days, he pulls her out of a state of complete paralysis resulting from a fall on the ice. She considers this a miracle and henceforth clings to her healer with wholehearted devotion. When the man dies less than a year after this incident, she inherits his writings which contain a rather curious mixture of religion, philosophy and medicine. She opens a school of healing and starts editing Quimby's manuscripts, adorning them with biblical quotations and commentaries which are often grotesque. She gathers around her a group of co-workers, only to quarrel with them when they acquire too much influence over the patients. The first edition of her book, *Science and Health*, is published in 1875, eventually to become the bible of the "Christian Science" movement.[100] After marrying Mr. Eddy in 1877, she settles down in Boston and starts a new religion, the "Church of Christ Scientist," in 1879. The movement spreads very fast, but all danger of schism is forestalled; Mrs. Eddy does not tolerate that a single letter be changed in her statements and forbids her disciples to read anything but her own writings. She eliminates every embarrassing trace of Quimby and tries to hide her own lack of education under the guise of erudite and obscure expressions. She soon rises to the rank of quasi-divinity and is honored like another Dalai Lama. At the age of ninety, with her reputation as an immortal being firmly established, she suddenly dies of pneumonia. Her disciples claim

[100] M. Baker Eddy: *Science and Health with Key to the Scriptures.* Published by the Trustees under the Will of Mary Baker G. Eddy (Boston, 1875).

that she is not dead at all, but has merely passed on to another phase of her existence. The movement is still in full swing, mainly because of the continuing American-style propaganda which uses press and radio as its media.

What are the doctrinal foundations of "Science and Health"? Any attempt to find a coherent system in this book would be quite futile, for it is hardly more than a haphazard collection of unrelated and often contradictory ideas, bearing the stamp of a grammar school mentality. The main thesis of Mrs. Eddy, however, is rather simple and may be expressed in a few words. Nothing is eternal but the divine spirit. Everything else (that is, the material world, evil, disease, sin and death) is merely an illusion, owing its existence to the lack of perspicacity in man who has become a victim of his mortal, human sense as opposed to the divine spirit which is the only actual reality in him. As shadows dissolve under the rays of the sun, so will disease, sin and death disappear in this divine perspective. "Christian Science" therefore consists essentially in the will no longer to believe in sin and disease. This cannot be achieved by merely hypnotizing ourselves into believing that we are free of a particular disease or sin. No; an absolutely universal act of faith is required which holds that neither disease nor sin exist. If man cannot rid himself of all ills through this mental act, that is merely a sign that his divine vision is still imperfect and the fog of illusion has not lifted. This "science" is called "Christian" because Christ was the One in whom the supremacy of the mind has found its most perfect expression, causing him to become the great healer and miracle-worker that he was.

The reader will find that neither the person of the founder, nor the original inspiration that gave birth to the movement, nor the "doctrine" put forth in the book bear any relation to genuine religious experience, except, of course, on the basis of H. Thurston's remark, "Christian Science makes health into a religion." [101]

The diagnosis is clear: hysterical desire of self-assertion vocalized

[101] H. Thurston: *art. cit.*, p. 132; in the same series of articles he writes: "It is precisely her lack of all sense of proportion and the selfcentered bias of her every thought that makes her the last person in the world whom one could or would willingly choose for a guide in the great affair of man's relation to God and the future life" (*ibid.*, p. 16).

in a vaguely religious style but orienting everything toward one focal point: the exalted and idealized ego. The success of Christian Science stems of the same cause: the same instincts of self-defense and desire of self-assertion are aroused in the disciples and become a theme for pseudo-religious suggestion. The egotistic preoccupation with the self, the naive self-sufficiency and complete lack of humor which characterize both the founder and her movement, find an unintended but ironical echo in the very dedication of her great work:

> *I, I, I, I itself, I*
> *The inside and the outside, the what and the why,*
> *The when and the where, the low and the high,*
> *All I, I, I itself, I!*

A conclusion, therefore, should not be hard to reach: the so-called miraculous cures in Christian Science are devoid of every genuine religious meaning, and by this very lack belong in the same category as the stories of bonesetters, healers and assorted charlatans.

This conclusion is confirmed by the experience we derive from reading the publications of the movement or listening to its radio programs. Assuredly, there are very frequent reports of cures of organic diseases and lesions. The difficulty is that these reports are invariably based on the testimony of the patient himself who, lacking as he does all medical training, offers a very vague diagnosis of his illness which has not been established or even studied by a physician. The historical validity of a testimony is never checked, and its very style is carefully edited so as to give the impression that it comes from a learned man, whereas far more often than not the actual source is an uneducated or even totally illiterate person.

Let us quote here the summary of the results of a thorough investigation conducted by a British physician:

> It is plain, from these evidences, and from the previous chapter, that Christian Science accepts all testimonials, even the most fantastical and illiterate. That she embellishes what she publishes. That she evades investigation. That her claim to cure organic dis-

eases breaks down under the most elementary rules of criticism. That she does cure "functional" diseases. That she has never cured, nor ever will, any disease, except those which have been cured, a hundred thousand times, by "mental therapeutics." [102]

A random example will give us a better idea of the settings and validity of Scientist miracles than any critical considerations. The following is a word by word quotation from a periodical of the movement:

> A banker, not a student of Christian Science, telephoned a Christian Scientist one day and said that auditors had for several nights been going over the books at his bank looking for a certain mistake that they knew had been made. The banker wondered if Christian Science could help in such a case. He was assured that it could, and treatment was accepted. Very soon the telephone rang again, and the happy report was that the error had been found. "How did you do it?" was the interested query.
>
> The Scientist replied, in effect: "The problem was approached by us from different standpoints. You were trying to find out the error by searching for it. Christian Science teaches that error is uncovered by the realization of the truth of being. I declared what was true about man as the reflection of God, unerring Mind, and when this truth was sufficiently realized, it uncovered and destroyed the error that man is material, liable to make mistakes." [103]

This example is sufficiently clear to make us appreciate the reaction of H. Thurston, who is an objective and moderate observer of paranormal manifestations, to the phenomenon of Christian Science. The words are few, but forceful enough to stigmatize the whole movement: "An astonishing example of the gullibility of a decadent age." [104]

•

[102] Stephen Paget: *The Faith and Works of Christian Science* (London, 1909), pp. 165-166; same opinion by A. Roozen: *op. cit.*, pp. 67-79; see also the third article by H. Thurston. Also, P. Janet: *Les médications psychologiques*, I (Paris, 1909).

[103] *The Herald of Christian Science* (French edition, Boston, Mass., May 1949), p. 101, quoted in H. C. Chéry: *op. cit.*, p. 278.

[104] H. Thurston: *op. cit.*, p. 132.

The various *Pentecostal movements* also use miraculous healing as their supporting theme.[105] Their followers expect an early end of the world and the return of Christ. The herald of these events is supposed to be the "latter rain" of the prophet Joel[106] which according to them is already pouring down on earth in the form of the charismatic gifts of prophecy and tongues, and the gift of healing through the imposition of hands, afforded again to the Church of today as once to the early Church. To further their cause, they administer a type of "baptism of the Holy Spirit" through immersion; they confess their faith at meetings resounding with alleluias and prayers in an inspired vein; they are opposed to church authority and claim to heal their sick by the imposition of hands. They freely admit that such healing sessions are their best means of propaganda.[107]

Reports of these cures often mention blindness, tuberculosis, cancer, leprosy, etc.

One of the miracle-workers of the movement, William Freeman, arrives in Stockholm in 1950. The advertising slogans heralding his coming declare that the "paralytics will walk, the deaf will hear, the blind will see; the sick will be healed; the diseases of kidney and liver will yield to new life for those who believe in the power of God." The trip, however, is anything but a success. Some newspapermen are so obsessed with doubts that they become indiscreet enough to investigate personally a particular case; they conclude that Freeman's healings are nothing but an empty parade. The bishop of Stockholm also voices his personal opinion: "God does miracles sometimes, but he is not an errand boy taking orders from pietistic adventurers." When passing through Oslo, Freeman is brought in by the police for questioning in connection with the death of a diabetic patient who under his spell had refused to continue his insulin treatment. His request for a Finnish visa is re-

[105] See the pages devoted to this sect by K. Hutten and H. C. Chéry who also furnish more extensive bibliographical data.

[106] Joel II, 23.

[107] See Pastor Nicolle: "Les Assemblées, de Dieu," *Réveil* (Oct. 1951): "L'unique moyen de recrutement dans les Salles d'Evangélisation est la Guérison Divine qui constitue l'attrait par excellence pour les foules (The only means of recruitment in the Gospel Halls is the Divine Healing which is the main attraction for the masses)" (p. 147).

jected on the grounds that charlatanism, even though disguised as religious activity, is not permitted in the country and that the authorities feel responsible for the sick. Freeman then returns to the United States.[108]

The pastor of Schwelm claimed to have known personally all those of his parishioners who said they were healed by Hermann Zaiss, another Pentecostal healer. The pastor's testimony is quite definite: he has not met a single person who was really cured; the patients merely had a temporary and subjective feeling of improvement. Once the euphoria induced by the healing was gone, the condition of the patient turned worse; the pastor eventually had to bury several alleged subjects of miraculous cures who died not long after voicing their loud claims of being healed.[109]

Here again, the prodigious events occur in a setting of systematic suggestion and quackish propaganda, which makes their acceptance as religious events difficult.

In conclusion we would like to mention a recent, comprehensive opinion concerning all of the various forms of healing under religious auspices. In January 1954, a special study was initiated by the British Medical Association upon the request of an archbishops' commission for cooperation between physicians and spiritual directors. The Association polled its members to determine if during their medical career they have ever encountered a case of evidently incurable illness being cured through religious causes, such as public worship, imposition of hands, anointing, public or private prayer, or pilgrimages. The official report calls the returns rather disappointing.[110] Only Protestants have responded; the majority of

[108] See K. Hutten: *op. cit.*, p. 407; the photographs toward the end of the book are very relevant for the informed reader.

[109] K. Hutten: *op. cit.*, p. 408; on Hermann Zaiss, see *ibid.*, pp. 379ff. Although a Protestant, the writer cannot help to notice the striking contrast with the Lourdes system of checking the facts.

[110] British Medical Association: *Divine Healing and Co-operation between Doctors and Clergy* (London, 1956). The texts quoted are on pp. 15-16. Appendix II contains a long list of samples of answers received (pp. 33-45). The pamphlet makes some references to the Lourdes facts, but the authors of the report do not seem to have taken cognizance of them. Their ignorance of these facts is explained by the refusal of Catholics to cooperate in the survey. The authors express their regret in the Introduction that three

the accounts were given by doctors who are themselves involved, one way or another, with "spiritual healing"; neither unbelievers nor Catholics have participated at all. The report deplores the fact that with one exception all of the facts were presented without any critical scrutiny, the terminology used was vague, and the accounts were based on prejudice and personal views rather than on factual data.

After studying the reports, the committee arrived at the following conclusion: "To summarize, we can find no evidence that there is any type of illness cured by 'spiritual healing' alone which could not have been cured by medical treatment which necessarily includes consideration of environmental factors. We find that, whilst patients suffering from psychogenic disorders may be 'cured' by various methods of spiritual healing, just as they are by methods of suggestion and other forms of psychological treatment employed by doctors, we can find no evidence that organic diseases are cured solely by such means."

One would find little benefit in studying some of the other sects that are even more primitive and eccentric in style, such as "Antoinisme" in Wallonia (Belgium) or the "Christ of Montfavet" in France. These various movements may be interesting to the doctors of body and soul, from a sociological and psychoreligious standpoint; they are irrelevant to the point we are concerned with here.

b · The Miraculous in the Russian Orthodox Church

The problem appears under an altogether different light when we consider Russian Orthodoxy where canonization is practiced as in the Roman Catholic Church. Like Catholicism, but even more exclusively, the Russian Church insists on miracles as criteria of the holiness of her great children. This outward similarity, however,

---

outstanding Catholic physicians who had been invited to join the Commission as co-opted members did not think they could accept the invitation (p. 5). A great deal of factual information is also gathered in D. Caradog Jones: *Spiritual Healing*, An Objective Study of a Perennial Grace (London, 1955). But the reader will not find in this book either a single fact supported by precise medical data and by competent persons. See also an article by K. Beth: "Heilung (religiöse)," in the new edition (1958) of *Religion in Gesch. u. Gegenwart*, VIII, cc. 194-198, and the attached bibliography.

should not prevent us from examining at a closer range the nature of Orthodox miracles.

We should bear in mind from the outset that Slavs in general, and Russians in particular, are inclined to speak of miracles far more freely than Occidentals. They see the miraculous element everywhere and accept it in full confidence; they would not think of making their assent depend upon an official approbation by the Church or a critical examination of the facts.[111] Consequently, the title of "miracle-worker" given by the people to a deceased holy person is even more fragile a proof of the reality of the miraculous events than in the Western Church.

Moreover, pre-canonization inquests in the Orthodox Church are very different from their Roman counterparts. Examination of the bodily remains is of primary importance; perfect preservation is a favorable and often conclusive factor warranting canonization.[112] The statement itself that the remains are "preserved intact" is taken in a conventional and broad sense, as indications and details below will show.[113] This would give us the right to assume that the norms applied in these inquests concerning miraculous events are not the same as the strict rules applied by the Catholic Church, and thus no purported miraculous facts may be accepted as such without prudent critical investigation in every case.

Let us study, for instance, the life of St. Seraphim of Sarov (died in 1833), the greatest miracle-worker of the 19th century. His biography, no doubt, presents an impressive number of facts which any Catholic would readily recognize as proofs of a supernatural intervention of God. He would, however, recognize just as readily that none of them qualifies as a major miracle, that is, one with an in-

[111] See A. Staerk's introduction to the French edition of Jean de Kronstadt: *Ma vie en Jésus-Christ* (Paris, 1902), pp. 244-245. Some typical features of popular credulousness are quoted in A. Martel: "Miracles et légendes de l'Ukraine contemporaine," *Irenikon*, 6 (1929), 517-526.

[112] See J. Bois: "Canonisation dans l'Eglise Russe," *Dictionnaire de théol. cath.*, II, c. 1663; P. Peeters: "La canonisation des saints dans l'Eglise Russe," *Analecta Bollandiana*, 33 (1914), 380-420; E. Behr-Sigel: *Prière et sainteté dans l'Eglise Russe* (Paris, 1950), II: "La canonisation dans l'Eglise Orthodoxe," pp. 24-35; Y. Congar: "A propos des saints canonisés dans les Eglises orthodoxes," *Revue des sciences religieuses*, 22 (1948), 240-259.

[113] See J. Bois: *art. cit.*, c. 1669.

trinsic apologetic value and of the kind we have so far found absent everywhere except in the Catholic Church.

There are two particularly striking instances among the cures attributed to him: the cases of Michael Manturov and Judge Nikolai Motovilov. Both are cases of functional paralysis which, judging by the way the illness and the manner of the cure are described, could have been cured, medically speaking, through spontaneous psychotherapy with religious motivation. At the Lourdes Bureau cases like these would not even be considered. We give here an account of one of the cures, inviting the reader to reach his own conclusions.

We find the following account among the writings of Judge Nikolai Motovilov:

> I was taken to Sarov on September 5, 1831. On the 7th, and again on the 8th, feast of the Nativity of the Blessed Virgin, the staretz granted me two interviews in his cell, one in the morning and one in the afternoon. On September 9, five men carried me to his hermitage which stood at a clearing in the woods. The staretz was talking to some visitors. I was put down under a large fig tree which is still standing. As I asked Father Seraphim to help me, he said: I am not a doctor; anyone who wishes to be cured should consult a doctor. I explained to him in detail that I had asked the best doctors of Kazan for help and consulted also a disciple of Hannemann, the famous homeopath, but to no avail. Then I added that I felt God alone could help me, poor sinner.
>
> —Do you believe in Our Lord Jesus Christ, God and Man, and in his Holy Mother the Blessed Virgin?
>
> I said: I do.
>
> —Do you believe that the Master who once could heal all suffering instantly, by a simple touch or word, could even now heal in an instant those who ask his help? That through his help and the assistance of his Holy Mother we are able to restore health instantly and by a simple word?
>
> I said: Indeed I do believe it with all my heart and soul. If I had no faith I would not have had myself carried here.
>
> —If you believe, you are healed.
>
> —How could I be healed, I said, when you and your servants must support me?
>
> —Not at all; you are completely cured.

The staretz ordered his servants to stand aside; he himself took me by the shoulder, lifted me, and made me stand on my feet, saying:

—Stand straight; put your feet firmly on the ground, and do not be afraid of anything: you are healed.

Then he added: You can see for yourself how well you can stand up.

I said to him: Yes, because you support me.

—No, you can start walking without my help, and you will remain able to walk. The Mother of God has interceded for you with the Father and he healed you completely. Do not hesitate, but start walking.

I felt an unknown strength fill my limbs and I took a few steps, but the holy man held me back, saying: That is enough for today. Three years of suffering have diminished your strength; be prudent in starting to walk again, and especially be careful for your health for it is now a precious gift of God. The Lord has taken away from you all evil and purified you of your sins. Remember what the Lord has done for you; be careful to keep your faith in his mercy.

I received the blessing of the staretz, then turned away slowly with the help of my servants and walked back to my wagon under the watching eyes of all my people.[114]

John Ilitsh Sergieff, better known as John of Kronstadt, is closer to our age and is a more famous and also more controversial figure. In his lifetime (1829 to 1908) he had a tremendous influence both at the Russian imperial court and among the people. A great number of miracles are attributed to him.

The miracles he reports (with an occasional touch of vanity)[115] in his book, *My Life in Jesus Christ,* were obtained by him in the name of the Blessed Sacrament to which he was very devoted. None of these accounts, however, show any fact that could be con-

[114] We borrow this text from I. Smolitsch: *Leben und Lehre der Starzen* (Vienna, 1936); from the biography of Seraphim of Sarov, pp. 209-257; the fact quoted is on pp. 228-230. On Russian saints and staretz's, see I. Kologrivof: *Essai sur la sainteté en Russie* (Bruges, 1953); N. Arséniev: "Le monde des saints et des staretz russes," *Dieu Vivant,* 6 (1946), 99-119; G. P. Fedotov: *Les saints de la Russie ancienne* (Paris, 1931); ID., *The Russian Religious Mind* (Cambridge, Mass., 1946), ch. IV and V; C. de Grunwald: *Quand la Russie avait des saints* (Paris, 1958).

[115] A. Staerk: *op. cit.,* pp. 173-174.

sidered more than an outstanding case of God's responding to prayer, or is such as could be called a major miracle.[116] His translator, a Catholic Benedictine monk who believes in the supernatural character and the historicity of the reported events, readily admits that we are very far here from any major prodigies.[117]

His admirers attributed to him some sensational miracles, and it seems that Father John was very reticent about these exaggerations. At any rate, his cult soon took an unhealthy turn, even giving rise after his death to a sectarian movement called "Johannism" which literally deified him, while one of the nuns in a monastery founded by him claimed to be the Mother of God risen from her death.[118] All of which evidently makes it difficult for us to accept the miracles claimed by his admirers, and creates doubts concerning their historical truth.

One could hardly help being skeptical also in the case of another alleged miracle-worker, Rasputin, this extremely shady character who enjoyed the strangest favors of the court. His curious power certainly did not come from his religious influence.[119]

c · *The Jansenist Miracles*

The one occasion that helped more than any other to set off the contrast between the Catholic and the non-Catholic miracle has definitely been the controversy about the Jansenist miracles. We are therefore justified in dealing with this subject at some length.[120]

[116] *Ibid.*, pp. 247-248.

[117] A. Staerk: *op. cit.*, p. 245: "If we are to believe a certain type of popular literature which sounds too much like propaganda and with which, we are sure, Father John has nothing to do, some of these cures show features of instantaneousness that seem truly miraculous; only these events took place ten to twenty years ago and thus exclude all possibility of checking." On John of Kronstadt, see an anonymous article in *L'ami du clergé* 23 (1900), 117-122; A. Retel in *Echos d'Orient*, (1906), pp. 44ff.; M. Jugie in *Echos d'Orient* (1913), pp. 57-60; G. P. Fedotov, A *Treasury of Russian Spirituality* (New York, 1948), pp. 346-416.

[118] See A. M. Ammann: *Ostslavische Kirchengeschichte* (Vienna, 1950), pp. 585-586.

[119] *Ibid.*, pp. 586-587.

[120] The chief contemporary testimonies, varying greatly in value, are those by Carré de Montgeron, Dom Lataste, Hecquet, Du Bonnaire, La Condamine; important excerpts of their works, with abundant bibliography but without any critical care, are available in H. Blanc: *Le merveilleux* (Paris, 1865), book I: "Le jansénisme," pp. 1-129 and 431-432. Of the more recent

The first extraordinary event took place at a crucial moment during the initial phase of the Jansenist crisis. On May 31, 1653, Pope Innocent X in an apostolic constitution entitled "Cum Occasione" condemns as heretical five propositions taken from the writings of Jansenius. The Jansenists promptly reply that with the Holy Father they too condemn these propositions (*quaestio juris*), but they deny that Jansenius had ever taught or professed any of them (*quaestio facti*). That marks the beginning of a heated controversy about the famous distinction "*de jure* and *de facto*." The center of the opposition soon shifts to a monastery of Cistercian nuns, the abbey of Port-Royal which since 1638 also shelters a group of "hermits" headed by Antoine Arnauld, the recognized leader of the movement since the death of Jansenius. Stubborn and violent as the opposition may be, it is not intended to trespass over the limits of outward obedience to the Church. Then Alexander VII, successor of Innocent X, declares that the five propositions have indeed been condemned in the very sense Jansenius meant them. The battle now becomes more violent than ever, although we still cannot speak of an open break with the Church.

The event known as the "miracle of the Holy Thorn" takes place on March 24, 1656, a few months before the publication of the new constitution. On this day the abbey receives for a few hours' display a reliquary containing, according to tradition, a thorn from the crown worn by Jesus during his passion. Little Marguerite Périer, a niece of Pascal, is among the children who come with their teacher to venerate the relic. The child is suffering of a fistula of the lacrymal duct. Despite all medical care her palate remains perforated, and pus is discharged not only through the eyes but also through the mouth and nose. The event that follows

---

literature on the convulsionists, see mainly J. Paquier: *Le Jansénisme* (Paris, 1909), ch. X: "Les miracles du Jansénisme," pp. 467-523; A. Gazier: *Histoire générale du mouvement janséniste depuis les origines jusqu'à nos jours* (Paris, 1922); G. J. Waffelaert: "Convulsionnaires," *Dict. apol. de la foi cath.*, I, cc. 705-713; R. Knox: *Enthusiasm*, ch. X and XI (on Jansenism), and especially ch. XVI: "The Convulsionaries of St. Médard"; J. Vinchon: "Les convulsionnaires de Saint-Médard ont-ils dépassé les limites de l'humain?" in *Limites de l'human*, Études Carmélitaines (1953), pp. 39-47; A. Mousset: *L'étrange histoire des convulsionnaires de St-Médard* (Paris, 1953).

is told by Jacqueline Pascal in a letter to Madame Périer, mother of the girl and sister of Pascal.

> When Sister Flavie, their teacher who was standing near the reliquary, saw Margie come forward, she signaled to her to let her eye be touched, then without much thinking she took the holy relic and held it against the eye of the child. After everyone had left, they gave the reliquary back to Monsieur de la Potherie. Toward the evening Sister Flavie, who had quite forgotten the incident, overheard Margie saying to one of her little friends: "My eye is healed, it does not hurt any more." She was very much surprised; she turned to the child and found that the swelling in the corner of the eye, which in the morning had been the size of the tip of a finger, very long and hard, was no longer there; the watery eye which had been a pity to look at before the relic had touched it, now appeared as healthy as the other eye and no one could tell the difference between them. She pressed the eye which no longer yielded pus or any thick liquid, but only what naturally belonged in it.[121]

At the time of this event, knowledge of the pathology of the lacrymal duct was still in a very elementary stage; nor is there any way of knowing whether the cure was instantaneous.[122] Yet everything seems to indicate beyond a doubt that this was a case of an organic lesion healing in a very short time; nor do we have any reason to reject the many serious witnesses who testified in the case.[123] Delancé, the attending physician, declared the healing to be absolutely beyond any medical explanation; other physicians consulted by Port-Royal abundantly testified to the same effect,

[121] See text in B. Pascal: *Pensées*, edited by L. Brunschvicg (Hachette, Paris), pp. 17-18, note.

[122] J. Lhermitte: *Le problème des miracles* (Paris, 1956), is exaggerating somewhat when he sees this fact as the prototype of genuine miracles, especially as regards "instantaneousness." (p. 70).

[123] Beside the testimony of Jacqueline Pascal, already quoted, one should read that of Madame Périer (Gilberte, older sister of Pascal) in her *Vie de Blaise Pascal* (see ed. of *Pensées* quoted above; pp. 17-18 in the text); that of Mother Angélique, abbess of Port-Royal, in J. Lhermitte: *op. cit.*, pp. 57-58; that of Racine in his *Abrégé de l'histoire de Port-Royal*, IV, pp. 482ff., or in J. Paquier: *op. cit.*, pp. 471-473.

and the vicar generals of the archdiocese of Paris, although very much opposed to Jansenism, did not hesitate to declare solemnly the miraculous nature of the cure on October 22.[124]

We have thus every reason to consider the "miracle of the Holy Thorn" a major miracle. But it is not yet a Jansenist miracle but a Catholic one, since at this time no one speaks of separation from the Church. In any event, the miracle and its setting are absolutely outside the sphere of the controversy. It is the answer of God to the sincere devotion and prayers of the people of Port-Royal, while being also, perhaps, a gentle invitation to fidelity to Christ within his true Church.

At any rate, that is how Blaise Pascal interprets the miracle. Not only did this event become his basic source of inspiration for a great apologetic work the outlines of which are preserved in the *Pensées*, but it has left a profound mark on his personal spiritual life. Sainte-Beuve, an author who can certainly be trusted in this case, states that the miracle marks the moment when the "Pascal of the *Provinciales*" became the "Pascal of the *Pensées*." [125]

This is not the way, however, in which most Jansenists understood the meaning of the miracle. The immediate result was a calming down of the storm over Port-Royal, and the various unfortunate developments do not begin to take place until 1661. By then the Jansenists have realized the advantage they could take of this miracle and they begin to use it as a means of propaganda. They construe it as a proof that the Jansenists are right and the Jesuits wrong. Also about this time more and more favors are being attributed to the Holy Thorn, their number growing year after year and soon reaching more than eighty. Many Jansenists become gradually convinced that in the crisis God himself is actually performing specifically Jansenist miracles.

This state of mind explains the events that take place some fifty years later when the condemnation of Quesnel and the papal bull

[124] See ed. of *Pensées*, p. 18.

[125] On the effect of this miracle on Blaise Pascal, see a chapter by J. Lhermitte: *op. cit.*, pp. 65-71. On the mental climate prevailing at Port-Royal at that time, see J. Orcibal: *Port Royal, Entre le miracle et l'obéissance.* Flavie Passart et Angélique de St. Jean Arnauld d'Andilly (Bruges, 1957), especially pp. 85-108.

"Unigenitus" (1713) finally break the peace established under Clement IX and force the Jansenists into open revolt.[126]

Partisans of the revolting faction call themselves "the appealing," and those in favor of submission, "the accepting." The former claim that the Church, through her own fault, has ceased to be the true Church and there is no salvation outside the small group that opposes the bull. From then on they live in a climate of prophetism and apocalyptic expectation, expressed in a commentary on the Apocalypse by Etamare, a Jansenist priest.[127] There follows in 1727 the death of Deacon Francis de Pâris, a real predecessor of Benedict Joseph Labre. This pious and devoted person who led a life of renunciation and extreme penance, fasting around the year and sleeping on an overturned wardrobe, eventually received the order of diaconate after repeated refusals and very much against his will, but steadfastly refused priestly ordination. He lived and died as a wholehearted Jansenist, an "appealer." [128] As an important detail, bearing on the events following his death and noted also by his biographer, his long fasts "were sometimes accompanied by bodily convulsions and unusual gestures." [129]

After his death miraculous stories begin to spread in a clandestine manner. At first no particular attention is paid to these stories. A year later, however, his admirers erect on his grave in Saint-Médard cemetery an ornate tombstone with a long epitaph. Visitors begin at once to flock around the grave. A tense atmosphere of apocalyptic expectation gives rise to desires to witness some heavenly sign produced in support of Jansenism; stories of miracles and prodigies are told and retold; written accounts, often signed by physicians and druggists, are being circulated. Vintimille, archbishop of Paris, orders a detailed study of a particular case, that of the supposedly blind and paralytic Anne Lefranc. Over a hundred witnesses sign their name in testimony to the reality of her cure. The investigation, however, eventually reveals that many signatures have been simply forged or extorted from victims. Anne's brother

[126] R. Knox: *Enthusiasm*, p. 227.
[127] R. Knox: *ibid.*, pp. 378ff.
[128] See J. Paquier: *op. cit.*, pp. 474-475.
[129] R. Knox, *op. cit.*, p. 375.

testifies that his sister has never been blind; her paralysis was real but existed after the miracle as well as before. Vintimille publishes these results in a pastoral letter. The Jansenists waste no time and keep offering other cases, not less than thirteen in a few weeks. One of the beneficiaries of these alleged cures, a man by the name of Le Doulx, is overwhelmed by qualms of conscience and admits to Bishop La Fare of Laon that the whole story was a deliberate hoax; he repeats his confession before the archbishop of Paris.[130] Moreover, the details of these miraculous accounts are enough to make any attentive and critical reader cautious.[131] Three years later the archbishop of Paris issues another letter on this question; he declares that the stories of Jansenist prodigies and miracles "were published temerariously, lack all proof and are unworthy of any belief." [132]

The events take a completely different turn in 1731. A young girl by the name of Mademoiselle d'Hardouin, suffering from paralysis, is taken to the grave of Monsieur de Pâris where she has a sudden convulsive seizure. The event is witnessed by a large crowd of bystanders who also see the young girl being healed. The first instance of seizures is followed by a real epidemic of convulsions, soon pushing the alleged cures into the background and yielding the stage to convulsionist scenes which become an original phenomenon in its own right.[133] At the height of the epidemic, toward the end of 1731, one could often see as many as four to five thousand spectators in the Saint-Médard cemetery, surrounding four to five hundred convulsionists.[134]

Louis-Baptiste Carré de Montgeron, a freethinker and member of the parliament, visits the Saint-Médard cemetery on September 7, 1731, in order to assess the events and arrive at a critical verdict.

[130] L. Pastor: *History of the Popes*, XXXIV (St. Louis, 1941), p. 443.

[131] Eight of these miracles are narrated with an abundance of detail, testimonies and apologetical analysis in L. B. Carré de Montgeron: *La vérité des miracles opérés à l'intercession de M. de Pâris et autres appelans, démontrée contre M. l'archevêque de Sens*, 1737, 1741, 1747, three vols. with engravings. See a critical discussion of these cures from the medical standpoint in R. Vander Elst: *Vraies et fausses guérisons miraculeuses*, pp. 158-162.

[132] See Pastor: *loc. cit.*, p. 447, n. 1.

[133] R. Knox, *op. cit.*, p. 376.

[134] Vinchon, *art. cit.*, p. 45.

He is so deeply moved by the spectacle he finds there that he throws himself at the grave of Monsieur de Pâris, is converted, and dedicates his fortune and the rest of his life to the publishing of a great book in which he collects a host of testimonies concerning the miraculous cures. The stories are adorned with beautiful engravings and the book is finally published in 1737. Without being invited, the author sneaks into the chambers of the king and manages to offer him a copy of his book, which causes him to be imprisoned in the Bastille and later exiled from France. During his exile he writes a second and a third volume on the convulsions, gathering all the evidence he can find on the subject.[135]

These books sparked a violent controversy; for fifty years countless brochures and pamphlets were written for and against the convulsionists. To distinguish between truth and falsehood in this mass of literature is an almost impossible undertaking. Assuredly, every student of the matter admits today that the evidence rendered by Carré de Montgeron is controversial, that the man himself is too unbalanced and fanatical to be trusted, and his books contain abundant proof of his own uncritical credulousness toward all manners of questionable evidence.[136] But does this mean that all of the events related are born of pure fraud, as the opposition sometimes would have them to be?

Perhaps our best chance to find an objective assessment would be to look among the very ranks of the Jansenists, especially those who themselves were surprised and shocked by the developments. On January 7, 1735, thirty Jansenists, all of them "appealers" and members of the Sorbonne faculty, issue with Du Guet, a Jansenist leader, a joint statement condemning and rejecting the convulsionist practices as contrary to the majesty of God, the holiness of his worship, the dignity of the Church, the purity of morals and common decency.[137] Doctor Philippe Hecquet, a staunch Jansenist, dean of the Paris medical school and house physician at Port-Royal, writes three pamphlets which in 1733 are reprinted in one

[135] Pastor, *loc. cit.*, p. 449.

[136] See, e.g., R. Knox, *op. cit.*, p. 387; Pastor, p. 448f.

[137] See P. F. Mathieu: *Histoire des miraculés et des convulsionnaires de St. Médard* (Paris, 1864), p. 469, note; see also H. B. Grégoire: *Histoire des Sectes religieuses* (Paris, 1828), II, p. 137.

volume, sparing no words in expressing his indignation over the Saint-Médard incidents which he explains as purely natural events.[138]

Let us review the actual facts. First, the convulsions: "Convulsions or violent contortions of the entire body; rolling on the ground; jumping around on the pavement; rigidity; frenzied agitation of arms, legs, head, and the entire body, resulting in difficulty in breathing, fast and irregular heartbeats." [139] A variety of automatic actions are observed: the convulsionist performs certain acts in a state of trance and partial unconsciousness. These performances would completely exhaust a normal person, but the convulsionist does not seem to show the least trace of fatigue.[140] Some of them imitate the way of life of Monsieur de Pâris; others enact a symbolic representation of the Passion; others again impose their hands on one another saying: "Receive the seal of the Holy Spirit"; there are some who mimic the Mass and hear the confession of participants; some spectators claim to recognize strange languages in the incomprehensible vociferation that accompanies these acts. There are again those who play with dolls or pull toy wagons around, which sympathizers interpret as a "heroic victory over human respect." [141] A 19th-century author sums up the whole matter in the following words: "In the midst of all of this, we hear sighing, singing, shouting, whistling, reciting, prophesying, caterwauling. The dominating activity in this convulsionist epidemic, however, is dancing. A priest by the name of Father Bécherand leads the chorus; he stands constantly on top of the Saint's grave so as to be better seen by everyone. That is where day after day he performs with matchless talent his favorite step, the famous "fish

[138] Full titles of these pamphlets: P. Hecquet: 1) "*La cause des convulsions finie;* 2) *Le naturalisme des convulsions démontré par la physique, par l'histoire naturelle et par les événements de cette oeuvre et démontrant l'impossibilité du divin qu'on lui attribue dans une lettre sur les secours meurtriers;* 3) *Le mélange dans les convulsions confondu par le naturalisme.* There is a summary of his argumentation in the article of Vinchon quoted above; Vinchon relies mainly on Hecquet's data. Other authors of the time have also offered a purely natural interpretation of the facts; e.g., Du Bonnaire: *Examen critique, physique et théologique des convulsions et des caractères divins qu'on croit voir dans les accidents des convulsionnaires* (without place, 1733).

[139] See H. B. Grégoire, *op. cit.*, p. 127.

[140] R. Knox, *op. cit.*, p. 378.

[141] H. B. Grégoire, *op. cit.*, p. 131.

jump," accompanied by the unabated admiration of the spectators." [142]

The leading parts are played by women, most of them illiterate and of very low class, usually mentioned only by their nickname, such as "Dizzy, Idiot, Invisible, Barker, Salamander, etc." [143] The few society people who join the convulsionists show grave and degrading symptoms: M. Pinault, an attorney, barks every day for two hours; M. Fontaine, an official of the Court, indulges twice daily, at 9 A.M. and 3 P.M., in a no less extravagant act: he keeps spinning around on one foot like a top while reading aloud Quesnel's *Réflexions morales;* this goes on for six months until all ten volumes are finished.[144]

As is evident from the outset, not all of the ultimate motives behind these acts are of the reassuring kind. Grégoire states that "the behavior of several participants shows that they are not Vestal virgins"; Hecquet also points out the erotic and sadistic aspects of these exercises, especially of the so-called "hurt and help" activity which achieves increasing prominence and commands the liveliest attention. Participants, mostly women, would experience violent pains during the convulsions, expecting—as in all other "brother and sister" sects—their "brothers" to comfort and assist them through these acts of "help." Only men can render this assistance which is as varied as suspect in nature. Sometimes the part of the body where the pain is felt is brutally beaten—Montgeron quotes the case of a thirteen-year-old girl sustaining more than a hundred blows from a 48-pound iron bar in the abdominal region—or again, a board is laid across the lower limbs to support eight to twenty dancing and jumping men; in other instances the subject is tortured with tongs and swords.[145] Hecquet also mentions that these "hurt and help" practices include certain "unmentionable" acts the nature of which explains "the frantic eagerness of girls in asking for this nameless help by the hands of the young men sur-

[142] L. Figuier: *Historie du merveilleux dans les temps modernes* (Paris, 1873), p. 369.

[143] Vinchon, *art. cit.*, p. 41; see also H. Blanc: *op. cit.*, passim.

[144] Montgeron, II, pp. 12-13; the text is reproduced in H. Blanc, pp. 65-66.

[145] See complete text in Montgeron, quoted by J. Paquier: *op. cit.*, pp. 481ff.

rounding them." [146] Some simulate diabolic possession in order to give free course to their instincts. Cases of prostitution under a religious pretext are not uncommon,[147] and pathological deviations, such as coprophagy, are not absent from the scene.[148]

It is not very surprising that in 1732 a royal ordinance should close the gates of the cemetery. But the convulsionists are far from being ready to surrender. The day after the publication of the ordinance the following sign appears on the cemetery gate: "God is herewith enjoined by royal decree from working any miracles at this place." The meetings are now held on private premises, and after another decree in February, 1732, forbidding even private meetings, they are held secretly. The convulsionists become an organized sect and appear almost as professionals in comparison with their amateur predecessors.[149] If Grégoire's figures are exact, there were some 800 such professionals in Paris and elsewhere.

At this stage the convulsions are pushed into the background and yield their place to the "help and hurt" practices which become independent phenomena evidencing increasingly sadistic tendencies. Some cases of crucifixion are mentioned, the subjects of which are invariably women; they sink into a state of infantile hysteria wherein reactions and language become childish and a certain insensibility develops in proportion with the degree of physical pain, varying from one case to the other. One of the crucified women dies a few days after the event, from injuries suffered in a trial by fire which she was expected to pass unscathed.[150]

Quite understandably many Jansenists were unspeakably mortified over these excesses. The modern student of history, however, still finds the events puzzling. How could men with deep religious culture, as were several of the defenders of the convulsionists, experience any feeling of respect or religious emotion at all in viewing these exhibitions?

At the same time, the basic question remains to be answered: Do the convulsionist performances surpass the limits of human powers, and are they in some way related to our "major prodigy?"

[146] Vinchon, *art. cit.*, p. 41.
[147] Pastor, *loc. cit.*, p. 448, n. 3; Knox, *op. cit.*, p. 378.
[148] Pastor, p. 448, n. 2; H. Blanc, pp. 26, 73.
[149] Knox, p. 382.
[150] Vinchon, pp. 45-46.

Most authors of the age answer affirmatively. No explanation of these events can be found in the natural order of things. Writers thus either attribute them to divine power or think that the dubious halo that surrounds them with extravagance, violence and corruption, proves that they are mere caricatures of the miraculous and bear the stamp of the "ape of God." [151] Some other contemporary critics, together with almost all modern historians, deny this supposition and state that all of the purported facts can be explained within the order of nature.[152]

This shift in the historical assessment of the convulsionist practices is based on the deeper insight we have today of both history and psychology.

In history, the passing of time broadens our total vision and facilitates the evaluation of the phenomenon as a whole; passions have subsided and the elements of life, blind fanaticism and naive credulousness can be sorted out more readily. These elements played a far larger part than originally supposed. Moreover, a study of some of the contemporary evidence, supplied by critical but obviously sincere witnesses,[153] renders inevitable the conclusion that the very facts contain a sizable proportion of conscious fraud and simulation.

These conclusions of historical research are in perfect accord with recent discoveries in psychopathology and the study of analogous manifestations in religious history. In this light the phenomena of Saint-Médard differ little from others brought about by psychoreligious disorders and pseudomystical fanaticism.[154] According

[151] Dom Lataste: *Lettres théologiques aux écrivains défenseurs des convulsions et autres prétendus miracles du temps* (Paris, 1740), was the first one to attribute the phenomena of convulsion to demonic interference. Among the more recent authors we have quoted above, J. Paquier, Msgr. G. J. Waffelaert, R. Vander Elst have adopted his conclusions.

[152] E.g., R. Knox, Vinchon, Pastor; J. Lhermitte: *True and False Possession* (New York, 1963), pp. 62-68, express the same views.

[153] See, e.g., the detailed minutes of the record, prepared by Du Doyer de Gastel at the occasion of a trial by fire and sword, and the ones prepared by La Condamine at the occasion of a crucifixion meeting, as published in H. Blanc, pp. 97-104 and 104-114. It must be mentioned also that Carré de Montgeron is practically the only one to introduce these improbable elements in the accounts of the St-Médard happenings.

[154] Knox, p. 378; see also J. Lhermitte: *True and False Possession*, pp. 68-70 and 81-85.

to Vinchon's highly pertinent judgment, they prove "the survival of mental states which are as old as mankind and continue to exist in a now latent, now acute form, as evidenced by developments in recent years. These states are characterized by a hypertrophy of instinctive activity mixing sex, aggressiveness and magic to a degree of tension where pleasure and pain become ambivalent and undistinguished." [155] There are other psychic troubles, such as hysteria, maniac excitement, schizophrenia, melancholic anxiety, that result in similar symptoms: resistance and unusual vitality of the muscular structure, at least as a temporary phenomenon; insensitivity to pain, enormous discharge of physical energy without fatigue, etc. Plasticity, suggestibility and simulation also have their counterparts in psychopathology.

The alleged miraculous cures must be placed in the total context of these manifestations. Thus we arrive easily at the same conclusion as expressed in this moderate indictment by Benedict XIV:[156] When the cures are genuine, they can be attributed without fear of error to the same natural causes as the convulsions. This is confirmed both by the nature of the illnesses—functional and nervous troubles—and by the manner of their cure.

We have dealt with these events in considerable detail because they seem the best available illustration of the monopoly of the Catholic Church on "major miracles." Jansenism displays a case of total and persistent absence of "major prodigies," despite fanatical and desperate expectations and appeals to external signs as God's stamp authenticating a body of religious tenets. If we were to interpret the convulsionist episode in a religious light, we would definitely see in it an instance of God's refusal to heed man's appeal to the miraculous. From the purely historical viewpoint which we have adopted in this chapter, we can only interpret it as an absence by incapacity.

[155] Vinchon, p. 46.

[156] "Medici scripserunt et ficta undequaque asserta miracula demonstrarunt; et, quatenus narrationes verae fuissent, nihil in eis interfuisse, quod vires naturae superat (Physicians wrote about and demonstrated completely fictitious miracles; but insofar as the accounts were true, there is nothing in them that would surpass the forces of nature)"; thus concludes Benedict XIV: *De servorum Dei. . . .* Book IV, Part I, ch. VII, n. 20. Dom Lataste, while attributing the convulsions to demonic possession, considers the cures as results of purely natural psychological causes.

This ends our long journey into the realm of the religious history of the miraculous and our futile quest for at least one fact that could be categorized as a major miracle. We believe that we have not overlooked any serious event or sequence of events. It is unlikely that any such events and facts, being as they are highly important in comparative religious science, would have remained hidden to the point of being altogether undetected in a conscientious and sincere inquiry.

Thus we may conclude that the Roman Catholic Church, while not claiming an absolute monopoly, which could not be proved because of the very nature of history, does have a *practical* monopoly on what we have called "major miracle."

4 · THE DISCERNMENT OF MIRACLES

The comparative study in the two previous chapters leads to the conclusion that the Roman Catholic Church has been and continues to be a stage of historically incontrovertible facts which have no counterpart either in secular situations or in other Christian or non-Christian communions. Moreover, these facts invariably occur in a context suggesting that they are God's answer to the prayer of man; their "*Gestalt*" is that of sign-events with a dialogical structure.

In the present chapter we shall seek an answer to the all-important question whether these events actually possess the sign value their outward appearance suggests, whether they truly are, or merely appear to be, signs of God. If it is possible to conclude from outward appearance to real signification, we would like to know whether such a conclusion is based on subjective religious feeling or rather on some rational, objective and universally valid argument.

A few preliminary observations must be made here to define the scope of the question.

As pointed out before, we are searching for a universally valid rational proof because we wish to comply with the laws of scientific apologetics. In practice, it makes little difference how an individual believer or unbeliever actually arrives at an appreciation of the sign value of miraculous facts, or how great a part scientific reasoning plays in the genesis of such an appreciation. It is doubtless rare, even among the stoutest champions of science, for anyone to accept the divine reality of a miracle solely because it has been firmly established through critical study and scientific analysis. As a rule, religious convictions are formulated through activities other than scientific research. Personal appreciation of the genuine nature of a prodigious event is itself a usually incommunicable experience. The passage from fact value to sign value follows an even more strictly personal logic, linked so intimately with the subject's own existence that reason alone is powerless to defend and support it, for this logic draws on intuition which is beyond the reach of apologetic reasoning. This does not make convictions thus born unreliable; on the contrary. Apologetics, however, aiming as it does at a scientific interpretation of the criteria of faith, must confine itself to universally valid aspects supported by logical reasoning.[1]

On the other hand, the scope of the "scientific" view which commands our reasoning here must not be narrowed down arbitrarily. Nineteenth-century apologetics has attempted to show on the level of the positive sciences that miracles are experimentally observed as exceptions to the laws of nature. Many even today cannot conceive of a scientific demonstration of the miraculous in any other way than within the limits of the positive sciences. We feel very strongly with L. de Grandmaison and numerous other authors[2] that while the positive sciences may furnish us with valuable tools for the observation of miraculous events, there would not be much sense in trying to demonstrate on the level of the strictly

[1] With reference to this distinction, see J. Mouroux: "Discernement et discernibilité du miracle," *Revue apologétique*, 60 (1935), 538-562.

[2] See L. de Grandmaison: *Jesus Christ*, III, pp. 243-244, "Can the Miraculous Be Verified Scientifically?" Ian T. Ramsey's inaugural lecture at Oxford University demonstrates in a conclusive and original fashion that the word "miracle" does not belong in the vocabulary of science but in that of history considered as the sum total of intersubjective relations. Miracle is a scientifically meaningless word which takes on a sense only in the area of history; see I. T. Ramsey: *Miracles*, An Exercise in Logical Mapwork (Oxford, 1952). The same idea is set forth in W. Born: *Glaube und Naturwissenschaft* (Bielefeld, 1954).

positive sciences a transcendental act of God. Fortunately, the positive sciences are not the only kind of science. The full, if not current, meaning of "science" encompasses every systematic effort by the human mind to solve problems at their own level, within the particular realm of thought in which they arise. Now, the discernment of miracles has only an indirect relevance to the positive sciences and belongs essentially in the level of metaphysics and in the domain of religious science; thus it can only be achieved through critical reasoning by a religious mind functioning on a metaphysical level. This method, when applied in a systematic and rational manner, is no less "scientific" in the strict sense of science.

These are the points of method which preside over the reasoning attempted in this chapter. We shall first examine the part history and the positive sciences play in the discovery of miracles, and mark its boundaries as plainly as possible. We shall then ask if these elements collected through positive science may be incorporated into a value judgment to be made by the human mind on all its levels of functioning, and eventually result in an apologetic argument of scientific nature. If such incorporation proves possible we shall examine the actual ways of arriving at this apologetic conclusion.

I • THE ROLE OF POSITIVE SCIENCE

The contributions of history and positive science to the discernment of the miraculous may be summed up in three points:

1) History and positive science guarantee on the level of scientific research the historical veracity and exceptional nature of a major prodigy. The direct witnesses are more often than not ill-prepared to establish the validity of their witness scientifically.

2) Positive science can demonstrate that there is a regular relationship between the prodigious events and a certain religious context with a dialogical structure.

3) Positive science shows that this relationship is an exclusive one. Through thorough study it may be able to exclude all other explanations, or even the possibility of any other explanation, and thus establish that this connection with the religious context of the

dialogue is the only demonstrable constant factor capable of explaining the facts.

Each of these points must be submitted to closer scrutiny.

a • Confirmation of the Facts and of Their Exceptional Nature

The part science plays in this connection has been clearly demonstrated in the previous chapters.

First, the certitude of the *reality* of the facts. Man's imagination and illusions, mirages inspired by his instincts and secret desires, exaggeration and adulteration of accounts handed down orally, are often the cause of serious deformations. Only scrupulous faithfulness to the rules of historical criteriology can eliminate this danger and establish the actual status of the facts. If historical study reveals a certain convergency of similar facts, the validity of each particular fact is reinforced. For a hypothesis of observational error, fortuitous coincidence or spurious testimony, which could be invoked for each particular case, becomes more and more improbable if the events, while remaining exceptional in nature, follow with a certain regularity and always in the same context, and the separate facts constitute an actual *series*.

Second, the *nature* of the facts. Quite evidently a substantial number of them may appear surprising and sensational to the common man while being perfectly normal, obeying laws well known to the expert. This is the case of certain primitive tribes to which the superiority of white man at the beginning of modern colonization appeared as a superhuman power. The same applies to the ordinary man in our own civilized lands, for he is often so unaware, e.g., of the mutual causality existing between psychic and somatic states that routine psychotherapeutic results will appear to him prodigious. In this sense there is some truth in the claim of certain psychotherapists that "miracles happen in their offices every day." When legitimate doubt arises concerning the exceptional nature of an event, especially if it is to be categorized as a major miracle, most often the only recourse is serious scientific investigation.

Throughout the two preceding chapters facts were submitted to study in a manner that illustrates abundantly the part science plays in this investigation. Genuine facts were isolated from spurious ones through rigorous critical scrutiny which, on the one hand, allowed us to reject a substantial number of vague and uncertain information, and, on the other, eliminated many apparent cures, together with cases of temporary improvement or disappearance of lesions that had been erroneously declared organic in a less careful examination.[3]

b · *Establishment of the Necessary Correlation Between the Facts and the Religious Context of the Dialogue*

The second task of science is the study of the regular relationship existing between the appearance of a miracle and a religious context with dialogical structure. Science will warrant the same conclusion to which the study of facts in the previous chapters has led: these events never take place outside a religious context, and the relationship between this context and a major prodigy appears invariably as a relationship between a request or appeal to the saving love of God or its divine witness, and a response embodied in the prodigy.

Establishment of this relationship as a scientific datum does not mean, however, that science pronounces any judgment on the real validity of the sign structure or on the existence of a causal link between a prodigy and its religious context. Science merely finds that this relationship is a *constant factor* and must be taken into account in any attempt at further explanation.

A comparison should help to understand the meaning of these scientific findings. Organic medicine and psychology operate at two different scientific levels. One is a natural science, the other is on the borderline of the positive and "mental" sciences. The clinical physiologist is often faced with syndromes that somewhat resemble those of an organic disease but do not seem to conform to the regular pattern of its course and cure. On the other hand, these

[3] For some typical examples of fraud, see F. Leuret and H. Bon: *Modern Miraculous Cures*, pp. 112-122; typical example of a psychogenic cure in H. Woltereck: *op. cit.*, pp. 242-243; P. Flood (ed.), *New Problems in Medical Ethics*, I, pp. 233-238; rejection of the case of G. Baillie by the canonical commission is typical of the severity of religious authorities (see chapter 2, n. 39); another ambiguous case is discussed in G. Siegmund: *Das Wunder im Lichte der modernen Medizin* (case of Théa Angele, sclerosis), pp. 40-64.

"abnormal" cases bear a constant and certain relationship to known psychic disturbances described in psychology; they come to exist with the appearance of a particular type of psychic complex; their intensity varies along the same curve as the complex itself, and they may altogether disappear suddenly with the disappearance of the latter, leaving no trace at all. Organic medicine is not equipped to determine the nature of the link existing between physiological syndrome and psychic complex, and even less the manner in which psychic complexes act upon somatic states. It must recognize, however, the reality of the link between the two and must reckon with it in establishing its therapeutic norms. Organic medicine, in categorizing these phenomena under the generic name of "psychogenic" disturbances, does not claim to establish an ontological relationship but a mere experimental correlation, and refers the cases to psychology for the solution of the problems they raise.

In the same manner and from the same purely scientific viewpoint, major miracles could be called "hierogenic." This does not imply that the facts depend upon some transcendental, metaphysical or supernatural, activity. The word only means that scientifically speaking, there exists a relationship between the facts and a certain type of religious context; for the eventual solution of the problems thus arising referral is made to religious psychology and philosophy.

c · *Establishing the Exclusive Character of the "Hierogenic" Relationship*

For a correct use of the word "hierogenic" as designating the one characteristic element in major miracles we may not be satisfied merely with the finding of an essential relationship between the facts and a religious context involving a dialogue. The correlation must also be found *exclusive,* that is, the *only* solidly established and constant link science can discover in the facts. If any other data appeared as consistently linked with the facts, it would be impossible to decide that the essential characteristics of these facts do not affect the other correlations and that their hierogenic character is not merely accidental.

Many contemporary psychologists maintain, e.g., that stigmatization occurs only in cases where all of the symptoms of a tendency to hysteria are present. Whether this theory is correct or not is irrelevant here; we merely quote it as an example. Its advocates like to conclude that stigmatization is a direct result of this propensity. A more accurate study of stigmatization, however, reveals another relationship: these phenomena are invariably linked with deep and strong religious emotions. With this second finding it would no longer be scientifically exact to say that stigmatization is a purely hysterical phenomenon, any more than it could be called a religious phenomenon without recognition of the typical hysteroid link. To remain within the boundaries of scientific accuracy we would have to describe and evaluate the facts in the light of a twofold relationship and say that stigmatization results from a religious event taking place in a psyche disposed to hysteria. For any further explanation science will have to refer to psychopathology as well as to religious psychology; these two will then decide whether the particular religious fact should be looked upon as a secondary manifestation of a hysterical disturbance, or contrariwise, whether the disposition to hysteria is merely a sounding board for a genuinely religious event.

If miracles are purely hierogenic facts to be explained further in religious psychology and philosophy, all other correlations and resulting explanations must be first excluded through strict scientific reasoning.

It is comparatively easy to establish the absence of spurious correlations in the case of cosmic prodigies, such as the multiplication of food and similar events. The difficulty resides elsewhere: it is almost impossible to reach a conclusive certainty concerning the historicity and the exceptional nature of the facts themselves; science will question the reality of the facts rather than attempt to find for them a nonreligious explanation. At any rate, precise verification of such prodigies is far more difficult than cases of cures and thus a skeptical attitude toward them might seem to be justified.

Since cures exclude by their very nature any reasonable doubt concerning their reality or exceptional character, objections will be based on the existence of other fundamental correlations, that is, on the probability of other explanations. We choose therefore to study the objections raised against miraculous cures and attempt to evaluate them with a mind free of prejudice.

One way the researcher may choose to follow is to appeal to still unknown but universally present *natural forces* as an explanation of prodigious cures. It does not take long to see how untenable this hypothesis is. For if such exceptional forces have a universal value and consequently no essential link with a religious element, it would be illogical to suppose that they do appear with a certain frequency and regularity within, but never without, a religious context. If there existed only one instance, the exclusive coincidence with a religious context could be attributed to chance. But such an explanation is altogether unthinkable when we are faced with a series of facts, as in the case of major miracles. An appeal to chance then ceases to be scientifically reasonable. Voltaire himself noticed this: "Believers are idiots, to be sure; yet it is strange that the exceptional forces displayed in a miracle should never work for anyone but these idiots."

The discovery of the purely statistical character of the laws of nature has produced in the last few decades a new and more subtle variant of the theory of unknown forces. Quantum physics has forced the natural sciences to recognize that the laws regulating the macrophysical phenomena (at the level of sense perception) are merely the global, statistically constant results of innumerable microphysical interactions which not only obey no laws we have yet been able to determine, but are altogether irreducible, at least according to some physicists, to any law whatsoever, and thus show a certain indetermination or arbitrariness in the physical sense. Some have hence concluded that a miracle could result from the highest statistical improbability and yet remain a completely normal exception within the boundaries defined by the statistical nature of laws.[4]

[4] The reader will find an excellent discussion of the statistical theory of the laws of nature in L. De Broglie: "Réflexions sur l'indéterminisme en physique quantique," *Travaux du IXe Congrès International de philosophie,* fascicle VII (Paris, 1937), pp. 3-9; also in *Matter and Light* (London, 1939), by the same author; see also A. Einstein and L. Infeld: *Drie eeuwen physica* (Amsterdam, 1938); B. Bavink: *Ergebnisse und Probleme der Naturwissen-*

Now, this theory would be perfectly acceptable in one isolated exception to the constant statistical regularity at a single elementary and very limited point. But no scientist engaged in concrete research would take into practical account such an eventuality because its probability is infinitesimal. Considering the complexity of a miraculous cure and the frequently numerous converging exceptions it supposes, theoretical probability remains but has no practical significance whatever, and the scientist cannot in good faith resort to this explanation as at all possible in practice. The improbability is even greater when we no longer view one isolated fact but a series of facts which furthermore are not uniformly distributed over the totality of individuals or groups statistics is interested in, but occur exclusively within a specific group and in a specific set of circumstances. Insistence on the theory of chanceful statistical exception as an explanation of a series of such facts would be a sign of an eminently unscientific attitude, a surrender to prejudice.

"If there had been only one miracle," says Theilhard de Chardin, "I could say that a chance combination of forces has touched

---

schaften[9] (1949) pp. 218-248 [Transl. of 4th ed.: *The Natural Sciences* (New York, 1932), pp. 193-222]. There is no doubt that the emergence of physical indeterminism has made many specialists more receptive toward metaphysical and religious problems in general, and in particular toward the possibility of a miraculous intervention of God in natural processes. See on this matter above, chapter 1, p. 189, n. 17.

Concerning miracles some have arrived at conclusions which, in our opinion, are exaggerated; see, e.g., H. Bergmann: *Der Kampf um das Kausalgesetz in der jüngsten Physik* (Braunschweig, 1929); W. Künneth in C. E. Braaten and R. A. Harrisville (ed.), *Kerygma and History* (Nashville, 1962), p. 104. For an answer to the objection based on the statistical character of the laws of nature, see E. Dhanis: "Un chaînon de la preuve du miracle," pp. 66-70, and especially pp. 74-76; W. Büchel: "Naturwissenschaft auf dem Wege zur Religion?" *Stimmen der Zeit*, 150 (1951-1952), 1-7; ID.: "Physikalisches Weltbild und christlicher Glaube," *Die Kirche in der Welt*, II, fasc. 31; ID.: *Wille, Wunder, Welt* (Kevelaer, 1956); J. Ternus: *Naturwissenschaft, Religion, Weltanschauung*, Chausthaler Gespräch (1948); G. Kafka: *Naturgesetz, Freiheit und Wunder* (Paderborn, 1940); G. Hennemann: *Philosophie, Religion, moderne Naturwissenschaft* (Witten, 1955), particularly pp. 66-69; F. Selvaggi; "Le leggi statistiche e il miracolo," *La Civiltà cattolica*, 101 (1950), 45-56, 202-213; L. Maier: "Der Wandel im Gesetzesbegriff der modernen Physik und die Analogie des Wunders," *Theol.-prakt. Quartalschrift*, 105 (1957), 100-116.

Pius XII made an allusion to this problem in his 1943 allocution to the Pontifical Academy of Sciences. See A.A.S. 35 (1943), 72.

the unknown but basically very simple controls by which life is regulated. As the lightest touch of a warm hand expands and effortlessly lengthens an iron bar that resists the strongest traction, so have these forces reorganized the tissues in a completely natural way. Or I might say that the cure was spontaneous, resulting from a capacity of reversal which mechanical theory attributes to every phenomenon, although it is made effective only in exceptional cases by the play of probabilities. Very well. There is, however, the fact that cures take place in Lourdes year after year, day after day, during certain pilgrimages. Not even the most accommodating set of probabilities would allow such a frequency of fortuitous coincidence." [5]

The *second* theory that arises seems far more acceptable at first glance. Special attention has been given in recent times to the reciprocal effects of psychic and somatic elements, and science has made great progress in this domain. No one was previously aware of the intensity and scope of the influence of psychic factors upon somatic processes. This is like an open invitation to consider so-called miraculous facts as results of psychic reactions which are religious in nature, or at least do not attain full strength and effectiveness except under the impact of very intense religious emotions. It is well known, in fact, how deeply the psychic state of a person can be altered by religious convictions and feelings, and to what paroxysm the force of religious emotions can sometimes lead.

This theory has been frequently set forth during the last half century. Its best known advocate was Charcot, author of *Healing Faith,* followed twenty-five years later by P. Janet whose comprehensive three-volume treatise is entitled *Psychological Medication.*[6] Modern man, who has been said, and not without reason, to be "psychology-stricken," will rediscover in these works some of his favorite temptations.

Upon serious scrutiny, however, this theory also turns out indefensible. In the first place, while recent psychological and psycho-

[5] P. Teilhard de Chardin: "Les miracles de Lourdes et les enquêtes canoniques," pp. 175-176.

[6] J. M. Charcot: *La foi qui guérit* (Paris, 1897); P. Janet: *Les médications psychologiques,* 3 vols. (Paris, 1919) [Transl. *Psychological Healing,* 2 vols. (New York, 1925)].

somatic discoveries have revealed the unsuspected scope of the effects of mind upon body, they have also marked more plainly the limits of such interactivity. Certain words, such as tuberculosis, cancer, sclerosis, blindness, are altogether missing from the index of Janet's book; his studies, in fact, do not cover any organic disease at all. Charcot himself has said that "faith healing," or healing through psychoreligious forces, can only occur in "special subjects and only for such special kinds of diseases as depend upon the effects of mind upon body." [7] When these authors nevertheless continue to expound their theory as the final explanation of Catholic miracles, their conclusions are based upon a lack of knowledge of the facts and a failure to submit them to serious scrutiny. No medical authority today would refuse, after a critical examination of all the facts, to admit that these fall beyond the realm in which emotive shocks and techniques of psychic influencing can regulate the activity of the human body.[8]

At any rate, psychoreligious treatment, such as practiced by Christian Science, is utterly incapable of yielding results even remotely comparable to Christian miracles, which illustrates superabundantly the limits of psychic causality. On this point psychological progress has not at all weakened the exceptional character of Christian miracles but has underlined it all the stronger and demonstrated it irrefutably. Contemporary science, in evaluating the differences between miraculous and psychogenic cures, does not find a continuity of mere difference of degree between essentially similar phenomena, but sees a certain jump, an irreducible hiatus, which forces the mind to conclude to a causal connection other than the causality of psychic activity, even when such activity must be termed psychoreligious.

Moreover, and this argument seems to be decisive, if miracles were effects of an intense religious emotion, they should occur, and with greater frequency, in religious bodies other than the Catholic

[7] J. M. Charcot: *op. cit.*, p. 37.

[8] The optimism shown in this regard in works such as Petersen's reedition of A. Lehmann: *Aberglaube und Zauberei*[3] (1925), and E. Liek: *Das Wunder in der Heilkunde* (1930), has not been confirmed by the progress of medical science. See on this matter A. Mellor: *Le problème des guérisseurs* (Paris, 1958), ch. X: "Les aspects religieux du problème des guérisseurs," pp. 222-257.

religion. In Catholic devotional practices, especially in the Western branch of the Catholic Church, even the peak moments of religious feeling, such as the thrilling—some would say, exalted—atmosphere of the Lourdes devotions, there prevails perfect self control and balance, characterized by sobriety and simplicity. This is in happy contrast with the manifestations of dionysiac frenzy, or the fanaticism and atmosphere of trance typical of devotional phenomena in many other rites. Accounts of religious rites in Tibet, or the exploits of Indian yogis and Moslem dervishes, or a perfunctory reading of *Enthusiasm* by Ronald Knox, would convince anyone that these other confessions offer a choice ground for disturbing psychoreligious emotions.[9] If the monopoly of major miracles seems to belong to a religion characterized by discretion and emotional discipline, explaining these miracles by some purely psychoreligious hypothesis would seem scientifically impossible.

Still another possible objection, based on what would be a *third* hypothesis, consists in supposing that the forces activated by a miracle are not the normal powers of nature. Instead, a specifically supernatural agency would act upon the psychic mechanism of man and would thus gain full control of the body. Such a result could only be obtained through genuinely supernatural faith. Science is not competent to pass judgment either on the nature or the value of such a faith; it may merely register the fact that the Catholic faith, and that faith alone, is capable of freeing in man powers that are over and beyond the natural.

A considerable number of scholars favor implicitly or explicitly this reasoning which appears also in the works of many Catholic authors, at least between the lines. Edouard Le Roy is the one who puts the elements together in a clear, coherent theory which rests on two premises.[10] One is the exceptional nature of the Catholic miracle which Le Roy claims to accept; the other is the observation that miraculous cures, as a rule, are the exact replicas of natural cures, except for the extraordinary speed with which they are achieved. His conclusion is that the supernatural effectiveness of

[9] See bibliographical data given in preceding chapter.

[10] E. Le Roy: "Essai sur la notion du miracle," *Annales de phil. chrét.*, 153 (1906-1907), 5-33, 166-191 and 225-259.

faith, while defying precise definition, is nevertheless great enough to give back to the human spirit its rightful supremacy over the body. Thus faith would cause man to regain "momentarily a portion of his inmost resources and powers." [11]

Miracles do not stem from some generous illusion, nor are they the ephemeral fruit of suggestion or psychic exaltation; they prove instead, says Le Roy, that faith has a *real causal power.*[12] Miracles, therefore, are truly supernatural by their ultimate source, but their mechanism remains entirely natural. While they cause an individual or a group to gain full possession of their natural powers over the body, they also presuppose in this process the supernatural grace of faith.[13] The miraculous thus explained may rightfully be considered as a sign of divine intervention. since the presence of faith presupposes a gratuitous gift of God. It may even serve as a proof of the truth of the Catholic religion, for by bringing to clear light the agreement of this faith with the nature of man and the destiny of his soul, it presents revelation as a genuine enrichment of the soul and the perfect actuation of its natural possibilities.[14] But strictly speaking the miraculous is not "hierogenic" in the sense that through it God himself answers a call of man; rather it stems, at least as its immediate source, from virtualities immanent to the very human soul.

It would be beyond our present intentions to determine whether this explanation is theologically satisfying or not. From the theological viewpoint, in fact, many objections could be raised against Le Roy's theory which seems to be based on an arbitrary, and even frankly inadmissible, view of the relationship between natural and supernatural.[15] The only point of his doctrine we are interested in here is the following: Can an explanation of the miraculous be derived from it, or does it open a path toward that goal? The answer to this question must be negative, for four reasons.

First, the theory is based on a very questionable view of the relationship between mind and matter. There exist no discoveries in

[11] *Ibid.*, pp. 242 and 247.

[12] *Ibid.*, p. 249.

[13] *Ibid.*, p. 250.

[14] *Ibid.*, p. 253.

[15] These objections are developed in detail in B. De Sailly: "La notion et le rôle du miracle," *Annales de phil. chrét.*, 154 (1907), 337-361.

any science that would prompt one to believe that the mind has an unlimited power over matter, or the soul over the body. Such a supposition could have only stemmed from exaggerated spiritualism which was, perhaps, a defensible view around the turn of the century but is no longer acceptable in the light of modern discoveries, e.g., in depth psychology.

Again, this theory fails to explain the monopoly of the Catholic Church on major miracles. The economy of the supernatural, as understood by the Catholic faith, includes the assurance that the grace of faith is granted not only to one who enters the Church in full consciousness but that it is also obtained through the so-called baptism of desire and is accessible to any man who, while erring in good faith, offers himself up to God as he knows him, and is ready to do anything God may ask him to do or accept anything God may wish to tell him. Thus pagans may well share the gift of supernatural faith. If, therefore, this faith by itself causes man to regain the native powers of mind over body, there is no reason why major miracles would not occur in the pagan world.[16]

Furthermore, this theory is incapable of accounting for the concrete circumstances in which major miracles usually appear within the Catholic fold. In particular, it remains irrelevant to all cases in which it would be very difficult to resort to a psychic, although perhaps supernatural, agency as an explanation. Let us quote, e.g., the cases of infants, or patients who are unconscious at the time they are healed, who are in a comatic or subcomatic state or who are healed in their sleep. In quite a few instances health was restored to patients who had never even thought of the possibility, or who were cured because another sick person prayed for them or offered his own continued suffering in exchange for their health.[17] Le Roy, no doubt, may try to explain this point through the collective action or power of faith within a community. It is questionable, however, whether this supposition, applied to the cases we have just referred to, would remain within the boundaries of scientific probability, all the more since in many instances cures occur

[16] See observation in Part I, ch. VII on the possibility of miracles in non-Christian religions.

[17] All of these elements have come up in the factual presentations in the preceding chapters.

outside of any actual experience of collective faith. Moreover, how are we to explain that unbelievers are also sometimes cured miraculously? Assuredly, they may possess the kind of hope and trust that contains the seeds of real faith. In actual fact, however, many of them have explicitly refused any allegiance to this faith. We have already quoted this conclusion of Carrel: "There is no need for the patient himself to pray or even to have any religious faith. It is sufficient that someone around him be in a state of prayer." [18]

Finally, Le Roy's theory not only fails to explain why miracles occur in certain definite circumstances, but more significantly yet, it fails to explain why they do not occur in other circumstances. If faith alone is responsible for the miraculous, why is it that miracles fail to materialize for men whose faith is great enough to remove mountains, yet are often achieved for the benefit of the doubting and for men of little faith? Le Roy says: "It is quite possible to be a believer without being a miracle-worker. But the reason is that in that case one's faith is wavering, uneasy and weak." [19] But this solution is so evidently incompatible with the established facts that it merely serves to reinforce our objection.

These three theories do not exhaust all the possibilities of attempted explanation. There remains a *fourth* avenue along which modern man may seek an answer to the problem of the miraculous.

Those who follow this fourth road agree that so far no essential correlation has been established between the miraculous and other factors, except its dialogical relationship with a religious context. They also agree that at the present we have no guidance as to where to look for a connection. At the same time, however, they put a blind trust in *future scientific achievements*, a trust inspired by what they call the "scientific experience of the past, especially the recent past." Their reasoning runs something like the following. A great many things in the past have been considered prodigious and miraculous but eventually turned out to be quite simple and obvious in the light of scientific progress. Who knows but that

[18] A. Carrel: *Man, The Unknown*, p. 149.

[19] E. Le Roy: *art. cit.*, pp. 249. B. Björnson in his well-known play, *Über die Kraft*, Act II, sc. IV, has Pastor Bratt recite a strong indictment of a cherished Protestant view, the impotency of faith to operate miracles.

some day we will have found simple and natural explanations for all those things that today we hold for prodigious and unanswerable? As the limits of scientific knowledge were pushed further and further, the realm of the prodigious kept shrinking, and we have every reason to expect that this process will soon reach its conclusion. The boundaries of science will eventually contain all the existing phenomena while the realm of the miraculous will have been completely overrun or reduced to an infinitesimal point. Half a century ago Sabatier predicted that "in this conflict between science and the miraculous the miraculous will necessarily be defeated, for its domain progressively shrinks and declines in proportion as the magnificent and sovereign order of the cosmos is being discovered." [20] These predictions have been reinforced by the incredible speed at which in the past few decades scientific achievements have surpassed even the most optimistic expectations. This boundless faith in scientific progress is not the monopoly of the specialist, for even the least competent and least educated seem to be ready with this stereotype answer to everything that appears puzzling: "We do not know yet, but we will certainly know some day." [21]

The first question we may raise about this attitude is whether it reflects a truly scientific disposition of the mind. There is definitely such a thing as scientific mysticism, one of the main components of which is intrepid optimism. The irresistible passion for knowledge drives the human mind toward ever new conquests and puts man under a constant compulsion to solve whatever problem or puzzle there remains for him to be deciphered. This passionate race propels him over all the hurdles of hesitancy, disappointment or temporary failure. Truly scientific mentality, however, must contain another, very basic element: objectivity and sound discretion. Science is scrupulously honest toward the facts, does not claim to have found an explanation where there is no hope for one, and recognizes the precarious nature of the fragmentary results obtained. It will never try to conceal the absence of knowledge behind empty formulas or unfounded hypotheses.

[20] See A. Sabatier: *Esquisse d'une philosophie de la religion d'après la psychologie et l'histoire* (Paris, 1897), p. 75 [Transl. *Outlines of a Philosophy of Religion* (London, 1897), pp. 76-85).]

[21] See A. J. Boekraad: "Perspectief van her moderne denken," *Streven*, 5 (1951-1952), II, p. 112.

The question is whether the blind faith of modern man in the achievements of science fits into a scientific frame of mind. Is it based on the registering of facts or rather on some untested myth, born of emotions and artificially nursed along from the outside? Could it be the present-day reincarnation of primitive superstitions, brought to new life by man's everlasting desire to palliate his human anguish, a desire shamelessly kept burning and constantly exploited by clever but unscrupulous propaganda?

But let us go on and ask further if the past achievements of science, old or new, warrant with any degree of probability the prediction that sooner or later the realm of major miracles will shrink to nothing.

First of all, the statement that the domain of major miracles has been constantly shrinking in the past under the pressure of science seems rather ambiguous. If it is supposed to mean that with a wider dissemination of scientific knowledge today the ordinary man is in a better position to tell a false miracle from a true one, the statement is quite correct, although one may wonder if with all the existing proliferation of superstitions and the widespread taste for the prodigious, among Catholics and non-Catholics alike, our age is so far advanced over the past. If it is supposed to mean that science has explained a good many events that formerly lacked explanation, again no one can quarrel with this evident fact. But the question is whether qualified specialists, such as ecclesiastical judges whose job is to ascertain the nature of these phenomena, have been guilty of calling miraculous certain facts that may have been puzzling in the past but today are fully explained. A close look at this question suggests rather that science has made it easier to draw and recognize the boundaries of the miraculous exactly along the same line that the Church has laid down several centuries ago, and any adjustment that has been made since concerns only details of borderline cases.

For the more distant past we could find no better support for this claim than the imposing work of Benedict XIV: *De servorum Dei beatificatione et beatorum canonisatione*.[22] As Prosper Cardi-

[22] See on this matter also C. S. Lewis: *op. cit.*, pp. 57ff. On the value of Benedict XIV's work, see his eulogy by Pius XII, published posthumously in *Docum. Cath.*, 56 (1959), cc. 602-605.

nal Lambertini the future pope was a "promotor fidei" in canonization trials. This assignment gave him the opportunity to collect a huge body of information which makes up the substance of his treatise, edited and published during his reign in 1750 by the Jesuit Emmanuel de Azevedo. This two-hundred-year-old book is still the standard authority on the subject. The question of miracles is dealt with in the first part of the fourth volume. Miraculous cures are discussed not only in a general way but according to their main categories, and the book lays down the conditions under which they can be called actually miraculous. Eminent as a canon lawyer, Benedict XIV was at the same time a highly cultured person with a wide range of interests. The book makes use of the best available medical authorities in setting the exact borderline which two hundred years ago separated the truly miraculous from that which was susceptible of scientific explanation.

Surprisingly, almost all of the cases of instantaneous healing that with our better knowledge of the psyche and its unconscious mechanism we ascribe today to natural causes are quoted by Benedict XIV as subject to natural interpretation. His reasoning may make the reader smile, as may the medical terminology which adorns his writing. But he is well aware of the *fact* of healings in secular contexts and even though he may not find the exact answer for them, he clings steadfastly to his principle: "If there is a possibility that the event may be caused by the powers of nature, it can in no way be called miraculous." [23] He quotes the instantaneous and purely natural cures of a deaf mute, a blind person, a paralytic patient, etc.[24] The circumstances which are part of his account, such as nervous panic, rage, and other violent emotions, underline the part of psychological shock in these cures. He draws his own conclusion by showing great distrust toward any cure of a purely functional disorder.

As a concrete example, in discussing certain cases of miraculous cures of blindness, he formally distinguishes between functional and organic disorders of vision: "Matta observes that sight may be regained by natural means if the functioning of the organ is im-

[23] *Op. cit.*, IV, ch. 33, n. 24: "*quidquid per naturae vires obtineri potest, non est miraculo adscribendum.*"

[24] *Ibid.*, ch. 10, n. 8; ch. 11, n. 11; ch. 12, n. 11, etc.

paired but the organ of vision itself has not been destroyed." [25] Therefore the cure of congenital blindness is considered a miracle if "the blindness is due to a grave organic lesion rather than to sticking eyelids, cataract, or some other trouble that can be eliminated by medication." [26] If the testimony, especially that of qualified physicians, is not unmistakably clear on the causes of blindness, the nature of the cure cannot be determined and the case may not be called miraculous.[27]

He rules out as a matter of policy the cure of any disease connected with psychic disorders. His opinion is quite clear on the cases of hysteria: "It is difficult to consider their cure as miraculous." [28] Concerning the paramystical phenomena, the pope carefully and formally points out that they must be distinguished from analogous but purely natural manifestations by strict criteria which he specifies. In his opinion any such manifestations as ecstasies, inner voices, visions, apparitions, prophecies, sweat and tears of blood, halo around the head or the body, fasting for months or years, are susceptible of purely natural explanations, therefore cannot by themselves be considered miraculous.[29] The same rule applies to the alleged flexibility or bleeding of a corpse. He personally believes in the miraculous boiling of the blood of St. Januarius but he dutifully registers the opinions to the contrary, together with the polemics about the case and the tests made.[30] He finally devotes a whole chapter to the "Power of Imagination." "Imagination" in his context means the same thing as "psychic" or "psychogenic" in our vocabulary. He concludes, relying on the authority of Matta, that "disease and cure often find their cause in the imagination, whereby we mean that the forceful imagining of disease or cure activates vapors and bodily fluids so effectively that they in turn produce the aforesaid results." [31]

An appraisal of this two-hundred-year-old circumscription of the

[25] *Ibid.*, ch. 9, n. 5: "*Notat Matta naturaliter recuperari posse visum, si impeditum quidem organum, at non destructa videndi facultas fuerit.*"
[26] *Ibid.*, ch. 9, n. 6.
[27] *Ibid.*, ch. 9, n. 17.
[28] *Ibid.*, ch. 13, n. 12.
[29] *Ibid.*, ch. 26 and 27.
[30] *Ibid.*, ch. 31, n. 10-18.
[31] *Ibid.*, ch. 33, n. 21.

miraculous in the light of modern medical science leaves us no alternative but to concur with this simple statement of Schleyer in his latest critical study on Lourdes: "The general criteria set up by Benedict XIV are still very much applicable today." [32] The basic reason of this stability is a twofold principle which implicitly guides the pronouncements of the Church on these matters: 1) If an event sometimes occurs in settings other than religious, this kind of event can never have a purely religious origin; 2) On the other hand, if an event is not attributable to exclusively religious causes, this type of event is not incapable of occurring in settings other than religious. The application of this double principle, along with a policy of ruling out any conclusions drawn from doubtful cases or from ones that appear susceptible of twofold interpretation, enabled the Church centuries ago to draw the boundaries of the miraculous along a line which modern science leaves practically intact.

The history of the more recent past confirms these conclusions. One of the important developments that in the last fifty years have helped the Christian wonder to gain the respect it deserves is precisely the progress of science which so many try to use against it as a weapon. Modern technological possibilities did not relegate the miraculous to the realm of illusions; on the contrary. The almost infinite variety of means available, e.g., in medicine for checking and testing, have made it possible to establish irrefutably both the factual nature and the mystery of miracles. Radiographs and laboratory tests of all kinds confront even the most skeptical specialist with evidence he cannot long ignore.

Yet it is sometimes objected that the progress of science has in fact reduced the number of miracles considerably; what has been gained in quality has been lost in quantity. This assertion, however, is based on a twofold optical illusion.

First, the statistical figures on which these conclusions are built are often derived from misleading comparisons. The number of Lourdes miracles, recently approved by religious authorities, is compared with the total number of older cases quoted by authors, although only a small number of these have ever been declared miraculous by the Church. Even if the basis of comparison were

[32] L. Schleyer; *op. cit.*, p. 195.

miracles accepted by the Church, we still could not tabulate the results on mere statistical data. Because of the extreme perfection of means available in modern medicine for the diagnosing of a disease or determining its organic nature, the evidence supporting a diagnosis must be far more stringent than was required in the past. There is a growing distance between the theoretical and the practical possibility of full certitude, the latter being often limited by financial or psychological considerations on the part of the physician in charge. Quite evidently, therefore, there are cases of healing in which detailed laboratory analysis would have eliminated all theoretical doubt concerning the diagnosis, and yet the case cannot be called miraculous because the physician in charge decided that the evidence concerning the nature and evolution of the disease was sufficient and that there was no need for further and perhaps costly tests. Furthermore, in an increasing number of cases physicians motivated by prejudice, considerations of personal advantage, or sheer bad faith, have refused to be involved in one way or the other in the proclamation of a miracle. All of which merely proves not that the facts are not miraculous but that the lucky combination of circumstances and other factors that would make the evidence fully conclusive is more complex and less often present than before. Yet, despite these growing difficulties in achieving full certitude, it seems that the number of miracles ultimately recognized by the Church, at least in places where it is possible to count them as in Lourdes, remains fairly constant.

Those who insist that at any rate miracles in Lourdes have not multiplied in proportion to the increasing number of visitors, suffer from another illusion. The norm applied in these quantitative considerations is faulty, for statistics cannot possibly take into account the very meaning a miracle as a religious phenomenon is supposed to have. Requirements of quantitative and proportional frequency would submit the miraculous to the very statistical laws it is supposed to defy. These laws, while governing secular phenomena, cannot bind the miraculous if the latter is to be what it purports to be, that is, a sign of salvation and supernatural reality. There is only one quantitative requirement in connection with miraculous events: while remaining exceptional, they must be frequent enough to qualify as permanent signs within the Church. The instances quoted fulfill this requirement.[33]

In other words, there is no indication that the Christian wonder may be progressively eliminated with the advancement of modern science. Those who today indulge in hypothetical predictions of this kind, do so without any serious warranty.

II • LIMITATIONS OF SCIENTIFIC INQUIRY

The conclusions drawn so far from our reasoning can be summed up in the following points. Science confirms the historical truth and exceptional nature of the Catholic miracle. It concludes furthermore that the relationship of miraculous events with a religious context of a dialogical structure is the only existing fundamental relationship common to all these events. From a natural standpoint science classifies them under the generic name of "hierogenic phenomena" which label does not explain their nature but merely refers the question to religious psychology and philosophy as the only disciplines capable of supplying the solid scientific background against which a rational explanation might be found.

Could science go a step further without leaving its legitimate ground and conclude that the facts lack not only a scientific explanation but absolutely all explanation, or that the answer suggested by the religious context is the true and strictly causal explanation of these phenomena?

No *science* true to its nature can ever declare a phenomenon scientifically unexplainable. Every phenomenon, in fact, presents a variety of aspects, not all of which concern science. Science is interested in a phenomenon only to the extent it is reducible to general laws.[34] Science must therefore proceed on the methodological pos-

[33] From the beginning of the Lourdes events to 1959, only 54 cases were proclaimed miraculous by the canonical commissions of investigation. Ten of them are from the last ten years of this period. It must be pointed out, however, that there are no canonically accepted miraculous cases between 1913 and 1946. See P. Miest: *Les 54 miracles de Lourdes au jugement du droit canon* (Paris, 1958).

[34] See H. Dolch: "Sind Wunder möglich? Kritik einer Fragestellung,"

tulate—without any metaphysical implications—that all natural phenomena are reducible to such laws. Once it renounces this principle, it automatically ceases to be science, for it forsakes the methodological postulate on which it is based. Any claim that positive science as such can verify an infraction of the laws of nature would seem nonsensical, contradicting as it does the very notion of natural law. When a scientist is confronted with the problem of reducing a fact to the laws of nature, he either finds a way of doing so or continues his search, but he can never positively exclude the possibility of a solution.[35] As Teilhard de Chardin says, he can only "shrug his shoulders" at a miracle or admit with Pierre Mauriac: "I do not know what to make of it." [36] As a scientist he cannot go any further.

Not that science can altogether deny the possibility of the miraculous. Its essentially limited view of reality cannot under any pretext be construed as a complete representation of reality. Therefore, by saying that science cannot pronounce on the miraculous or nonmiraculous nature of a fact, we merely mean that the word "miracle" does not belong in a scientific vocabulary and has no meaning in scientific reasoning, but belongs to the language and vocabulary of another field of knowledge.[37]

Theologie und Glaube, 41 (1951), 210-218. He insists on this point: "The purpose of research in the natural sciences may be defined as the discovery of the great functional connections between the various natural processes *insofar* as the latter depend on other natural processes. The word 'insofar' is all-important, for the purpose is not the observation, description and understanding of processes of nature *which* depend functionally on other processes of nature, but *insofar* as they so depend . . . This outlook altogether defines the scope of pronouncements in the natural sciences. The conclusion is that if reality is viewed within the scope of the natural sciences, that is to say viewed from the very outset *as* functionally dependent upon other processes of nature, then it is impossible to decide within *this* scope, after the whole system is built up piece by piece, whether or not a portion of reality came to being through intervention from the outside." (p. 215).

[35] See, e.g., E. Le Roy: *art. cit.*, pp. 8-9. But Le Roy is wrong in making this scientific view an absolute one and thus concluding that miracles in the traditional sense are impossible.

[36] Teilhard de Chardin: *art. cit.*, p. 117; Pierre Mauriac quoted in J. M. Tauriac: *Miracles à Lourdes?* p. 67.

[37] See I. T. Ramsey: *art. cit.*, p. 8: "All talk about the laws of nature is in the case of the miracles a sheer waste of breath: whether or not they are broken is a pseudo-question. The word 'break' cannot be used of 'law' as it

To confirm this conclusion, let us recall what a miracle is supposed to be. If there are miracles at all, they are divine signs at the heart of a religious setting, meaningful not only for the scientist but to all men who think and search. They will achieve their purpose only if they are discernible as properly miraculous by all men capable of sound judgment. The apologetical evaluation of this judgment must be carried out at the level of religious criteriology.[38]

III • AN EVALUATION THAT INVOLVES THE WHOLE BEING OF MAN

Apologetic reasoning at this point must rise above the horizon of the natural sciences. The various elements collected through scientific investigation will now be gathered up by man who takes the momentous step of committing himself as a person. Science discovers the miraculous *fact*, but only man can discern it as properly *miraculous*.

A comparison may clarify this shift in viewpoint. A doctor finds his patient suffering from a specific syndrome. He takes advantage of all the available means to determine, through laboratory analysis, the nature and course of the disease with the greatest possible accuracy. But when the reports are in and actual treatment begins, the scientific data gathered are suddenly placed within a much larger, live situation. The doctor is no longer a mere scientist and diagnostician; he is now a true healer, a living person who enters into a very personal relationship with another person calling for help in his human need. He is expected not merely to perform a material task but to act as a man bound by the duties of his vocation; the illness has become a distress signal, a call for rescue. If the manner of medical intervention does not bear the mark of this total humanity, if the physician, however spectacular his results

---

occurs in the logic of science. When scientific laws are generalizations at different abstractive levels, when they are more or less tentative directives of procedure, then scientific language can have no place for 'miracle' and the less we embroil ourselves in irrelevant scientific discussion the better." But he adds immediately that one could therefore conclude to the impossibility of the miraculous only "if scientific language were the only language and were itself all-sufficient."

[38] See on this matter L. de Grandmaison: *Jesus Christ*, III, pp. 243-244 and the article of J. Mouroux quoted in the beginning of this chapter (n. 1).

may turn out to be otherwise, concentrates on a scientific goal and views his patient as an interesting case that lends itself to some new therapy or may enrich his experience, his rejection of the personal bond called for by the disease amounts to a betrayal of his professional mission.[39]

The study of the miraculous presents a similar case. With the scientific research completed, the investigator faces a religious situation soliciting his attention as a live human being. The whole problem of the supernatural, of revelation in its concrete totality, arises before him as a sign at the occurrence of a miraculous event and solicits his response as a person now totally involved in the process. Assuredly, he can choose to fall back on the lines of science and leave everything unanswered, but by doing this he would merely evade the religious problem arising from the prodigy and buy his peace at the price of his dignity as a man.

If man is to be faithful to himself, he must be present with all that he is, for then only will he be ready to examine critically the whole complex of the miraculous fact instead of the limited aspects it offers to positive science, and to ask in all honesty whether this fact is a divine sign or not. Once he has asked this question with all that is in him as a living being, he will be faced with a further *choice*.

Either he accepts the major miracle as a divine sign and recognizes the truth and reality of the divine message signified by the miracle; the facts would thus be fully explained. Science would favor such an interpretation, for the religious setting surrounding the sign is the only constant factor that scientific analysis of the facts has been able to discern. From the philosophical viewpoint the supposed existence of a supernatural revelation is the only hypothesis that would explain the emergence of such facts. Finally, from the religious viewpoint, this recognition will endow the facts with an enriching and full meaning.

Or he may refuse to interpret major miracles as divine signs. In this case the facts remain absolutely enigmatic for any scientific

[39] J. Maritain: "Le discernement médical du merveilleux d'origine divine," in *Foi et mystiques humaines*, Etudes Carmélitaines (1937), pp. 95-104, observes that a physician must appraise a miracle as he would a disease, that is, not as a scientist but as a person exercising his medical vocation.

approach, for the only road along which a solution might have been sought is blocked. Philosophically, the facts will have to be called highly improbable. In religion, they will appear inept, displaying as they would a deceiving appearance of divine meaning while resisting any attempt to find the author of this subterfuge or discover any motivation for such a monstrous fraud.

Any honest and unbiased mind will unhesitatingly arrive at the certainty that the facts in question are signs of the presence of God. It is hard to see how one could then avoid accepting with the sign the reality it signifies, that is, Christian revelation as presented by the Roman Catholic Church.[40]

This kind of certainty is essentially different from the one generated by a mathematical equation of scientific experiment. Even in the apprehension of faith, the supernatural can only be grasped as a dim anticipation, beyond all human evidence. A fortiori, no merely natural event can present the supernatural with evidential

[40] When one discerns the prodigious as a divine sign, does he thereby automatically recognize in it a transcendent intervention by God? If such intervention is meant in the general sense of God's using nature as an instrument, the thing is evident. If the word is used in the strict sense of producing an effect which surpasses the proper forces of nature and thus exempts the phenomenon from "the laws of nature," the conclusion is no longer evident. It certainly would not apply to minor prodigies, although these too, as noted before, may well be genuine miracles. There are many major prodigies which even at the stage of scientific appraisal turn out to be merely cases of extreme acceleration of some natural process. Others would suggest, at least by their external appearance, a case of altogether surpassing every natural possibility. This latter idea is totally alien to scientific thinking, but ceases to be unthinkable if one views the facts within a total human scope. If, therefore, a fact which from this standpoint has been discerned as a divine sign appears to science as contradicting the best established scientific laws, the theory of such a strictly transcendent intervention by a divine cause acquires a certain probability. Yet, there is too great a gap between our scientific knowledge of the phenomena and their innermost structure to allow, even with moral certitude, a metaphysical definition of the precise manner of the divine intervention apparent in a miracle. It would be perfectly possible, e.g., to reintroduce in a more modern garb the Augustinian explanation of "semina seminum." "If some phenomenon is explained by a free intervention of human consciousness," says very much to the point J. H. Walgrave (in a review of the Dutch edition of the present book, *De Maasbode*, Nov. 13, 1958), "this would not be a 'natural' explanation, and yet the intervention has not violated any natural law. In the same manner, if one says that God achieves his miracles in nature not in contradiction to its laws but utilizing them in his own divine way, this does not mean at all that the phenomena are given a purely natural explanation."

clarity. The signs are only indications of its presence. The certainty they generate does not dispel the darkness of faith; it merely supplies the moral guarantee that the journey into darkness is a safe one, that undertaking it would be wise and reasonable, whereas the refusal to do so would be foolish and morally insincere. That is why we have called the certainty whereby one assents to the miraculous *moral certitude.*

All of this is far from warranting a conclusion that any such certitude is merely personal or has a purely subjective validity.[41] On the contrary. Being based as it is upon unquestionable proofs with universal validity, it attains in its proper area the level of *scientific* certitude. In other words, it is not a mere practical certitude, but a speculative moral certitude as well. We might say with Dubarle[42] that the person engaged in apologetical reasoning about the miraculous arrives at his conclusions not as a "scientist" but as an "expert." He works at a different level from the positive sciences but

[41] Several recent authors, Catholics as well as Protestants, have described the Christian experience of the miraculous in terms that would attribute to it a purely subjective value. Among them are E. Carp: "Wonder en geneeskunde," II: "Het beleven van het wonder," *Annalen van het Thijmgenootschap* (1955), pp. 227-238; J. Van Den Berg: *Metaboletica of leer der veranderingen,* Beginselen van een historische psychologie (Nijkerk, 1956), ch. IV; W. Sikken: *Het wonder* (Kampen, 1957). Some of these authors offer a penetrating analysis of the experience of the "prodigious," this particular domain situated at the borderline between the esthetic and the religious. But they are mistaken in identifying this experience with that of the Christian miracle. An experience of the prodigious prescinds totally from the objective sign value of the object or event experienced as prodigious; it is precisely the experiencing subject who construes the object or event as a symbol of his religious astonishment. Now, the essential element in a Christian miracle is the fact that it symbolizes not only a human religious experience but also a divine intention. The miraculous displays a divine, not human intentionality, as do also the sacraments, although in an altogether different fashion. Therefore, the structure of a Christian experience of the miraculous is basically different, even from the simple phenomenological viewpoint, from a simple experience of the prodigious, for it consists not in symbolizing man's divine astonishment but in perceiving an objectively signified divine element. A description of the Christian experience of the miraculous which overlooks this objective aspect would be, in our opinion, unacceptable in Catholic theology.

[42] D. Dubarle: "L'attitude du savant chrétien en face du fait miraculeux," lecture delivered at a meeting of the International Medical Commission of Lourdes on February 21, 1954, *Bulletin de la Société Médicale de St. Luc, Côme et Damien* (1955); reprinted in a special issue on the miraculous, *Lumière et Vie,* 33 (1957), 321-350.

he reasons, in the sense defined above, with "scientific" competence in the field typical of the miraculous, the field of symbols which religious criteriology seeks to discern.

This certitude, therefore, is a moral one. As such, it is rooted more deeply in personal life than is abstract scientific knowledge; it is influenced by the orientation and *previous options* of man as a person. As Leibniz says: "If geometry were as contrary to our passions and worldly concerns as ethics, we would fight and violate it as much as we do with the latter." [43] As we have pointed out before, the God who appears through wonders as signs of salvation disrupts our natural feeling of security and our attachment to the things of this world. It is not difficult to understand that man whose autonomy is thus threatened should rise against him, refusing to surrender to him humbly, and should take refuge in the inevitable ambiguity of the signs, or cling to his so-called scientific objectivity. "The mind that has reason not to want Him," says Teilhard de Chardin, "will always find some ignis fatuus by which to wander or some opiate to dull its perception." [44]

But there is no honest way to avoid the decisive choice. Once again the words apply: "He who is not with me is against me." The man who refuses to take a stand may be sure of finding again the miraculous facts stored away in his subconscious mind, repressed as it were but all the more irritating. It would not seem rash to say that the thinly veiled distaste many unbelievers or even many Catholics feel whenever the question of miracles comes up is based not so much on legitimate intellectual distrust as on a defense reflex: man is reluctant to give up his distinction as master of the world and yield his absolute right to do with it as he pleases; he refuses to submit without defense to the judgment of God.

Once the existence of genuine miraculous signs has been accepted in principle, scientific inquiry plays a lesser part in the discerning of actual miracles, whereas the importance of total human appraisal grows. Let us suppose a major miracle the proofs of which are scientifically incomplete or do not exclude all possible doubt. The person involved may conclude, through critical study of the

[43] Leibniz: *New Essay on the Human Understanding,* I, II, 12.
[44] Teilhard de Chardin: *art. cit.,* p. 179.

religious setting and the sign itself, but still aside from any assent inspired by faith, that God has really appeared through the sign; he may arrive at complete human certitude in excluding a natural explanation, even though doubt would remain scientifically possible.[45]

Facts which do not belong in the category of major prodigies, and are therefore susceptible of natural as well as supernatural explanation, will also be investigated through attentive study of their religious setting and their structure as religious signs. The observer may often arrive at a moral, although not strictly scientific, certitude that the particular event is a genuine sign of salvation.[46]

In making an official pronouncement about the genuineness of a miraculous event, the intention of the Church is simply to issue a warrant to those who are not in a position to undertake a scientific study of the facts and could not personally verify the genuineness of the sign. All the Church says in effect is that such a study has been made and the sign has been discerned. These pronouncements make no appeal to faith which is not involved in them; they are intended merely as a help and guarantee which allow even the least equipped Christian to form in his own conscience a prudential judgment concerning the miraculous events appearing in the Church.

In achieving this task the Church may adopt either one of two viewpoints. If her message is aimed at those who deny the actual reality of miraculous events, she will demand from science the strictest guarantee; she will require that all natural explanations be scientifically excluded, and thus she will lead the human mind toward the inevitable dilemma of which we have spoken. In speaking to the faithful or to those who at least accept the possibility of major miracles, she will balance the strictly scientific data by emphasizing the warranty resulting from the study of the total religious picture and the human context, which may sometimes cause her to vouch with moral certitude for the genuinely religious na-

[45] A case such as G. Baillie's (ch. II, n. 39), which is controversial from the exclusively scientific viewpoint, should be accepted in our opinion as a genuine miracle if its concrete setting is viewed from a human and religious standpoint; see A. Deroo: *op. cit.*, p. 170.

[46] Beside the often quoted work of Benedict XIV, see on this matter also J. de Tonquédec: *Merveilleux métapsychique et miracle chrétien*, pp. 61-69; J. Lhermitte: *Mystiques et faux mystiques*.

ture of the facts in case, even in the absence of decisive scientific indications.

Whether the Church uses the first or the second approach will depend on the prevailing intention that governs the inquiry. As an example, the study of miracles in a canonization trial is conducted in a climate of faith, and in a way calls for different criteria from those required for the acceptance of the miracles of Lourdes which by their nature and setting lend themselves directly to an apologetic application. In the case of apparitions, mystical or paramystical manifestations or private relevations, religious criteria are the only ones that would apply and thus any declaration the Church may make in their regard is based on these alone.[47]

Finally, the witnessing of major miracles in our times opens our mind for a full appreciation of the *Gospel miracles.* Once we admit, in fact, that true miracles can happen, we can no longer doubt the genuine character of the miracles narrated in the Gospel, for they bear the stamp of authenticity down to their smallest details. Their sober simplicity and characteristic starkness, the dignified, grave and self-forgetful manner of Jesus in achieving them, their perfect accordance with the personality of the Lord, his teaching and the work of salvation, their harmony with sacramental symbolism and the language of the parables—all of these authenticating signs (as explained above in detail), which place the miracles of Christ at the opposite extreme from prodigies typical of apocryphal accounts or modern charlatans, reveal their full apologetic meaning in the light of the contemporary miracle.[48]

[47] It would seem desirable that the official agencies of the Church make it clear in proclaiming a cure miraculous whether they are speaking from a standpoint of Christian religious attitudes only or have also apologetic considerations in mind, directed at unbelievers.

[48] A. Oepke: "'Ἰάομαι," *Theol. Wört. z. N. T.* III, p. 206, compares from an apologetical standpoint the miracles of Jesus with those of pagan wonder-workers. We have pointed out several characteristic differences in Part I, ch. 6. A further element that should be pointed out in an apologetical treatment of the Gospel accounts are the numerous small details which are so far from being tendentious that they could not have been invented, and, on the other hand, are so typically human that they betray the presence of an eyewitness. Moreover, the Gospel miracles cannot be attributed to ancient man's thirst for the prodigious, for nothing like this transpires from the Gospel stories; on the contrary, no miracles are attributed, e.g., to John the Baptist, great prophet as he was; and several events that would seem perfect

•

We have thus reached the conclusion of our apologetic appraisal. There appear in the Roman Catholic Church, and in that Church alone, certain phenomena called "major miracles." Positive science is a precious help in their analysis, but the final verdict depends on the decision of the person involved in the inquiry. Finally, when man as a religious person who also follows the rules of critical thinking is confronted with the facts and their background, he has no choice but to recognize them as genuine divine signs and to open his whole being to the contents they signify: the message of the living God.

---

occasions for the building of legends are treated as simple historical events (e.g., Acts XIV, 20; XX, 10; XXVIII, 5). See also B. Brinkmann: "Die Erkennbarkeit der Wunder Jesu," *Scholastik*, 29 (1954), 345-362. On the harmony between the miracles of Christ and the institution of the sacraments, see the inspiring pages of M. Brauns: *Jesus als Dichter* (Tielt, 1954), pp. 30-38 and 75-78.

· CONCLUSION

As a conclusion of this book we would like to condense its results in a very modest image suggested by simple human psychology. The reader has perhaps met the kind of person who, despite all his valuable manly assets and a very sensitive soul, cannot open up and communicate with others because he is suffering from some real or imagined incapacity. His powers are paralyzed; he is a prisoner of himself, incapable of calling attention to his inner riches through word or gesture. His handicap may result from poor childhood training which has failed to established a firm link between him and his environment, or perhaps broke that link too brutally; or again his anxiety and doubt are the fruit of hope blighted once too often. The real cause may never be known. In any case, he is now enclosed in a fatal circle no cry of his heart will ever be able to break. But because he desires very much to escape from his anguished solitude, he makes one last attempt. He tries to communicate through signs, but using symbols very remote from the true language of the heart. In his fear that the world wherein he wishes so much to gain a foothold is closing its gates forever, he resorts to a childish fraud. He translates the message of his heart into the language of business or in figures. He composes a "small ad" and sends it to the newspaper.

Readers will notice his "ad" as they read the various advertising messages down the column. The person who wrote it is described in a language normally used in selling a product, and the reader may not suspect at all that this masquerade hides an offer of human love. Depending on his mood, he may think either that the message is in bad taste or is highly comical. One reader, however, may be capable of seeing through the disguise: the one who can rise above the concerns of business and reads the anonymous words and brutal abbreviations with the eyes of the soul and with a heart yearning for tenderness. This reader alone can measure the depth of anguish and passion beneath the strange and unsuitable wording. The sign, no doubt, is glaringly inept. But this very inadequacy, more moving than the most beautiful love poem, reveals the violence and despair of love forced to resort to this disguise in its search for freedom.

The person who reads the lines with nothing but business in mind is certain to miss the secret message altogether. The happily married family man who reads them with superficial attention may capture some of their hidden meaning but would still not understand the whole reality of the contents. The only person really able to pierce the veil of mystery is the one whose own anguish and loneliness have attuned him to understanding; he alone can throw on the words the light of his own offer of love which will uncover their richness. . . . Many years go by when something brings back to two hearts a long-forgotten memory whose faded charm makes them lean over a newspaper clipping yellowed with age. With the unerring feeling of their mature love they will know that the promise of their first message has been fulfilled.

Let us try once more to clarify the meaning of Christian wonders in the light of this humble example. Holy Scripture itself uses the image of marital love to symbolize from the very beginning of time the desire of God to share his love with his creature. The covenant of Yahweh with his chosen people is described as a marriage union, and the unfaithfulness of Israel is called adultery.[1] After God has

[1] See, e.g., the bride symbol in Is. LXI, 10; LXII, 5; Zeph. III, 17; Hosea II, 18-25; the symbol of adultery in Is. I, 21; III, 6; Jer. II, 20. 24. 32; XIII, 22; Ezek. XVI, 37-39; Hosea II, 2; etc.

finally revealed in the language of man the abundance of his Word made flesh in the fullness of time, the inspired authors of the Bible, Church Fathers and mystical writers of all ages will call incarnation the marriage feast of the Redeemer with fallen mankind. God is a "king who made a marriage feast for his son." "For God so loved the world that he gave his only-begotten Son." [2] John the Baptist is "the friend of the bridegroom, who stands and hears him, rejoices exceedingly at the voice of the bridegroom." [3] Mankind is the bride. The mystery of union is achieved in the virginal womb of Mary, the secret chamber "where he wedded this bride, our human nature, uniting it with his own Person through the most pure blood of the noble Virgin; the priest blessing this union was the Holy Spirit; Archangel Gabriel proclaimed the banns; and the glorious Virgin gave her consent." [4] Through Mary's acceptance mankind says "yes" to the Lord and thus becomes the Church of Christ, his spouse "not having spot or wrinkle." [5]

Continuing the same symbolism, we may consider the miraculous as God's latest attempt, repeated throughout the centuries, to recapture the attention of his fickle spouse too distracted by a thousand childish games to understand his message of love. Having been so often cheated by his wayward spouse, he would for a while set aside any appeal to the mystery of faith, which is his own proper language, and forsake the voice of prophets and the telling sacrament of the incarnation of the Word, in order to speak to his fleeing lover, swept away by unbelief and sin, in a language she can understand in the exile of her earthly mediocrity.

> *"And in that day . . .*
> *I will espouse thee in justice, and judgment,*
> *And in mercy, and in commiserations.*
> *And I will espouse thee to me in faith;*
> *And thou shalt know that I am the Lord.*
> *In that day*

[2] Matt. XXII, 1; John III, 16.
[3] John III, 29; see also Matt. IX, 15.
[4] Ruysbroeck: *The Adornment of the Spiritual Marriage*, preface.
[5] Eph. V, 27.

I will have mercy on her that was without mercy,
And I will say to that which was not my people: Thou art my people.
And they shall say: Thou art my God." [6]

But many would not heed even this last, desperate message of love, for it seems a burden, a killer of petty joys. Countless are the unwilling guests who are kept away from the banquet table by ambition, job, money, politics, science or the pleasures of life. Carried away by all these currents they do not pay the least attention to the loving grace of God who is calling to them through wonders. There is always that farm, that yoke of oxen as a ready barrier between the searching love of God and man's reluctance and mediocrity; or man's heart is drunk and his mind befuddled with earthly love which keeps him from understanding a single word of the message of salvation.[7]

God then sends out his wonders as servants into the street and crossroads to invite the poor, the crippled and the lame to the great supper. If the newly invited get over their natural reluctance and enter the banquet hall, they will catch a sudden flash of the glory heralded by the servants. Many indeed will catch no more than a passing glimpse for they refuse to exchange their earthly rags for the wedding garment their host has offered them. But there will be some who will enter the fullness of the mystery; having been purified by the sacrament of water and word, they offer themselves to the love of Christ and are admitted to the wedding feast of the Lamb;[8] they will taste for the first time the full richness of the wonders which have drawn them, and they will understand the greatness of the love of God in stooping down to man in the garments of a lowly slave. Every time the faithful servant enters again the banquet hall, these guests will relive with an ever-deepening and intimate understanding the memory of the original invitation. And every time they hear the voice of the servant while union with the Bridegroom remains momentarily veiled, their eagerness gathers intensity and they become more and more receptive to the

[6] Hosea II, 20-25.
[7] Luke XIV, 14-25.
[8] Eph. V, 26; II Cor. XI, 2; Apoc. XIX, 7. 9; XXI, 2. 9.

pressing word of the Beloved who whispers in their ears: "It is true, I come quickly!" [9] The time will come when the veil is finally lifted, all signs are set aside, and the true meaning of wonders is fulfilled, and not at all destroyed, through the transcendent wonder of a face-to-face vision which will have no end.

[9] Apoc. XXII, 17. 20; see also Matt. XXV, 6.

INDEX